T0339718

STRIKE AND DESTROY

STRIKE AND DESTROY

When Counter-Insurgency (COIN) Doctrine
Met Hellraiser's Brigade
Or,
The Fate of Corporal Morlock

Stjepan G. Mestrovic

Algora Publishing
New York

Library of Congress Cataloging-in-Publication Data —

Mestrovic, Stjepan Gabriel.
    Strike and destroy: when Counter-insurgency (COIN) doctrine met Hellraiser's
Brigade or, the fate of Corporal Morlock / Stjepan G. Mestrovic.
        p. cm.
    Includes bibliographical references and index.
    ISBN 978-0-87586-909-4 (pbk.: alk. paper)— ISBN 978-0-87586-910-0 (hbk.: alk.
paper)—ISBN 978-0-87586-911-7 (ebook: alk. paper) 1. Afghan War, 2001—Atrocities—
De Maywand Kariz. 2. United States. Army. Infantry Division, 2nd. Stryker Brigade, 5th. 3.
Tunnell, Harry D. (Harry Daniel), 1961- 4. Morlock, Jeremy. 5. War crimes—Afghanistan—
De Maywand Kariz. 6. Sociology, Military—United States. 7. Counterinsurgency—
Afghanistan. 8. Counterinsurgency—United States. I. Title. II. Title: When Counter-
insurgency (COIN) doctrine met Hellraisers Brigade. III. Title: Fate of Corporal Morlock.
    DS371.4123.D45 2012
    958.104'742—dc23

                                    2012013694

Printed in the United States

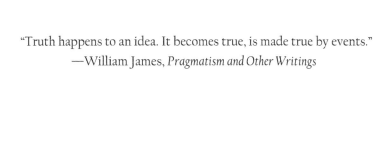

"Truth happens to an idea. It becomes true, is made true by events."
—William James, *Pragmatism and Other Writings*

TABLE OF CONTENTS

PREFACE

This book discusses a set of war crimes committed by U.S. soldiers in Afghanistan between January and May of 2010, the so-called Maywand District Killings. As a sociologist, I testified as an expert witness at the court-martial of Jeremy Morlock, one of the soldiers involved. Thus, the book is a sociological study; it explores the structure and dynamics of the social environment in which the U.S. soldiers were operating, broadly at first and then more specifically as regards Corporal Morlock.

My approach is inductive. This means that I begin with observations, interviews, and other facts, and arrive at generalizations which emerge from those facts. As a sociologist, I am constantly mindful of, and remind the reader of, various social contexts for what was said, done, written, and expressed by various actors in this study. In taking the inductive approach, I necessarily clash with approaches taken by some lawyers, journalists, military officers, military theorists and others who are not as mindful of social context and who are more deductive in their approaches.

But I do not take a "strike and destroy" attitude toward approaches that are different from mine. Instead, and in the spirit of one of the major themes in this study, COIN (counter-insurgency) doctrine, I seek cooperation, mutual understanding, and the fruitful resolution of differences in opinion. Yes, I do adopt the sociological attitude that combat is not restricted to the military but applies metaphorically to other social institutions, including law, academia, and journalism, among others.

I ask the reader not to take a strike and destroy approach in reading my study, but to entertain more fruitful readings. For example, to those lawyers who might be reading this study, and who might be tempted to judge hastily that "this author clearly does not understand the law," I would respond as follows. I do not pretend to understand "the law," but I have spent many years carefully observing what lawyers and judges say, do, write, and interpret as they are *creating* "the law." Perhaps some lawyers and judges will find my approach useful.

To those military theorists who will think, "this author does not understand COIN doctrine," I say: my study of officers and soldiers who were tasked to carry out COIN doctrine shows that they were hopelessly confused as to what COIN meant and means. What can we learn from their confusion?

Some journalists have asked me, "How can you defend a war criminal?" I ask them: Who is responsible for war crimes, given the military's doctrine of command responsibility?

In general, I ask the reader to set aside dogmatic pre-conceptions and to join me in an intellectual journey of discovery.

Legal considerations

The present study is distinctive because of my access to an internal army report that is still under a military judge's protective order.

The AR 15-6 investigation of command climate and responsibility was conducted by Brigadier General Stephen Twitty. The Twitty report was sent to me by the prosecutors in the case of US v Corporal Jeremy Morlock. I relied upon it to prepare for my expert witness testimony at Morlock's court-martial. However, since his court-martial in March of 2011, this report had been leaked to the media. Several news sources, ranging from *The Army Times*[1] to the *News Tribune*, have quoted extensively from this report in published news articles.[2] Several attorneys have advised me that because of the leak and the 1st Amendment to the U.S. Constitution, the report is now public. However, they advised me that in quoting from this report, I must not quote from the copy of the report which was given to me by the prosecutor. Instead, I must have obtained another copy of the report from a news source. I hereby declare that I did receive a copy of the Twitty report from a news source. Furthermore, I declare that my quotes and citations in this book are only from the leaked, news source copy, and not from the copy given to me by the prosecutor. It is lawful for me to quote from this public document, based upon the news source copy.

In this book, I also quote from Morlock's Record of Trial (ROT) and Article 32 hearing. These records are considered public. Furthermore, my testimony at Morlock's trial on the Twitty report is considered to be public record and may not be restrained by the government.

I also obtained a news source copy of the AR 15-6 investigation on the phone calls made by Adam Winfield's father to the government in order to report the killings. Again, this news source copy is considered to be public.

Corporal Morlock has given his permission for me to quote and describe what he has said to me as recorded in this book. I am grateful to him for his permission. His defense attorney, Mr. Frank Spinner, has vetted these disclosures by his client.

Privacy and other issues

It is my understanding that the names of and statements by soldiers who were convicted in the many companion cases to the Morlock case are considered public record. Similarly, various news sources have already named various officers and soldiers in the Twitty report, and quoted them extensively. It is lawful for me to name the officers and soldiers in this report in the quotations I take from the report. Nevertheless, and in keeping with a COIN-like spirit which I adopt in this book, I have decided to be as respectful as possible of the privacy of the various actors in this drama. For example, I avoid using the real names of most officers and soldiers. Thus, I refer to officers as Colonel A or Major U or Lieutenant General J, and so on. Those readers who are formerly from 5/2 SBCT may figure out who these people are, but most readers will not, and in any case, linking the quotes to specifically named individuals is *not* my intent. However, I do offer brief descriptions of the roles and formal positions these various officers and soldiers held in 5/2 SBCT, because that is an integral aspect of this sociological study. For the purposes of this study, it does not matter who these individuals were but what their social roles were.

The major exception to this rule is my citation of and quotations from the brigade commander, Colonel Harry Tunnell IV, as well as what other officers and soldiers said about him in the Twitty report. The publication of these quotations is lawful, given that the news-source leaked copy of the Twitty report is now public. More importantly, the focus on Colonel Tunnell is unavoidable given the remarkable fact that the Twitty report is much more about him and his philosophy of war than it is about the soldiers who were accused and convicted of war crimes. There is simply no way for Colonel Tunnell to remain anonymous when almost every single sworn statement in the Twitty report mentions him, or in many cases focuses on him, COIN doctrine, and counter-guerrilla doctrine. Moreover, his statements in the Twitty report have already been made public in news reports.

Nevertheless, I am scrupulous in this book in using Colonel Tunnell's name only when quoting or discussing what officers and soldiers said or wrote about him. I refer to his persona as "Hellraiser" when I interpret, digress, or make connections to myths, archetypes, or theories in discussing "him." The label Hellraiser is not arbitrary; this was one of Colonel Tunnell's call signs in the field in Afghanistan (the other was Destroyer). Soldiers and officers actually referred to him as Hellraiser. His real name was almost never used.

I capture this strange aspect of life in Stryker brigade by referring to him in the way that his soldiers referred to him—Hellraiser. But I wish to make it clear that when I make comparisons between Hellraiser's statements and those of Captain Ahab (from Melville's *Moby Dick*), for example, I am not making assertions about the individual, Colonel Tunnell. I am making allusions and interpretations based upon his persona, the myth he created by choosing the call sign Hellraiser, in the context of other things he said and what has been said about him. Thus, the reader will find references to Colonel Tunnell based upon precise quotations of what he said and what others said about him in public documents. The reader will find references to Hellraiser when I am engaging in the sociological imagination, namely, interpreting the brigade commander's statements and actions in a sociological manner.

I wish to make it unequivocally clear that I do not assert or imply any criminal wrongdoing by Colonel Tunnell or any other soldier or officer whom I mention or quote in this book. I present many instances of wrongdoing and "questionable" kills neutrally, and as a sociologist, not as a criminal investigator.

Regarding the confusing array of military names, ranks, and acronyms, I provide a brief glossary for the reader. When I first introduce a military term, rank, or acronym, I explain it. However, it would be cumbersome to use the formal terminology for each and every instance. Thus, when I refer to Stryker brigade, I am referring only to the 5/2 SBCT commanded by Colonel Tunnell, and no other Stryker brigade. Regarding the battalions within that brigade, I refer to them by their numerical designations most of the time. For example, Corporal Morlock was in 2-1 Infantry Battalion, which I abbreviate as 2-1. The other important battalion in this story is abbreviated simply as 1-17. Again, these moves on my part are not arbitrary but reflect how soldiers and officers discuss their units on a daily, informal basis.

Similarly, I abbreviate Counter Insurgency doctrine as COIN, and the opposing counter-guerrilla doctrine as CG. However, I go beyond the strict definitions of these terms as found in manuals, to include COIN-like spirit, actions, and behaviors that are focused upon cooperation. Similarly, I extend CG doctrine, captured with the motto of Stryker brigade, "Strike and Destroy." I refer to CG-like philosophy, actions, orientations, and attitudes in non-military settings. For example, I distinguish between COIN-like aspects of academia which focus upon cooperation and discussion versus CG-like aspects of academia which are combative and in line with a "publish or perish" philosophy.

ABBREVIATIONS, ACRONYMS, AND DEFINITIONS

1-17, or 1/17	1st Battalion of the 17th Infantry Regiment
2-1 or 2/1	2nd Battalion of the 1st Regiment
5/2 SBCT	5th Brigade, 2nd Division, Stryker Brigade Combat Team (referred to as Stryker Brigade or as 5/2 in this book)
1SG	First sergeant or E-8, the highest ranking sergeant in a company of soldiers
ANSF	Afghan National Security Forces
AO	Area of operations
AR 15-6	A formal investigation in the US Army
Article 15	Non-judicial punishment in the US military
Article 32	The rough equivalent to a civilian preliminary hearing
BDE	Brigade, or an army unit consisting of several battalions
BG	Brigadier general, one star, sometimes referred to as O-7
BN	Battalion; an army unit consisting of several companies
CG	Counter-guerrilla, referring to a doctrine, philosophy, or manual. Counter-guerrilla operations are aimed only at the military elements of an insurgency. The inherent ambiguity in the CG concept is that it is a part of counter-insurgency (COIN) operations, but does not aim at defensive or stability goals.
CID	United States Army Criminal Investigation Command
CO	Company, or an army unit consisting of several platoons. May also refer to the Commanding Officer.

COIN	Counterinsurgency, referring to a doctrine, philosophy, or manual. I distinguish between "doing COIN" versus adopting, embracing, or believing in COIN. COIN is an ambiguous concept, because it joins lethal and nonlethal tactics and behaviors. It may refer broadly to "winning hearts and minds" but also includes offensive operations, and has stability as a goal. The relationship of COIN to CG is problematic, and that is the subject of this book.
COL	Colonel or O-6
COP	Combat outpost
CPL	Corporal or E-4, the lowest ranking non-commissioned officer
CPT	Captain or O-3
CSM	Command Sergeant Major or E-9, the highest rank for a non-commissioned officer. Additionally, the CSM is in charge of all non-commissioned officers in a command such as a brigade or a battalion
CWO	Chief Warrant Officer
FM	Field manual
FM 3-24	COIN (counterinsurgency) Manual
FM 6-22	Army Leadership Manual
FM 90-8	Counter-guerrilla Operations Manual
FOB	Forward Operating Base
GH/K or GHK	Guerrilla Hunter Killer
HMMWV	High mobility multipurpose wheeled vehicle or humvee
IED	Improvised explosive device
IN	Infantry
IO	Investigative officer
ISAF	International Security Assistance Force
JAG	Judge Advocate General's Corps, or the military's legal branch
JBLM	Joint Base Lewis-McChord, referred to as Ft. Lewis
KIA	Killed in Action
LG	Lieutenant General, three stars, or O-9
LN	Local National
LT	Lieutenant, sometimes used as an abbreviation for a 1LT (O-2) or 2LT (O-1). Lieutenants are the lowest-ranking commissioned officers.
LTC	Lieutenant colonel or O-5
MAJ	Major or O-4

MG	Major general, two stars or O-8
MJ	Military judge
MSG	Master sergeant or E-8
NCO	Non-commissioned officer
NTC	National Training Center at Ft. Irwin, California
PL	Platoon; several platoons comprise a company, and a platoon is comprised of four squads.
	Also may refer to Platoon Leader.
PTSD	Post Traumatic Stress Disorder
RCF	Regional Correctional Facility
RC-S or RCS	Regional Command South (in Afghanistan)
ROT	Record of trial
S2	Intelligence staff
S3	Operations staff
S4	Supply staff
SBCT	Stryker Brigade Combat Team
SFC	Sergeant first class or E-7
SGM	Sergeant major or E-9
SGT	Sergeant or E-5
SSG	Staff sergeant or E-6
Stryker	An eight-wheeled, all-wheel-drive armored fighting vehicle
Stryker Brigade	In this book, refers only to the 5/2 SBCT. Otherwise, refers to a brigade that relies upon Stryker vehicles
TDS	Trial Defense Services or military defense lawyers within JAG
TBI	Traumatic brain injury
UCMJ	Uniform Code of Military Justice
USDB	United States Disciplinary Barracks, commonly known as Ft. Leavenworth military prison
XO	Executive officer

CHAPTER 1. DISCOVERING CONNECTIONS

"In the law, you have to make connections," Frank Spinner said to me. He was the lead attorney in the Jeremy Morlock case as of December 2010.

"What does the law regard as a connection?" I asked Spinner.

He just smiled, as he often did in our conversations. I eventually came to the conclusion that anything can be a "connection" to the law so long as it "works" in the courtroom. Connections, for the law, are applied to just about anything, from fibers, e-mails, and conversations to command climates. A connection "works" (even if it is not necessarily "true" in some pristine, academic way) if it survives cross-examination and convinces a jury or a judge. Working with lawyers, I had become used to cryptic answers, or no answers. The first time I ever went on a witness stand as an expert witness, the lead attorney's only advice to me was, "Whatever you say, just don't crash and burn." That advice was not much to go on. Lawyers do not seem to reflect on the meanings of the words they use for non-lawyers: they just go about the business of what I would label as "lawyer-ing." So long as the judge, jury, and other attorneys in the courtroom seem to know what they are saying and doing, they seem to be satisfied. A courtroom trial in the US in the 21st century is analogous to the Catholic Mass as it was celebrated in Latin well into the 20th century: most of the observers had no idea what was really going on. Law-speak might as well be in Latin, from the point of view of the layperson trying to make sense of a trial. (Of course, some of it literally *is* in Latin.)

Spinner and I had been wrangling—always in a friendly way—about the meaning of legal terms for the common man or woman ever since we met in 2005. In that year, we worked together in the Sabrina Harman court-martial, which was one of the Abu Ghraib cases. In order to understand each other's professional vocabulary—his as a lawyer and mine as a sociologist—we tried hard to translate legal and sociological terms into the universal language of common sense. We both would laugh, because some strange combination of our temperaments as well as mutual respect prevented both of us from ever crossing the line into heated discussion or argument. Our differences in opinion always ended with humor, but the insight remains: when professionals communicate with each other, they interact more as social roles than as individuals, and they carry the enormous weight of the cultural lag of their roles on their shoulders. Spinner became a lawyer through the weight of all the lawyer-ing he had done during his career. I became a sociologist; and Morlock would eventually become a convicted criminal. But when I first met Morlock, he was still a young soldier who had only recently emerged from his cocoon of being a high school hockey team captain in Wasilla, Alaska.

The "connections" made in the courtroom must be deemed "relevant" by the equivalent of the high priest in the courtroom, namely, the judge. One of the most common—and damning—legal connections is that of a "conspiracy." In my experience over the course of a decade as an expert witness in sociology, I have noticed that legal terms such as "relevant," "conspiracy," and "connection" do not hold the same meanings for the legal profession that one finds in dictionaries. More importantly, the decisions in the courtroom as to what these terms mean do not always fit legal definitions of them. Dictionaries capture shared meanings for the everyday person, but lawyers think and work in a separate social universe that they superimpose upon the rest of us. Echoing William James and pragmatism, I would say that *truth happens to the ideas* "relevant," "connection," and "conspiracy" (among other ideas) in the courtroom. It is *not* the case that the ideas which send people to jail or exonerate them are "truly" relevant, connected, or indicate conspiracy. No two trials are alike, even if they involve the same crime or events, because the way that the "connections" are received by a particular judge or jury is always distinct and unique.

Lawyers are in this world, but not of it. This linguistic and conceptual Tower of Babel is magnified when one considers other professions, such as the military, journalism, sociology, and psychology—among other professions—as each of these types of professionals tries to describe aspects of a crime or trial in their own idiosyncratic ways. Then there are the families of the accused, who understandably cannot comprehend what these others professions have to say about the actions of their sons and daughters in war, or the outcomes of courts-martial.

Spinner's client, a young 22-year-old soldier named Jeremy Morlock, was charged with three counts of premeditated murder as well as conspiracy to commit premeditated murder. Moreover, because these crimes occurred during his deployment in Afghanistan in the year 2010, he was being charged with war crimes, albeit through the military justice system—more precisely, through the Uniform Code of Military Justice, or UCMJ, established in 1950. (Before the UCMJ, the US military court-martial system had been practically the same since the days of George Washington.)[3] Three particular words—relevant, conspiracy, connection—were important for understanding what happened, what the charges were, who was charged, who was not charged and what really happened during Morlock's deployment in Afghanistan.

In the everyday life of the common person, the word "relevant" means pertinent, significant, and important. Spinner thought that an internal army report (over 500 pages in length) on Morlock's brigade commander and the aggressive command climate this commander created was highly significant and important for defending Morlock. Predictably, the military prosecutor, Captain (CPT) Andre LeBlanc, argued that this report was not "relevant" and should not be introduced into testimony. It does not matter whether CPT LeBlanc sincerely believed the report was irrelevant. He was doing his job as a lawyer by arguing that it was irrelevant. Prosecuting and defense attorneys sparred on this issue in front of the judge as well as outside the purview of the judge. Prior to Morlock's court-martial, military judge (MJ) and Lieutenant Colonel (LTC) Kwasi Hawks finally ruled that this report was relevant, but he also issued a protective order that kept it out of public purview. The judge's ruling in favor of Spinner was a significant victory: out of the five courts-martial for five separate soldiers who were on the so-called "kill team," the army's furtive report was used in testimony only in Morlock's court-martial.

But the judge's favorable ruling still left Spinner with the problem of *how* to introduce its relevance into testimony, the trial record, and ultimately, history. Facts do not speak for themselves. The seemingly obvious solution was to have me testify as an expert witness on the general's interpretation as well as the facts in the report, and to be cross-examined by the prosecutor. During my testimony at Morlock's court-martial, the prosecutor again objected that my testimony was irrelevant, and the same judge again overruled him. But it could have just as easily gone the other way. Prior to and during some of the courts-martial in the Abu Ghraib trials, the military judge sustained the prosecutor's objections that the Taguba and Fay reports were irrelevant.

The important point is that internal army reports (and other evidence) are not inherently, innately, "really" or "truly" relevant or irrelevant. They become relevant or irrelevant through a unique and particular interaction in a courtroom.

What these internal reports have in common is that they were the results of research conducted by and written by army generals on a phenomenon the army calls, "command climate." In formal army vocabulary, such a report is referred to as an AR 15-6 Investigation. General Stephen Twitty conducted the research and wrote the AR 15-6 report in Morlock's case. The Taguba and Fay reports were also AR 15-6 documents, parts of which eventually made public. The generals who conducted the research and wrote these reports are not sociologists, but their reports are profoundly sociological. This is because their AR 15-6 investigations were focused mainly on "command climate" and related issues such as leadership, group cohesion, the "circulation" of officers with troops, and so on. But these phenomena are typically the domain of the sociologist.

The reader should also be aware of the fact that some of these reports eventually become public while others remain undisclosed forever. An example of the latter is the AR 15-6 for the Operation Iron Triangle case (see Mestrovic, 2009), which was never allowed into testimony for any of the soldiers who were prosecuted and which will most likely never be released.

Whether they become public or remain closeted, some of these reports make it into the court record while others do not. General Twitty's AR 15-6 is a hybrid of these possibilities: it was placed under a protective order, but eventually leaked to the media, and it was used in Morlock's court-martial but not in the courts-martial of the companion cases. It *became* relevant in Morlock's case because of Spinner's strategy and lawyering skills, but remained irrelevant—even invisible—in the other cases. It may or may not become relevant for the readers of this book despite the intentions of the author. This is because the meanings and dynamics of "relevance" are completely different for communication within and outside the courtroom.

And apart from the pre- and in-courtroom drama of declaring these reports relevant versus irrelevant, an important issue remains for the common man and woman, as well as scholars: Is the understanding of the crimes under discussion here, as well other war crimes, changed significantly when one takes into account the social climate and social context of the crimes in question?

Can this or any other war crime be fully comprehended as a purely private event involving an individual, with the social backdrop taken out of the picture? To put the matter plainly: the crime in question involved an entire platoon, not just Corporal Morlock. The platoon was connected to a company, which was connected to a battalion, which was connected to a brigade, which was commanded by a colonel who confused everyone in the brigade about their mission in Afghanistan.

The degree of "involvement" is open to debate and was never finally established in any courtroom trial of any of the defendants: The entire platoon "knew" of the crimes and the scenarios which led up to them. Journalists and prosecutors were quick to label these five defendants as "the kill team." But murder charges were dropped against the fifth member of this alleged kill team; the fourth member reached a pre-trial agreement for involuntary manslaughter; and three members were convicted of premeditated murder. Two out of the three convictions for premeditated murder were the result of pre-trial agreements, so that only one out of the five soldiers (Gibbs) was truly convicted of premeditated murder by a military panel (jury). In the end, reality did not conform to the truths the prosecutors tried to impose upon it. To repeat: truth happens to an idea, including a criminal charge, in the courtroom.

Of course, a related question on the far horizon of this discussion is whether *any* crime, including crimes in the civilian social world, should be understood solely as the actions of isolated individuals. The knee-jerk response seems to be that the law—at least, in contemporary societies—can only prosecute individuals, not the groups and societies to which these individuals belong. Deeper reflection on this issue reveals that war criminals are connected with "bad" platoons, companies, battalions, brigades, and other military societies. Similarly, criminologists have documented that civilian criminals come from "bad" families, corporations, work settings, and other social groups. These various insights and findings from various professions fail to form a coherent whole for comprehending crime. Moreover, these insights all constitute conceptual connections. Inside or outside the courtroom, one may connect an individual to a crime and stop any further inquiry, or one may—as we will in this study—connect the individual to a social group to a crime.

Thus, the legal charge of "conspiracy" is very problematic. The legal definition of conspiracy does not have a time limit, does not require an overt plan, and does not remotely resemble the layperson's dictionary understanding of conspiracy as a plot, scheme or plan:

> The agreement and conspiracy does not have to be in any particular form or expressed in formal words. It is sufficient if the minds of the parties reach a common understanding to accomplish the object of the conspiracy, and this may be proved by the conduct of the parties. The agreement does not have to express the manner in which the conspiracy is to be carried out, or what part each conspirator is to play... A member of a conspiracy is criminally responsible under the law for any offense which is committed by any member of the conspiracy in furtherance of that conspiracy [in Mestrovic, 2009, p. 223].

Five soldiers were charged with conspiracy to commit premeditated murder in this case (while only three were convicted of this particular charge). Yet evidence revealed that Morlock's entire platoon and several other platoons knew about and in some manner tacitly approved of these and other, related killings. What is the full roster of soldiers who were involved in the conspiracy to commit these killings? The most precise legal answer is that the charge of conspiracy to commit murder "happened to" five soldiers, of whom three were convicted of this charge. But this is not a satisfactory explanation of the involvement of various social groups in the killings.

The meaning of the Latin root for the word "conspiracy" is "to breathe together." Herein lies the mystery and profundity of comprehending war crimes: all military units "breathe together" or "conspire" (in a non-legal sense) each and every time they go out on any mission. A military society is like traditional society due to its group cohesion and authoritarian structure. In a very real (but not legally binding sense), Morlock's entire "brigade" conspired—in some sense of the term—in the killings under discussion here as well as other killings. This claim is not hyperbole: in the course of this study, we shall be analyzing the aggressive mottos, symbols, scenarios, and climate of Stryker brigade. How does one distinguish "lawful" killings versus war crimes? If the answer to this question were easy—and it is not—officers would not have referred to "questionable kills" in the Twitty report. Where does one draw the line between collective and individual responsibility?

These and related questions merge into theology, sociology, and numerous fields other than the law. This is because they revolve around the question, "Who was responsible?" The law does not allow for this truth to happen in any courtroom: that the entire brigade and especially the brigade commander were "responsible" in this wider, non-legal sense.

I shall repeat that I am not accusing the brigade commander of any criminal responsibility for the killings under discussion here. Nevertheless, I will demonstrate that the brigade commander set the tone with his "Strike and Destroy" motto and other words and actions which created a toxic social climate, which in turn predisposed the killings. A sort of plan (or scenario) was established without being in any particular form and without being expressed in any particular words, but it was connected to the killings.

MAKING CONNECTIONS AND "OPENING DOORS"

Spinner and I were sitting in Captain Mark Opachan's office in the law office building on the base that is formally known as Joint Base Lewis McChord but is still commonly referred to as Ft. Lewis. CPT Opachan was Morlock's appointed military attorney. He was absent on that day due to a family emergency. His office was at the end of the hall on the third floor of a sprawling brick structure that, on the outside, looked like a building one would find on any Ivy League campus. On the inside, it was dilapidated and showed its age. It was built in the 1920s. Morlock was down the hall in a room labeled as the library, still in his role as the pre-trial accused and technically innocent until proven guilty. This tiny room had a few legal books and had absolutely no air vents. It was the size of a small conference room and served as such. Morlock was in the window-less library with twenty-six members of his extended family who had come from Alaska to support him during his court-martial, which was scheduled for the next day, March 3, 2011. (At the last minute, the first court-martial was postponed until March 23, 2011, due to CPT Opach-an's emergency leave.) On the outside, the building presented a beautiful façade from the Gilded Age which belied a decaying infrastructure.

I turned to Spinner and asked: "Frank, is it a connection that Sergeant Calvin Gibbs was the brigade commander's personal bodyguard right before he was transferred to his new position as one of the squad leaders in Jeremy's platoon?" Take careful note of some factual details, dear reader, so as to avoid confusion later in this narrative: Gibbs was not Morlock's immediate squad leader. There are four squads in a platoon. Sergeant Sprague was Morlock's immediate squad leader. Sprague invoked his 5th Amendment rights as soon as the investigation into the killings began, and he was never convicted of any crime. Morlock later told me, "Sprague did not know because we kept him in the dark."

Morlock's platoon did not score any kills of any sort, lawful or otherwise, until Gibbs's arrival in the platoon; and Gibbs's leadership apparently spilled over from his immediate squad into Sprague's squad and other squads. Gibbs was widely regarded as the ringleader of the so-called "kill team," which was the nickname the media invented for the five accused soldiers. But Gibbs was not merely one of the brigade commander's many bodyguards. In one of his statements, Gibbs described his relationship with Colonel Tunnell as follows: "There was one person close to him, and that was my role. My role was standing right next to Colonel Tunnell." Spinner's face lit up: "Yes, that's a connection. But you have to support it with other connections."

"Is it a connection that all the soldiers I've worked with in other war crimes cases were nice, normal young men and women, while in each case, from Abu Ghraib through Operation Iron Triangle and the Bagh-dad Canal killings, to this case, the brigade commanders established poi-soned work environments?"

"You would have to make the connections in that pattern," Spinner said, and smiled again. It was always a friendly smile, like your favorite grandpa's or uncle's. I had learned that Spinner's grandpa-like demeanor is deceptive, though not in any intentional or mean-spirited way. Beneath the warm demeanor there lies a brilliant strategist who is fiercely devoted to his clients and to his profession. He catches opposing attorneys off-guard and is pugnacious in a mild-mannered sort of way. Spinner's reputation always precedes him: opposing government attorneys invariably respect him based on what they've heard about him. Other lawyers typically say, "Oh Spinner, I've heard good things about him." Morlock later told me that some of the army prosecutors "were scared of Spinner." Spinner continued: "But you can't say on the witness stand that Jeremy was nice. You can't say anything personal about him at all. You must not mention anything at all based upon your conversations with him."

"What? I've been speaking with him on the phone every week, at least twice a week, for the past six months. Why can't I talk about the young man I have come to know? And it's a fact that he is a nice young man."

"Because that would open doors for the prosecutors," Spinner said.

"Oh no, not the ole 'open doors' and 'close doors' thing again," I said. "Do they really teach about opening and closing doors in law schools?" This time, we both laughed. The first time I heard a military judge say to an attorney in the courtroom, "Counsel, be careful, you're opening doors"—I had no idea what the judge was talking about. This is because the main actors in a courtroom drama, namely, the judge and opposing attorneys, know—pretty much, more or less, yet with enough uncertainty to score brilliant victories or shameful defeats—ahead of time which doors they will "open," "close" or keep "closed." The metaphor of the trial process as a long corridor is apt. The goal of each attorney seems to be to get through the corridor as efficiently as possible and to block the opposing side from "opening doors" which could lead to another, different, and far more dangerous corridor than the one in sight. The accused, jury and family members, witnesses, and the outsider often have no idea as to why certain "obvious" facts are kept out of proceedings while seemingly "irrelevant" facts are admitted. Lawyer-ing is about strategy carried out by insiders in front of an audience who do not really know what the insiders are intending.

Spinner closed the conversation: "Your job is solely to connect Colonel Tunnell's poisoned command climate with what Jeremy did. I will show that Jeremy was a good person through the testimonies of his mother, coach, school principal, uncle, and previous squad leader. You will be sworn in as an expert in sociology and nothing but sociology. I know you wear a hat in psychology. You wear another hat in theology. And you wear a hat in sociology. On the witness stand, this time, you will wear only your hat in sociology." Spinner was referring to my three graduate degrees in the aforementioned professions. An academic might dispute whether these three professions are that insulated from each other. A scholastic discussion of this sort would have been futile with Spinner.

He had told me long ago: "Remember, I'm the decider." "You and George Bush, yes, I know," I replied. If I had said on the witness stand that Morlock was a nice, normal, young man, I would have 'opened the door' for the prosecution to argue that he was not. But the prosecutor would not challenge his mother, coach, principal, uncle, and squad leader, because they knew him like the prosecutor could never know him. If I could open the door on the disastrous command climate that Colonel Tunnell established, the record of trial (ROT) would force everyone who read it in the future to confront the question of what happened to this nice young man who was thrust into a poisoned social climate—and to wonder about other young war criminals in similar social circumstances. More precisely, Spinner would open that door, the prosecutor would try to keep that door closed, and I was expected to walk through it if possible.

It was the third of March, 2011. Morlock's scheduled court-martial had been postponed due to CPT Opachan's emergency leave. Spinner and Opachan had the option to waive the requirement that Opachan be present at Morlock's court-martial, and to proceed, but Spinner asked for a postponement because, as he told me, "I want the prosecutor to know that we mean business." This fortuitous delay gave me more time to sort out how to open some new "doors." At Morlock's trial, and in this book, I will have attempted to open the conceptual and emotional doors to the connection between a social group's dysfunctional climate and resulting war crimes.

While this connection will appear more or less obvious to most sociologists, it seems to be completely foreign to lawyers, judges, journalists, psychologists, psychiatrists, and other professionals who involve themselves in the narratives of war crimes. Most professionals and laypersons alike are used to the idea of "hunting monsters" (Ressler & Schachtman, 1993). In other words, most people suppose that a heinous crime was committed by a sociopath, or "monster." But Morlock is not a sociopath. Additionally, Morlock committed his crimes in the context of a "bad platoon," or dysfunctional social groups at many levels (squad, platoon, company, battalion, and brigade). The typical response by the profession of law is to judge and punish some of the individuals in the lowest levels of this group hierarchy, namely, the squad and platoon—but not to walk through the door of examining how "bad social groups" in general lay the foundation for heinous crimes. The consequences of this new way of conceptualizing war crimes—namely, in the social context of the groups in which the criminal is embedded—are enormous. If the social groups contributed to the crimes indirectly through their dysfunction and the establishment of a poisoned work environment, then the responsibility for the crimes is partly collective *as well as* individual. At the present moment in history, it does not seem to be the case that the law is able to account for this insight, habituated as it is to hunting and punishing individual "monsters" only.

One is used to psychologists, historians, psychiatrists and numerous professions serving as expert witnesses in trials and courts-martial. But it is very rare for sociologists to testify as experts, in general, and especially at war crimes courts-martial. I have never come across a fellow sociologist as an expert witness at any of the courts-martial which I studied or in which I participated. Opening the sociological door to understanding war crimes is relatively novel.

Spinner's legal focus on connecting Corporal Morlock's actions to the brigade commander's dysfunctional climate is a very specific "door" that he wanted me to walk through as a sociologist. I carried out my role in Spinner's legal strategy. However, in the present study, I intend to open many other "doors" in the long corridor connecting Morlock's actions with society. I intend to connect the crimes under discussion here with COIN doctrine, anti-COIN doctrine, the ambivalence in American culture toward "warfare" as a metaphor for fighting phenomena ranging from drugs to cancer, and many other phenomena. Spinner was right about the importance of making connections, but the connections I will be making in this book will go beyond the narrow, legal scope of connecting evidence to crime.

Spinner and I finished talking for the time being. I walked down the long corridor to the so-called "library," opened the door, and asked Morlock if he was ready to go outside for a break. "I'm ready, there's no oxygen in this room," he said. He complained frequently that there were absolutely no vents in that tiny room full of people. (Like all the other soldiers I had met who served in Iraq and Afghanistan, he immediately and by habit evaluated all buildings and rooms which he entered with regard to possible dangers.) My "crew," as Spinner called them, Dr. Ryan Caldwell and Dr. Keith Kerr, would join us for the break. They are my former doctoral students who were professors of sociology on opposite ends of the country at that point. Morlock peeked into a room across the hall and requested a guard to accompany him downstairs. The guards were always members of his brigade, and they were not "real" guards in the sense of formal training or police status. They were simply his colleagues. He knew them, and they were always friendly.

We walked about fifty yards to an area which was located at the edge of a beautiful parade ground, underneath several huge pine trees. The commanding general's ornate residence—a veritable mansion—was at one end of the parade ground, while his equally ornate and imposing headquarters building was at the other end. Every social setting in the world has its leisure class and symbols of power (Veblen, 1899), and an army base is no exception to this rule. On that same morning, I had finished looking at several thousand photographs of Morlock's deployment in Afghanistan, under the watchful eyes of army CID agents. (Those CID agents were very friendly and helpful to me in explaining what they knew about the context and background of the photos.) Most of those several thousand photographs would remain sealed forever and out of reach of the American people, although a few would be leaked to the news media. This, too, was a common pattern in all the war crimes trials in which I have participated: the public makes its judgments based upon a tiny fraction of leaked photos while the overwhelming bulk of photos are never seen. Spinner arranged for me to see them as part of my preparation for testimony. On that particular day, I was struck by the photographs of Morlock's entire platoon painting their platoon motto, "Death Dealers," onto a piece of plywood.

I said to Morlock: "Jeremy, why were you guys calling yourselves the 'death dealers' when your mission was COIN?" COIN refers to the official U.S. military policy of counter-insurgency, which purportedly aimed at winning the hearts and minds of the Afghan people.

Morlock replied: "You still don't get it. Our mission was COIN, but our brigade motto was 'Strike and Destroy.' Every unit in the brigade had violent mottos. COIN was treated as a joke."

Morlock's guard chimed in: "Yeah, my platoon motto was 'Shoot Them in the Face.'" "You're kidding, right?" I said. The guard, who was from Morlock's brigade, answered gravely: "No, I'm serious. It was 'Shoot Them in the Face.'"

Caldwell, Kerr, and I looked at each other in disbelief. Morlock and his guard proceeded to educate us on other nicknames in their brigade: Morlock's Battalion was nicknamed the Legionnaires. His company was nicknamed Black Watch, and its motto was "There is no hunting like the hunting of men." Morlock explained that Black Watch referred to the 3rd Battalion of the Royal Regiment of Scotland, which has a long and bloody history going back the 17th century, including the more recent fighting in Fallujah, Iraq. The company with which his company was merged was nicknamed Arikara, named after one of the Native American tribes which General George Custer faced at the Battle of Little Big Horn. The nickname for Alpha Company in Morlock's battalion was Attack. Charlie Company was nicknamed the Spartans, and the headquarters Company were the Trojans.

"Why am I learning about this literally on the day before your trial?" I asked Morlock. "I tried to tell you on the first day we meet at the navy brig," Morlock replied. It is true. Caldwell, Kerr, and I first met Morlock at the naval brig that was about an hour and a half drive away from Ft. Lewis, on September 25, 2010. (The army placed Morlock in the navy brig so that he would not have any contact with the other accused soldiers, who were at the army detention facility at Ft. Lewis.) Morlock did tell us that the motto, guidons, pistols, stationery, and other symbols used by the brigade were all marked with the words "Strike and Destroy" or "counter-guerrilla." He did tell us that his platoon's motto was "Death Dealers." But his words did not fully register with me until I saw the words in a photograph, in the context of a platoon of smiling soldiers. "And your platoon leader, Lieutenant Ligsay, is in the photograph too," I said. "Of course," Morlock replied, "we were all pumped up." The reason I brought up the platoon leader is that a commissioned officer was encouraging his troops in this violent symbolism, and he later got in trouble for this after the battalion commander learned of it.

When I later tried discussing these violent symbols and nicknames with Spinner, he was not impressed. He said: "We had similar nicknames at the Air Force Academy." Perhaps some readers will share Spinner's reaction and conclude that violent nicknames are acceptable and to be expected among military units, sport teams, and other social groups bent upon combat, real or metaphorical. Nevertheless, one should consider the discordance between these typically violent nicknames and symbols with the official and new policy of the US government, as of the year 2007, to "win hearts and minds" through COIN doctrine. How could one expect—in any realistic sense—soldiers to suddenly shift from the mind-set of "Shoot them in the face" to one of "Go have tea with the village elders?"

Conversation with a battalion commander, Colonel A: "Colonel Tunnell sought revenge"

"Colonel Tunnell's comment sums it up best, when he said to me in his office, prior to our deployment, that he was after revenge for being shot in the leg while serving in Iraq." This is how one of his battalion commanders, Colonel A, remembered his boss, adding: "Colonel Tunnell kept the metal rod from his leg on his desk in his office, and would use it as a pointer." The metal rod had held Colonel Tunnell's leg together while he was recuperating from the injury in Iraq. All of Hellraiser's battalion commanders described him similarly in words that are refractions of some sort of archetype pertaining to Captain Ahab, the tragic anti-hero in Herman Melville's novel, *Moby Dick*, who invites destruction upon his entire crew as the result of his obsession for revenge upon a whale. Ahab and Hellraiser both had their legs destroyed. Archetypes exist, and persist, for a reason. Fictional characters from novels become memorable across generations for a reason. The reason is that archetypes summarize innumerable impressions by millions of people to capture a "social type"—not just an individual personality—and they capture it immediately, emotionally, and collectively. Archetypes also capture the meaning of a type of person more succinctly than scholarly explanations, theories, and verbiage. And perhaps COL A is correct that the image of Hellraiser bent on revenge *sums it up best*. But COL A's opinion is itself a summary of thousands of events and interactions he had under Hellraiser's command, as well as of COL A's own experiences as a battalion commander in Hellraiser's brigade.

I spoke with COL A over the phone as part of my preparation for my testimony, and I contacted him only after Spinner gave me permission to do so. Spinner instructed me: "Experts are allowed to investigate and to testify on what others tell them. The prosecutor will make the objection that it is 'hearsay' and inadmissible, but typically, the judge will allow it." And that is exactly what happened on the date of my testimony at Morlock's court-martial, March 23, 2011. Spinner also advised me: "They are not required to speak with you, and if they decline, you must hang up immediately and not persist. But anything they tell you is not protected under the law." Several officers refused to speak with me, but Colonel A seemed eager to speak.

When I reported to Spinner that three battalion commanders agreed to speak with me, he seemed pleasantly surprised, and said: "How did you get them to talk with you?" The wily lawyer told me that I could try to speak with them, but he did not really believe they would agree to do so. I said to Spinner: "It's human nature, Frank. If Hellraiser was in fact as he is described in reports, the battalion commanders must have suffered under his command. And anyone who suffers unjustly for a long period of time will want to talk about their suffering." After all, the fictional character, Ishmael—the sole survivor of Ahab's vengeance—wrote an entire book (through Melville), because he and the rest of the crew of the imaginary Pequod suffered grievously under Ahab's command. Metaphorically speaking, Stryker Brigade was the Pequod. This brigade with no previous history was doomed from the moment that it was created artificially from portions of other regiments and assigned to Hellraiser.

My first phone conversation with COL A took place in late February, 2011. I found his sworn statement in the internal army report, previously mentioned, that had been handed over to the defense team, albeit under a gag order. Were it not classified as a report, this document could pass for a very long book. And it is not exactly a report or a book, but is more accurately a compendium of sworn statements made by Hellraiser's battalion and company commanders, commissioned as well as non-commissioned officers or sergeants. A sworn statement is a legal document, the civilian equivalent of an affidavit. COL A and all the others who made sworn statements had to raise their right hands, swear that the statement was true, and sign it in the presence of a witness. It is important to emphasize that the report is mostly about Hellraiser and his brigade, as seen through the eyes of his subordinates, *not* about Corporal Morlock and his squad or platoon. It is not even about the crimes in question, but is mostly about COIN doctrine versus counter-guerrilla doctrine, and about the passions concerning duty, responsibility, and the confusing mission that were unleashed by Hellraiser. The prosecutor released the Twitty Report to the defense team about a week before Morlock's court-martial was scheduled to begin at Ft. Lewis. Ours was the only defense team to obtain access to this remarkable document at the time, because of brilliant strategizing on the part of Spinner. Spinner convinced the prosecutor to include my testimony on the Twitty Report as part of the pre-trial agreement which Morlock, the prosecutor, Captain Opachan, and the base commander, Lieutenant General Scaparrotti, signed in late January, 2011. The prosecutor knew that this report opened thousands of doors to facts that the government wanted to keep hush-hush. He did not give me much time to study it. After weeks of frustration and back-and-forth e-mails between the defense team and the prosecutor, the Twitty Report finally arrived on my doorstep via FedEx in late February. Morlock's first court-martial (which was postponed after we all arrived at Ft. Lewis) was scheduled for the first week of March, 2011.

The clock was ticking. I e-mailed COL A and explained who I was and why I wanted to interview him. He eventually called me on my cell phone. I told him that I was surprised at the strong negative views of Hellraiser that he and other battalion commanders expressed in their sworn statements that were included in the report. For example, I reminded COL A that he wrote that Hellraiser was the most difficult commander with whom he had ever served, and that he would never want to serve with him again in the future.

"Do you really feel that strongly about your former commander?" I asked.

"That's right. And if the army were ever to assign me under his command again, I would resign and take an early retirement rather than serve under him."

"One of the other battalion commanders did precisely that: he resigned. Why did some of you and some of the other commanders feel that strongly?

"Colonel Tunnell is bad for the army."

"Did people really refer to him as Hellraiser or Destroyer, rather than by his name?"

"Those were his call signs, yes."

"But when he came by to visit your battalion in the field, did you guys say, 'Colonel Tunnell is on his way' or did you say 'Hellraiser is on his way?'"

"Hellraiser. But that's the point. He almost never came to visit. We almost never saw him. I would say that in the entire year of deployment, I saw him only four times. On the other hand, I met with General McChrystal many times and McChrystal's staff officers visited weekly."

"Colonel, I know this is a somewhat sensitive question, but the report makes it clear that Colonel Tunnell's subordinates were split into two opposing camps, pro-COIN and Colonel Tunnell's anti-COIN camp. Which side were you on?"

"I was pro-chain-of-command. Colonel Tunnell was interested in one thing only and that was destroying the enemy. He did not allow the word COIN to be used around him." Take careful note, dear reader, that COL A did not take sides for or against COIN doctrine, but answered that he was following orders from the chain-of-command. Even though COIN was the official policy of the US government at the time of my investigation (and in fact, since the year 2007), not a single officer or soldier with whom I spoke ever said that he was pro-COIN. To be pro-chain-of-command was the safe answer. But was the chain-of-command truly pro-COIN, even though it proclaimed it as the official policy of the US government after the year 2007?

"Okay. It seems that you were more directly under the influence of General McChrystal and his staff officers than your own brigade commander."

"Colonel Tunnell was 108 kilometers away and I hardly ever saw him."

"Let me switch gears. I read in the report that the company which was involved in the crimes initially came from your battalion. I think the slang term for this process is cross-leveling. And this company was further cross-leveled by moving two platoons out and two platoons in from companies in 2-1 battalion."

"That's right. Colonel Tunnell requested one of my companies, because we are a reconnaissance unit, and in turn he gave me one of his infantry companies from 2-1. But he took it back."

"He took it back?"

"That's right. I gave him my best company. Captain Q was the company commander. Captain M was the executive officer. Sergeant Major H was the first sergeant. They were my most outstanding soldiers, the most professional, the most trustworthy. A month later he took back the company of infantry soldiers that he gave us, and left me exposed. I commanded one of the most sensitive and volatile areas in Afghanistan, right on the border with Pakistan. Colonel Tunnell and I had a falling out about that."

So that the reader is not overly confused, let me explain that COL A gave Colonel Tunnell his Alpha Troop ("companies" are called "troops" in cavalry battalions), which was further cross-leveled in 2-1, and he received Charlie Company from 2-1. The reasoning seems to have been that COL A, whose battalion was primarily involved in reconnaissance, needed an infantry company to protect it on missions. But Colonel Tunnell took back Charlie Company, while he left a cross-leveled A Troop/B Company within 2-1, and Morlock was left in this cross-leveled hybrid company, and separated from his original, habitual B Company Commander, Captain T.

"What do you mean, a falling out?"

"Very harsh words were exchanged."

"OK. This is really hard to follow and I want to make sure I get it just right. The company involved in the crimes initially came from your battalion. Then that company was assigned to a battalion under the command of LTC B, who in turn had replaced LTC C, whom Colonel Tunnell had in effect fired right about the time of the pre-deployment training. And in exchange for giving up your company, you received a company from a battalion under the command of LTC B. I mean, all this switching around of soldiers and units is mind-boggling."

COL A seemed to think that this and other instances of cross-leveling were not mind-boggling, but routine. I switched gears to approach the topic of which battalion commanders Hellraiser liked and disliked. I said: "And it's my impression from the report that the 1-17 commander was Colonel Tunnell's favorite because he was the most aggressive."

"Initially, I was Colonel Tunnell's golden boy. Then we had the falling out, and that changed. Nobody could get away with disagreeing with Colonel Tunnell"

"Colonel, here is another sensitive question. If this company you gave up to 2-1 was your best one, how do you explain that it was the very one involved in the killings that are going to trial soon?"

There was a pause on the other end of the line. "I can't explain it. I had absolutely no contact with Captain Q or his company after they left my battalion. But I will always insist that Captain Q was one of my best officers."

"Okay. What about the cross-leveling itself? Don't they teach at war colleges that cross-leveling destroys morale and trust because it moves soldiers around as if they were chess pieces without regard for the emotional ties they had established with their leaders and peers? That's well known in sociology, ever since Samuel Stouffer's classic study, *The American Soldier.*"

"Cross-leveling is an established part of Army doctrine."

"Okay. So let me see if I have the facts straight. Your best company was the one in which these crimes occurred, but they occurred only after this company had left your command. You had a falling out with Colonel Tunnell even though initially you say you were his golden boy. You and other battalion commanders were trying to follow General McChrystal's directives to implement COIN, while your brigade commander openly mocked those directives and forbade you from using the word COIN around him."

"That's right."

"Are you aware that Gibbs was one of Colonel Tunnell's personal bodyguards and was transferred into Captain Q's company, and that the killings started shortly after Gibbs was transferred?"

COL A repeated that he did not know anything about his company after it was taken away from his command. And so we left unresolved the mystery of how COL A's outstanding company came to be involved in the war crimes under discussion here. How did COL A's *best* company become a "bad" company in a different battalion?

Conversation with Corporal Morlock's new battalion commander, LTC B

I e-mailed LTC B, who had been Morlock's battalion commander at the time of the killings in Afghanistan, and asked him for an interview. I knew from reading the Twitty report that prior to being assigned to Hellraiser's brigade, he had been an instructor in COIN doctrine. He called me on the phone the day before Morlock's court-martial. What he told me was entirely consistent with the Twitty report, and with what the other battalion commanders had told me, only more detailed. "Let me ask you an uncomfortable question, colonel," I said. "I have the impression that the entire brigade was split into two camps, pro-brigade commander and anti-COIN versus anti-brigade commander and pro-COIN. Which side were you on?"

"I was pro-chain-of-command," he said. (At this point, I was seriously beginning to wonder exactly how one should characterize the split within the brigade, because it was clear that no one was precisely pro-COIN.) And he added that during the first two months of his battalion's deployment in Afghanistan, he was not under Colonel Tunnell's command at all but was directly under General McChrystal's command in South Afghanistan. COL A had said something similar about the influence of McChrystal upon him.

"How is it possible that you were not under Colonel Tunnell's command, given that you were a battalion commander in Colonel Tunnell's brigade?" I asked.

"That's just the way it was," he said.

LTC B said that he "did COIN" because that was General McChrystal's policy, and because it was Army doctrine in Afghanistan. One should note LTC B's precise words: "Doing" COIN is not necessarily the same as believing in COIN doctrine or being pro-COIN. He added that COL Tunnell knew that LTC B was *doing* COIN, and therefore wrote him off, so to speak.

"How often did Colonel Tunnell 'circulate' or visit your battalion?" I asked.

"Really, never. He came by a couple of times to award medals, and left." Morlock confirmed this observation, which is consistent with all other reports. Ironically, COL Tunnell pinned the Combat Infantryman's Badge onto Morlock's chest on one of those rare occasions that he visited the battalion. This fact was entered into the trial record at Morlock's court-martial.

"Is it true, what COL A told me, that he had a 'falling out' with COL Tunnell about the brigade commander's anti-COIN mindset versus COL A's desire to follow the chain of command, namely, COIN?"

"Everybody knew about their conflict."

"And COL A told me that COL Tunnell ordered him to give your battalion an entire company of soldiers, in return for one of your companies? I keep forgetting the formal term for this, but it's cross-leveling." At this point, I could hear LTC B sigh deeply on the other end of the phone, and he said "yes."

"And was COL A's company further cross-leveled such that two platoons were taken out of one of his companies, while two platoons were put in from your battalion?"

"Yes." But LTC B explained that the situation was more complicated than that. Basically, all of LTC B's infantry companies were hybrids composed of platoons from other units.

"And this strange hybrid company, led by Captain Q, who was, according to COL A, his best company commander, was the one involved in the killings now going to trial?" Again, LTC B confirmed this fact, as well as the fact that Sergeant Gibbs was transferred from COL Tunnell's bodyguard company into this new amalgamated company led by Captain Q.

I asked: "So how did this transfer take place? Did you sign papers? Did you have a say in the decision to transfer Gibbs into your battalion?"

LTC B told me he had been "left out of the loop" on the decision and really did not know who ordered it or why. He did not sign any papers. He learned after the fact that Gibbs was what the Army called a "rehabilitative transfer," basically a second-chance after receiving an Article 15 for stealing a motorized vehicle called a Gator.

I continued: "Colonel, as painful as this question is, I have to ask you. How do explain the fact that COL A's best commander was in charge of the company that was involved in these killings, and that his former company was under your command?"

There was a long pause in the conversation, and I could hear LTC B sigh again on the other end of the phone. He said: "I've been asking myself that question for months, over and over again. All I can tell you is that my battalion had no problems until Gibbs came on the scene." I said: "Is it something like, 'Gibbs was the Typhoid Mary who contaminated the platoon with Colonel Tunnell's infectious doctrine?'" LTC B seemed relieved at my metaphor: "You have to follow the facts. Everything was fine; then Gibbs came to us from Colonel Tunnell's detachment, and the killings started."

My conversations with LTC C, Corporal Morlock's former battalion commander

LTC C was Corporal Morlock's original battalion commander at Ft. Lewis prior to deployment to Afghanistan. In fact, LTC C was forced into retirement by Hellraiser immediately prior to the brigade's deployment. In plain language, LTC B replaced LTC C. I spoke with LTC C several times over the phone, and at considerable length, in addition to meeting him at Ft. Lewis. LTC C's first words to me, after exchanging introductions, were the following:

"I firmly believe that Colonel Tunnell suffers from a personality disorder."

I was taken aback by this statement, including the fact that an army battalion commander would use the language of professional psychologists. I attempted to clarify his statement: "I assume you mean a diagnosis like Narcissistic Personality Disorder or one of the other so-called character disorders?" "Yes," he replied. In the present study, I do not take a position on whether or not Hellraiser suffered from a personality disorder, because I have no access to any diagnostic facts to support LTC C's contention. It is important for the sake of historical record to note the fact that LTC C expressed this opinion even though I am not in a position to verify it. *If* LTC C's contention were true, it would be in line with consistent research in marketing and business journals which show that CEOs who suffer from personality disorders bring ruin to themselves and their corporations. It would also be in line with the classic work in this field, Sam Vaknin's (2007) *Malignant Self-Love*. Vaknin demonstrates that the malignant narcissist boss destroys social relationships in his or her milieu. The one area in which such research is lacking is that of military commanders. But all this is merely an interesting digression. Spinner had cautioned me to "never lead the witness" in my interviews, and my own training in sociology follows a similarly neutral maxim. I asked LTC C to elaborate as to what he meant by his statement. He elaborated at length:

Well, first off, I should tell you that Colonel Tunnell in person is completely different from his aggressive memorandums and persona. He projects aggression in his image, but in person, he is a recluse. He is completely asocial. I'll give you an example. On one occasion, all the officers received free tickets to an NFL game in Seattle, and it was decided that we would go as a group and sit as a group. We all showed up, and were looking for Colonel Tunnell. He wasn't there. It turned out that he sat on the other end of the stadium, alone, and left alone. He never socialized with the other officers. You never dared to disagree with him about anything. He would seethe quietly and you knew that he would carry out his revenge. One of his most peculiar habits was that anytime you made a request, he would listen, not grant it, and then ask you at the end of the meeting, "So, you didn't get what you wanted, did you?"

As I listened to LTC C, I thought about the author Herman Melville's depiction of Captain Ahab as a loner, as the invisible leader who incited his men to kill Moby Dick, but did not eat with or socialize with his men in any manner. Of course, I did not bring up Melville with LTC C, but I asked him about Hellraiser's attitude toward COIN. LTC C again gave a long reply:

All the commanders knew that we should never say the word COIN in his presence. He lectured and issued memorandums on what he called counter-guerrilla doctrine, which is just about killing the enemy. That's where I ran into trouble. I was the only one among the battalion commanders who confronted him openly at a meeting about following the chain of command, which was to do COIN. My punishment was that he relieved me of command. But he did that his way. He allowed me to go through the motions of being the commander of my battalion during the National Training Center (NTC) exercises, though we both knew that I would not be deployed to Afghanistan. NTC was a debacle. He immediately got on the wrong side of all the trainers, who wanted us to do COIN, while he wanted to do counter-guerrilla. Our brigade was the laughing stock of the NTC.

"So how did that work? If he did not want to do COIN, and all the trainers wanted you to do COIN, something had to give. I don't understand how that is possible." LTC C replied:

"The way it worked is that I would fill out one training program for the trainers who wanted us to do COIN, and I would fill out a different training program and file it with Colonel Tunnell."

"You're kidding. That's like double-bookkeeping."

"I'm not kidding. That's what we all had to do."

"I read in the Twitty report that several generals were called in to advise Colonel Tunnell to comply with COIN. What do you know about that?"

"Look, his attitude was anti-COIN during the entire existence of Stryker Brigade. He got a dressing-down from generals at several different meetings, in front of all the subordinate commanders. He did not react. The rest of us just watched in silence."

"I really have a hard time imagining that. But I also read that some of the generals contemplated not certifying him or the brigade as fit for deployment. How did Stryker Brigade get certified under such conditions?"

"You'd have to ask those generals. My opinion is that those generals are partly responsible for what happened."

"Are you referring to the killings that are going to court-martial?"

"Yes."

"What do you know about the whole cross-leveling thing and changes in leadership that occurred in Morlock's battalion?"

"I don't know anything about any of that. I wasn't there."

"Switching gears a little bit, this case reminds me somewhat of the Operation Iron Triangle case, in which the brigade commander, Colonel Michael Steele, also espoused a very aggressive attitude which was at odds with the official Rules of Engagement. Do you have any thoughts on that?"

"You should know that Colonel Steele came to NTC to give a pep talk to Stryker Brigade."

We discussed this last point at some length. I expressed surprise that after being reprimanded for the Operation Iron Triangle fiasco, and in the aftermath of three soldiers sent to Ft. Leavenworth, the army would allow Colonel Steele to lecture Tunnell's soldiers on similarly aggressive attitudes, all in the shadow of COIN as official doctrine. LTC C did not express surprise. He added that at the time of this visit to Stryker brigade, Steele was an adjutant to General "Hondo" Campbell, who was the commander of FORSCOM [U.S. Army Forces Command]. "What does that mean?" I asked. "It means he was in charge of all operations in the theater." This general went by his nickname, "Hondo," and not his real name.

The connection to Steele is very important. I have published two books on Steele's infamous order to his troops to kill every military-age male on sight during Operation Iron Triangle (Mestrovic, 2008, 2009). A recent book, *The Fourth Star*, documents how General Peter Chiarelli tried to rein in Steele and other commanders like him who held a "strike and destroy" philosophy toward Iraqis. Three low-ranking enlisted soldiers were sent to prison for the killings during Operation Iron Triangle, while Steele received a reprimand. But even the act of issuing the reprimand was like a scene out of an old Western film: "On the day Steele arrived for his punishment, several of Chiarelli's staff were so worried about what the volatile colonel might do they insisted his aide, Major

Gventer, stand outside his office with a round chambered in his side arm" (Jaffe and Cloud, 2010, p. 237). General Chiarelli was criticized by other generals for trying to restrain an aggressive fighting philosophy that is similar to the one under discussion here and which was apparently not restrained by Hellraiser's commanders.

Prior to the first scheduled court-martial (which was postponed), Spinner and I both met LTC C in person. The three of us had breakfast together at the International Guest House in Dupont, Washington, which is approximately two miles from the main gate of Ft. Lewis. Spinner considered having LTC C testify at Morlock's court-martial on the dysfunctional command climate in Stryker Brigade. LTC C was willing to testify, as he was now retired and had nothing to lose. Spinner asked him why he wanted to testify, and LTC C gave the now familiar reply: "Because I believe that Colonel Tunnell is bad for the army." LTC C recounted for Spinner all of the major points which he had made to me and elaborated further on issues raised by Spinner. In the end, Spinner decided against having LTC C testify because of the acrimonious professional relationship between Hellraiser and LTC C.

Conversation with the Chaplain for 1-17

I wanted to speak with the chaplain for a battalion to which Corporal Morlock did *not* belong, 1-17, for several reasons. I noticed that in the Twitty report, 1-17 was depicted as the "murderous" battalion because of its many "questionable" kills. Morlock was in 2-1, which was known for doing COIN, and not for scoring kills. How is it that the questionable kills in 1-17 were not investigated and did not result in any charges against anyone? Furthermore, I noticed that sworn statements from members of 1-17 were conspicuously rare, while sworn statements from members of 2-1 were plentiful. Why was there this discrepancy? In sum, I wanted to speak with an officer from 1-17 to verify these and other intriguing patterns.

To make a long story short, I finally asked the prosecutor—in Spinner's presence—for the chaplain's phone number. This was because, as I explained to the prosecutor, no one answered the phone when I called the chaplain or the chaplain's office at Ft. Lewis—the phone would just keep ringing, and never switch to an answering machine. The prosecutor, CPT LeBlanc, responded with gallows humor: "Imagine calling the chaplain, your life is in ruins, you need spiritual guidance, and there's nobody there!" He laughed, and his laughter was contagious, so that we all laughed. He ordered his assistant to track down the chaplain's cell phone number for me.

I finally reached the chaplain on the phone, introduced myself, and explained the reason for my call. He had retired from the army after his deployment in Afghanistan had ended, and was a pastor at a church in a large, metropolitan city in the U.S. The chaplain almost immediately said that he would only tell me things that would not violate any sort of confidentiality or privileged information from his role as the former chaplain to 1-17. I asked him about the negative reputation of his former battalion as overly aggressive. He said, "Our battalion had the most casualties as well as kills because we were thrust into the Arghandab Valley. It was unpopulated and laced with IEDs."

"Wasn't the battalion's presence in that valley against COIN doctrine?"

"Colonel Tunnell wanted us there, and LTC N [the battalion commander] complied."

"Did Colonel Tunnell play favorites with LTC N and 1-17?"

"I wouldn't say that. It's true that Colonel Tunnell visited 1-17 more than any other battalion. I saw him several times a week. But it wasn't a question of playing favorites as much as Colonel Tunnell wanted to be where the action was. And we were where the action was." The chaplain also explained that Colonel Tunnell always visited in a Stryker vehicle, accompanied by two other Stryker vehicles, each filled with soldiers from his personal "security detail." This came to more than fifty bodyguards on each visit—and up to December 2009, Gibbs was one of them. This security detail, known as the A 5/2, ate, slept, and associated separately from all the other soldiers.

"I read a lot in the report about the opposing teams in the brigade regarding COIN doctrine versus counter-guerrilla doctrine. What can you tell me about that?"

"It consumed a lot of mental energy, and nobody ever really resolved what we were doing, COIN or counter-guerrilla. The real problem was that 1-17 had the worst discipline in the brigade, and the lack of discipline caused a lot of unnecessary deaths among the soldiers."

He elaborated that because soldiers in 1-17 were doing most of the fighting in the brigade, they and their non-commissioned as well as commissioned officers stopped paying attention to normal army standards of discipline. Soldiers stopped addressing superiors as "sir." They did not meet standards for wearing their uniforms. Cliques developed in which soldiers became overly friendly with superiors and were exempt from routine standards. He gave the example of wearing seatbelts: this standard ceased to be enforced. As a result, when IEDs went off, many soldiers died because the vehicle rolled over and they were not properly strapped in. He also complained that soldiers went on missions that he considered unnecessary, through orchards, in pursuit of the Taliban, which resulted in many deaths to soldiers from IEDs.

What about the battalion's reputation for questionable kills? "Yes, there were questionable kills, but the commander refused to investigate them." He did not elaborate on this theme.

The chaplain also recounted the story of how Captain Joel Kassulke, the Charlie Company commander, was fired by Colonel Tunnell for reasons nobody in the battalion could comprehend. "Kassulke was loved by his men," the chaplain said.

Chapter 2. Hellraiser's Commanders Assess Him

One of the most distinctive and informative elements of the Twitty report is that it includes sworn statements by three generals who were Hellraiser's superiors. These statements offer a rare glimpse into the politics and dynamics of the highest echelons of the army's power structure. The three generals refer to a number of other generals who became Hellraiser's commanders once Stryker brigade deployed to Afghanistan. However, the Twitty report does not include sworn statements by those additional generals. Taken overall, the generals were clearly unhappy with Hellraiser's attitude prior to and during deployment in Afghanistan, and they express regret that they did not relieve him of command. However, they do not explain why they did not act on their judgments that Hellraiser was not fit to lead and that Stryker Brigade was not fit for deployment.

Statement by Brigadier General D: the National Training Center Operations Group Commander

Before a brigade is deployed to Afghanistan or Iraq, it undergoes a training and assessment period at a place called the National Training Center (NTC). In the case of Stryker brigade, the NTC exercises took place at Ft. Irwin, California. The training involves more than field exercises, the use of equipment and weapons, and other tangible drills. The brigade and battalion commanders also submit written plans for what they hope they will accomplish on their mission.

Hellraiser did not hide his intent to defy General McChrystal's orders at the National Training Center. He openly defied the existing norms of the Army and the U.S. government, and thereby exasperated the train-ers and the Operations Group Commander of the NTC (whom we shall call Brigadier General D, and refer to hereafter as BG D). At the time of the NTC exercises, BG D's rank was that of a colonel; he was later promoted to the rank of brigadier general. As the operations group com-mander, and as a colonel at the time, BG D and Hellraiser clashed openly. The commander of the NTC, Brigadier General P, is mentioned in sev-eral sworn statements by other generals, but he did not write a sworn statement for General Twitty's report. In any case, BG D chose his words carefully when writing about Hellraiser in his sworn statement in the Twitty report:

> The unit had an aggressive, combat-seasoned commander who attempted to apply an internally-generated doctrinal framework that was *outside the commonly accepted norm*—his counter-guerrilla approach could be char-acterized as exclusively enemy-focused. Those who actively or tacitly followed along *were part of the team*; those who did not were viewed as *non-believers and marginalized.* During my 2 year and 20 rotation tenure as the NTC Operations Group Commander, this was the most challenging rotation, *due in part to the late change of scenarios* but more due to the re-luctance by the 5/2 Stryker commander to follow and train his formation using *current doctrine.* The commander set the *tone* for his organization to *ignore doctrinal fundamentals* that many applied in previous tours in Iraq and Afghanistan.... The *cumulative effect* of an *uncooperative leadership su-perstructure* coupled with *open disdain* for contemporary Army doctrine created a divide—the *scenario* and organization aligned to COIN-related multi-echelon skills and a unit chain of command tied *exclusively* to an enemy-centric approach and *unwilling* to adapt [emphasis added].

This general's statement is eloquent. The information he conveys in the paragraph above is so tightly packed, it requires meticulous unpack-ing. First, Hellraiser's doctrine was private or "internally-generated." It failed to connect with the "commonly accepted norm" of the army to such an extreme extent that the general characterizes it as "outside" the commonly accepted norms—at the time—of the US government and the US Army. Hellraiser's private doctrine cannot be characterized as merely "pushing the envelope" or as an example of the benign sorts of aggression one finds among athletes at a sporting event, who come close to break-ing a norm but do not take that final step that would compel a referee to throw them out of a game. No. Had the general been a referee, and the training exercise were like a baseball game, the general should have yelled at Hellraiser, "You're out!"

Second, and because the generals who were his superiors failed to re-move him from command, Hellraiser divided the "team" that was his and America's brigade into two opposing "teams." Those who followed Hellraiser were considered part of *his* team, but this means that they were not part of America's normative team. Hellraiser's team was actually the anti-team relative to the larger context. On the other hand, those officers who defied Hellraiser were seen as "non-believers and marginalized," but they were the normative ones in relation to the larger army culture. To be on Hellraiser's team was to be a "true believer," in contrast to the "non-believers" who opposed him, but who thereby supported the norms of the US government. BG D's choice of the label "non-believers," which automatically invokes the contrast of "true believers," is loaded with multiple connections to fundamentalism, fanaticism, and blind loyalty. It reverberates with echoes of the phrase, "You're with us or against us," found in numerous American films, literature, and political speeches— including the speeches of former President George W. Bush. Hellraiser's true believers necessarily had to become anti-chain-of-command, while the non-believers who remained pro-chain-of-command were necessarily pitted against Hellraiser's private team.

It is not merely the case that the brigade was split into two opposing teams: such a state of affairs is dysfunctional from the perspective of overall group cohesion, and group cohesion is one of the core values and goals of the US Army. In addition, Hellraiser's true believers were on the wrong team, from the perspective of "commonly accepted norms" of the United States at this period of time. To be right (follow the chain of command) was to be wrong in Hellraiser's eyes. To be wrong (defy the government's norms) was to be right in Hellraiser's eyes. This state of affairs in Stryker Brigade illustrates the sociological concept of anomie as it was originally understood by the intellectual who coined it, sociologist Emile Durkheim—namely, as a breakdown, derangement, or disorganization of group structure and cohesion (see Mestrovic, 1988).

Third, the general refers to the "late change of scenarios." Elsewhere in his statement the general explains that "The I Corps staff, 5/2 Stryker Brigade and the NTC staff had approximately three weeks to re-design the scenario and adjust training requirements from an Iraq-based scenario to an Afghan-based scenario." In plain language, Stryker brigade's mission was changed from Iraq to Afghanistan at the last minute, and the environment was going to be entirely different.

The general adds: "Normally, six months is allotted for rotational planning and prep." Morlock explained to my crew and to me what this meant to the low-ranking soldier: "We had been training for months on how to enter and clear out houses as part of our urban warfare training and getting ready for Iraq, and suddenly we were told we'd be walking through orchards to go have tea with the village elders in Afghanistan." This last-minute change in the mission would have been a difficult challenge to the brigade in itself, and it and clearly violated the norm of at least six months that was considered adequate to allow an adjustment to such a change.

Further, at this point in the war—in Iraq as well as Afghanistan—COIN, or winning hearts and minds so as to defuse the rage that spurred insurgent uprisings, was the official policy of the US Army. This fact made no difference to Hellraiser. Whether the mission was to be in Iraq or Afghanistan, Hellraiser did not change his private, aggressive, and anti-chain-of-command doctrine either way.

Fourth, note that the general referred to "scenarios," in general, and with regard to Iraq and Afghanistan. In fact, the words "scenario" and "scenarios" permeate the Twitty report and this entire story. Gibbs is described by his comrades as running "scenarios" past the other soldiers. It is clear that Gibbs did not invent the idea of constructing scenarios. And the particular scenarios of killing unarmed Afghans were not the private, idiosyncratic inventions of Gibbs or any other particular soldier, but were a reflection and extension of Hellraiser's aggressive scenarios. Many pages in the Twitty report document the organized practicing of COIN scenarios such as having tea with village elders, how to manage the cultural taboos pertaining to interactions with Afghan women, greeting Afghan children, and so on. The brigade also practiced counter-guerrilla scenarios such as baited ambush. The important point is that in splitting his brigade into two competing teams, Hellraiser also split them into two opposing scenarios, aggressive versus COIN-oriented.

But this characterization does not exhaust the many dimensions to the scenarios used in these respective yet opposing "teams." The general refers to his and the government's "COIN-related" scenarios versus "exclusively enemy-centric" scenarios promoted by Hellraiser. These two grand scenarios each produced thousands of smaller scenarios. "COIN-related" scenarios ranged from having tea with the village elders, to hesitation in pulling the trigger when confronted with a suspect, to avoiding orchards as an unnecessary exposure to IEDs, among thousands of other scenarios. Conversely, Hellraiser's grand scenario promoted acts that were prohibited by COIN, such as deliberately walking through orchards in order to hunt down insurgents, and prohibited scenarios such as building clinics for Afghan women solely to win favor among the locals. The soldiers rehearsed in their minds the aggressive scenarios they would act out once they arrived in Afghanistan, including "baited ambush" scenarios. The collective mental rehearsal of the soldiers, or the establishment of scenarios—what sociologists call anticipatory socialization—was already poisoned at the NTC.

Fifth, the NTC operations commander does not accuse Hellraiser of any direct or criminal responsibility for the killings that went to trial. But he does hold Hellraiser responsible for the "tone" he set in the brigade—a tone that was divisive at the same time that it was aggressive—and for the "cumulative effect" that his "tone" created. Words are important, and BG D chose his words carefully. He avoids the word "cause." Indeed, all the players in the legal drama that emerged in the subsequent courts-martial avoided the word "cause." Nobody said or implied that Hellraiser "caused" any of the killings. But Hellraiser did create a social climate whose slow, steady, and "cumulative effect," over the course of three years, in thousands of incremental steps and scenarios, was the tragedy of the war crimes that were committed.

Like so many other generals whose reports I have read over the course of many years, BG D wisely avoids the "why" questions and presumed answers, and opts for the "how" questions and answers. One will never know *why* Hellraiser chose an attitude of "open disdain" for existing government policy (or how many years it took for his choice to solidify through thousands of small choices) or why the convicted soldiers engaged in their killing scenarios. But the NTC group operations commander describes *how* Hellraiser's attitude progressively created a command climate which set the stage for the war crimes that occurred.

BG D writes that Hellraiser was "stubborn and maladaptive" in clinging obstinately to his private, aggressive doctrine even though "most if not all of his battalion commanders had successfully applied some form of a COIN strategy on a previous tour to Iraq or Afghanistan." Interestingly, BG D notes that "command climate is not normally addressed as part of formal collective training experience at the NTC." (Perhaps command climate should be part of the formal training.) Nevertheless, he opines that Hellraiser caused a "drag" or "negative effects on unit progression." BG D continues: "In retrospect, there are several indicators that did not allow this unit to grow to its potential in the training environment, and those indicators are attributable to the 5/2 commander's adherence to the counter-guerrilla approach." One of these indicators was that Hellraiser relied on an obsolete training manual, FM 90-8, while the NTC relied on the current-at-the-time FM 3-24, authored by a team under the supervision of General Petraeus. As a result, BG D writes, "we could not move forward during the rotation." "The unit leadership was unable to adjust its mindset" from Hellraiser's doctrine to official army doctrine, and this divide "created confusion." BG D offers a complex, multi-layered account of this confusion:

> Company and Battalion level leadership were *hamstrung*, having to choose between remaining silent when it came to the application of COIN doctrine at their level or applying COIN on the margins or going against the flow of the Brigade's counter-guerrilla approach [emphasis added].

The sociological term "double-bind" exists to capture the mental agony of making a decision under the deranged rule, "You're damned if you do and damned if you don't." BG D is describing an intolerable situation that might be called a triple-bind: the battalion and company commanders were damned if they followed COIN doctrine *and* if they sneaked in COIN doctrine without Hellraiser's knowledge *and* if they openly defied the brigade commander. There was no way to be right without being wrong in the eyes of Hellraiser or the chain of command. BG D writes: "To summarize, there was a reluctance to embrace COIN doctrine. It is my recollection that there were several officers who thought that they would be ostracized for using the term COIN and this feeling was generally prevalent throughout the command." This was because "Colonel Tunnell was quick to marginalize those whose opinions/recommendations differed from his own." BG D adds: "The opinions of others didn't count."

SWORN STATEMENT BY BRIGADIER GENERAL H, THE DIRECTOR OF OPERATIONS FOR RC-S

Brigadier General H, hereafter referred to as BG H, was the Director of Operations for RC-S (Regional Command South), which refers to the command in charge of southern Afghanistan. RC-S fell under the command of General Stanley McChrystal, whose overall command is referred to in the statements as COMISAF. BG H ends his sworn statement in the internal report as follows: "Looking back on my relationship with him [Colonel Tunnell], I regret that I wasn't more involved in his professional development during his tenure as a brigade commander" and "I should have specifically told him that Major General C and I had lost confidence in his ability to command from his failure to follow instructions and intent." Major General C (who did not write a sworn statement) was the Commanding General of RC-S. MG C was also British, which seems to have bothered Hellraiser, who clearly objected to taking orders from British, Dutch, and other foreign NATO generals in Afghanistan. In fact, and regardless of nationality, not a single general among Colonel Tunnell's superiors expressed confidence in his ability to command. Yet they all allowed him to command.

BG H starts his sworn statement with the following sentence: "Inside the brigade, it seemed that the brigade staff were a little intimidated or reluctant to communicate with Colonel Tunnell." He added: "The battalion commanders and staff seemed distant from their commander." This general's assessment is consistent with *all* the characterizations by *all* the commissioned officers who made sworn statements in the Twitty report, namely, that Colonel Tunnell was asocial, distant, and intimidating. BG H added:

> Something that did strike me as odd was the brigade motto "Strike and Destroy," which was unusual since there was no historical significance for this and it seemed counter to what we were trying to accomplish, but I failed to bring this issue up with him as it related to his mission Afghanistan.

Many differences in opinion will exist with regard to the issue whether the brigade motto was "odd" in that it was defiant of then current Army doctrine to win hearts and minds in Afghanistan.

It is significant that this particular general, who was one of Hellraiser's commanders, found the motto to be odd. This admission by the general begs the question: Why did this general, as well as several other generals who were Colonel Tunnell's commanders, fail to order him to change the brigade motto to something more in accordance with public and official US policy? BG H observes that "The battalion commanders did not seem to follow his [Colonel Tunnell's] counter-guerrilla intent but instead did COIN within their area of operations." The reader should note carefully the general's choice of words, which is consistent with what the battalion commanders told me in interviews: the battalion commanders *did* COIN, but no commander admitted to embracing COIN. However, the general does not seem to notice that in order to "do" COIN, they had to "go against" Hellraiser's orders: they had to disobey him, defy him, and do COIN behind his back. How did Hellraiser's commanders fail to notice the negative effects on group cohesion of forcing battalion commanders to lead double-lives?

The friction between Hellraiser and his commanders in the United States carried over when Stryker brigade arrived in Afghanistan, and involved several generals. According to BG H:

> The mission of Stryker [brigade] was to assure the freedom of movement along highway 1 and highway 4 from Kandahar. The expectation of Colonel Tunnell by MG C was to not just run Strykers up and down the road, but to get involved with the local populace. It seemed to me that Colonel Tunnell never bought into the mission, which became a point of friction for us. Either Colonel Tunnell did not grasp the concept or just refused to follow MG C's intent. However, it is difficult for me to think that Colonel Tunnell did not grasp the intended concept.

If BG H did not believe that Colonel Tunnell failed to grasp the COIN concept, then his unstated conclusion seems to be that Colonel Tunnell "just refused to follow" COIN. Notice the polite chicanery BG H uses to avoid stating this conclusion bluntly. Several different generals privately counseled and publicly rebuked Hellraiser for not being a team-player in Afghanistan. Hellraiser's response, which was silence, "seemed almost childish and cadet-like to me," BG H wrote. He added: "The situation [in Afghanistan] was again embarrassing the Army." By using the word "again," BG H apparently meant that Hellraiser had already embarrassed the Army at the NTC in the United States. Apparently, Hellraiser's only direct reply to the criticisms leveled at him by his superiors was that "he didn't believe that the tactic of being civilian-sensitive worked since these tactics did not work from his experience in Iraq."

A THREE-STAR GENERAL ASSESSES HELLRAISER

One of the highest-ranking generals out of all of Hellraiser's commanders was Lieutenant General (three star) J, or LTG J. At the time that Stryker brigade was being deployed to Afghanistan, LTG J was the Deputy Commanding General of Ft. Lewis and of I Corps. He refers to several other generals in his sworn statement, including MG P (the commander of NTC) and LTG Q, who was the I Corps Commander prior to the arrival of LTG Scaparrotti.[4] LTG J wrote in his sworn statement that Hellraiser's brigade almost failed the NTC exercises. He refers to MG P who "expressed his concerns to me that the brigade would not be certified to deploy."

In response to this disturbing piece of news, LTG J telephoned Hellraiser: "I explained to Colonel Tunnell and directed Colonel Tunnell to stop his references to counter-guerrilla operations and to focus on the feedback the NTC trainers were attempting to provide his unit." Note, again, the genteel language: the general writes that he "directed"—but did not "order"—Colonel Tunnell to "focus on the feedback" of NTC trainers, who were teaching COIN. Apparently, in the present era, generals do not order colonels to follow established doctrine. This general's "counseling" did not change Hellraiser's attitude at all. Nevertheless, Hellraiser and his unit were certified to deploy, despite the misgivings of at least three generals who admit their misgivings in sworn statements. LTG J refers to another "telephone conversation with Colonel Tunnell where he expressed frustration with his NATO and US chain of command" upon the completion of Stryker brigade's mission in Afghanistan. "The tone was decidedly negative as compared to any of the similar discussions I had with other returning units."

How can the common person relate to the news that Hellraiser's commanders pondered not certifying his brigade for deployment, but decided amongst themselves to deploy him anyway? Most people will never have access to the secretive, social world of US Army generals. But most people know someone who should have failed a driver's test, a university exam, or some other certification. Common sense says that passing someone who deserved to fail is a socially irresponsible act: the person who is barely certified or is given another chance may end up hurting a person, or society, through his or her incompetence or willful negligence. Let me repeat: one of the battalion commanders said to me that in his opinion, the generals who certified Hellraiser as fit to command and his unit as fit to deploy bear some of the responsibility for the tragedies that ensued.

Hellraiser's negligence—in the social, not legal sense—was extensive. Because he was focused exclusively on his aggressive scenarios, he neglected administrative issues and obligations such as obeying a law passed by Congress which required all returning veterans to be given thorough physical as well as mental examinations, especially for brain injuries. LTG J wrote:

> I became even more concerned when I discovered that Colonel Tunnell was allowing his Soldiers to initiate block leave without finishing redeployment processing. This caused us to change our redeployment model and reiterate the requirement for all Soldiers to complete their face to face behavioral health (BH) interviews prior to being allowed to start block leave. Any soldier determined to be at high risk was required to further complete BH appointments as required by medical assessments and not start block leave until cleared by a medical professional....We subsequently found that many Soldiers had not completed this requirement. [This] caused me to question the overall organizational health of this unit.

CHAPTER 3. HELLRAISER'S MINIONS: THE TRUE BELIEVERS

The generals who assessed Hellraiser seem to be correct that there existed a cadre of officers who opted to appear to be on *his* team. It is less clear whether these officers were pro- or against COIN or CG or doing COIN or doing CG or some other weird, hybrid of believing and doing COIN and CG. The point is that these officers were loyal to him. These officers, Hellraiser's true believers, are easily recognizable in the sworn statements by the following uniform characteristics in their statements: They praise their commander lavishly. They claim that morale in the brigade was high, when command climate surveys and General Twitty's report suggest that it was dismally low. Their answers to General Twitty's specific questions about command climate and the commander's lack of circulation within the brigade are evasive or non-existent. Some chose simply not to answer at all. In summary, they exhibit the "immature" defense mechanisms that psychologists call denial, projection, and shifting of blame onto others.

For example, a major who was on Hellraiser's brigade staff writes: "I interacted with Colonel Tunnell on a regular basis." This major simply did not answer any of General Twitty's questions about Hellraiser's interaction with other officers. Similarly, a lieutenant colonel who claimed that he was very close to Hellraiser simply evaded the questions posed by General Twitty, writing: "I cannot speak to the closeness or the lack of closeness he shared with his commanders." Hellraiser's minions uniformly blame the crimes under discussion here on a handful of allegedly bad soldiers. They rationalize Hellraiser's contempt for COIN doctrine as nevertheless incorporating or doing COIN in some manner.

Let us examine some of these sworn statements in detail, keeping in mind that there is more to their narratives than meets the eye. It is important to pay attention to the tone of their statements, the particular words and phrases they use, and the words and phrases they steadfastly avoid.

LTC K or the Deputy Brigade Commander:

"Colonel Tunnell is the finest leader with whom I have served in my career"

Hellraiser's deputy brigade commanding officer, LTC K, offers a spirited defense of his boss: "Without question, Colonel Tunnell was responsible for establishing what I would characterize as an ethical climate and organization." He elaborates:

> It has been suggested that Colonel Tunnell's use of FM 90-8 counter-guerrilla doctrine may have contributed to unnecessary or indiscriminate application of lethal force during combat operations. First of all, that is patently absurd. Secondly, in truth, counter-guerrilla was more an appellation, a literal *nom de guerre*, a matter of stylizing the brigade and instilling a winning spirit. The brigade's performance proves that we embraced all facets of COIN doctrine that were appropriate in southern Afghanistan... I cannot recall one instance where our soldiers, without good cause, killed or wounded civilian non-combatants with direct fire, and only two incidents where we did so with air delivered munitions (both of which were later determined to be justified). We were models of restraint consistent with ROE. Given the complexity of the deployment and environs therein, there can be no question that our unit performed magnificently.

The charge that Hellraiser's doctrine may have contributed to the tragedy under study here is not "patently absurd," given that so many generals and high-ranking officers have entertained it. This connection is open to discussion and debate, but is not simply absurd. LTC K's second point, that Hellraiser's doctrine was "in truth" a matter of style, not substance, is problematic because it obfuscates the question of which philosophy truly informed the brigade's missions, the COIN doctrine or the Counter-Guerrilla doctrine (or, more plausibly, some weird hybrid of COIN and CG doctrines). There is something odd about referring to anything that is style over substance as being "true." LTC K is incorrect that the brigade embraced "all facets of COIN doctrine," given the sworn statements by other commanders, who state that they were fearful of using COIN openly—or even using the word, COIN, in Hellraiser's presence. Finally, LTC K betrays an astonishing lack of awareness of the problems in his brigade by claiming that there did not exist a single instance of unlawful killings. Quite apart from the killings that were formally charged as murders, we have seen that there were charges made of several instances of questionable killings. It is understandable that LTC K may have wanted to believe that the brigade performed magnificently. But it is a dangerous sign for a leader to state that "there can be no question" about his belief. The Twitty report raises numerous questions which must be taken seriously.

LTC K is aware that "within days of arriving in Kandahar, it became common knowledge that there was concern within RC-S that 5/2 was an 'over-lethal' unit." RC-S refers to the command over the Southern region of Afghanistan. But Hellraiser's deputy explains away the discrepancy between his perception and the perception of his superiors by belittling his superiors:

> Very quickly our relationship with RC-S deteriorated. I would attribute this *entirely* to RC-S, who quickly demonstrated that they were a pathetically inept staff, devoid of fundamental training, systems, understanding, and competence.... RC-S frequently queried 5/2 as to whether we possessed "extra" items that might be cross-leveled to other non-US units within RC-S. I can remember requests for DUKES, Boomerangs and RAID cameras. Additionally, RC-S gave a disproportionate allocation of US resources to British units. All of these factors contributed to significant rancor. Colonel Tunnell did a very good job keeping this from his subordinate commanders [emphasis added].

Similarly, LTC K is apparently aware that his boss was aloof, asocial, and did not circulate with his subordinate commanders or troops. But again, he rationalizes away these perceptions, and makes his boss out to be the misunderstood victim:

> For reasons I cannot explain most of the battalion commanders in 5/2 had difficulty communicating with Colonel Tunnell. I found him very approachable, personable and generally affable. Colonel Tunnell can appear imposing to some but I never saw him lose his temper or even raise his voice. I am confident he never made a decision based on emotion—he was very detached in that sense. I think most of the battalion commanders did not get the kind of feedback and encouragement they wanted from the Commander and as a result many of them called or queried me to ask what the commander was thinking. I do know that Colonel Tunnell was very confident in his field grade officers and did not feel the need to praise them regularly. It is my personal opinion that *the only mistake* Colonel Tunnell ever made regarding the counter-guerrilla subject was not engaging in the war of perceptions. Had he made more of an effort to explain why he chose to use certain language there may have been less concern by senior leaders and less friction for the brigade. I am not aware if any senior leader ever discussed the subject with him or whether any suggested or directed that he change his philosophy. I think Colonel Tunnell was also surprised that other Army officers would go to such lengths to undermine or criticize a deploying brigade commander... Lastly, I want to go on record having said

that Colonel Tunnell is the finest leader with whom I have served in my
career and it was a great honor to have served in 5/2 [emphasis added].

LTC K loses credibility for his views by claiming that the *only* mistake Hellraiser made was that he failed in impression management, or
what he calls the "war of perceptions." Army doctrine requires that commanders circulate with and mentor their subordinates, and Hellraiser
defied this doctrine like he defied other army norms. The more important
point is that LTC K's narrative demonstrates that Hellraiser converted
his deputy commander, and presumably others on the brigade staff, to
his counter-chain-of-command perspective. This is not the story of Hellraiser as the lone wolf who tried to follow army norms in a brigade that
defied army norms, as LTC K implies. LTC K unwittingly suggests that
it is the story of Hellraiser who made his immediate staff hostage to his
idiosyncratic doctrine. It is as if LTC K and the rest of the brigade staff
were suffering from a sort of Stockholm Syndrome: LTC K seems positively unable to entertain the thought that all those generals, all those
subordinate commanders, and army norms might be right—if that were
true, then Hellraiser might be wrong. A reasonable person would suspect
that if so many persons, above and below Hellraiser in rank, were unhappy with him and his doctrine, there might be something wrong with
him and his doctrine. Instead, LTC K lionizes Hellraiser and portrays
him as the misunderstood victim of everyone else, his commanders as
well as his subordinates.

Given what is known about similar social dynamics in dysfunctional
families, one is better able to appreciate how difficult it must have been
for anyone in that brigade who wanted to follow army norms to be able
to defy Hellraiser. Any such person would have faced not only Hellraiser's intransigence, but also the stone wall of his slavishly loyal staff. In
dysfunctional families, the most pathological and authoritarian member
usually finds confederates in the group. Any reasonable, sane questioning of his or her private norms is immediately invalidated by a social faction, not only by the pathological member. It is beyond the scope of the
present study to explain the workings of this group pathology, which is
extremely complex. However, one should note, for example, that LTC
K claims that absolutely no one challenged Hellraiser about his counter-guerrilla doctrine at the same time that he claims that this doctrine
was mere style, a show, a pretense. This discrepancy alone betrays false
emotions as well as facts. What good could possibly come from someone challenging Hellraiser regarding his doctrine if the reply would have
been that it was mere show, that "in truth," Hellraiser supposedly was
following COIN doctrine?

Moreover, numerous sworn statements, as well as my interviews with battalion commanders, show that some officers did challenge Hellraiser, and the consequences for the dissidents were consistently negative. My aim here is merely to suggest that Hellraiser's pathology was not only private but that it contaminated his deputy and most of the brigade staff, and it thereby neutralized any healthy questioning, growth, or function in the rest of the brigade.

CHIEF WARRANT OFFICER P: "BODY COUNT TRACKER"

Chief Warrant Officer (CWO) P is an important member of Hellraiser's inner circle in that he developed a body count tracker for the brigade. A neutral observer or reasonable reader might raise his or her eyebrows at this fact, and connect it to the other assertions made by subordinate commanders that Hellraiser was overly-aggressive. It is important to note that like LTC K, CWO P rationalizes and neutralizes this fact; lionizes his boss; and demeans all who disagreed with Hellraiser. It is also important to note that CWO P worked under Hellraiser "since March 2007" where he served his entire time "as a member of the brigade staff involved in targeting, IPB and operations planning." In other words, CWO P worked very closely with Hellraiser and had a long gestation period for absorbing his philosophy. Ironically, COIN doctrine became the official doctrine of the US Army as of June 2007, while CWO P and Hellraiser worked together in a counter-COIN direction. CWO P writes: "Over the course of 3 years in the brigade, I was often asked by battalion staff members (captains and below) about the Counter-Guerrilla concept and the reasoning behind it. I believe that battalion commanders did not fully buy into the concept and did not effectively translate Colonel Tunnell's intent to their battalions." In CWO P's mind, the battalion commanders, not Hellraiser, were at fault. But why would anyone expect the commanders to "translate" Hellraiser's intent if they "did not fully buy into" it?

Under the astonishing subheading CWO P wrote into his sworn statement, "Pressure to inflate body counts," he recounts and describes this pressure in a matter-of-fact tone, but with very helpful details:

> Within approximately 2 months in Afghanistan, Colonel Tunnell directed the S2 section and MICO to produce a weekly Battle Damage Assessment (BDA) tracker, aka, a body count tracker. The BDA tracker was a tool at the brigade level only; battalions were not required to maintain their own tracker nor were the battalions required to provide input to the tracker. All data for the BDA tracker was pulled from the CIDNE database. At no time during my discussions with Colonel Tunnell was the term "body count" ever used, nor did I hear that term throughout the brigade staff. The BDA tracker was used as a tool to measure enemy strength through-

out the brigade's operating area in order to update IPB products, assessments and to determine if security levels were high enough for GR&D projects. I assisted in developing the BDA tracking and adding information to it although the S2 Operations section was the section in charge of its production. At no time during the deployment was I pressured to inflate the numbers of enemy dead or wounded nor did I see or hear about battalions being pressed to do so.

The brigade used the euphemism, BDA, for the reality of establishing a body count tracker. Perhaps it is true that nobody used the words "body count," but it appears that everyone on the brigade staff knew what it was. Similarly, CWO P may be telling the truth that Hellraiser did not pressure him or the battalions to inflate the body counts, but the reality of the "pressure" could have been covered up with other euphemisms. The very existence of the body count tracker implicitly put pressure on the entire brigade, including the battalions, even if battalions did not keep their own separate trackers. This is because the battalions fed information about kills into the database which CWO P used for the BDA. In a very evasive, convoluted, and distorted manner, CWO P has unwittingly betrayed Hellraiser's euphemism-covered pressure on the brigade to produce high body counts.

CWO P betrays another important connection, namely, that prior to working for Colonel Tunnell, he had worked for Colonel Michael Steele at the 101st Airborne Division. Colonel Steele's own aggressive style precipitated the Operation Iron Triangle war crimes in 2006, a year before COIN doctrine became official policy. Sworn statement from that case shows that Colonel Steele also had a body count board at his brigade headquarters, which *did* influence his brigade to kill unarmed Iraqi civilians. CWO P does not mention Steele by name, but he does make a direct link to his same role as the body count tracker at both Ft. Lewis and Ft. Campbell (which was the base for Steele's brigade):

> My overall assessment of the 5/2 (SBCT) command climate: 5/2 (SBCT) was my 2nd consecutive assignment on a brigade staff and I now have 6 years as a brigade staff member between assignments at Fort Campbell, KY in the 101st [Airborne Division] and here at JBLM [Joint Base Lewis-McChord]. Additionally, I worked as an LNO [liaison officer] with the 172d SBCT during operations in Baghdad, Iraq. From my perspective, the command climate in 5/2 was the best I've experienced.... Col Tunnell was not a "rah rah" commander, he did not give very many motivational speeches and I never heard him glorify or glamorize killing the enemy. It was simply part of our role within the COIN doctrine.

As a very important aside, let us note the following about unit 172d SBCT, with which CWO P worked in Iraq prior to his deployment in Stryker Brigade in Afghanistan. The 172d SBCT was comprised of the exact three combat, infantry battalions that would later become a part of 5/2 SBCT under the command of Colonel Tunnell, namely: 2-1, 1-17, and 4-23. The 172d SBCT was stationed in Alaska. The names, guidons, and symbolism of these three combat battalions were artificially transferred from the 172d SBCT to the 5/2 SBCT. This is an important point, because one of the background stories in our overall story is the cross-leveling and artificial destruction as well as construction of hybrid military units. This cross-leveling was occurring at many levels, from brigades through battalions and companies to the platoon level. Another important point is that CWO P, the officer in charge of assessing body counts, had been doing this for many years, in the old as well as the new brigade.

Furthermore, these connections between Steele and Hellraiser, the 101st and 5/2, the same body count tracker (namely, CWO P), and war crimes in both brigades, seem to be more than a coincidence. And each connection, in turn, leads to other connections. Recall that LTC C told me that Steele and General "Hondo" Campbell visited Hellraiser's brigade during its exercises at the NTC. It seems to be a consistent description of Hellraiser that he was not a good, motivational speaker. But CWO P conveniently omits the other ways that Hellraiser glorified and glamorized killing, which are well-documented in the Twitty report: the streamers, memorandums, kill boards, scenarios, power point presentations, and indoctrination of his commanders.

Major T: "The brigade commander had the utmost respect for the Afghan people"

Major T was the executive officer for one of Stryker brigade's support battalions. Given the lack of interaction between the brigade staff and subordinate commanders, it is significant that Major T interacted frequently with Hellraiser's inner circle: "I had frequent interaction with the Brigade Staff and the various units within the brigade." He writes: "I can say with 100% confidence that proper training across the Brigade relative to ISAF directed Escalation of Force training was implemented."

Like other officers who were in frequent contact with Hellraiser, he disconnects the responsibility for the killings under discussion here from the command climate created by Hellraiser: "I believe that the command climate of the Brigade did not in any way contribute to the soldiers conducting murders, assaults, and drug use." Rather, "the soldier's actions were driven by what appears to be the unfortunate mental instability and dissociative mental nature of one Squad Leader [Staff Sergeant Gibbs] controlling several young and impressionable junior soldiers. That, matched with the frustration and intense nature of combat in Afghanistan were the proximate causes." In other words, Major T attributes responsibility to an allegedly mentally ill Sergeant Gibbs. In fact, an army Sanity Board investigation concluded that Sergeant Gibbs was not mentally ill. The second part of his statement, about frustration and intense combat in Afghanistan, is intriguing, but it remains undeveloped by MAJ T.

In complete contradiction to General Twitty's findings, Major T asserts that "the brigade commander's thoughts on counter-guerrilla vs. COIN substantiated the concept that the operations conducted by 5/2 were in line with current COIN doctrine." Major T's sentence seems nonsensical. If two concepts are described as being "versus" each other, one cannot in the same breath be described as being "in line" with the other. Major T seems to be aware that Stryker Brigade had an anti-COIN reputation, but dismisses this thought: "Stryker Brigade efforts to clear routes, secure culverts from IEDs, and protect the people became overshadowed by the ridiculous myth of a rogue Brigade." But Major T does subscribe to the typical "few bad apples" theory that has become the mainstay of explaining war crimes in the current War on Terror: "The rogue squad resulted from leadership failures at the Company and below level."

Major T's rationalization for the tragedy that occurred is elegant, even though it is false: Companies and platoons do not go rogue spontaneously, because they are linked to battalions and brigades. Major T, like Hellraiser's other minions, does not wish to question the leadership above the company level. And, who or what, exactly, is rogue in this story? Was Hellraiser's aggressive CG philosophy rogue? Or was Hellraiser's interpretation of COIN rogue? There is no easy answer to these questions.

CAPTAIN Q: CORPORAL MORLOCK'S NEW COMPANY COMMANDER

Captain Q was Corporal Morlock's company commander following the cross-leveling or re-task organization (as it is formally known) that took place in July of 2009, following the NTC training and lasted during the entire deployment in Afghanistan. Captain Q was not Morlock's original company commander (his original commander was Captain T, who is mentioned many times in the sworn statements, but does not have a sworn statement in the report). The reader may recall that COL A, who seems to have despised Hellraiser, spoke glowingly of Captain Q as his best company commander. The mystery of how this supposedly outstanding commander, Captain Q, could have been in charge of the company that was involved in the killings is deepened, not resolved, by an exceptional fact that jumps out of his sworn statement: Captain Q had been Hellraiser's right-hand man. Captain Q writes:

I worked closely with the brigade commander as he developed the counter-guerrilla framework for operations in Iraq and Afghanistan. Because of my duty position, I often assisted in developing briefing products, training OPORD's and FRAGO's, and brigade internal correspondence that *helped the brigade commander formalize the counter-guerrilla framework throughout the brigade. Further, because I had to understand Colonel Tunnell's intent, he often took time to explain in detail to me his understanding of FM 90-8 (Counter-guerrilla Operations)....*After I took command of A/8-1 in Nov 08, I found that my fellow company level commanders did not have as thorough an understanding of either the commander's intent or the counter-guerrilla operations as I did. I believe that there was confusion at the company level in the competing doctrines of counter-guerrilla and COIN. I observed that battalion commanders often decided to pursue a more COIN-focused campaign plan [emphasis added].

Hellraiser's idiosyncratic philosophy, based upon an obsolete counter-guerrilla manual (FM 90-8) was intended by him to apply in Iraq *and* Afghanistan. The troop build-up in Afghanistan, ordered by President Obama, was entirely different in its mission orientation from Iraq, at least according to the army doctrine of COIN. Hellraiser made no distinction between these two theaters of war. Captain Q involved himself intensely in Hellraiser's project. Far from questioning it, as so many officers did, the captain found the critical reactions of his fellow commanders to be odd. The captain states that his fellow company commanders were *confused* as to whether they should follow COIN versus Hellraiser's doctrine, but that the battalion commanders threw in their lots with COIN. This divide in loyalties—perhaps similar in some ways to the confusion of children prior to the divorce of their parents—must have produced anguish among the other company commanders. Captain Q does not betray any anguish. On the contrary, he was Hellraiser's helper in "formalizing" the anti-COIN, anti-chain-of-command doctrine that tore the brigade apart. He worked "closely" with Hellraiser for an entire year before being assigned to the battalion led by COL A, who was originally Hellraiser's "golden boy" but became his nemesis. Because of cross-leveling, Captain Q eventually worked for LTC B in a different battalion. LTC B told me that he was "doing" COIN. Clearly, there is much more to this interpersonal drama among various commanders than meets the eye. Captain Q never criticizes Hellraiser in his sworn statement. But he does hint that he understood Hellraiser's doctrine better than any of the other commanders. He adds: "Throughout the brigade, counter-guerrilla operations became more of an identity for the soldiers and leaders within 5/2 than either a tactical imperative or a cohesive campaign plan. It was a distinction that separated the brigade for better or worse from the rest of the RCS."

What were Captain Q's loyalties? Was he pro-COIN, pro-chain-of-command, or pro-Hellraiser? I wanted to ask him these and other questions, but when I finally reached Captain Q by phone, he said he did not wish to speak with me.

Captain Q gives the most detailed account of the mind-numbing re-shuffling or "re-task organization" that took place at battalion, company, and platoon levels:

> I deployed as the A/8-1 cavalry commander. In July of 09, A/8-1 was attached to 2-1 Infantry. Once we had consolidated in Kandahar we were re-task organized. I maintained one of my original recon platoons (1 A/8-1 CAV) and gained 2 infantry platoons from 2-1 IN, 3/A/2-1 and 3/B/2-or 3rd platoon. This task organization occurred within 72 hours of our first combat mission in Afghanistan. This was the first opportunity I had to meet the leadership of the 2 platoons attached to me. 1LT L was the platoon leader of 3rd platoon. My initial impression of LT L was that he was very inexperienced and potentially a liability. As a brand new platoon leader, he had never been on a Stryker, let alone led a platoon and especially not one in combat. Initially, I was shocked. SFC B was the platoon sergeant for 3rd platoon. I felt he lacked the tactical expertise that I would have liked in a platoon sergeant. SSG Gibbs came to 3rd platoon in November 09 reassigned from the brigade commander's personal security detail. I observed that he did not exhibit the same ease of communication with either subordinates or superiors that the other squad leaders within 3rd platoon had. *SSG Gibbs seemed to avoid conversations altogether and exhibited a detachment from his soldiers that I saw as awkward.* I believe he specifically targeted the mentally and physically weaker soldiers to coerce them into killing civilians [emphasis added].

The Army's euphemism "re-task organization" (more widely referred to as cross-leveling) conceals the *disorganization* that occurs when soldiers are moved about as if they were lifeless chess pieces. Missing in Captain Q's description of the cross-leveling is any acknowledgement of the emotional turmoil for the soldiers who were ripped from their previous social networks and friendships. Perhaps Gibbs was awkward compared to the other squad leaders for the simple reason that he was new to the platoon. Captain Q regarded both the platoon leader (LT L) and platoon sergeant (SFC B) as liabilities. On the other hand, CPT Q protected both of these "liabilities" and refers to both as "valuable assets" in another section of his sworn statement. In addition, soldiers told me that they rarely saw Captain Q. There is nothing to suggest that the soldiers who were accused of the crimes at issue here were mentally or physically weak or weaker than other soldiers. And one should never lose sight of the fact that the entire platoon knew—directly or through rumors—of the killings that were taking place, so that there is no good reason to isolate the five soldiers who were charged with crimes as essentially different from the other soldiers.

One detects a strenuous effort in Captain Q's statement to make himself seem not responsible for the crimes that occurred, and to connect, shift, or otherwise attach responsibility to others. For example, he writes:

> There were several incidents of indiscipline within the platoon. I asked for a dismounted footbridge for a canal crossing. Battalion executive officer saw the bridge had been painted with a slogan referring to a "crusade," clearly a disaster had it gone unnoticed. Once it was brought to my attention I explained to LT L and SFC B why this could have ruined progress within the battalions.

> Private Holmes had a negligent discharge with an M203 round that destroyed an unoccupied CHU on the FOB for which he received an Article 15 from the BN commander. In March [there was] a report from the Maywand district leader that stated that village elders from a village within 3rd platoon area of operations had complained that soldiers had gone through the village, shot at dogs, killed chickens and kicked in doors. I was shocked. LT L and SFC B denied it. Although the [battalion] commander [LTC B] wanted to replace both LT L and SFC B, I argued that the platoon had become a valuable asset and I did not want to lose the platoon leadership. LTC B basically gave the platoon leadership one more chance. I specifically expressed to LT L that he was out of chances and the next mistake would result in his removal as platoon leader. *Two nights later the platoon conducted an escalation of force.... From the report that I received over the radio I was angry. The individual was not a threat.* I was not present during any of the three incidents that led to allegations of murder against members of 3rd platoon (I was on leave during the month of February 2010) [emphasis added].

The killing of this particular Afghan national—which will be discussed at several junctures in this analysis—occurred *after* the first killing in January which was judged to be murder. No charges were ever leveled against anyone for the questionable killing of this Afghan man, hereafter to be called the EOF (Escalation of Force) killing. Captain Q may or may not be correct that the EOF killing was completely unjustified; formally and officially, it was justified by the chain of command. But he fails to mention that in this incident approximately eight soldiers opened fire on the unarmed man at the command of LT L, and Morlock was not involved in the EOF killing at all. Clearly, the aggressive attitude in the platoon extended well beyond the five soldiers who were charged for other killings.

The fact that the EOF killing occurred almost immediately after LTC B and Captain Q warned LT L that he would be removed from command suggests an extreme problem in leadership. It was as if the entire 3rd platoon believed they were above the law and beyond the reach of discipline. The EOF killing merged into the first killing in January and was indistinguishable from it in the eyes of the soldiers. Questions surrounding the EOF killing, and why it was not prosecuted, will remain a historical mystery. The EOF killing involved the planting of an AK-47 magazine on the corpse, and involved the entire platoon. It was, in its own way, a "scenario" killing. To put it another way, the EOF killing, which was never prosecuted as a war crime, is connected in many ways to the killings that were prosecuted as war crimes, and especially by the unofficial doctrine of planting weapons on dead bodies to make the kills seem legitimate.

I have read dozens of sworn statements concerning this EOF killing, and most of the soldiers describe the victim as mentally handicapped. Captain Q does not refer to the victim in this way—but the majority of soldiers and officers do. They arrived at this conclusion because the unarmed Afghan male seemed dazed and confused by the confrontation with the soldiers, paced, and did not seem to comprehend what was going on. There is no way to determine whether or not he was, in fact, mentally handicapped or even "crazy" (as some soldiers described him). Hereafter, I shall refer to this victim as a mentally handicapped Afghan national, based upon this common perception of him. The EOF incident haunts the Twitty report and my narrative from start to finish.

Captain Q was not physically present with the platoon during the entire month of February and was not present for any of the killings that were later prosecuted. He did not learn about the killings of the chickens and dogs until March, but Gibbs had begun killing animals in December. While Captain Q is successful in making himself seem not responsible for any of the killings in a direct sense, one must wonder how he failed to grasp the problems in his company until it was too late. And why did he implore his new battalion commander to give the platoon leader and sergeant a second chance?

Similarly, it is difficult to believe that Captain Q—along with all the other commanders—had no idea of the rampant drug use in the platoon. In Captain Q's words: "Despite living in close proximity to 3rd platoon and conducting many patrols alongside them, I did not have any indications of drug use or behavior that was in violation of the Laws of Armed Conflict." In the conclusions to his report, General Twitty faults Captain Q for not living with his men (Captain Q claims he lived "in close proximity" to them). He also faults Captain Q for failing to interact or "circulate" with his men.

Captain Q became suspicious that two of the killings involved grenades. Following the last killing, in May, Captain Q writes: "I took the picture to LTC B and we discussed this incident further. My impression was that if the first grenade event was an anomaly, then two similar attempted attacks were potentially the beginning of a trend."

MAJOR H: "THE BRIGADE HAD A REPUTATION OF 'NOT GETTING IT,' NOT 'BEING TEAM PLAYERS,' AND THEY WERE 'MISSING THE BIG PICTURE.'"

Major H was on Hellraiser's brigade staff as the "S2X counter-intelligence and human intelligence coordinator" officer. He begins his 5-page-long sworn statement with a description of two in-house leader retreats for commanders and non-commissioned officers. Both retreats were held in preparation for a mission to Iraq, which again suggests that Hellraiser saw no essential difference between the missions for wars in Iraq and Afghanistan. The first retreat was centered on Hellraiser's presentation entitled, "Sometimes War is Just War." Major H concluded that Hellraiser's overall point seems to have been that COIN would "put the cart before the horse" in warfare. In addition, "he wanted everyone to understand that there was a difference in essential services (food, water, sewage) that was covered under the Geneva Conventions and projects that were not essential (schools, soccer fields)." Furthermore, "he did state that the non-essential projects needed to relate to the effects the Brigade was attempting to influence on the battlefield." Major H helps to explain why many other commanders stated that they had to justify non-lethal (COIN) projects with reference to Hellraiser's lethal objectives. In other words, subordinate commanders had to justify repairing a school, for example, with fictitious accounts of how the school project would result in the deaths of Taliban fighters.

The second retreat was held in November of 2008 and included lectures on "US Army policies and activities in the Reconstruction Era (1865–1879), Survival Strategies in a Segregated Society (1890–1965), Tribal Interactions and the US Bureau of Indian Affairs, and ended with a round-table with all these presenters." Reconstruction, segregation, and the extermination of Native-Americans are extremely painful episodes in American history. What possible connection did they have to US Army policies in the wars in Iraq and Afghanistan? Major H writes: "The briefing on Southern Reconstruction was highlighting the policies and procedures of the US Army during a period of occupation that required small-scale military activities to suppress revolts/paramilitary groups, while also conducting rebuilding and governance." It seems that in Hellraiser's mind, the equivalent of the suppression of revolts by the US Army during Reconstruction coupled with rebuilding was akin to his own policy of counter-guerrilla operations coupled with doing some COIN so long as COIN activities were secondary to lethal objectives. The rebuilding and governance during the Reconstruction seems to have been the equivalent of COIN, in Hellraiser's lectures. Perhaps these historical parallels and connections are intellectually stimulating to Hellraiser and some others. Nevertheless, one would expect that contemporary historians would be sensitive to the plight of African-Americans and Native Americans at the hands of the US Army during those historical periods, and perhaps historians would evidence some sense of regret or apology. But Hellraiser sought to apply these unsavory lessons (how to crush the revolts by African-Americans and Native Americans) to Iraq and Afghanistan. Major H writes dryly: "This was difficult for many folks, because you had to take this information and see how you could apply it to the situation we would face in Iraq (later Afghanistan)."

Major H documents the many training exercises in the brigade which involved *scenarios* wherein soldiers "had to seize the town, while also interacting with a civilian population." Film crews, translators, and soldiers were involved, "populated by role-playing insurgents and towns people." An apt summary of Hellraiser's approach seems to have been: Rule with an iron fist, but hide the iron fist in the velvet glove of COIN.

Major H blames the catastrophe of the exercises at the National Training Center on the NTC staff, not on Hellraiser: "Overall, the NTC rotation was a very negative event that neither prepared the Brigade to operate under a NATO command or to understand the types of threats the Brigade would face starting in July." He does not mention the disagreements between Hellraiser and his superiors on implementing COIN which are documented by General Twitty.

Similarly, Major H blames the leadership problems in Afghanistan on Hellraiser's superiors. He notes that in November of 2009, Hellraiser's commanders "required 1-17 Infantry to turn over control of the Arghandab River Valley to 2-508 PIR, and required 4-23 Infantry to leave Zabul Province and move to Helmand Province on the other side of Kandahar." According to Major H, the main effect of these orders were that "by moving off Kandahar Airfield, the Brigade would lose its 15-megabyte line-of-sight connection with the Upper Tactical Internet hub, and would be forced to only use a 2-megabyte satellite-based link with the Upper TI." Major H make it seems as if Hellraiser had issues with losing Internet and satellite connections, not with COIN. He continues: "When Colonel Tunnell could not make any headway with either Brigadier General Hodges or Major General Carter, he briefed Major General McDonald. Basically, Colonel Tunnell's position was that he did not want to have a scenario where he was not able to communicate with his subordinate elements during a significant activity." The context of MAJ H's description suggests that Hellraiser briefed MG McDonald as a way to bypass the other two generals, who opposed his wishes. Major H concludes: "It was after this point the Brigade had a reputation of 'not getting it,' not 'being team players,' and we were 'missing the big picture.'" It does not seem to occur to Major H that there may have been some basis in fact for this negative reputation.

The intelligence expert, Major H, gives an interesting but idiosyncratic explanation of the problems between Hellraiser and his superiors. His superiors unanimously objected to his intransigence and insubordination regarding COIN philosophy. No one else in the Twitty report supports Major H's interpretation that the problem had to do primarily with losing good Internet connections.

Of greater interest is the fact that Major H claims that he did not know anything about any unlawful killings until he returned to Ft. Lewis from Afghanistan: "I did not really hear anything else, until returning to Joint Base Lewis-McChord, when I was appointed as an Article 32 Investigations Officer in the cases of US v SSG Bram and US v SSG Stevens." Remarkable! A commissioned officer from Hellraiser's inner circle was chosen by the army to serve as the investigative officer at the equivalent of pre-trial hearings (Article 32s) for two of the accused soldiers!

Much has been written about command influence in the army's military justice system, yet it continues to prejudice the outcomes of courts-martial. Surely the army could have found a more neutral investigative officer for the Article 32 hearings of Stevens and Bram, who were both eventually convicted of various charges. Not surprisingly, Major H ascribes all the blame for the killings on 3rd Platoon, B Company, 2-1 Infantry, and absolutely none to Hellraiser or the command climate: "I do not believe the unit [platoon] was properly supervised and the platoon leadership was incapable of overseeing the organization." Moreover, he blames 2-1's former battalion commander, LTC C, who did not deploy to Afghanistan! He writes: "The organization that LTC B inherited from LTC C did not trust its Battalion leadership due to the climate LTC C created." Furthermore, "the poisonous environment that LTC B inherited would also have contributed to the mistrust apparent in 2-1 Infantry to their higher leadership." (I should add that Hellraiser had ordered an AR 15-6 investigation into LTC C's leadership and command climate, and the report exonerated LTC C. It seems to be the case that Hellraiser and MAJ H were scapegoating LTC C.) Major H does not attribute any responsibility, of any sort, for any of the brigade's problems to the brigade commander.

LIEUTENANT L: CORPORAL MORLOCK'S PLATOON LEADER

LT L, who has been mentioned several times already, was Morlock's platoon leader in B Company, 2-1 Infantry Battalion. He held this position from May, 2009 to March 18, 2010, when he was relieved of command by LTC B. It turns out that LT L was also one of Hellraiser's minions. In his sworn statement, he describes several killings which occurred during his command, all of them questionable, including three killings that were never investigated or charged as murders. These uncharged, questionable killings are of great interest because they provide context for the killings which led to charges of murder.

The first questionable killing occurred in October of 2009 and involved an Apache helicopter attack on "one male running." LT L writes: "We found the body during our search and we found that the body had been blown in half." They interrogated the nearby villagers "and they didn't have any information about it [the body]." Then, "SSG Bram and I took a picture with the dead body." By this, LT L meant that he posed for a trophy photo with the badly mutilated torso, half of which was missing. Absolutely no evidence was presented that this dead Afghan was an insurgent, a member of the Taliban, or an enemy in any other way. One wonders what sort of signal this sent to the platoon, and also, the PTSD-producing effects of being required to photograph and examine this mutilated corpse. Soldiers told me later that the platoon members had concluded that the US helicopter pilots had mistaken a farmer for an insurgent. However, the platoon members also noted that the helicopter pilots got the "credit" for this kill.

The first killing which resulted in a murder charge occurred in January. LT L was not aware that it was murder at the time it took place. More significant is LT L's account of the killing of the handicapped Afghan male a few weeks later—the infamous EOF incident—which was never charged as murder:

> About Jan or Feb time frame we were coming back from a mounted patrol on Highway 1. My vehicle commander, Specialist Winfield, identified a crouched figure on top of a hill, near the road, at night. I told my driver to slow down so that I could identify what he saw. I was able to identify a crouched figure too. I told my driver to stop and I informed the rest of my platoon of the situation. We dismounted to move to the individual to search his person. I know SFC Bruno called it up to our higher. We dismounted with interpreters. They asked the man to come down and he did. They asked him to stop. He complied. Then finally we asked him to raise his shirt so we could identify if he had anything on him. This time he had no reaction and my interpreters continued to ask him to raise his shirt. My Soldiers and I also asked him to raise his shirt and he did not comply. The man walked forward and we told him to stop again. He stopped and paced back and forth. We had white lighted him and green beamed him to make him stop. He started pacing back and forth again and someone gave him a warning shot to stop. The man did not stop. He approached us again and we stepped back and fired another warning shot, to include

myself. At this time, I felt threatened for my platoon and myself. I felt the advancement of the local national displayed a threat. I gave the order to engage if he advanced and he did. We engaged and killed the local national. I explained to CPT Q that the man posed a threat, so we shot him. I explained that we followed the escalation of force (EOF) rules and the LN [local national] did not comply. CPT Q instructed me to do a very thorough search in the area. After talking to CPT Q I was pretty worried. We had a negligent discharge (ND) the night before and now my CO is telling me that to him this didn't seem like a threat. I knew that my platoon had to do a thorough search of the area... SSG Bram called over and said that they had found an AK-47 magazine.

What LT L does not disclose is that the AK-47 magazine was planted on the corpse; that Sergeant Bram was later convicted of planting false evidence on the corpse; and that the entire platoon knew of the planting of the magazine on the corpse—except, apparently, that LT L did not know. Clearly, the entire platoon was prepared at that point to make any "questionable" kill seem like a "legitimate" kill. The entire platoon was "in on it," prepared to make any "scenario" seem like the genuine killing of the enemy.

In February, another killing took place in the village of Kari Kheyl. This one was later charged as one of the murders, but LT L apparently had no reason to perceive it differently from any of the other killings. An AK-47 was found on the corpse, which was later found to have been planted. LT L says that he questioned the villagers: "They responded that he [the victim] was a very religious man and did not know how to use an AK-47."

Finally, on the very day that he was relieved from command, March 18, 2010, yet another questionable incident took place:

On my last patrol, 18 March 10, we were on our way back from to Kandahar for retrofit. As we entered Kandahar City there was a road block so I told SSG Sprague to take a bypass. We took the bypass and didn't have any issues, but as we were getting back onto Highway 1 we had an RPG [rocket propelled grenade] shot at us. It landed between my vehicle and the vehicle behind me.... I turned to look and saw a small black figure duck down on the roof. So I did not have positive identification. SSG Gibbs and SGT Jones returned fire, at the men on the roof top. We have no confirmed kill or wounded because I ordered them to push through the kill zone.

It seems that LT L was not sure if the men on the rooftop were the ones who fired the RPG. He was also not certain whether or not his platoon had killed anyone in this incident. What is of greatest interest here is that all of these incidents, charged and uncharged, merge into one another. All of them fit the lethal "scenarios" which Hellraiser had used for training purposes. It is truly difficult to differentiate allegedly "staged" scenarios from "genuine" scenarios, because a scenario is fake by definition.

A CID agent asked LT L: "Do you know if someone planted the AK-47 magazine?" "I do not," he replied. The interrogation continued:

Q: Do you know anyone who has staged scenarios in your platoon to kill local nationals?

A: No, I do not.

Q: Have you ever staged scenarios to kill LNs?

A: No, I have not.

Q: Have you ever received any photos from the soldiers in your platoon?

A: Yes, I have.

Q: Did you take these photos?

A: Some of them I did, the rest were given to me by platoon members...

Q: What kind of pictures are they?

A: Some are dead people, some are regular patrol pictures, cars, culverts, people, villages, or if we found any type of ordinance....

Q: The incident coming back from Kandahar City, are you sure you were fired on by an RPG?

A: No, but that is what was reported.

Regarding the last incident described by LT L, soldiers filled me on details which never made their way into official, sworn statements. Gibbs and Jones threw a grenade so that it would seem as if an RPG had exploded. Apparently, the unofficial rule in Stryker brigade was that if an IED or RPG went off, the soldiers would shoot at anyone in the vicinity. (In the next chapter, we shall see that Major O and Major S describe several such "questionable" killings based upon this unofficial rule, which goes completely against the ROE.) The explosion in this last incident was staged so that soldiers would seem to have a legitimate reason for shooting at whoever was in the vicinity. This incident was never investigated, and one does not know whether the soldiers killed any Afghans in this incident. In LT L's words, "I ordered them to push through the kill zone."

MAJOR U: A BRIEF ENCOUNTER

Major U was assigned to the headquarters of 1-17, the aggressive battalion favored by Hellraiser, where he "served as the battalion operations officer" known as S3. He begins his narrative with the tale of how he arrived in Afghanistan in January of 2010 immediately following his graduation from a course at the Command and General Staff College. Note that by the time Major U arrived, 1-17 had already been in Afghanistan since

July of 2009. Hellraiser asked him, "What did they teach you at school about COIN?" Major U responds:

> I explained that we only discussed COIN operations in the broader context of tactics and doctrine. I also explained that we did not receive any instruction about "how to" conduct COIN operations. COL Tunnell then explained that he believed his brigade headquarters had a greater responsibility to conduct COIN while his subordinate battalions conducted lower-level operations. He explained that he did not believe that battalions were appropriately staffed or resourced to properly conduct COIN operations. He explained that he had organized his Brigade Special Troops Battalion, under the command of LTC Gaydon, to lead the brigade's COIN effort in support of the subordinate battalions.... I always received support from brigade to conduct both lethal and non-lethal operations.

It would be important to conduct further research on exactly how COIN is taught at the army's war colleges. Major U claims that they did not teach him "how to" do COIN. Hellraiser's explanation that a special battalion would do COIN, while the infantry battalions would not, adds a new twist to the already confusing account of the vicissitudes of COIN doctrine in this brigade. Major U's account is out of sync with other sworn statements which make it clear that various infantry battalion commanders were doing COIN, despite the existence of this Brigade Special Troops Battalion for doing COIN. Finally, one is struck by Major U's line that he was supported in conducting both lethal and non-lethal operations. We shall examine this Jekyll and Hyde aspect of COIN in future chapters.

Major U's very short statement is important because of his position—he was in charge of planning the lethal as well as non-lethal missions in 1-17—and because of the confusion he implies in the brigade as to what they were doing and why. He had just graduated from a war college, where he was taught the theory of COIN—but not how to do COIN—and was assigned to the most aggressive battalion, which by all other accounts was doing CG more than COIN. Nevertheless, Major U rationalized this discrepancy as doing COIN in far-fetched ways: that he was supported in conducting lethal as well as non-lethal missions at the same time that Hellraiser told him that he did not want combat, infantry battalions doing COIN.

Chapter 4. The Team of Non-Believers Who Opposed Hellraiser

While there can be no doubt that Stryker brigade was split into two opposing teams or camps, Hellraiser's minions or true believers versus the non-believers, the full extent of the issues that divided them is less clear. We have seen that COIN versus counter-guerrilla philosophies seems to be one of the divisive issues. But we have also seen that no commander admitted to fully embracing COIN as a doctrine—only to doing COIN. Hellraiser's minions tried to rationalize that COIN doctrine and counter-guerrilla doctrine were somehow compatible. This is a debatable point, but we are less interested in a logical, academic solution to this problem, and more interested in how other commanders made sense of the contradiction between COIN and CG. In addition, attitudes toward Hellraiser as a leader seem to be a mixture of contempt and respect. One must accept reality as it truly is, even when it seems to be ambiguous. In the end, ambiguity and ambivalence regarding loyalty in the brigade emerge as the most important factors in explaining its social dysfunction. Let us read the sworn statements by the commanders who fall under BG D's label, the "non-believers."

COL A's sworn statement: "I would not work with or for him [Colonel Tunnell] in the future"

COL A is to Hellraiser as Starbuck is to Captain Ahab in Herman Melville's *Moby Dick*. This analogy includes the many nuances of a relationship that is a mixture of the subordinate wanting to follow his leader, wanting to be the leader's favorite, and yet eventually becoming his nemesis. No other battalion commander's criticisms of Hellraiser are as strong as the condemnations made by COL A in his sworn statement. Moreover, COL A's sworn statement, which consists of a five-page, single spaced letter, is the most erudite document in the Twitty report. Let us clarify that COL A was a lieutenant colonel during the deployment in Afghanistan, and that Hellraiser blocked his promotion to colonel by writing a negative evaluation. COL A appealed the negative evaluation, and was promoted to full colonel despite Hellraiser. During the deployment, COL A was the commander of 8-1 Cavalry, which was the scout reconnaissance battalion.

COL A chose his words carefully and expressed himself eloquently. He begins with the lines: "I view Colonel Tunnell as the most difficult senior leader I have worked alongside in my twenty-six plus years of military service. I would not work with or for him in the future." COL A then launches into a critical assessment of Hellraiser as a leader:

> In my opinion, Colonel Tunnell served as a commander with "no ears"; subordinate commanders' input was not requested, valued, or weighed in most tactical situations. Colonel Tunnell was only interested in actions that pertained to his view *and his view was solely focused on the destruction of the enemy*. At no time would I say that Colonel Tunnell portrayed or professed a balanced approach to command—in training, combat, outside relations or administratively. Colonel Tunnell's private comment to me prior to our deployment sums it up best when he stated in his office that he was after revenge for being shot in the leg while serving in Iraq. Colonel Tunnell kept the metal rod from his leg on his desk in his office and would use it as an illustration.

In his report, General Twitty noted COL A's judgment that Colonel Tunnell was motivated primarily by revenge. But he concluded that he could not find any corroboration for COL A's testimony, although he did not indicate that he sought any confirmation. Plenty of other officers substantiated COL A's perception that Hellraiser was focused solely on destroying the enemy. In his opening paragraph, COL A does not try to frame Hellraiser's motives in terms of any formal doctrine, COIN or counter-guerrilla, but solely as a philosophy of wanting to destroy the enemy. Taken as a whole, COL A's assessment conjures up the archetype of Captain Ahab: unbalanced, uninterested in his men, and obsessed solely with wanting to destroy the great white whale, his private revenge. COL A continues:

> Additionally, as a commander, Colonel Tunnell mainly commanded through his staff, direct interaction was infrequent at best. Battalion level input was rarely sought in my opinion, and brigade commander feedback was routinely funneled through his staff. His lack of interaction stretched deeper than just the tactical arena as well. Throughout my tenure working

for Colonel Tunnell, he never once counseled an individual from my unit on their efficiency report when he served as the individual's senior rater. Colonel Tunnell expressed to me that he was not required to counsel or mentor them; it was strictly the rater's responsibility. In my view, Colonel Tunnell's direct interaction, understanding and personal knowledge of the individuals he senior rated within my unit was poor at best and truly less than the professional standards set by the US Army. Additionally, *as a self-proclaimed A-social individual, Colonel Tunnell refused to interact with his subordinate commanders and leaders outside of an official military setting.* Informal mentoring and counseling in an Army unit is imperative to unit cohesion, bonding, and building trust among each other. His demeanor in this capacity set a tone throughout the SBCT; the SBCT consisted of different battalion level organizations, not a collective Brigade level entity [emphasis added].

Again, COL A strikes a chord in the archetype represented by Captain Ahab, the commander who was not seen by his men. Hellraiser simply did not interact with his subordinate leaders or any troops as he was required to do by army standards. One should note that this depiction of Hellraiser as an asocial leader is consistent across the assessments made by all of Hellraiser's subordinate commanders. COL A's conclusion that, as a result of Hellraiser's poor leadership style, Stryker brigade did not exist as a cohesive social entity, is important sociologically. All the other evidence in this case supports the view that the battalions existed independently of each other, and that they were split into opposing camps. Evidence will point to the conclusion that Stryker Brigade was a dysfunctional society. COL A turns to the issue of how Hellraiser's private and idiosyncratic counter-guerrilla (CG) doctrine translated into actions:

Throughout our train-up for deployment, Colonel Tunnell continually espoused a Counter Guerrilla philosophy, in thought, word, and deed. During our Mission Rehearsal Exercise (MRX) at the National Training Center (NTC) in Feb '09, the focus of the unit's training (Counter Guerrilla operations) came under immediate scrutiny; his views were immediately debated upon our arrival at NTC.... Simply put, the brigade's stated training plan was not the view of subordinate commanders. During our MRX rotation, unbeknownst to Colonel Tunnell, I worked with my Task Force Senior Observer/Controller at NTC to execute the same STX [Situational Training Exercise, COIN] lanes Colonel Tunnell had canceled. Based upon my view of the skill sets required for our pending deployment to Afghanistan, *I shaped this training without his approval or knowledge*.My view of the situation was that I needed this time to properly prepare the unit for the mission I saw us executing in Afghanistan....I advocated more COIN-centered situational training scenarios.... I openly admit that I worked to shape the training received at NTC to meet the needs I assessed were of value for our pending deployment. I did not agree with Colonel Tunnell's philosophy on the focus of the rotation [emphasis added].

In no uncertain terms, COL A proclaimed in a sworn statement that he sneaked COIN training behind Hellraiser's back. LTC C had already told me that he did the same thing at the NTC exercises, and we shall see that other "non-believer" commanders also snuck COIN into their missions even though COIN was the official policy of the US Army at the time. The price COL A paid for this insubordination to Hellraiser (who was being insubordinate to his commanders) was a negative evaluation for promotion by Hellraiser. The important points for the purposes of this study are the following: COL A trained his soldiers in COIN, albeit, without the brigade commander's approval or knowledge. COL A does not claim that he embraced COIN as a doctrine, only that he followed it and trained his subordinates in it. COL A was put into a difficult position by the chain of command in being forced to choose disobeying Hellraiser's unlawful orders versus disobeying official army doctrine (namely, COIN). Sociologists refer to this as a "double-bind" situation, or what the layperson would call a lose-lose situation. COL A would get in trouble for obeying and disobeying Hellraiser and the chain of command. But all the other battalion commanders were in a similar double-bind situation.

COL A's exact choice of words in describing how he followed COIN in Afghanistan—despite Hellraiser's anti-COIN stance—is important to note. COL A does not get lost in the theory of COIN, but focuses on its population-centric orientation. He writes:

> Upon our arrival in theater, I routinely addressed my unit and expressed the views I believed were necessary to be successful in southern Afghanistan, all of which were centered around COIN *fundamentals*. These views centered on dignity and respect, working with the populace, building cooperatives and working together with the District government and the local Afghan Security Forces. In this capacity, we did *not* follow the guidance of Colonel Tunnell and seek to solely hunt down the insurgents in our area of responsibility. Rather, we took a more population focused approach to the problem set. In this capacity, I endeavored to abide by the tactical directive published by COMISAF; from this document I took my direction, *not* from Colonel Tunnell. I worked around Colonel Tunnell's directives in order to adhere to COMISAF's directives and the additional guidance received from other visiting senior leaders [emphasis added].

COMISAF refers to the commander of ISAF, namely, General McChyrstal. One reason among many that COL A could get away with openly defying Hellraiser regarding COIN is that the visitors to his battalion were from General McChrystal's staff. McChrystal's staff visited

COL A's battalion frequently, while Hellraiser visited rarely. In addition, COL A's area of operations was at Spin Boldak, which was over a hundred kilometers from Hellraiser's headquarters. (Soldiers explained to me that traveling a hundred kilometers in Afghanistan took approximately four hours and was always dangerous.) COL A elaborates:

> Spin Boldak, Afghanistan sat on a strategic border crossing with Pakistan. The battalion routinely received senior level visitors, to include COMISAF, who issued direct guidance and expressed clear guidance and expressed clear views on the importance of the border crossing site as well as the way ahead for this area. Additionally, Colonel Tunnell made rare visits to Spin Boldak (I believe he visited Spin Boldak a total of five times in a one year period and none of the visits lasted more than twenty-four hours in duration.) Additionally, when external senior leaders visited Spin Boldak, he refused to allow me or the Battalion staff to update him on the current situation and the way ahead. On one visit, he actually pulled me in my office and lectured me for having the TOC called to attention when he entered the building and the staff standing by to give him and update brief. His interaction with the unit during his visits was almost non-existent; even today, I do not see what he accomplished or gained from his brief visits to Spin Boldak. At the end of the tour in Afghanistan, the relationship between the Battalion and Colonel Tunnell and Colonel Tunnell and me was not good; it was reported to me prior to our redeployment that Colonel Tunnell had verbally stated to the Brigade staff that he hated my Battalion. As I left Afghanistan, Colonel Tunnell told me that he felt like an outsider when he visited the unit, and truthfully to me, he was an outsider. In my opinion, Colonel Tunnell was not interested in the mission, challenges, or approach of the unit. He clearly did not understand the problem set in Spin Boldak, nor did he understand the direct guidance issued to the unit from other senior leaders.

It seems that COL A ran his battalion as he saw fit, and that the brigade commander was an "outsider" to him, and a nuisance. COL A took his orders and guidance directly from General McChrystal's staff. (One should recall that Corporal Morlock's battalion commander, LTC B, similarly stated that he took his orders directly from General McChrystal's staff.) It appears that Hellraiser realized he had no influence upon COL A, and this might be one of several reasons why he did not want to be briefed on what COL A was doing. The professional relationship between COL A and Hellraiser was not normative.

COL A is connected to the story of Corporal Jeremy Morlock and his platoon because Morlock's company commander, Captain Q, was cross-leveled from COL A's battalion and re-attached to LTC B's battalion. To put it another way, a supposedly outstanding company commander in COL A's battalion was artificially detached and then re-attached to an entirely different battalion, and became Morlock's new company commander. Cross-leveling has become a routine process in the US Army, and its usage has increased dramatically since the war in Afghanistan began in 2001. COL A is connected to the other story in our analysis, the story of COIN doctrine. It seems that COL A took considerable risks to his career by doing COIN, but Captain Q had spent two years undoing COIN with Hellraiser prior to be assigned to both COL A and LTC B. Yet COL A never mentions Captain Q's pro-Hellraiser and anti-COIN history. COL A writes of Captain Q, the company commander he lost to cross-leveling: "Throughout our tenure together, CPT Q always displayed a competent, trustworthy, dependable professionalism that equally matched his reputation. I never had any reason to question CPT Q's ability to command, make sound decisions, and lead soldiers. I still hold this true today." Nevertheless, it is a fact that the war crimes that are the subject of this book occurred under CPT Q's command, even though CPT Q was never charged with any wrongdoing. It is also a fact that CPT Q worked closely with Hellraiser for two years as the main writer and promulgator of his counter-guerrilla philosophy. Objectively, there is a strain or dissonance between COL A's pro-doing-COIN, anti-Hellraiser views and CPT Q's anti-COIN and pro-Hellraiser's views (which we will examine in increasing detail throughout this book). Was COL A aware of CPT Q's history as one of Hellraiser's most important true believers? If he was, he never mentions them in his sworn statement. It appears that COL A was trying to show support for CPT Q and his staff so that they would not be charged with any responsibility for the war crimes which occurred in CPT Q's company. CPT Q was investigated, but never formally charged with any wrongdoing.

COL A's sworn statement opens many doors into understanding the dynamics of the brigade, but it also begs many questions and leaves some mysteries which may never be solved. An additional layer to the stories of COL A's connections to COIN doctrine and Corporal Morlock via CPT Q is the story of COL A's personal relationship with Hellraiser. General Twitty must have noticed the curious fact that COL A was Hellraiser's favorite battalion commander yet had a "falling out" with him which was known to the entire brigade. A month following COL A's sworn statement, General Twitty made a follow-up interview, and issued a brief memorandum:

> COL A stated that he felt "golden" before 5/2 SBCT deployed, referring to his status in the eyes of the Brigade Commander. However, he felt that the final OER that he received effectively ended his career progression. He believed that the change is due to how "he went after the problem set."

Sergeant First Class (SFC) R was one of the platoon sergeants in Morlock's battalion. In fact, he was Morlock's original platoon sergeant, before the cross-leveling that dispersed Morlock as well as the sergeant into a succession of other units. SFC R and Morlock lost their connection after the cross-leveling under discussion here. Let us be precise: After the fateful cross-leveling, SFC R was moved to the battalion staff and his official title was 2-1 IN Operations NCO (non-commissioned officer), a position he held from June 2009 to July 2010. SFC R begins his sworn statement with this blunt assertion: "Platoon discipline as a whole in 3rd platoon Bravo Company 2-1 IN was lacking." Even after SFC R left his former unit, he observed them "sleeping behind their vehicles" and "with minimal manning on security." Although he was no longer a platoon sergeant, he engaged the soldiers: "I actually confronted them after this and they said it was no big deal." SFC R gives a concrete assessment of the lack of "circulation" within Stryker brigade in terms that anyone can understand:

> Platoon leadership interaction with the soldiers was low. After returning from patrol, leadership would return to their sectioned tents. Face time with leaders was minimal. Discipline broke down in this platoon because senior leadership let cohesion be controlled at a junior level, squad and team. Soldiers who would never make poor choices when it was known they would be held accountable for their actions, were able to form their own ideas of right and wrong. People who should have been setting the example were unavailable.

SFC R also noted that "urinalysis were not regularly conducted while at FOB Ramrod. I only know of one urinalysis that was conducted during the entire time, which was of 3rd Platoon B Company after the allegations that they had been using drugs." I was present in the courtroom when Morlock's new platoon leader, Lieutenant Moye (who replaced LT L), similarly testified under oath that there were absolutely no random drug tests on any soldiers in the brigade during the entire year of deployment in Afghanistan. No lawyer asked the question, "Why not?" Army doctrine requires monthly random drug testing. The answer seems to be that at the top of the leadership hierarchy, Hellraiser paid no attention to the administrative requirement that infantry soldiers should be drug-free. Perhaps this is because drug testing, mentoring, counseling, and face to face interaction between commanders and troops were deemed as irrelevant to Hellraiser's overall, aggressive philosophy. SFC R recalled that "Companies received counter-guerrilla streamers for guidons" in order "to focus units" on Hellraiser's "mindset."

SFC R's assessment of the confusion in the brigade that was noted by generals and colonels is blunt: "I felt confusion in the coexisting concepts of counter-guerrilla and COIN. The counter-guerrilla tactics I understood concentrated on directly engaging the enemy, then returning to the Forward Operating Base (FOB). Contact with the populace was solely to find the enemy and *winning hearts and minds was crap*" (emphasis added). If other platoon sergeants agreed with this platoon sergeant that winning hearts and minds—which is an apt summary of COIN doctrine—was "crap," it is easy to imagine that Morlock and other low-ranking soldiers would slowly but surely come to feel the same way. In a brigade wherein commanders avoided face-to-face contact with their subordinate officers, sergeants, and troops, sergeants would have the most contact with troops. The sergeants were confused, but the accent of the confusion fell on the belief that COIN was "crap," *not* that Hellraiser's aggressive philosophy was "crap."

Nevertheless, SFC R, like other sergeants and officers in the brigade, were able to figure out that Hellraiser's private doctrine was harmful to their soldiers and to the mission: "Finding the enemy by flooding an area with soldiers provided the enemy with high priority, low risk targets to attack with IEDs. From my point of view this did not work as every time we flooded an area the enemy would activate their IEDs and hide until we left." SFC R's assessment of army doctrines was not based upon abstractions, but upon a practical analysis of the consequences of these doctrines for the welfare of the soldiers under his care and command.

Captain C's take on Hellraiser's philosophy: "Let's kill those mother fuckers."

Captain C was the Brigade Senior Engineer (BDE EN) and adviser to Colonel Tunnell. He cuts through the polite, learned language and chicanery used by generals and colonels to describe the meaning of Hellraiser's private doctrine for soldiers:

> Colonel Tunnell made a speech prior to deployment. During the speech, it was obvious that his philosophy was to search, capture, and then destroy the enemy. To my memory, no reference of aiding the Afghan population was made. If I were to paraphrase the speech and my impressions about the speech in a single sentence, the phrase would be: "Let's kill those mother fuckers."

Captain C acknowledges that, despite Hellraiser, some of the commanders were doing COIN. But like SFC R and so many others, he noticed confusion among the soldiers, and admits that he was also confused:

> There is a distinct disconnect between the mission focus in Afghanistan and General McChrystal's philosophy. Although the battalions and companies conducted many governance type missions, the driving focus was to search and destroy the enemy. This focus was top driven. Being able

to travel between and work with three of the four maneuver battalions, I could sense confusion among the ranks and at times was confused myself.

Captain C's words, "distinct disconnect," seem to capture what the officers and soldiers were feeling. Hellraiser's personal philosophy was distinctly the opposite of General McChrystal's and the government's doctrine. There was no ambiguity in the minds of the troops that Hellraiser was defying General McChrystal. As if they were suffering from some weird form of *collective* Stockholm Syndrome, the soldiers and officers acted as if they were Hellraiser's captives, unable to follow the chain of command's directives as they knew they were supposed to do. Captain C explains:

> My interpretation of the Afghanistan focus was to create a secure environment for the local populace. My interpretation of the brigade focus was to develop intelligence on the enemy, create targets of opportunity, develop and execute plans to engage and destroy the enemy, and then move onto the next "search and destroy" mission, or long term plans to hold and build areas. The guidance pushed from the top was to protect Soldiers at all costs and no matter the circumstances. To protect the populace *at all times* seemed to be a foreign subject and was often pushed to the side.... It was mandated that all soldiers read the new rules of engagement and philosophy of General McChrystal. Following the readings many questions arose. Based on the soldiers' questions, it was evident that our operational focus and the Afghanistan ROE/philosophy were different. The COIN emphasis was talked about among soldiers and leaders *knowing that our mission focus was not in compliance*. The brigade knew that our philosophy was counter-guerrilla and threw in COIN when convenient [emphasis added].

Captain C uncovers the disconnections between philosophy and action, believing and doing in the brigade. Commanders were *doing* COIN without necessarily believing in COIN. Any soldier in his right mind could not fail but to be aware that COIN doctrine and the lawful ROE were charades. The officers who comprised Hellraiser's brigade staff knew that they were giving orders, from top-down, that defied General McChrystal's orders. Those who tried to take on the role of Starbuck on Ahab's ship, namely, COL A, LTC B, and LTC C, were quickly marginalized by Hellraiser and their careers were destroyed. I leave it up to the reader to imagine the agony every soldier and officer experienced every morning that they woke up and knew that they had to pretend to be following General McChrystal's directives, but in reality, they had to follow Hellraiser's anti-chain-of-command philosophy. Leading a double life is never an easy task.

Major D observes:
Colonel Tunnell's name was almost never spoken

Major D's official status in the brigade is difficult to decipher. It is listed formally as "TF Zabul XO, LNO to RC-South." It is very important to examine Major D's self-description of his formal position, because it captures the nature of the maddening, widespread cross-leveling in Stryker brigade. Major D writes:

> I arrived at Ft. Lewis, WA at the end of June 2009 and joined 5/2 Stryker Brigade Combat Team (SBCT) at the beginning of July 2009 and deployed on 20 Jul 09 to Afghanistan, assigned as the Executive Officer (XO) for Task Force (TF) Zabul at Forward Operation Base (FOB) Lagman. TF Zabul was an ad hoc organization formed from the nucleus of the brigade Tactical Command Post (TAC) personnel and equipment, under command of the Deputy Brigade Commander, LTC Karl E. Slaughenhaupt, charged with command and control of Zabul Province, Afghanistan as part of 5/2 SBCT's battle space in Regional Command-South (RC-S). Lacking key staff enablers (e.g., a Judge Advocate General (JAG) officer and Public Affairs Officer), TF Zabul remained subordinate to and reported to the brigade headquarters, and it commanded 4-23 IN, 1-508 PIR, the Zabul Provincial Reconstruction Team (PRT), and the Romanian-American Battle Group (ROAM BG), composed of a motorized Romanian infantry battalion with an embedded US light infantry company from 1-4 IN at Hohenfels, Germany. This arrangement lasted from Aug 09 to Dec 09, when RC-S directed a major change-of-mission and re-alignment. From Jan 10 to Mar 10, the BDE TAC displaced to Military Operating Base (MOB) Lashkar Gah, the headquarters of (British) TF Helmand to coordinate with TF Helmand within whose battle space 4-23 IN now operated on Highways 1 and 601 in Helmand Province and, along with TF Leatherneck, with whom 4-23 IN would operate as part of Operation Moshtarak, Phase II, known colloquially as the clearance of Marjah and central Helmand. The Brigade TAC was folded back into the Brigade Tactical Operations Center (TOC) at the beginning of April 10, and I served from then until redeployment (17 July 10) as the 5/2 SBCT liaison officer (LNO) to the headquarters of RC-S at Kandahar Airfield (KAF).

Let me try to make this passage seem somewhat intelligible to the layperson. What Major D calls TF Zabul is basically the equivalent of Colonel Tunnell's brigade. TF Zabul was sort of a brigade, though not a real brigade, and "it commanded 4-23," which was formally a part of Stryker brigade. Note that TF Zabul was created artificially from several battalions, including an infantry battalion from Romania. (One should keep in mind that Romania is a member of NATO, and the US military presence in Afghanistan is depicted as an international and NATO operation.) By "artificial," I mean that none of the component battalions of TF Zabul have a history of working together. Major D uses the words, "ad hoc," to describe how TF Zabul was created. Major D seems to imply that had TF Zabul been assigned a JAG officer and a public affairs officer—it would have been a full-fledged brigade, on par with Stryker brigade and other brigades. But it was not assigned these positions, and so it was a sort of quasi-brigade. Note that TF Zabul was under the command of Hellraiser's deputy brigade commander! In other words, Hellraiser's deputy brigade commander, who had mandated duties within Stryker brigade, was also the commander of this other, hybrid, quasi-unit, TF Zabul. Note also how TF Zabul was further cross-leveled, and its mission changed, after December 2009 (the same month that Staff Sergeant Gibbs was assigned to Morlock's platoon). Major D's description of his position—which is ambiguous and complicated—gives us yet another glimpse into the widespread cross-leveling that was occurring not only within Stryker brigade but in other units in Afghanistan. I shall repeat that from a sociological perspective, and based upon the research by Samuel Stouffer in the classic, 1949 book, *The American Soldier*, cross-leveling is devastating to any unit's morale and overall functioning, regardless of the unit's size. In addition, cross-leveling calls into question the loyalty of soldiers and officers. For example, to whom did soldiers in 4-23 answer, and to which commander were they loyal, given that they sort of belonged to Stryker brigade, but not really, and sort of belonged to TF Zabul, but not really? This same issue of divided, hybrid loyalties was an issue for Morlock's platoon, which was sort of a part of Alpha Troop 8-1 Cav, but not really, and was sort of a part of Bravo Company 2-1 IN, but not really. On daily missions, CPT Q was their commander, but on paper, CPT T was their commander, but not really, because he was leading the "habitual" B/2-1 IN which no longer had contact with Morlock's platoon. We have seen that commanders refer to this cross-leveling as routine. In fact, it is extremely problematic.

Because Major D was in the peculiar sociological category of "the stranger," he was at home everywhere yet nowhere; he was near and far to soldiers and officers at the same time. This lack of rootedness and commitment to any particular unit gives Major D a predictable edge of objectivity. Major D observes the lack of something everyone takes for granted, namely, that people refer to each other by their names. If they are friends, they call each other by their first names. In more formal social relations, it is common to refer to a Mister or Miss or Doctor or Colonel and Sergeant, followed by the last name. Even when people talk about another person in the third person, in their absence, they "obviously" refer to them by first or last name, with or without a title. The exceptions to this rule usually occur in families and in relation to children: "Mom," "Dad," "Grandpa," "Nana" and other monikers are used. Families also sometimes use pet names and nicknames. But in a formal work setting, most of the time and in most places, one does not refer to "the boss" with a nickname, pet name, or moniker. Major D found it "odd" that in the brigade under discussion here, Hellraiser's real name was not spoken. Major D writes:

> I have conflicted feelings on the climate within the brigade staff. There was a subtle but palpable feeling of fear among staff officers. Staff members were scared to go to the brigade commander with bad news or contradictory info as in the "Emperor Has No Clothes" story. They were unwilling to pass on messages to Colonel Tunnell, which I found strange. *I also found it odd and different from all previous units I had served with that the words Colonel Tunnell were almost never spoken*—he was referred to almost exclusively by his call-sign, mostly "Hellraiser 6" or "Destroyer 6." (emphasis added)

Some readers may try to dilute the impact of Major D's observation by rationalizing that call-signs are necessary in battlefield situations in order to deceive the enemy or protect the commander. Of course that is true. But even the fictional James Bond, whose codename was 007, became James to his secretary and friends. Another example is that Jeremy Morlock was referred to by the army prison staff as "pre-trial Morlock" prior to his court-martial and as "prisoner Morlock" afterwards. (I remind the reader that at the navy brig, he was always known as Mr. Morlock.) The system gave him a number, but they did not take away his name. Prisoners at Fort Leavenworth wear their names on their prison uniforms. One's name becomes a part of one's self, and to refer to others by their names is part and parcel of humanizing them. Melville did not take away Ahab's humanity in *Moby Dick*: Ishmael always refers to him as Ahab or Captain Ahab. True, Captain Ahab's nickname was "Old Thunder," but the crew never confused his nickname with his name. But Colonel Tunnell became his nickname: he was Hellraiser or Destroyer to his men. This is significant, because names and designations matter in social groups. The words "COIN" and "Colonel Tunnell" became taboo in Stryker brigade—they were not to be spoken. I agree with Major D that this state of affairs is strange.

The call-signs used to designate Colonel Tunnell are themselves aggressive. Perhaps the choice of these words speaks to the image Hellraiser wanted to project. From the perspective of his subordinates, however, reducing Colonel Tunnell to a call-sign is also an aggressive act. It is akin to referring to one's boss as "the bitch" or "f___" There is a sado-masochistic element in dehumanizing someone with an aggressive nickname that the wearer of the nickname eventually adopts. Major D observes that Hellraiser's staff feared him. Fear is closely related to loathing, and loathing that is unresolved can degenerate into self-loathing. Major D continues:

> Staff would develop courses of action that were not feasible or reasonable in their professional opinion and no senior staff members were willing

to seek additional guidance ... the staff unquestionably followed ... Based on how my peers reacted to Colonel Tunnell, I too developed an apprehension of briefing or interacting with him. I am very confused about the cause of this *climate of fear and stunted staff* [emphasis added].

Major D's sworn statement is a deep psychological analysis of Hellraiser and the "climate of fear" that surrounded him. Yet, Major D makes the curious statement that, "Although I don't think the staff climate was healthy nor did it encourage free thinking, my interactions with Colonel Tunnell don't indicate he directly caused this unhealthy staff climate." It is curious because of the phrase that Hellraiser did not "directly cause" the poisoned command climate. Who else could have "caused" this climate of fear?

Major D continues: "Colonel Tunnell did have a very dim view of any role for 5/2 in mentoring (outright prohibited) or partnering with ANSF units with Afghan partners being viewed only as a tool to help our forces get at insurgent forces." Of course, Hellraiser's attitude in this regard was directly contrary to COIN doctrine. More importantly, Major D fills in the gaps of our knowledge regarding mentoring *in general and across the board* in Stryker brigade and NATO forces in Afghanistan. For example, he notes that the relationship between Hellraiser and two generals who were his commanders in Afghanistan was "rocky from the start." These high-ranking officers avoided speaking to each other to work out their differences, which resulted in "irrational decision-making." Major D adds: "I was shocked that US soldiers would be denied protection as a consequence of turf-wars and command squabbles." Regarding MG C, who was the army commander of RCS in Afghanistan, Major D writes: "I would summarize that relationship as professional but cold and as minimized as duties and professional obligations would allow: MG C rarely interacted with Colonel Tunnell." In addition, "there was an ultimate mutual loss of confidence between RCS and 5/2." Major D explains the lack of communication and mentoring in helpful detail:

> The straw that broke the camel's back was Operation Stryker Guardian, a brigade operation which was to take advantage of a traditional lull in fighting in April west of Kandahar city, when nearly all able-bodied men would participate in the poppy harvest.... MG C summarily dressed down Colonel Tunnell in front of a large group of subordinates and Afghan National Army partner leadership. In my opinion, the real disapproval of Operation Stryker Guardian was because Marjah was continuing to be a bleeding ulcer.... President Karzai in a Kandahar shura to local elders said that "Kandahar will not see operations like Marjah." ... On RCS part there was a general groan given at almost any mention of 5/2 ... Foreign officers asked me whether it was normal in the American army that subordinates exercised reactive obedience.

It is important to note that the war crimes under discussion here took place during the same time period in which the US government launched its infamous offensive into Marjah, Afghanistan—which was touted by both the government and the news media as the ideal example of COIN doctrine. According to the government and the media, the US military was supposedly going to drive out the Taliban and win the hearts and minds of Marjah's citizens. Of great interest for the purposes of the present story is the fact that portions of one of Hellraiser's battalions, 4-23, was involved in the Marjah mission. (Again, we have seen that 4-23 was sort of under the command of Task Force Zabul.) But overall, Marjah was a fiasco.[5] The Taliban were not driven out. Civilian as well as US casualties were high. Nobody won the hearts and minds of Marjah's frightened residents. The President of Afghanistan condemned the US military devastation of Marjah. Major D alerts us to the fact that Hellraiser wanted to launch his own, separate imitation of the Marjah incursion, albeit in Kandahar Province. MG C would not allow Hellraiser to carry out his goals, no doubt because Hellraiser made it clear that he had no COIN aspirations whatsoever. Major D sensitizes us to the nuance that it was not Hellraiser alone who failed to implement COIN doctrine and who failed miserably in his mission in Afghanistan: Hellraiser's failure is part of the texture and fabric of the overall failure of COIN doctrine in Afghanistan.

First Sergeant W from Charlie Company, 1-17: "We were completely enemy-focused the entire time"

First Sergeant (1SG) W is a high-ranking non-commissioned officer from Hellraiser's favorite battalion, 1-17. He was in Charlie Company, which gained notoriety in the news media because of Hellraiser's firing of its company commander, Captain Joel Kassulke, who dared defy him on the issue of doing COIN (Naylor, 2009). 1SG W does not mince words about the real mission in Afghanistan: "From the very inception of the brigade, counter-guerrilla had been the focus. We had streamers on our guidons, and it was widely accepted as the way we were going to operate." He adds: "We were given a copy of General McChrystal's guidance on COIN. After reading it, I immediately realized that the kinds of operations that I assumed we would be conducting would have to be altered to fit this strategy." Regarding the sometimes strained, overly intellectual, and highly abstract discussions of COIN versus counter-guerrilla strategy that are found in other sworn statements (as well as the literature by theorists of warfare), 1SG W writes succinctly: "We were trained to always be enemy focused and only be population focused in such a way that allowed us to attack the enemy." He elaborates:

I was surprised to find that the brigade commander was unhappy with this location [Arghandab River] and made us relocate to areas that weren't co-located with the major population centers. We then began to conduct more operations in the unpopulated enemy infested area along the river. This effectively stopped us from developing ties with the local population leaders and affecting larger towns that were in our sector... These types of operations dominated our entire time in that sector. Time and again we would go for a day or three days into unpopulated area and search for the enemy. Rarely did we see or talk to anyone, as the local villagers had moved to other towns and abandoned their property. This is specifically addressed in General McChrystal's guidance and *is in direct violation of it. It speaks specifically about going into areas with a low population density for short durations and then leaving. It tells everyone that this is not the desired course of action; however, that is what we did on a daily basis.* All of this conflicted with our efforts to win the support of the locals. We were completely enemy focused the entire time [emphasis added].

1SG W also exposes the real, inside story behind Hellraiser's firing of Captain Kassulke, the popular company commander in 1-17. Captain Kassulke was featured in a news article in *The Army Times,* under the headline, "Stryker Soldiers Say Commanders Failed Them."[6] The article noted the "mixed signals" (doing COIN and doing CG) in the brigade as well as the high casualty rates among soldiers in this battalion due to Hellraiser's sending them into unpopulated areas. 1SG W writes:

Shortly before Captain Kassulke was informed that he was going to change command, Colonel Tunnell, along with is personal security detail, showed up to spend the night and check on us. He was on a routine battlefield circulation patrol out to units in sector and we were an easy way station along his route to overnight at. Captain Kassulke had confided in me that he was unhappy about the current track that the unit was taking for operations. He let me know that he thought we were too enemy focused and we were neglecting major population centers in our sector. He thought that battalion level clearance operations were the wrong strategy and that we should more closely align with the guidance put out by General McChrystal. I agreed with him. He then told me he thought he should approach the brigade commander with his ideas. He wanted to express his concerns personally and try to convince the brigade commander that we should focus on the larger population centers in our area of operations versus continuing to execute clearance operations in an IED-ridden area with low population density. I told him that I was sure that Colonel Tunnell could not be convinced that this was a better strategy. I also felt that approaching him with these ideas could be perceived as *subversive* and may be detrimental to his career. That night I overheard Captain Kassulke talking with Colonel Tunnell. Captain Kassulke told him all of the things that we had discussed. Soon after that, once again conducting another of these types of operations, we had a mass casualty event. Later that day or early the next, Captain Kassulke was informed that Colonel Tunnell was worried about him and that he would be changing command. Battalion commanders felt that if they briefed what they believed to be the best course of action, it would be denied because it was not enemy focused. What was being shown on the slides and what we were conducting were action changes not intent changes [emphasis added].

1SG W's inside dope allows us to grasp the fact that Hellraiser fired Captain Kassulke in order to cover up his own mistakes, and to scapegoat Captain Kassulke for the high rates of US casualties, which were the very issue which Captain Kassulke sought to prevent. Captain Kassulke dared to disagree with Hellraiser, and to voice the normative opinion that the brigade should be following General McChrystal's directives. The COIN strategy manual is explicit on the fact, as noted by 1SG W, that low population density areas are not worth the cost of the lives of American soldiers. Such unpopulated terrain makes it easy to plant IEDs, and offers no opportunity to win the trust of the local population. Like Melville's fictional character, Starbuck, Captain Kassulke confronted his Captain Ahab, namely, Hellraiser. Given that Hellraiser ignored the advice of generals and his own battalion commanders to follow chain of command directives, there was no possibility that he would listen to a captain. Yet, Hellraiser could not simply, openly remove Captain Kassulke from command for disagreeing with him and agreeing with General McChrystal. Moreover, Kassulke was loved by his men. So, Hellraiser fired Captain Kassulke for allegedly sustaining high casualty rates in his company, when, in fact, Hellraiser was responsible for putting his soldiers into physical environments which invited such high casualty rates. (Let me remind the reader that General Twitty did not interview Captain Kassulke.)

1SG W's descriptions illustrate that everyone in Hellraiser's brigade was leading a double life: pretending to be following Hellraiser's directives and also pretending to be following General McChrystal's directives. Soldiering in that brigade was like an exercise in double-ledger bookkeeping. 1SG W could see through the double-hypocrisy of constantly lying to both sets of commanders (those on McChrystal's versus Hellraiser's staff). Captain Kassulke's fate was sealed, and his career ended, when he dared to be honest with Hellraiser. To be honest in any dishonest social climate is to be perceived as subversive and disloyal.

1 SG W also alerts us to one of the background themes to this story, namely, that Hellraiser's exclusive focus on aggressively killing the enemy detracted from a focus on the real needs of soldiers, such as supplies. In 1SG W's words: "I was literally fending for myself on things that I needed to upgrade the standard of living for my men at our company headquarters. Things were very expeditionary for a long time. I received

basically no support from either my battalion or my brigade headquarters." I had heard similar testimony from the supply officer at Abu Ghraib, who said on the witness stand that he felt abandoned by the army as he tried to obtain water, toilet paper, and other essentials for his soldiers.

MAJOR O: "ONE COMPANY ABSOLUTELY EMBRACED THE BRIGADE
COMMANDER'S MENTALITY"

Major O was the operations or S3 officer for 1-17 Infantry—the aggressive battalion, Hellraiser's favorite battalion—but he was opposed to Hellraiser's philosophy. Major O was not a true believer, even though his battalion commander, LTC N, was perceived by his peers as one of Hellraiser's minions. Like other soldiers and officers I have interviewed, MAJ O singles out 1-17 as the battalion that was most in line with Hellraiser's mentality. Within 1-17, he singles out Bravo Company: "One company absolutely embraced and adopted the brigade commander's mentality, B Company, 1-17 IN." One cannot repeat often enough, in order to avoid confusion, that Morlock and the so-called kill team were *not* in 1-17. They were in 2-1. However, 1-17 collectively engaged in more instances of war crimes or at least, "questionable kills," than 2-1 did. None of the war crimes committed in 1-17 were investigated, and none went to court-martial. By itself, this discrepancy is not unusual. Scores of war crimes were not prosecuted in the Abu Ghraib courts-martial as well as the notorious cases of Operation Iron Triangle and the Baghdad Canal killings. The important point is that war crimes come in tribes, groups, clusters, or whatever word one wishes to use to capture the fact that war crimes are never isolated events. The cases that are prosecuted and reported in the news media are the ones that are the easiest to prosecute.

Let us explore Major O's focus on 1-17, and especially Bravo Company, in relation to the brigade, which corresponds very closely to what the battalion chaplain told me over the phone, and what he wrote in his own sworn statement. MAJ O is very clear about his objectives in his sworn statement:

> I was asked to write this statement covering the following areas: my view of the effects on command climate due to the brigade commander's pursuit of a counter-guerrilla strategy instead of following current COIN doctrine; my impression of B/1-17, particularly the effects of them adopting the counter-guerilla strategy and as compared to A and C Companies; the reluctance of the 1-17 commander to conduct 15-6 investigations; and the discipline problem in 1-17 IN. The brigade commander's strategies caused frustration at multiple levels. The XO and I were frustrated as we tried to plan operations according to our current doctrine, but were continually pressed from higher to conduct continual offensive operations attacking enemy "formations." These operations were not tied to protecting the

population, but rather completely enemy oriented, *using enemy attrition as measures of success...* The brigade commander wanted us to attack, to close with and destroy "enemy formations." He wanted us penetrating into the green zone, despite there being no population, to hunt down and destroy the "guerrillas," as he called them. He repeatedly told us we needed to "seize and maintain the initiative." He was not interested in us gaining the initiative in any other way, like partnering with local governments, leaders, and security forces... We were forbidden to focus on the population as the center of gravity. We were forbidden to use the term "cells" to talk about adversarial forces. There were only "formations," organized into companies, groups (platoons), and teams (squads) *[emphasis added]*.

One should connect Hellraiser's references to the Taliban as supposedly operating in "formations," "companies," "platoons," and so on with similar claims by him in the counter-guerrilla manual which he wrote (Tunnell, 2009). There is something bizarre about perceiving insurgents and the Taliban as a mirror image of US army formations. MAJ O continues:

All of this put me in the awkward position of attempting to carry out the commander's intent when I felt it was very much at odds with what I, and the XO, and most times the battalion commander, and most of the staff all felt was "the right way," the "doctrinal way" to prosecute our operations. These guys have been to the career course. They've been deployed before. They know how it's supposed to work (emphasis added)

MAJ O adds that when the 1-17 battalion commander "wanted to move to larger population centers, brigade commander denied his request." To clarify, moving one's troops to larger, urban areas is part of COIN doctrine, but Hellraiser wanted this battalion to stay in the unpopulated and more dangerous (in terms of exposure to IEDs) areas. I inquired from the chaplain and other battalion commanders, who would speak with me, whether the 1-17 battalion commander was pro-COIN or pro-Hellraiser. This is because the 1-17 commander did not respond to my request to speak with him. His colleagues said that he was as pro-chain-of-command as they were, with the major difference that he was more directly under Hellraiser's thumb whereas the other battalion commanders were in more frequent contact with or under the direct supervision of General McChrystal's staff. Hellraiser established a temporary headquarters at 1-17, and visited frequently, often staying for days. MAJ O writes that Hellraiser would constantly inquire from soldiers returning from missions whether they saw any Taliban fighters. (This is another similarity to Captain Ahab, who inquired of sailors from every passing ship whether they sighted Moby Dick.) In general, Hellraiser did not circulate among his troops, but he circulated obsessively with 1-17. To rephrase the matter: Hellraiser contaminated 1-17 with his aggressive mentality more than any other battalion. The 1-17 commander was not able to build metaphorical walls of resistance to Hellraiser's contagion, whereas the other battalion commanders were more able to resist. Within 1-17, Hellraiser adopted a particular company. Major O goes into some detail on this point

> One company *absolutely embraced and adopted the brigade commander's mentality, B Company 1-17*. It was positioned on the West side of the Arghandab River geographically isolated from the paved road and the government center. While there were two larger population clusters in their area of operations, Jelawuhr and Adira, B Company spent most of their time in the orchards hunting guerrillas and their caches. The company was *completely enemy focused and could not be made to come off of conducting ambushes, raids, and clearance operations. They were held up by the brigade commander as a company who was getting it right. He [Colonel Tunnell] routinely positioned his TAC at the B Company COP demanding personal debriefs from the company commander. He routinely called the company commander directly for tactical discussions or debriefs. While the brigade commander seemed obsessed with B Company, he visited A and C companies two or three times or once throughout the entire year. The other companies were not in the Arghandab River valley where the enemy formations cold be concentrated and massed and they were not perceived by him to be aggressively hunting down and destroying enemy formations. It is my belief that Captain Kassulke was, in fact, relieved by the brigade commander because he was perceived to be placing too much effort into partnering with local government, police, and army, and engaging the population [emphasis added]*.

There is much information condensed in the above statement that requires careful explication. Major O named the object of Hellraiser's obsession as B Company, 1-17 IN (consisting of approximately 200 soldiers). Sitting in the CID office at Ft. Lewis, with a CID special agent seated behind me, I have seen photographs of squads and platoons in Bravo Company posing with their trophy kills. I viewed the photos lawfully, and under CID supervision, as part of my preparation as an expert witness. But the photos of the kills by Bravo Company, 1-17, never came up in any trials. I learned from soldiers that B/1-17 followed the rule of engagement that if any Afghan man was seen after curfew, he was to be shot on sight. Indeed, the photos showed what seemed to be farmers lying dead next to their shovels. Soldiers explained to me that once they learned that Afghan farmers irrigate their fields at night, due to the excessive heat during the day, these raids by Bravo Company ceased. As of this writing, the army still forbids the public dissemination of these and other photos. A portion of them were published by *Spiegel* and *Rolling Stone* magazines in the Spring of 2011 (Boal, 2011). In fact, these magazines published some of the photos of kills by B Company in 1-17, but wrongly attributed them to Morlock's company and battalion. Morlock, his platoon, and company had nothing to do with the activities that Major O describes by Bravo Company 1-17 IN. Major O's observation that no formal investigation was ever made of these questionable killings screams for attention. But no one in the army seemed to notice. It is instructive to read MAJ O's detailed account of several "questionable" kills by B and C Companies 1-17:

> Around April 2010, two different platoons in the battalion had direct fire contacts which appeared to both the S3 and me to need further investigation. One event involved a platoon from C Company. A platoon was attacked with an IED and when a second platoon moved to assist they observed who they believed to be the trigger man and others fleeing the scene. At some point during the pursuit, this individual was shot and killed. Upon further exploitation of both the IED strike site and the scene of the shooting, the lack of evidence prompted both the S3 and I to recommend for the commander to initiate an investigation. The IED turned out to be pressure-activated and there was no cell phone or weapons found on the killed individual. However, the commander said no investigation was needed.... Within a few days, while manning Ops to isolate an objective for a MEDCAP mission in a village with questionable loyalties, a team from the BN RECON PLT made direct fire contact, killing three males. Initial reporting to the BN TOC was that they received direct fire and then returned fire, killing the three. Those reports also indicated finding IED components and weapons/ammunition. However, C CO CDR, who was conducting the MEDCAP, exploited the site and called back to the BN TOC with concerns. He told me that he felt the shooting was not within the ROE. After I received the photos of the site, including the three bodies, I agreed. The BN S3 had the same concerns I did. The IED "components" were some old, used AA batteries and a couple strands of electronic wire. The ammunition was old, discarded brass. These items amounted to no more than the average Afghan pocket litter. Additionally, the photos of the deceased appeared to me to indicate two were killed with head shots and the third was hit multiple times on the left, back, side. Again, the S3 and I both recommended to the commander that he initiate an investigation. Again, he said he had talked to the members of the platoon and didn't think it was necessary. While consolidating the reporting and submitting our impression reports and story boards, I began to see inconsistencies in reporting between the RECON PL, RECON PSG, and C CO CDR. There was confusion about who initiated fire, whether or not warning shots were fired, and whether or not the entire event took place before anything was reported to the C CO CDR. (The RECON PLT was OPCON to the C CO CDR for the operation.) While on a separate mission in the C CO AO, I stopped at their CP and talked at length with the C CO CDR and reviewed their CP duty logs. The C CO CDR was adamant that the shooting was outside the ROE and what I saw of the duty logs furthered my belief that something was not right. The S3 and I again had a lengthy discussion with the BN CDR, insisting that he initiate an investigation. Eventually,

he capitulated and said he would call the BDR CDR first, though. Afterward, he said that the BDE CDR told him to investigate, but to have someone in the BN do it. The commander told me to do one and give the other to the S3. The S3 and I both insisted that he request IOs from outside the BN, but he refused. He said he did not want anyone from outside the BN coming here and poking around because they don't understand the BN and they won't have any idea or context for "the kind of fight we've had here." While I don't remember all specific discussions, I remember that the BN CDR was absolutely reluctant to do any type of investigation of direct fire contact....I believe his reluctance to conduct investigations was based on a number of factors. First, he did not want to expose anything that would reflect negatively on the BN, and further, on him. I believe his mentality was that if there was anything negative going on, as long as it wasn't exposed, everything was fine. Secondly, I think he knew that his training and leadership of these platoon leaders and their platoons was lacking. He did not want that exposed. Finally, I think it was a function of his broader failure to supervise.

In this one incredible passage, one finds reference to multiple instances of "questionable kills" and probable war crimes that were never investigated. Shots to the head suggest execution. The planted and fake batteries and wires lead to further suspicions. Note that the C Company Commander, Captain Kassulke, was the one who most questioned some of the killings by Bravo Company—and he was later fired. Major O's overall description of 1-17 suggests that B Company was the most aggressive while C was the least aggressive, and A company was somewhere between the two in terms of Hellraiser's philosophy. MAJ O also uncovers the lack of a standard operating procedure for investigating questionable kills or possible war crimes. Hellraiser wanted the investigation to be internal to 1-17, but the battalion commander resisted, knowing that any such investigation would reflect badly on him, not on Hellraiser. Major O also resisted, given the overall climate in which it was widely known that any bearer of bad news would be sacked or blamed. The point is that the chain of command failed miserably in reporting and investigating "questionable" kills.

As I have stated at the outset, I have no interest or expertise in Hellraiser's legal responsibility for any of the tragedies that resulted from his command: this is a sociological study, not a criminal investigation. But it is clear that Hellraiser, like the fictional Captain Ahab, acted as a sort of negative "contagion" to his troops: He was obsessed—to use Major O's word—with 1-17 as a whole, and within this battalion, with Bravo Company. He circulated with Bravo Company more than any other company. And by most accounts, Bravo Company was the most troubled, undisciplined, and tragic company in a battalion that was infected by the same, aggressive contagion. Major O writes:.

1-17 was the most ill-disciplined BN in which I have served. The BN contained multiple drug offenders who were given simple UCMJ action and
not processed out of the Army. The BN was in poor physical condition,
with multiple fat soldiers. Uniform standards, personal hygiene, unit and
field hygiene, and vehicle safety standards were simply and routinely ignored. CSDP was non-existent. Part of the problem was the CSM [com-
mand sergeant major]. The CSM was the worst I have ever seen. He rarely
left the wire, was never in the TOC [tactical outpost command], and put
his own comfort and safety above those of his Soldiers. The other problem
was that no one was ever held accountable. Partly due to the commander's
lack of supervision, and partly because it was too hard for him to actually
hold anyone accountable. CSM was never held accountable. B Company
was the most ill-disciplined company in the BN. The CO CDR was never
held accountable. B Company had a Soldier die and one Soldier had a leg
amputated in a roll-over because they were driving too fast and were not
restrained. CO CDR was not held accountable. B CO had the worst CSDP
in the BN. CO CDR was not held accountable.

MAJOR S: "COLONEL TUNNELL TOLD HIS MEN: 'KILL FIRST, THEN CAPTURE'"

Major S initially served as the S3 or operations officer in the problematic 1-17 battalion and was subsequently cross-leveled to another battalion, 4-23, where he was the battalion executive officer. He is blunt in
his assessment: "Colonel Tunnell failed to properly define the counter-
guerrilla strategy in relation to COIN and therefore created confusion,
animosity, and uncertainty among leaders in the brigade." And he elaborates on the ways that Hellraiser kept criticisms at bay:

> No one that I remember publicly challenged Colonel Tunnell on counter-
> guerrilla operations because of fear of retribution and being on "his bad
> side." It is commonly known that once Colonel Tunnell made up his mind
> about an officer in a negative manner professionally, his career was termi-
> nated or the officer was severely marginalized. The confusion I mentioned
> on the previous page along with the following topics I believe *led soldiers
> and some leaders to think that their sole purpose for the deployment was to kill the
> enemy* [emphasis added].

Major S's hypothesis is very precise sociologically. He does not claim
that Hellraiser's philosophy led directly to the murders. Instead, he argues plausibly that the *confusion* generated by Hellraiser led—or in some
sense, indirectly "caused"—a tendency to solely kill the enemy. When
doubts or further confusion is introduced as to who constitutes the enemy, it is easy to grasp that soldiers and commanders would be bent on
solely on killing a *perceived* enemy, and then justifying the kills with drop
weapons. As I will point out later, Morlock's platoon, along with many

other soldiers, came to regard anyone and everyone in Afghan villages as the enemy. An obsessive reading of the sworn statements by low-ranking soldiers shows that they knew that the three villages in which the charged killings occurred were regarded as pro-Taliban in intelligence reports. Major S expands upon the precise mechanisms involved in these complex connections, and he typed his statement in all capitals—as if he were some prophet who grasped a mystery, and wanted to convince his future readers. His long explanation is worth quoting fully:

> Colonel Tunnell in his few speeches to soldiers, motivated them by telling them they were the most technologically advanced and most lethal force assembled *made only for war and fighting.* He used similar terminology in his change of command speech. Field grade officers took sides in the approach to executing orders. *There were two camps,* those that supported and followed the *lethal approach* of COIN from Colonel Tunnell's version of counter-guerrilla operations and those who attempted a *hybrid concept of counter-guerrilla and COIN* to keep Colonel Tunnell relatively satisfied while executing the mission. In my perception this broke down as follows: 2-1 commander supported the counter-guerrilla approach. 1-17 IN has a mixed approach (B/1-17 IN company commander, CPT James Pope, and his inability to operate in a team environment, drove the battalion to be more counter-guerrilla operational by Colonel Tunnell while the other companies were attempting less CGO [counter-guerrilla operations] and more COIN). 4-23 IN and 8-1 Cavalry were more COIN throughout the process. The field grades at the brigade level as a result, put significantly more emphasis into 1-17 IN and 2-1 IN over the other combat units in the brigade. This was evident by the behavior of Major McClean (S2) in allocating (supplies), Major Kuth (S3) in prioritizing training and operations, and Major Doogan (XO) in providing resources and support for sustainment. This emphasis of support by the brigade S2, S3, and XO drove battalion field grades to have some animosity toward each other [emphasis added].

Major S is very sensitive to nuance. He does not portray the two teams as pro-COIN or anti-COIN, but more accurately as a team that sought to rationalize CG as a part of COIN versus a team that tried to incorporate CG while doing COIN. Major S alerts us to the reality that Stryker brigade was not following COIN or counter-guerrilla doctrine, but was following various hybrids of the two philosophies. Doctrinally speaking, there can be no such thing as "lethal COIN" doctrine, yet the practical reality of everyday life in Stryker brigade is that this Frankenstein monster of pieces of COIN cobbled together with CG doctrine was the doctrine they followed. The important point is that all the soldiers and officers were confused. Moreover, and in the abstract, Hellraiser's version of CG philosophy is simply not compatible with COIN. Yet, his subordinates made CG compatible with COIN in a dysfunctional and monstrous way.

Major S offers a fascinating interpretation of the leanings by various battalions vis-à-vis COIN and CG. It is curious that he associates Battalion 2-1 (Morlock's battalion) with Hellraiser's counter-guerrilla doctrine, not primarily COIN, given that this battalion's former and then current commanders told me they were leaning toward doing COIN. However, he attributes this shift by 2-1 toward Hellraiser's philosophy to Captain Q, who, as the reader may recall, had worked closely with Hellraiser prior to being assigned first to 8-1 and then to 2-1. 1-17 was "mixed" in Major S's view, but the confusion within this troubled battalion drove it into a more distinctly pro-Hellraiser (CG) approach. (This view is consistent with Major O's description of 1-17 as mixed in the sense that B Company was the most aggressive and C Company was the least aggressive.) In summary, Major S seems to be claiming that units either faked COIN in order to follow Hellraiser's philosophy (1-17 and 2-1) or faked CG in order to do COIN (4-23 and 8-1). Soldiers and officers engaged in chameleon-like behaviors in order to avoid being on Hellraiser's bad side. Like a disturbed father-figure, Hellraiser played favorites by funneling supplies and support to units which adopted his views, and withholding such favors from commanders who opposed him. Major S's description of the dynamics within the brigade is very similar to descriptions of favoritism and dynamics in dysfunctional families. Major S continues:

> Colonel Tunnell on two or three commander conference calls in the fall of 2009 where I listened in, made statements about the commanders providing him feedback, as to why units were not killing the enemy.... I specifically remember discussing with Major McClean 08 December 09 about our move from Zabul to Helmand, where I was asking why we were not the main effort, even though we were supporting the RCS [Regional Command South] main effort. He specifically stated, "Sha Wali Kot has all the bad guys, we are here to kill bad guys." The focus of every brigade level mission planned or executed went specifically after kill/capture individuals in the area of operations (please note that kill/capture versus capture/kill. Colonel Tunnell specifically *told every commander that it will be kill first then capture as he did not want hesitation by soldiers—stated in commander meetings in 2008 and in the week of 20-28 July 2009 in meetings)* (emphasis added)

It is worth noting that Maywand District, where the killings that went to trial took place, had a reputation for harboring "bad guys" before Stryker brigade arrived. But it is a sparsely populated area, and according to COIN doctrine, it should not have been a focus. Major S makes an important distinction between the orders to "kill/capture" versus "capture/kill." Sometimes the news media reports such missions as "capture or kill," as if it were a soldier's choice, and as if capture was the first option. Major S alerts us to the fact that Hellraiser went out of his way to drill into his officers that the soldiers should be trained to kill first. But the order to "kill first, then capture," makes no sense. One cannot capture someone who has already been killed. On the other hand, the more conventional order of capture/kill makes more sense, as it implies that one is permitted to kill an enemy if the soldier is unable to capture him. These are fine, philosophical, and abstract distinctions. In practice, the kill first and capture later philosophy—even though it makes no sense—helps to explain why members of the so-called kill team did *not* hesitate to try to kill a perceived enemy from the moment that they believed that they were confronted by a "bad guy." They heard a grenade go off, saw a comrade go into lethal mode, or heard someone open fire, and they supported each other in eliminating the perceived enemy without thinking, questioning, or even considering the capture option. Hellraiser's philosophy had, indeed, trickled down from the high-ranking officers to the lowest grunts. Major S continues:

> Colonel Tunnell did not provide an environment where commanders could communicate with him... During these discussions, the officer that was most involved was COL A, who did what in my interpretation was the most work in *replicating* COIN during the deployment. He tried to clarify every point. Colonel Tunnell got somewhat but not visually irritated, but he gave the guidance to the effect that "All of you work for me and you need not worry about what I do." ... Colonel Tunnell was against mentoring officers. On 23 July 2009, Colonel Tunnell specifically told me in counseling something to the effect that "mentoring is some bullshit that the Army came up with to keep officers around. The reality is that officers, especially field grades, do not require any mentoring." He further went on to comment that I was high maintenance for requesting counseling for my Officers Evaluation Report (OER). This verbiage went throughout the staff and other majors who then decided not to seek counseling. So it became apparent to all field grades that you only got counseling when things were wrong or when an officer was to be fired [emphasis added].

It is beyond the scope of the present work to review the nine, single-spaced, typed pages of Major S's sworn statement. I shall summarize some of the remaining key points in this officer's erudite, nuanced analysis. Major S quotes Hellraiser as saying to his commanders at a meeting: "You are here to kill the enemy" and "I am not interested in the people—that is someone else's problem." Major S witnessed conversations between Hellraiser and two generals who criticized him at the NTC exercises. He summarizes: "Colonel Tunnell engaged in friction type conversations." One general tried to tell Hellraiser that "a brigade may have a lot of kills of enemy, but would not be making a difference in the lives of the people." Hellraiser argued that USAID and other institutions should be helping the people, but this was not his job. When another general was giving a lecture on COIN, "Colonel Tunnell made a facial expression during Brigadier General Nicholson's brief on the Rules of Engagement and the directives they would have to follow." Major S concludes: "You could sense the tension based on what we had been trained and been told to execute by Colonel Tunnell and what we were being briefed by Brigadier General Nicholson."

The cumulative effect of everyone's energy spent on the COIN versus CG philosophies "led to the perception that no one cared about soldiers." This is because army directives concerning health, supplies, and work obligations were pushed to the background. As a result, there were constant rumors of "sexual activity, adultery, and drugs," and these rumors "created a perception of one big party and that they did not care or had a reality check on what was going on in the field." Regarding LTC B, commander of 2-1, Major S opines that initially, this commander boasted about "the lethal behavior of units and the way he was going to focus after the enemy." Referring to the double-life we have already uncovered, Major S notes that LTC B "was often able to convince Colonel Tunnell for support because of the lethality opportunities that he saw available to him." But, LTC B later "changed his discussion to population centric opportunities being more of a focus." Major S writes that "Colonel Tunnell specifically questioned him" about his switch of allegiances from CG to COIN. If these assertions are true, one can imagine that the infantry soldiers in 2-1 would have been confused by their battalion commander's switch from lethal mode to the mode of having tea with the village elders. Major S notes that LTC B made his conversion to COIN in January of 2010, but that is the month in which the killings under discussion here began. And Major S's assessment contradicts LTC B's statement to me that he was initially under the command of General McChrystal and was doing COIN from the outset. Perhaps this ambiguity is best resolved by assuming that LTC B, like the other battalion commanders, was forced to live a double-life and presented contradictory personas regarding COIN or CG depending upon his audience.

In line with statements by other officers, Major S singles out 1-17 as the most lethal and murderous battalion, even though no one from this battalion was ever charged with murder:

> There were rumors about 1-17 in conducting a murder of an innocent civilian during the fall of 2009, but I don't remember that ever being substantiated. I believe that they were first with the "murder" reputation as blowback for the casualties they had. Again, nothing I can substantiate, but it left the reputation that we were hunting only after the enemy.

Finally, Major S compliments Hellraiser on some of his good qualities, but in a subtly back-handed sort of way: "Last, I want to acknowledge that while there were command climate issues, I firmly stand that Colonel Tunnell had some strengths as a leader." For example, "When you are on his good side, he is great to dialogue with." He was an excellent motivator: "He could motivate soldiers to believe they were in the most lethal unit in the army." And he was highly skilled in the art of persuasion: "On multiple occasions with senior officers, I watched him convince soldiers on how his CG doctrine was related to COIN. The issue was that the articulation and translation of what he stated did not make it clear for leaders and soldiers to understand and ultimately confused many."

Major S also appended an additional three pages in which he listed the names of officers who could give specific information on "the numerous doctrinal violations" of orders by Hellraiser "to execute a lethal operation against the enemy instead of COIN operation."

Major K: "Culture in the brigade of not holding anyone accountable for anything"

Major K was the operations officer for 4-23 IN. His attention to particular details gives the reader further and deeper insight into the dynamics of Stryker brigade. He begins with a detailed analysis of lack of discipline and administrative issues, concluding that "The lack of enforcement of any kind of standards overflowed to every aspect of daily operations." He also describes his role in Operation Longview in Afghanistan. Major K was assigned the task of giving the brief on this operation which was supposed to have had a "population-centric focus," according to Hellraiser's commanders. In other words, it should have been in line with COIN. According to MAJ K, "Before I could finish the brief, Colonel Tunnell interrupted me and disapproved our plan." MAJ K continues:

> As a result, we changed the concept to an enemy-centric clearance operation (Exhibit 3). During the back brief for this operation, Colonel Tunnell was particularly concerned about our concept to arrive on target with an overwhelming display of combat power... Colonel Tunnell seemed disappointed that our plan did not *bait the enemy* into firing on a small element so that we could respond with more combat power and destroy them in the village. LTC Shields [Battalion commander] and I agreed it was best not to provoke a firefight in the middle of any Afghan village and thus we executed accordingly.... I ensured it was heavy with counter-guerrilla terminology, i.e. "target the insurgent auxiliary" by using "*small kill teams,*" etc. in order to get it approved by Colonel Tunnell but we really had no intention of conducting aggressive interdiction operations—especially with the impending winter in the mountains. By the time this operation was approved, we began receiving warning orders that would eventually require the battalion to move to Helmand Province. (emphasis added)

One should pay careful attention to MAJ K's exact choice of words, "bait the enemy" and "kill teams." It is important to connect MAJ K's description of Hellraiser's emphasis on "baited ambush" tactics with Staff Sergeant Gibbs's scenarios. The baited ambush tactic comes up several times in the sworn statements. Soldiers told me that Gibbs complained frequently to his platoon leader and company commander that B Co was not using this tactic. In this sense, he was echoing Hellraiser. Another connection is that instead of viewing the killings under discussion here as random killings, it is possible to view them as distorted efforts to use baited ambush tactics. Basically, all the scenarios imagined by Gibbs and described by soldiers in numerous sworn statements involve provoking the appearance of hostility by Afghans (the bait part) that would be met by ambush. This connection does not negate the fact that the scenarios were murderous, but it does suggest that Gibbs did not invent the scenarios out of thin air.

Major K's account is in line with other accounts of the double-lives all of Hellraiser's subordinates had to create in order to survive in that dysfunctional social environment. The initial order was to develop an operation in line with COIN doctrine. Hellraiser disapproved it despite the approval of his superiors. It was re-written in order to trick Hellraiser into approving it. Major K and the battalion commander had no intention of carrying out the false plans they submitted to Hellraiser in order to appease him. The operation was never executed.

General Twitty asked Major K the question, "How did Colonel Tunnell's counter-guerrilla strategy cause confusion throughout the ranks?" Major K's long and detailed reply is worth quoting at length:

> The first I heard of the counter guerrilla strategy was during my initial phone contact (about 60 days prior to my arrival at the unit) with Major S, the 4-23 Infantry Battalion Executive Officer, who mentioned that the brigade was "definitely enemy focused." I found this curious since much of the year at ACSC [army command staff college] was devoted toward educating us on a population-focused COIN strategy and I questioned Major S about how the enemy-focused strategy reconciled with the population-focused strategy. I remember that he could not adequately explain to me how the enemy-focused strategy could be reconciled with FM 3-24 [COIN]. .. Upon arriving at Fort Lewis in early July 2009, my wife and I were moving into on-post housing when one of the movers happened to mention that he had recently helped Colonel Tunnell move out of his on-post residence. The moving company employee mentioned that Colonel Tunnell had told him that the Brigade was "going to Afghanistan to kill." I chuckled and insisted, "no, we're not.".... [upon arriving in Afghanistan] LTC Shields [battalion commander] told me "continue to focus on the population." I experienced some fairly significant conflict with the company commanders because I was disapproving many of their night "small

kill team" ambush operations in favor of forcing them to conduct more key leader engagements and more patrolling in villages. I sensed that the battalion was not adequately trained in population-centric operations—after all, the companies had been "validated" in counter-guerrilla operations and had been awarded the Counter-Guerrilla Streamer for it. It was challenging to change this dynamic since there appeared to be *so much institutional momentum to go out and kill the enemy.* After Operation Longview was disapproved by Colonel Tunnell, I was so *mentally and physically exhausted from trying to get the battalion focused on the population, I relented and published Operation Longview2 and allowed the companies to chase the enemy with minimal success.* Shortly after, we received a document from the Brigade S2 section, a faux Field Manual entitled "Guerrilla Hunter Killer Operations." *Initially, I thought it was a joke, but after perusing it for a couple of minutes, I realized it was a real attempt at putting Taliban organization into an OPFOR [opposition forces] order of battle structure.* Henceforth, we were pressured to describe insurgent organization in terms of Guerrilla Hunter/Killer (GH/K) teams, groups, and companies [emphasis added].

Note that Major K was a Johnny-come-lately to the brigade dynamics, having been assigned to the brigade in the summer of 2009, immediately prior to deployment in Afghanistan. He had no idea of the in-fighting that had already occurred and was ongoing in the brigade. It is of great interest that his battalion commander urged MAJ K to pursue COIN, knowing full well that this advice would, and did, get MAJ K in trouble with Hellraiser as well as the company commanders. We do not have sufficient data to ascertain the battalion commander's motives or evaluate his ambivalence. But MAJ K was set up to fail by the battalion commander. Exhausted by the resistance he met on all sides, MAJ K admits that he finally relented and started writing up lethal operation plans, in defiance of COIN.

MAJ K's allusion to the GH/K [Guerrilla Hunter Killer] manual, which was commissioned and partly written by Hellraiser, is also important. I have read this manual (see Tunnell, 2009), and while I did not think it was a joke, I found it to be as troubling as it was to MAJ K. It is true that in this strange and idiosyncratic manual, Hellraiser wrongly ascribes modern-day army organization to the Taliban. In plain language, Hellraiser falsely claimed that the Taliban was comprised of teams, groups, companies, and battalions, just like the US Army. In Hellraiser's mind, the US Army was engaging its mirror image when engaging the Taliban. In the reality described by his subordinate commanders, the Taliban coerced villagers and sympathizers into small-group operations which focused primarily on IEDs. The "confusion" which surrounded MAJ K existed on multiple levels: Hellraiser's private manual competed with authorized US Army manuals; his battalion commander advised him to pursue COIN even though the battalion was following counter-guerrilla operations; and Hellraiser's superiors advised doing COIN even though they knew they were doing CG.

MAJ K describes instances in which Hellraiser ignored the COIN-centered guidance of his superiors. One such example is worth citing as an illustration. MAJ K writes:

> Contact [was] made in the Yakchal area in Helmand Province. During the firefight, one of the A Company platoon leaders cleared a hellfire strike on a residential compound. He claimed it was the only way he could secure the withdrawal of one of his squads that was "pinned down" in a cemetery in front of his position. Our airstrikes resulted in a minimum of 8 civilian casualties (deaths). Four of the casualties were fighting age males and were declared to be insurgents, which I'm not certain was true. Regardless, in my opinion, the airstrikes were unnecessary and unauthorized. The unit was not in sufficient danger to merit the risk of civilian casualties and the appropriate level of authorization was not sought, nor received, to authorize the strike.

These questionable kills of civilians were not investigated. MAJ K recounted the "lack of discipline across the brigade." He begins with "basic uniform violations" which "affected the unit on a massive scale and the NCO chain of command/responsibility, nor my commander, seemed interested in correcting the problem." He generalizes broadly: "The lack of enforcement of any kind of standards overflowed to every aspect of daily operations." He lists some of the violations that he witnessed:

> Uniforms not worn correctly (trousers not properly bloused, headgear not worn correctly, no rank or nametape, watch caps worn in unauthorized manner, sleeves rolled up. Soldiers not carrying a minimum of 2 quarts of water when they get off the Stryker. Soldiers not carrying NODs on their equipment during daylight operations. Soldiers sitting down on patrol instead of pulling security. Machine guns not put on tripods when stopped. Smoking cigarettes in the Stryker. Continuing to wear tinted eye protection in violation of the Tactical Driving Directive. Not policing the FOB and allowing trash to build up attracting files and rodents. Allowing interpreters to taunt the Taliban over ICOMs. Continuously calling in the MEDEVAC at the point of injury. KIA/WIA Soldier equipment not being handled properly and subsequently lost. Leaving water bottles full of urine in the MWR tent. Throwing trash (specifically water bottles) everywhere while on patrol. Soldiers not wearing restraints in the Stryker (resulted in the death of SPC ___). Soldiers not wearing IOTV and helmet when firing mortars (resulted in the death of SPC ___). Many of these issues are documented in Exhibit 10.

MAJ K ends his sworn statement abruptly with this statement: "We have raised an entire generation of young leaders who have never seen what right looks like, and the person singularly most responsible for this is being rewarded with another position of great responsibility where the same will no doubt be repeated."

I am able to corroborate some of MAJ K's claims regarding the lack of discipline based upon my examination of several thousand photographs and dozens of film clips in the CID office at Ft. Lewis. It is true that in the photographs I saw, soldiers were smoking cigarettes and marijuana inside the Stryker vehicles. Some of them were also consuming black tar heroin inside the vehicles. They wore tinted shades, whereas COIN doctrine specifically calls for clear eyewear. The CID officer who showed me the photographs pointed out additional and serious discipline violations. For example, soldiers frequently engaged in what the CID agent called "muzzle violations." That is to say, soldiers pointed weapons at each other and at the person who was taking their photographs. The CID agent told me, "It doesn't matter whether it's loaded or unloaded, we teach soldiers from the get-go that you never point a weapon unless you intend to engage." (As an aside, it is important to note that I have read CID reports of numerous cases of negligent discharge, resulting in death or paralysis of fellow soldiers, that were the result of soldiers "playing" with each other by pointing weapons at each other while deployed in Afghanistan.) I saw videos in which soldiers as well as translators were taunting Afghan children and throwing stones at them. Soldiers were singing or sleeping in Stryker vehicles, and in general did not give the appearance of disciplined soldiers going out on serious missions. There were numerous photographs of soldiers "clowning around" by photographing each other's naked genitals. In line with MAJ K's observations, I saw sergeants and lieutenants, who were supposed to be enforcing army standards and discipline, joining the grunts in this open defiance of army rules. It seems to be true—and is not an exaggeration—as MAJ K claims, that the lack of enforcement of *any* standards affected *all* aspects of everyday life in Stryker brigade.

THE CHAPLAIN'S SWORN STATEMENT: "IT SEEMS THAT OUR BATTALION COMMANDER'S OVER-RIDING CONCERN WAS LOOKING GOOD TO HIS BOSS."

This is the same chaplain who gave me an interview over the phone, and I shall continue to refer to him as "the chaplain." I remind the reader that he was chaplain to 1-17, Hellraiser's favorite battalion, the one with the worst discipline problems, the highest casualties, and the murderous reputation.

The chaplain begins his sworn statement with a legal disclaimer: "None of the following comments are derived from chaplain/confessor confidential conversation, privileged communication, or any formal act of religion but are solely my observations based on first person experience, public conversation with Soldiers, or communication from Soldiers to me with their stated goal of improving morale/welfare within the unit." He then launches into a detailed analysis of the problems in the command climate in his brigade and battalion:

> Many soldiers in 1-17 have expressed to me or publicly that they believed the brigade commander's counter-guerrilla (CG) strategy was in defiance of the COIN strategy we were supposed to be following. That the brigade commander was dedicated to CG was clear to us before we deployed, when he visited each company and gave the companies "counter-guerrilla" streamers to be hung from their guidons and spoke to the companies about the importance of the CG training they had been conducted. As a chaplain, I was not well-versed on differences between CG and COIN and had no idea that these would be at odds with one another. At NTC, I became aware that staff considered our brigade "very aggressive" and somewhat out of step with a COIN fight. In the first few months of our deployment (August to November 2009), I watched as our battalion conducted mission after mission in the Arghandab River Valley. The pace was hectic and it felt rushed and poorly planned. It was at this time that I heard a lot of discussion among Soldiers that *we were running the wrong strategy.* They strongly believed that we were fighting in the way the brigade commander wanted *in defiance of General McChrystal's orders (CG vs. COIN).* The Soldiers complained that they didn't have time to conduct COIN because they were constantly running clearing operations. They saw these operations as useless because they believed *areas were being cleared and then not held.* They also saw these operations as essentially picking fights with the Taliban, which resulted in Taliban killed, but turned the local populace against us because these Taliban were relatives of the local populace. *Many Soldiers believed we were creating more Taliban by upsetting the local populace.* Our Charlie company was the most vocally upset about this *discrepancy* and posted quotes from General McChrystal. One sign posted read: "Apparently COIN stands for Counter-guerrilla Operations in November." The perception of the brigade's aggressiveness and *CG-in-defiance-of-COIN* would eventually lead to Soldiers referring to the brigade's motto, "Strike and Destroy!" in a mocking way. Near the end of the deployment some Soldiers would refer to anything that was jacked-up, or poorly planned, or overly-machismo with a mock "Strike and Destroy!" Or in reference to disgust with the battalion, Soldiers would say, "Well, it's a Buff Life," meaning it was a Buffalo's lot in life to be mistreated.[7] Many Soldiers (all ranks) expressed that they believed our battalion commander did whatever the brigade commander wanted without looking out for their best interests. They expressed that they believed he was afraid to give the brigade commander info or observations that would defy him in any way. I am in agreement with that observation. It seemed that our battalion com-

mander's over-riding concern was looking good to his boss. He did not want to appear to contradict him in any way [emphasis added].

The chaplain makes it clear that not only officers but soldiers perceived Hellraiser's philosophy as being in "defiance" of established army policy. The soldiers also perceived correctly that Taliban are persons with families, so that killing Taliban created more enemies from the local population. The COIN manual teaches explicitly that the goal is not to kill the enemy, but to win them over. The chaplain also portrays the battalion commander as a weak leader who dared not defy Hellraiser. The chaplain elaborates:

> One example of this was in the planning of the memorial for SPC ____ who had been killed as a member of our Alpha Company. SPC ____ had only been with A Company for one month. As we were planning for his memorial, the brigade commander decided that the memorial would be conducted by the brigade headquarters company outside of our area of operations. This decision infuriated the Soldiers of A Company. When I advised my battalion commander that his action was not good for our Soldiers' morale or healing and suggested that we conduct two memorials (one with A Company and one with the brigade) or that he talk with the brigade commander to try to change his mind based on our Soldiers' feelings, my battalion commander acted upset that I would "dare" advise him in this way. He said, "No, the brigade commander has made his decision and we are not going to show him our ass in any way." In this instance, as well as in others, I observed that our battalion commander related to the brigade commander in the same way he expected his subordinates to relate to him, which was *a blind reception of orders with little opportunity to offer a view from under those orders.*(emphasis added)

Funerals, memorial services, and other varieties of what sociologist Emile Durkheim (1912) called "piacular rites" serve the important social function of reintegrating a social group (usually a family) that had been devastated by the loss of one of its members. This social function of funerals and related memorial services is particularly important in military units, whose morale is always damaged by the death of its members. It is not without reason that soldiers routinely refer to the comrades in their units as "family." Instead of serving the healing, integrative social function that piacular rites are supposed to achieve, Hellraiser's handling of the memorial made the brigade as a whole less socially integrated by enraging A Company 1-17. They would not be allowed to hold their own memorial for their comrade. This task would be performed by a brigade company to which the fallen soldier did not belong. At the very least, Hellraiser's decision is insensitive to established protocol in the army.

The chaplain connects this instance of insensitivity to other, similar acts. One of these acts violates one of the most sacred (respected) norms in the US Army, namely, to never leave one of its fallen members behind:

> Prior to the deployment and during the deployment, I heard 1-17 company commanders complain that the battalion commander did not listen to them and took feedback like defiance. They did not feel like they were heard by him. I heard battalion staff observe that the commander needed to form better relationships with the company commanders, but he would not. Some guys also observed that anyone who tried to give him advice (to improve the way he did things) was treated as if they were insubordinate and put on the "shit list." ...On 18 August 09, one of those battalion-company commander relationships completely broke down during an operation into the orchards where two Soldiers were KIA and one lieutenant lost both his legs. While the Soldiers under Captain Pope's command were looking for PFC ___'s body they sustained more WIA [wounded in action] to the point where the battalion commander ordered Captain Pope to give up the search and pull out. Soldiers at the operation report that CPT Pope was openly defiant on the radio and gave report that he basically turned off his radio to continue searching a little bit longer. I believe that because CPT Pope did not trust LTC N to hear him he made the decision to follow the Army Value: I will never leave a fallen comrade, in spite of the consequences that could follow from disregarding the order. The fallen Soldier's body was not found. The fallout from this event was that some Soldiers distrusted our battalion commander for leaving a fallen comrade and other Soldiers distrusted their company commander for keeping them in harm's way when he was ordered to get them out of harm's way. LTC N barely spoke with CPT Pope after this event and the battalion staff treated CPT Pope like the odd man out as he was on the shit list.

The chaplain's overall point seems to be that communication between the battalion commander and his company commanders had broken down drastically. Soldiers later told me that this fallen soldier's body was never found. Moreover, the chaplain depicts the battalion commander as a mirror image of the brigade commander: both commanders were authoritarian and failed to listen to their subordinates. Finally, one should not lose sight of the overall context. According to COIN doctrine, the soldiers should not have been risking their lives in the orchards. COIN doctrine specifically forbids such missions as too risky and with no benefit in winning hearts and minds. Hellraiser's philosophy permeated every aspect of everyday life in the brigade, ranging from the constant push to conduct lethal missions to insensitivity to army values, which took second place to the lethal goals.

In the following passage, the chaplain links the high level of social dysfunction in the brigade and battalion to the unnecessary deaths of several US soldiers:

In my opinion, 1-17 was not a very disciplined unit except for pockets where there was strong NCO leadership. I think the cause of the lack of discipline was due to the *dysfunction in command relationships* and due to a very uninvolved Command Sergeant Major. This lack of discipline I believe is partly to blame for why some of our Soldiers were KIA and WIA. Lack of basic discipline and good convoy briefs led to Soldiers *doing whatever they pleased* as far as seatbelts and "safety lines" for those in air guard positions, which eventually contributed to the death of Sergeant ___ in a rollover accident on 4 March 2010. After that date, the battalion started getting serious about seatbelts. Likewise, I believe a lack of tactical discipline contributed to the deaths of four Soldiers on 25 August 09. Another example is when one platoon failed to dismount their Strykers prior to rolling over a suspicious chokepoint (when the platoon right in front of them did dismount in order to minimize the risk of getting an entire Stryker full of troops killed) and the end result was 7 Soldiers and 1 interpreter KIA by a massive IED hidden in that chokepoint and detonated by a patient triggerman (27 October 09). Another example on 5 Nov 09, involved using a Stryker to deliver MREs and water to a patrol base using a very dangerous road when these supplies could have easily been trucked in from the COP nearby, thereby minimizing some of the risk. This resulted in 2 KIA and 2 WIA. These types of basic tactical disciplines must be learned prior to deployment. I have heard from those I consider the disciplined NCOs comment that they don't think those disciplines were practiced prior to deployment.

Taken in context, the chaplain's description suggests that Hellraiser was so obsessed with his CG philosophy, and his battalion and other subordinate commanders were so obsessed with trying to reconcile CG with COIN (which are irreconcilable), that everyone neglected army fundamentals concerning discipline. The lack of discipline, in turn, was connected in a myriad of ways to unnecessary casualties. For example, soldiers not wearing seatbelts led to deaths when accidents occurred. The chaplain states that "the battalion command sergeant major was not very well respected among the NCOs, officers, or junior enlisted," and "I heard him referred to as ROAD (Retired on Active Duty)." But no one in the chain of command removed or disciplined this command sergeant major for his own failures to maintain discipline in the battalion. Again, the chaplain comes across as an amateur sociologist—and a very good one, at that—in his description of the social context for the lack of discipline:

I think low morale, a rushed pace, and hardships contributed to a bit of entitled mentality that became they are "real warriors doing the real deal" and they don't have to follow all the rules and standards that other Soldiers in garrison would. It was an environment where it was hard to discern what the standard was and what would be enforced. Instead of a uniform UCMJ, there was a buddy code of military justice practiced where NCO's would let Solders get away with standard violations as long as the Soldier was their buddy. But if the Soldier was not their buddy, then that Soldier could expect to be disciplined for the most minor infraction of the standard (which others were not practicing). These entitled standards violations did not include war crimes or illegal activities, but they did include the tolerance of *unprofessional behavior that went against COIN and could undermine the US public's support for our mission. Examples include how Soldiers responded to children throwing rocks at them while riding past their village. Some Soldiers threw candy back which seemed to stop some of the children. Others fired pen-flares near the children's location (but not at them) in order to warn them. Some Soldiers kept rocks on the Stryker to throw at the children who threw at them. Another example is Soldiers who cursed at locals and would say obscene things to them and to children because they knew the locals did not speak English.* Another example is senior NCOs who abused their rank and would dole out punishments outside of regulations and in the realm of "hazing."...Another event which Soldiers have spoken to me about and which undermined their trust in the leadership happened during Operation Blowfish. Soldiers of 1st Platoon Charlie Company ran out of water and some became so desperate that some *drank their own urine*. When I told the battalion commander about the incident, he sternly told me that it did not happen. The Soldiers were so angry that they vowed to report it to the Inspector General and beyond [emphasis added].

Note again the intricate connections between the poisoned command climate created by Hellraiser and the specific events which the chaplain describes. The result of Hellraiser's poor leadership was that everyone was focused on being lethal and hardly anyone communicated with each other. This meant that ordinary issues such as ensuring adequate supplies of water were neglected. Through a myriad of intermediate steps, the end result was the shocking fact that some US soldiers felt forced to drink their own urine, because they ran out of water. I leave it up to the reader to perform the thought experiments necessary to understand how soldiers would regress to the level of storing up on rocks to throw at children, yell obscenities, haze each other mercilessly, and so on for the other events described by the chaplain. The point is that the scope, range, and incidence of the barbaric behavior is too great to explain with any variation of "the few bad apples" theory. Clearly, the social environment in 1-17 and the brigade as a whole was dysfunctional.

In closing, one should also pay attention to this particular chaplain's role in the military's system of morality. He states at the outset that he is not reporting anything from the perspective of any formal religion. But clearly, his sworn statement evidences what might be called a universal morality of all social systems, applied especially to the military, and to his battalion. For example, the chaplain is loyal to army values. He reported violations of norms as well as values to the battalion commander,

who consistently rebuffed him. He has empathy for the needs of the soldiers to grieve, to have access to real justice, to have faith that leaders
care for them, to be as safe as possible in a dangerous environment, and
so on. These are all norms and values that make any social system function, ranging from the family to a military unit. In a word, the chaplain
took on the role of the battalion's conscience. He was this unit's moral
compass, faithful to universal standards of morality and not the commander's skewed system of vengeance. There is no way to tell how many
lives this chaplain affected positively. But in the end, he could not be
effective against the deranged moral system of his particular society, a
dysfunctional brigade and an undisciplined battalion which was led by a
commander who sought mainly to look good in Hellraiser's eyes. The real,
non-fictional relationship between this chaplain and his battalion commander is reminiscent of the fictional relationship between Chaplain
Tappman and Colonel Cathcart in Joseph Heller's (1955) novel, *Catch-22.*
The commander oriented solely toward lethality views the chaplain and
his morality with contempt.

COMMAND SERGEANT MAJOR FOR 2-1: "THIS OPEN HOSTILITY BE-
TWEEN THE NTC LEADERSHIP AND OUR BRIGADE LEADERSHIP WAS
GREATLY DISTRACTING"

The command sergeant major for 2-1, whom I shall call CSM P, gives a
crisp, no-nonsense account of leadership problems at all levels. CSM P is
the only CSM out of ten whose sworn statement made it into the Twitty
report. He was the highest ranking NCO in Morlock's battalion. Regarding Corporal Morlock's immediate platoon leader and platoon sergeant,
CSM P writes that "they were not a good match." He adds:

> It was not because of major failures in execution of their missions but a
> series of lower level incidents that gave LTC B and I cause for concern:
> negligent discharge of an M203, failure to properly clear weapons upon
> entering the FOB, shooting of dogs, the "Crusader" bridge, a Soldier be-
> ing injured on the FOB due to a lack of enforcement of safety standards,
> and my observation of a separation of the Platoon leadership and Squad
> leaders, upon completion of the mission, not being engaged with their Sol-
> diers. The LTC and I spoke with them [platoon leadership] several times
> about our concerns. This eventually led to LTC B and me sitting down
> with CPT Q and 1SG H to discuss 3rd Platoon, B Company leadership and
> possible replacement of both [LT L and the platoon sergeant]. I believe
> this was around late November. As I stated before this discussion was
> not triggered over any single incident but due to the constant flow of mi-
> nor incidents and our, LTC B and myself, perception that they [platoon
> leadership] were not responding to our counseling or meeting our intent
> in taking care of our Soldiers. During the discussion CPT Q and 1SG H as-

sured us that 3rd Platoon, B Company was their best platoon and that they had total faith and confidence in their leaders.

There is a contradiction here between CSM P's statement that the new company commander (following the fateful cross-leveling), Captain Q, defended the platoon leaders as being among his best, and Captain Q's own statement in which he stated that these platoon leaders were his worst. Something is amiss here. In any case, LTC B and CSM P replaced Corporal Morlock's platoon leader, LT L, in March 2010, not due to any specific incident, but due to the accumulation of "minor incidents."

Regarding the NTC training, CSM P writes that "the major focus seemed to me to be to convince us to follow COIN strategy as opposed to a counter-guerrilla strategy." The NTC staff and Colonel Tunnell's staff "were openly combative with each other over these different strategies." In CSM P's assessment, "this open hostility between the NTC leadership and our Brigade leadership was greatly distracting to the purpose of the NTC rotation."

LIEUTENANT J: "THE PLATOON BEGAN TO SEE EVERY PERSON AS AN ENEMY" AND "OUR NON-LETHAL SUCCESS OCCURRED NOT BECAUSE OF, BUT DESPITE THE ACTIONS OF COLONEL TUNNELL"

LT J served as 2-1's battalion S5 officer, or "lead advisor on non-lethal operations" to LTC B. LT J was a contributing author to the GR & D (Governance, Reconstruction, and Development) report, titled, *Maywand Report: The Pride of Afghanistan.* LT J met with village elders in weekly "shuras" [meetings]. At one such meeting in January of 2010, the elders told him that a platoon had shot an innocent villager, as well as dogs. At first, LT J told the elders flatly that "the US Army does not simply shoot local nationals for no reason." The elders persisted: "The following week at the regular shura with the local leaders, there was an abnormally large contingency of approximately 75 elders." The elders "repeatedly explained that the man who was killed would never have thrown a grenade at US forces." In addition, "they claimed that the soldiers who killed the man with the grenade had also killed dogs and chickens." The elders were so persistent that LT J began to take them seriously. The parting words by the elders were: "Please investigate and find out why your soldiers in this area are treating our people badly."

LT J still refused to believe that any of his soldiers had committed murder, but he did believe that something was wrong: "I personally informed LTC B of this information that night." In response, "LTC B seemed furious." LT J continues:

It was obvious throughout the deployment that he [LTC B] cared not only about the mission, but also about "doing the right thing" and protecting the Afghan people. Two days later I remember hearing that LT L was no longer the platoon leader and LT Moye had replaced him. I never heard any complaints about the treatment of Afghans in the villages west of FOB Ramrod after LT Moye became the platoon leader.

We have seen throughout the Twitty report that LTC B had threatened to fire LT L as early as January of 2010 and finally did relieve him of command in March of 2010. Nobody suspected murder during this timeframe, but there was plenty of evidence that something was wrong with this platoon. LT J was one of the rare officers who circulated frequently and went out on patrol with almost every platoon in the battalion. In his words, "3rd Platoon acted differently." He elaborates:

> They did not seem to have the same level of respect and care for the populace as the other platoons did. For example, most platoons go out of their way to show local nationals that they are friendly while walking around their village armed. In my experience with 3rd platoon, while LT L was platoon leader, the villagers seemed very scared of them and the platoon leadership seemed to think this was normal and desirable It is my opinion that this was because they were desensitized to local nationals. I believe that their zone reconnaissance missions required them to spend so much time observing people from a distance and getting attacked by an unknown enemy with IEDs *that the platoon began to see every person as an enemy* [emphasis added].

LT J's lay-sociological explanation resonates with findings by academic, established sociologists. The village was a community, and was in a position to know whether that particular victim was a member of the Taliban or not. The Afghan national who was killed was not an anonymous target, as he is portrayed in CID statements. He was a member of a community, and his death caused a reaction by his community. Similarly, the soldiers who killed him were not just anonymous persons, but members of a platoon, which in turn was part of a company. This platoon had a reputation for frightening the villagers and killing their chickens and dogs. They adopted the nickname, "The Death Dealers," for themselves. The killings did not come out of the blue, but emerged as "secondary deviance" which followed the "primary deviance" of shooting chickens and dogs. Shooting someone's dog is an important symptom, and harbinger of future actions. It is symptomatic of the contagion effect by which the dogs and chickens are perceived as extensions of the village and villagers. Hatred toward the animals indicated a hatred of the villagers. LT J hints at some of the reasons for the hatred: this particular platoon did not circulate frequently with the members of the village, and therefore did not come to know them as persons. soldiers in this platoon gradually came to perceive all the villagers as the enemy. LT J states precisely that the reconnaissance missions which this platoon carried out were "reconnaissance in force" missions, a term invented to capture yet another hybrid of CG and COIN philosophies. Let me repeat that because of the cross-leveling which occurred, Morlock's platoon was no longer doing "real" infantry or COIN work, but was assigned to protecting the reconnaissance work of Alpha Troop under the command of Captain Q. Having diagnosed the problem sociologically, the remedy is immediately evident: Had the platoon circulated with the villagers and had they come to know them like LT J came to know the village elders through the shuras, there would have existed social barriers toward the killing of animals or villagers, or any other unfriendly action. It is an axiom in sociology that all crime occurs more readily against victims who are perceived as anonymous or are otherwise dehumanized.

According to LT J, "2-1 Infantry COIN operations were completely populace focused." This was because "LTC B informed us that our mission would be focused on 'winning the argument' against the Taliban for the support of local nationals." LTC B said much the same thing to me during our phone interview. But LT J paints an entirely different picture of Hellraiser in relation to LTC B's efforts:

> To the best of my observations, Colonel Tunnell did not support these efforts. While I do not have many specific examples, the pattern seemed to be that the only non-lethal efforts that Colonel Tunnell wanted to focus on were those that would create a large media victory for 5/2, or those that would aid his lethal fight. Colonel Tunnell set the tone for this lack of support with the initial review of CERP [Command Emergency Relief Program] projects. Three days before the first project approval meeting, CPT Pan informed me that "no project will be approved unless Colonel Tunnell can be shown how the project will help us kill enemy forces." This stuck in my memory as I had previously gone through training that warned of the legal repercussions of using CERP funds for any project that would support combat operations. Four of the five projects that we presented received approval and funding because we were able to show how they would help us kill enemy formations. We were unable to show how building a wall around the local clinic to give privacy so that women could receive health-care would kill enemy formations. Ironically, the clinic wall was the most important of the projects to the local populace. Throughout the rest of the deployment we primarily used a source of funding that required no approval from Colonel Tunnell so that we would not have to satisfy his counter-productive requirements. This issue with funding set a pattern throughout the deployment. Whenever I needed funding or resources for our non-lethal fight, *I would go around Colonel Tunnell and directly to the actual resource, secure the resource, and then inform the brigade....*[there were] countless agencies that I had to establish contact with and "sell" on working with us (2-1 Infantry) because they did not want to be associated with TF [Task Force] Stryker. Some examples of these include US Army

Psychological Operations teams and equipment, and several US government agencies such as USAID, USDA, etc. In my opinion, the lasting effect of 2-1 IN was to turn the previous Taliban safe haven of Maywand into a stable area... I believe that we were able to act in this manner because *Colonel Tunnell was not paying attention during the fall when we established most of our programs.* By the time he began to visit 2-1, our COIN operations had been wildly successful and we were used as his examples of success. In my opinion, *our non-lethal success occurred not because of, but despite the actions of Colonel Tunnell* [emphasis added].

LT J's account is consistent with most other accounts of the seemingly eternal struggle between COIN and CG philosophies in this troubled brigade. But his account still begs the question why 3rd platoon was out of step with LTC B's philosophy, which ran counter to Hellraiser's philosophy. This question does not have a simple answer. But it is worth repeating that Morlock's former company commander (prior to the cross-leveling), Captain T, went on to do outstanding COIN work for which he was commended, while Morlock's platoon was put under the command of Captain Q, who was not doing COIN. But what is immediately apparent from LT J's account is that the efforts to sneak COIN behind Hellraiser's back were confined to the higher-ranking commissioned officers. These high-ranking soldiers formed their own reference group, which was distinct from the reference group of the lower-ranking grunts. The lower-ranking soldiers, like Corporal Morlock and others, would not have been privy to the machinations which LT J describes. However, they were exposed directly to Hellraiser's symbols, memorandums, and numerous signs which pointed toward a lethal orientation. It seems that in the battle between Hellraiser and LTC B for winning the hearts and minds of the ordinary platoon soldiers—not the villagers—Hellraiser won, even if LTC B won the hearts and minds of the villagers. And the reader should always keep in mind that the company commander, Captain Q, was Hellraiser's right-hand man in drafting and disseminating the counter-guerrilla, and by extension, counter-LTC B, and counter-COIN philosophy.

CONCLUSIONS

We have seen in the sworn statements of the "non-believers" that the division of Stryker brigade into two opposing teams created desperate measures by all the soldiers and officers to reconcile the cognitive dissonance between Hellraiser's CG philosophy and COIN doctrine. Some officers tried to rationalize the disconnection between the two philosophies by creating various, abstract hybrids such as "lethal COIN" or "COIN in the service of CG" or "CG first, then COIN" or "COIN for essential services only"—among many other fine nuances. Others gave up trying to make sense of the discrepancy and concluded that COIN "was crap." Still others resorted to sneaking COIN or doing COIN "behind the back" of Hellraiser. 1-17 stands out as a particularly troubled battalion because soldiers began to conclude that their commanders were more interested in the intellectual aspects of wartime philosophy more than they were concerned with the safety of their own troops. Some officers, such as Captain Kassulke, tried to disagree and discuss their misgivings with Hellraiser, only to be relieved of command. Morale plummeted, discipline suffered, and some of the descriptions of the command climate resemble the artistic depiction of social dysfunction found in William Golding's (1959) novel, *Lord of the Flies*. The connection between this work of literature and the reality of life in Stryker brigade is that authority slowly but steadily disappeared in the brigade, leaving every officer and soldier to feel as if they were alone in a fight for personal survival during the deployment. Leadership cannot be divided without eventually eroding the practical reality of leadership.

One distinct difference between the accounts given by believers versus the non-believers is that the believers seem to have been oblivious to the command climate while the non-believers were keenly aware of problems in their social environment. The non-believers noticed and complained about the low morale, problems in discipline, negligent discharges, drug use, confusion, and so on. By contrast, the true believers seemed to be concerned only with the abstract principles of Hellraiser's philosophy, and in a very dogmatic sort of way. To phrase the matter in another way: the true believers ignored the facts which contradicted their abstract dogma while the non-believers were immersed in the facts of their everyday life which prevented them from believing in Hellraiser's doctrine.

CHAPTER 5. OMISSIONS IN THE TWITTY REPORT

The Twitty report conveniently lists the names and positions of all the officers, sergeants, and soldiers whom he interviewed. In addition, he lists their positions and exact date and time that they were interviewed. Seventy-six officers, sergeants, and soldiers are listed as having been interviewed. Their ranks range from a three-star general on one end of the stratosphere of power to lowly privates on the other end. However, there is an interesting discrepancy in that the sworn statements of thirty-three officers, sergeants, and soldiers on this master list are *not* included in the report. Thirty-three out of seventy-six is a sizeable chunk of evidence that is missing. It is important, for the sake of completeness and historical accuracy, to examine briefly whose sworn statements were omitted in the report. I shall not use the real names of these individuals, unless they have been identified in the news media or other sworn statements, but I shall list their ranks and positions. Their social roles and relationship to the brigade are important to note. The missing sworn statements are those of:

A brigadier general who was the chief of staff of I Corps

A lieutenant colonel who was the chief of military justice at Ft. Lewis

A colonel who was the commander of 6th Criminal Investigative Division

A brigadier general who was the deputy commander of I Corps

A major who was the brigade Judge Advocate General

A major who was the brigade chaplain

A major who was the brigade supply officer

A command sergeant major who was Colonel A's sergeant major in charge of operations

A captain who is listed as the brigade battle captain

A sergeant major who was in charge of operations in 4-23, one of the infantry battalions

A captain who was Corporal Morlock's former company commander prior to the cross-leveling that has been discussed at length, and who is mentioned frequently by others in their sworn statements. I refer to him as Captain T

A first sergeant who was the B Company 2-1 first sergeant

A major who was the brigade executive officer.

The first sergeant for B Company 1-17 IN, the company labeled by some officers in the report as "the murder company"

A captain who became the commander of C Company 1-17 IN, the position which Captain Kassulke held until Hellraiser fired him over disagreements about following COIN doctrine

A captain who is listed as the commander of B Company 1-17, the company labeled by some officers in the report as "the murder company." His tenure for command is listed as March 09 to "present." However, the captain who is listed as the B 1-17 commander is not the captain who is named by MAJ O, MAJ S, and other officers in the report as the real B 1-17 commander.

The first sergeant formerly in COL A's battalion who became Corporal Morlock's First Sergeant

The first sergeant of A Company 2-1

The command sergeant major for COL A's battalion

The command sergeant major for battalion 1-17

The command sergeant major for 4-23

The first sergeant for B 2-1

A captain who was the RC-S liaison officer and brigade S3

A captain who was the A 2-1 IN company commander

The command sergeant major for 8-1 Cavalry

A lieutenant who was a platoon leader in the "murderous company," B 1-17 IN

A sergeant first class in the "murderous company," B 1-17 IN

A lieutenant who was a platoon leader in C 1-17 IN

A staff sergeant who was the platoon sergeant in C 1-17 IN

A sergeant who was a team leader in B Co 2-1 IN

The command sergeant major for the entire brigade.

A colonel who was the brigade commander for yet another Stryker brigade at Ft. Lewis, namely, 4-2 SBCT

A colonel who was the brigade commander for yet another Stryker brigade at Ft. Lewis, namely, 3-2 SBCT

An immediately discernible pattern is that the sworn statements by *all* the command sergeant majors (CSM) except for one are missing from the report. The most significant omission of the command sergeant majors is Hellraiser's CSM. A CSM is the highest-ranking non-commissioned officer in the army, and their importance in the army cannot be overstated. The term, Command Sergeant Major, means that an E-9 or Sergeant Major is assigned a command position in a brigade or battalion. CSM's are the most important link between the reference groups of the commissioned officers and the enlisted soldiers. CSM's implement the theories and strategies of the commanders. And the army has a long-standing tradition in which the CSM shadows and accompanies his or her commander to all briefings and meetings. In plain language, the CSM is the most important conduit for brigade and battalion policies reaching the low-ranking enlisted soldier.

The missing CSM statements are important for another reason. One of General Twitty's conclusions is that the intellectual debates among Hellraiser's commissioned officers as to what they were doing vis-à-vis COIN, CG, or hybrids of these doctrines did not affect the enlisted soldier. Twitty assumes that the enlisted soldier could not have been privy to the doctrinal confusion we have been analyzing. However, Twitty seems to forget that the role of the CSM is to act as the *connection* between the enlisted soldiers and the commissioned officers. Officers confirmed for me that CSMs did, in fact, accompany the commissioned officers to all briefings. This means that CSMs would have known and been privy to all that we have covered so far concerning the doctrinal confusion in the brigade. Twitty's omission of the CSM sworn statements prevents us from knowing how the CSMs reconciled this confusion, and what information they passed on to the other sergeants and enlisted soldiers as to what they were supposed to be doing in Afghanistan.

Another one of the most striking omissions is that of the sworn statement by Captain Casey Thoreen, who was Corporal Morlock's original company commander. In other words, CPT Thoreen was the commander of B 2-1. This connection is confusing because Captain Quiggle is listed as the commander of B 2-1 after it was cross-leveled and renamed as A Troop 8-1. The practical, important point is this: CPT Thoreen went on to lead his hybrid portion of B 2-1 and became known for doing so much COIN and doing it so well, he received a letter of commendation from General Petraeus. After CPT Q took over Jeremy's hybrid unit, the company went on to commit war crimes. In practical terms, Morlock went from training with and seeing CPT Thoreen regularly, to not seeing him at all following the cross-leveling. CPT Thoreen's sworn statement would have been a crucial piece of the puzzle we are trying to solve as to how the war crimes under discussion here occurred.

The Omission of Key Personnel Pertaining to B Company, 1-17

We have seen that several officers refer to B Company 1-17 as "the murderous company," and cite numerous instances of questionable kills in that company. It is striking that the Twitty report omits the sworn statements by the company commander, a platoon leader, the first sergeant, and a team leader in B 1-17. More importantly, the captain who is listed by General Twitty as the company commander of B 1-17 was *not* the company commander during deployment in Afghanistan. I have no intention of speculating on the reasons for these omitted sworn statements, or for the fact that the wrong company commander is listed for B 1-17. It is sufficient to point out that given the importance of B 1-17 to the overall story, these omissions are significant.

Regarding the overall narrative of the war crimes in this book, it is important to observe that Morlock's platoon and company were singled out for scrutiny in the Twitty report, while the questionable kills in B 1-17 fade into the background of Twitty's account. Contextually, Morlock's platoon had no kills at all prior to the arrival of Gibbs in December 2009. However, B 1-17 is cited for multiple, "questionable" kills throughout the entire deployment in Afghanistan.

Officers Who Were Not Interviewed at All

So far, I have discussed the omission of sworn statements by thirty three officers and soldiers who were apparently interviewed by General Twitty. It is also intriguing to examine the officers who were not interviewed by General Twitty at all: LTC Richard Demaree, Captain Joel Kassulke, and Captain James Pope. I list the names of these officers because they have all been named and discussed in the news source articles I have already cited. Demaree was the original battalion commander of 2-1, and his clashes with Hellraiser have become legend in the brigade. Captain Kassulke (sometimes referred to as Captain K in the sworn statements) was the company commander of C 1-17, and was fired by Hellraiser for disagreeing with him about doing COIN. Finally, Captain Pope was apparently the real company commander of B 1-17, which is cited by several officers in the Twitty report as the most problematic company in the most problematic battalion in Stryker brigade.

What is missing from the Twitty report is a fuller understanding of the contrasts within 1-17: Pope's company apparently embraced Hellraiser's philosophy, while Kassulke's company rejected it. The contrast between these two captains, Kassulke and Pope, is important for understanding what happened within 1-17, and also for understanding how the mythical image of 1-17 as the warrior battalion influenced 2-1 and other battalions. The omission of Kassulke and Pope is significant for this story.

Finally, the omission of LTC Demaree is almost tragic. Spinner chose not to have him testify—for purely pragmatic reasons pertaining to legal strategy. Twitty chose not to interview him. Demaree's views are published in several newspaper interviews, but his views never made it into the official story of what happened in this brigade. The significance of the fact that Demaree was Corporal Morlock's original battalion commander cannot be overstated. There is a general pattern here: Morlock's original battalion and company commanders, as well as his squad leader—were taken away by cross-leveling. One cannot avoid asking the question: Would Morlock and the other soldiers have committed the crimes under discussion here had their original commanders and leaders remained in charge? What would the story of this brigade have been without the widespread cross-leveling that was destroying bonds of trust, loyalty, and cohesion?

THE OTHER STRYKER BRIGADE COMMANDERS

General Twitty omitted sworn statements by two colonels who are Hellraiser's peers: the brigade commanders of two other Stryker brigades, 4-2 SBCT and 3-2 SBCT. 3-2 SBCT emerged in the news during the week of March 12, 2012, after it was reported that a sergeant from Ft. Lewis had killed seventeen Afghan civilians, including women and children.[8] This sergeant was from 3-2 SBCT. These are connections, not coincidences. Two of the major war crimes committed during the war in Afghanistan were perpetrated by soldiers from two different Stryker brigades at Ft. Lewis. It seems that the "poison" in the toxic climate at Ft. Lewis is not confined to Hellraiser's Stryker brigade. Had the sworn statements by the other two Stryker brigade commanders been included in the Twitty report, one would be in a better position to assess the overall social climate at Ft. Lewis.

In summary, it is important to note the personnel General Twitty included in his report as well as the personnel he omitted. I am not implying anything sinister about these omissions and shall not speculate as to the reasons for the omissions. For the sake of context and completeness, I note them. This story, like any other story, is always the result of what is known and what is not known, of what was said and documented, and of what will remain forever unsaid and unknown.

Chapter 6. Hellraiser's Assessment of COIN Doctrine And History

Like the other officers who spoke with General Twitty, Hellraiser made his comments on the record, in several sworn statements. Unlike any of the other officers, above or below him in rank, Hellraiser attached long, prepared statements he had made prior to his interviews with General Twitty. There is no ambiguity or nuance or shade of grey in any of Hellraiser's statements or supporting documents. According to him, he was and will remain right about everything. On the other hand, and again without any nuance whatsoever, the army, his superiors, and the subordinates who questioned or challenged Hellraiser were and will remain forever wrong. He attached his scholarly papers, power point presentations, and lectures on counter-guerrilla philosophy to his statement, and these are all included in the report. In all, Hellraiser takes up ninety-four pages of the Twitty report, including his sworn statements and attachments. The average officer took up three pages each. Given his insubordinate and inflammatory views, there is no plausible explanation as to why he was not relieved of command other than that his views represent the latent views of scores of other colonels, brigade commanders, and generals in the army. The student of this case is grateful that Hellraiser does not hide his views at all. On the contrary, he wears his insubordination on his sleeve.

Hellraiser's sworn statement of November 16, 2010 is really a sort of treatise on military history. There can be no doubt that Hellraiser is an intellectual. Indeed, some of his subordinates and General Twitty refer to him as such. He begins by citing the US Army's obsolete counter-guerrilla manual, FM 90-8: "According to FM 90-8 counter-guerrilla operations are appropriate to use against many kinds of irregular forces, to include those conducting military operations in support of an insurgency." He illustrates his point immediately by referring to the American Civil War. He tags the Confederate forces as insurgents and Union forces as necessarily using counter-guerrilla methods to suppress the American Confederate insurgents: "For example, in the United States' own War of the Rebellion—an insurgency by Confederate states—most Union military operations were characterized by conventional military maneuver and counter-guerrilla operations were complementary operations conducted by certain units throughout the various theaters of operation." In Hellraiser's way of thinking, there is no tradition of COIN in American military history. There is only insurgency (by Native Americans, the Confederate states, and other groups), and only one sure remedy: counter-guerrilla doctrine. One could extend Hellraiser's thinking metaphorically: he is basically equating American Confederacy soldiers with the Taliban and other insurgents while he sees the Union and current US Army forces as using counter-guerrilla tactics to cripple any insurgency.

Perhaps he is correct to claim that, "historically, counter-guerrilla operations are part of a long established military framework for US Army forces." It is historically accurate to claim that the US Army did use lethal, counter-guerrilla methods to put down insurrections, rebellions, Confederate uprisings, Native American resistance, strikes, and other forms of "insurgency." But these many episodes in American history are not typically depicted by historians as the normative way that the US Army should have behaved or did behave in all these instances. It is beyond the scope of this study to inquire as to the actual use of COIN-like strategies in US military history. The important point for the present discussion is that according to Hellraiser, counter-guerrilla doctrine is the American way of dealing with any insurgency, foreign or domestic, and COIN doctrine is a foreign import. Hellraiser adds: "Counter-guerilla operations is a doctrinal concept that pre-dates September 11, 2001 and still exists in doctrine today." Much hinges on the meaning of the word "exists" in his claim. A host of generals, from Petraeus through McChrystal to Twitty have made it clear that COIN superseded counter-guerrilla doctrine as of June 2007. Nevertheless, Hellraiser's academic claims concerning US military history do beg the question: was the post-2007 shift toward COIN doctrine sincere or was it a brief footnote to a long tradition of counter-guerrilla doctrine?

Hellraiser goes much further, by attacking COIN doctrine directly as dangerous for the US Army, and as an un-American, colonialist, imperialist, and otherwise flawed doctrine. Perhaps he was taken seriously by the generals who were his commanders and the lieutenant colonels who were his battalion commanders because Hellraiser was one of the official reviewers of COIN doctrine for the military. It is important to quote Hellraiser's criticisms of COIN doctrine extensively and precisely:

> Counter-insurgency operations have a valuable role in American military art and science. FM 3-24, however, is *not* reflective of an *American* tactical, operational, or strategic framework for counter-insurgency. Soldiers' lives are routinely put at hazard because the doctrine has not been written within a context of American military art and science, organization, or capability. US Army forces are not organized, trained, or equipped to implement the doctrine and Americans are not culturally suited to accept predominantly European, *colonial and imperial* tactical, operational, practices—the foundation upon which FM 3-24 rests [emphasis added].

Note that Hellraiser grants to COIN the status of playing a "valuable role" in American military art, but that he does not grant it the status of historical doctrine. We shall return to this point later. It is a fact that US forces were and continue to be organized, trained, and equipped to implement the official doctrine of the US government in the last phase of the War on Terror, namely, COIN doctrine. The rest of his statements are opinions that might play well on some extreme Conservative talk show. What could Hellraiser mean with the claim that FM 3-24 is not an American document culturally speaking? Let us grant him the argument that European history includes imperialism and colonialism. However, it is flawed history to attribute all colonialism and imperialism to the Europeans. Every high school graduate knows that in its history, the United States, too, went through its colonialist and imperialist stage (specifically, the Philippines, Puerto Rico, Hawaii, Guam, and elsewhere). Hellraiser continues his strident attack on COIN doctrine:

> Many of FM 3-24's drafters do not have much significant practical military experience applying American military art and science in training or combat. Many of the people involved in the process have academic credentials but lack practical experience about American military activity and they prefer to rely *on concepts from European colonial and imperial activity to write American military doctrine.* (See *Small Wars Journal* interview with Dr. John Nagle in which he states that a David Galula, a French officer, was the "single biggest influence on FM 3-24") [emphasis added]

I encourage the reader to check Hellraiser's claims. In the interview which Hellraiser cites, Dr. Nagle does state that Galula's "book is probably the single biggest influence on FM 3-24."[9] Galula passed away in the year 1967, and his influential book, entitled *Counterinsurgency Warfare*, was published in 1964. It is true that Galula's *book* is highly influential at the various US Army war colleges and among military theorists. It is not true that the French officer and scholar, Galula, was personally the biggest influence on FM 3-24. It seems to be a fact that contemporary American military strategists were highly influenced by a book authored by a

French scholar who was most influenced by Mao Tse-tung's example in the pacification of China. Perhaps Hellraiser is offended by the fact that Mao's, Chinese, Marxist, Communist, version of COIN doctrine could have—and did—influence the American COIN doctrine of 2007, but he never mentions Mao in any of his statements. The straw man argument seems to be that Galula was French, and therefore implicitly "imperialist," "colonialist," and bad for the American version of COIN.

Hellraiser continues his intriguing *ad hominem* attacks on the co-authors of the American COIN doctrine:

> Regarding the practical experience of contributors, we can use Dr. David Kilcullen, a retired Australian Army Lieutenant Colonel who contributed to FM 3-24 and has been an advisor to Secretary of State Condoleezza Rice, General Petraeus, and most recently General Stanley McChrystal in Afghanistan, for comparison. The Australian Army's permanent (regular) strength is a little under 30,000 personnel and the Army does not have much highly sophisticated equipment... The consequence of relying on a retired Australian Army Lieutenant Colonel for strategic and doctrinal advice means that many of our senior leaders have been advised by someone with the equivalent practical experience of a US Army Infantry captain. The other contributors to our counter-insurgency doctrine have even less practical experience in many respects than Dr. Kilcullen or our generic Infantry captain.

Again, I shall not take up Hellraiser's personal opinion about this particular Australian officer and theorist who influenced an American Secretary of State, faculty at various war colleges, and other military theorists. Hellraiser has a right to dislike this Australian theorist. But the sociology of Dr. Kilcullen's rise to influence in important seats of power is important to note: Kilcullen's influence stems from the fact that numerous social *groups* took up his ideas, not from Dr. Kilcullen as a solitary, Australian individual. Hellraiser is attacking an isolated straw-man when, in fact, he is opposing a *group consensus* among notable military strategists who threw their collective lot with Kilcullen's ideas. Again, Hellraiser fails to mention that Kilcullen was influenced by Chinese leader Mao Tse-tung and French scholar Galula. Hellraiser continues his attack upon the other individuals who influenced COIN doctrine:

> The lead writer of FM 3-24 is Dr. Conrad Crane, a War College history teacher and the Director of the US Army Military History Institute ... Dr. Crane acknowledges the emphasis in FM 3-24 on lessons from colonial and imperial military leaders. Dr. Montgomery McFate, a leader in the development of the Army's Human Terrain System program and co-author of the FM 3-24 chapter on intelligence, noted during discussion as a member of a November 17, 2006 American Anthropological Association panel that colonialism was used as a model for COIN... It is also germane to

address the general research quality of FM 3-24 since part of its allure is the academic credentials of its authors. The contributors to the manual include contractors, academics, or others with little practical American military experience. It contains plagiarized material from academic and military journals and many of the ideas it presents about operational design, intelligence, and information operations have little foundation in prior doctrine are not descriptive of widespread best practice.

Hellraiser includes five footnotes to support various parts of the paragraph above. Let us check the ones he uses to attack Crane and McFate. I could not find a single sentence by Crane which supports Hellraiser's view that he was supposedly inspired by colonial and imperial military leaders. On the contrary, Crane cites his inspirations for COIN in the first paragraph of his paper: "Along with the propagation of ideas from Mao Tse-tung, Ernesto Che Guevara, Carlos Marighella, and Vo Nguyen Giap came a corresponding attempt by counterinsurgents to develop their own set of practices and principles. The tenets of these mostly British and French writers were a product of many years of struggle in theaters from Algeria to Malaya to Vietnam, along with observation of many case studies. David Galula, Frank Kitson, Robert Thompson, and Roger Trinquier still have much useful information for current practitioners of counterinsurgency (COIN) ."[10] The particular leaders cited by Crane are regarded as Marxist revolutionaries and Leftist intellectuals, but are never regarded as colonialists or imperialists. Regarding the attack on McFate, Hellraiser cites Roberto J. Gonzalez, "Towards mercenary anthropology?: The new US Army counterinsurgency manual FM 3-24 and the military anthropology complex," *Anthropology Today*, Volume 23, Number 3, June 2007, pages 15-17. Again, there is no support for Hellraiser's assertions concerning imperialism and colonialism in the article. It is true that the American Anthropological Association has engaged in vigorous internal debates concerning the morality of helping any military force win a war vis-à-vis its institutional commitment to "cultural relativism" and disdain for "ethnocentrism." But this complicated debate, which is beyond the scope of the present study, cannot be summarized with Hellraiser's inflammatory claim that "colonialism was used as a model for COIN."

I have taken up Hellraiser's apparently scholarly claims, because he tries to pass himself off as an intellectual in the context of providing a sworn statement that is part of an internal army criminal investigation. *That* is the significant point. Who would typically provide a sworn statement in a criminal investigation that resembles a pseudo-scholarly treatise? The common sense answer is that Hellraiser breaks commonly accepted social norms in every social interaction which comes up for discussion. He reacted with insubordination to his superiors when they ordered him to implement COIN. Intellectual discussion about COIN among military theorists is one thing, but a brigade commander is part of a chain of command, and is obligated to obey lawful orders. Instead of exhibiting the common, human responses of pausing, reflecting, and wondering whether his intractable attitude might have contributed to the tragic killings that are the subject of the present discussion, Hellraiser continues to insist that he is right and that the entire chain of command and all of the many military theorists and co-authors of COIN are wrong. What he finds most wrong in this vast literature is that most of the authors of and inspirations for COIN doctrine are from the political left, Marxist in their orientation, and foreign. When he is forced to give a sworn statement, he seems oblivious to the directive that he must explain whether or not he holds command responsibility for the killings in his command. Instead, he launches into highly inflammatory, ethnocentric, and intellectually vicious attacks on the allegedly un-American, colonialist, and imperialist framework of COIN doctrine. Hellraiser's sworn statements, taken in conjunction with what his superiors and battalion commanders said about him, give us an insight into his intractable personality. He truly does come across as a man obsessed with his personal version of counter-guerrilla doctrine, much like Melville's fictional Ahab was obsessed with killing Moby Dick.

Yet, there are some grains of truth in Hellraiser's treatise/sworn statement. And there can be no doubt that there will be conservative intellectuals who will agree with Hellraiser's ideas. My purpose here is not to engage with Hellraiser as an intellectual, but to connect his dogmatism to the perceptions by most officers in the Twitty report that he was a failed or toxic military leader. It is true that the most recent version of American COIN doctrine is *not* home-grown. It is also true that its original inspiration is Mao Tse-tung, and that this inspiration was codified into military theory by the French scholar, David Galula. Hellraiser attacks Galula for being French, but does not mention Mao's indirect influence on COIN. It is beyond the scope of the present study to pursue the cultural migration of the ideas central to COIN from Communist China via NATO countries to United States military war colleges. For the purposes of the present study, the more important fact is that Hellraiser confused his subordinates with his jingoistic and ethnocentric attacks on COIN as an un-American doctrine. American culture demands that military leaders follow the orders of its chain of command, which includes civilian leaders. Let the reader recall that all of the lieutenant colonels in Hellraiser's brigade told me that they were pro-chain-of-command, but none stated that they were unequivocally pro-COIN. General Twitty accuses Hellraiser of creating "confusion" among the ranks, but he never accuses Hellraiser of being wrong in his criticisms of COIN. Hellraiser tapped into a fundamental ambivalence among his superiors as well as his subordinate commanders, namely: To follow COIN is to do one's duty in following the chain of command, but it is also to follow an un-American doctrine. One may place this agonizing dilemma in the more universal context of provincialism versus cosmopolitanism: Should American COIN doctrine be rooted in American history and be authored by American-born intellectuals (provincialism) or should the United States adopt international ideas about how to win over a population during war even if those ideas come from as far away as China and are authored by French and other non-American intellectuals (cosmopolitanism)?

The cultural issues which Hellraiser uncovered go far beyond COIN doctrine *per se*, because COIN doctrine relies upon the current base of knowledge in anthropology, psychology, and sociology. General Petraeus invited and relied upon social scientists, and especially anthropologists, to inform and co-author the COIN manual. Although Hellraiser does not make this connection, it is important to note here that all three of these disciplines were established by Europeans, and this sense, are "un-American" disciplines in terms of their origins. The French intellectual, Emile Durkheim, established both sociology and anthropology approximately a century ago. The founding fathers of sociology were all European: Durkheim, Max Weber, Karl Marx, Georg Simmel. Psychology was established by the Germans, Sigmund Freud and Wilhelm Wundt. American social sciences relied upon and continue to rely upon their initial insights into the nature of society and personality. Using Hellraiser's logic, one should be as suspect of the social sciences—which form the bedrock of COIN doctrine—as of the COIN manual because they are all foreign imports intellectually. The extreme divisiveness Hellraiser created in his brigade is reflected in the equally extreme divisiveness Hellraiser creates among the community of scholars.

Hellraiser's reflections on the NTC training and NATO command climate in Afghanistan

Not surprisingly, Hellraiser faults the NTC leadership and his NATO commanders for the overall tragedy that resulted from his leadership. He begins by claiming that "Many of the training objectives addressed in our 180-day letter were not supported by NTC leaders." His commanders and trainers failed to support *his* objectives. Of course, his objectives were completely opposite of the COIN objectives of his superiors and of the United States government. This discrepancy does not seem to matter to Hellraiser, who writes: "There is a long history of American military success employing counter-guerrilla operations, our doctrine supports the concept, units are organized and equipped to conduct such operations, and we had designed a training program for the SBCT that would make the successful implementation of counter-guerrilla operations possible." Note that Hellraiser had designed *his* own training program for his doctrine, and it does not seem to occur to him that he was expected to follow the NTC's training program in COIN. According to the army, CG doctrine (FM 90-8) was obsolete at the time of the NTC training. According to Hellraiser, "FM 90-8 was still current doctrine at the time and NTC was not supportive of the fact that it was our doctrinal framework." In sum, from Hellraiser's point of view, the NTC staff failed to support him and his doctrine, which he believes is an orthodox, traditional, and above all, American military doctrine. He does not seem to want to grasp the fact that he failed to follow orders and COIN doctrine.

For support of his views, Hellraiser cites several of his "publications within Department of Defense." One of these is his *Guerrilla Hunter Killer Operations Field Manual*, which was indeed published by the Department of Defense (Tunnell, 2009). As we have already seen in the previous chapter, one of his commanders initially thought the book was a joke, because it argues that the Taliban make use of modern, Western military formations and organization. From an anthropological and sociological point of view, Hellraiser's claims simply cannot be true. The Taliban, and Afghani society as a whole, are traditional, and simply cannot rely upon Western military models. For Hellraiser's claims to be true, the entire edifice of sociology and anthropology would have to be false.

Hellraiser also wrote a book entitled, *To Compel With Armed Force: A Staff Ride Handbook for the Battle of Tippecanoe* (Tunnell, 2000). Hellraiser takes up the leadership issues at the Battle of Tippecanoe, which was fought on November 9, 1811 in what is now the state of Indiana. The antagonists were US Army General William Henry Harrison versus a Native American chief called The Prophet. Of course, Harrison's troops defeated the Prophet and his band of Native American "insurgents," and thereby established government control over Indiana. His intellectual argument is that Harrison was the superior leader in contrast to the Prophet. The point he seems to miss completely is the obvious one that Native American "insurgents" were absolutely no match for modern, Western firepower. If one reads his book from the perspective of seeking to gain insight into his role as Stryker brigade commander in Afghanistan, the following issues jump out of his text: The Prophet sought compromise, accommodation, and COIN-like interaction with General Harrison. However, Harrison was motivated solely to annihilate the Prophet and his band of "insurgents," and rejected all such COIN-like efforts. If one likens the Taliban to the Native Americans and Hellraiser to General Harrison, one captures the gist of his counter-guerrilla doctrine in a flash: the enemy must be annihilated.

Turning to some of the other attachments to his sworn statements, one comes across photographs of various symbols Hellraiser created for his brigade. The brigade symbol was, in his words, a "helmet and tribal stripes." One would have to turn to Sigmund Freud's writings to comprehend Hellraiser's and other US Army uses of Native American names and symbols—such as all those helicopters named Apache, Chinook, Blackhawk, Kiowa, Iroquois, Creek, Lakota, and so on. Given that the US Army practically annihilated Native Americans, the meaning of Native American names and symbols in the contemporary US Army cannot be explained without recourse to the concept of the unconscious and defense mechanisms such as reaction formation. Space does not permit such an analysis in this study. Hellraiser features the counter-guerrilla streamers he developed in order to promote "unit identity." There are also photographs of pistols, guidons, and other physical objects inscribed with the words, "counter-guerrilla." Morlock told me the story of how these pistols were offered for sale to everyone in the brigade with a discount: they normally cost $1300 but were sold for $750. The pistols carried other symbols on them: they were inscribed with the symbol "9/11" and with a map of Afghanistan. It is beyond the scope of this study to venture into the emotional power of symbols (see Durkheim 1912), but it is worth noting that the juxtaposition of 9/11, Afghanistan, counter-guerrilla, and an elite pistol forms a powerful symbolic brew. "However," Hellraiser muses, "we realized that many of our efforts were constantly misunderstood so we discarded most of them." He does not acknowledge in any way how his efforts were "misunderstood." Presumably, streamers that read "counter-guerrilla" during a military mission that was supposed to follow COIN doctrine was contradictory and offensive to the local population as well as to his superiors.

Regarding the mission in Afghanistan within the framework of NATO, Hellraiser writes: "There was friction from the start and we worked very hard to change this and develop a positive relationship with the NATO command in RC(S)." He names three generals who were his commanders, and who—in his view—failed to understand his vision. "Things did not work well under UK leaders," Hellraiser writes. Again, in the larger social context, it is important to note that the United States mission in Afghanistan was presented to the world as part of a cosmopolitan and specifically NATO operation. Yet Hellraiser clearly resented having to answer to British and other non-American generals who were among his NATO commanders. It is clear that part of Hellraiser's resentment of these generals is that they were foreign. NATO, like COIN doctrine, is comprised of "foreign" and "un-American" ideas and persons who contribute to them. Nevertheless, his professional relationships with his American commanders were also strained. Regarding one such American general, the deputy commander of RC-S in Afghanistan, he writes that "the relationship with BG Nicholson was inconsistent." The same was true for yet another American commanding general: "The relationship with BG Hodges started out well but deteriorated as time progressed." Hellraiser only hints that the source of the friction was that his commanders wanted him to follow COIN doctrine while he wanted to follow his own, CG doctrine. At one point he claims: "I do not remember restricting the use of the term COIN." This claim contradicts sworn statements by numerous officers who claimed that he forbade the use of the word, COIN, in his presence. Perhaps to account for this inconsistency, he adds: "Members of the brigade used the term in public and in essays and articles." But this shallow rationalization does not contradict the evidence that his subordinate commanders were forbidden to use the term, COIN, in his presence.

HELLRAISER'S PRESENTATION ON COIN, COUNTER-GUERRILLA DOCTRINE, AND WAR

On August 27, 2007, Hellraiser gave a presentation to his brigade staff entitled "Sometimes War is Just War." He includes the power-point slides for the talk in the attachments to his sworn statement. It is very instructive to go through his presentation and to assume the role of the lieutenant colonels, captains, or other subordinate commanders in his audience. One should also keep in mind that the commissioned officers in his audience were paired with a high-ranking non-commissioned officer, such as a command sergeant major, so that Hellraiser's views affected the highest and the lowest ranks under his command simultaneously. How did Hellraiser convince the leadership core of his brigade that he was right and that the US Army was wrong about COIN?

The opening slide features the head of a Native-American wearing traditional head-dress, which is superimposed onto a star. This is the symbol for the 2nd Infantry Division (which extends all the way from army bases in South Korea to the Pacific Northwest) and is not Hellraiser's creation. The "agenda" for his talk was as follows: Commander's philosophy, Introduction: The Nature of War, Information Operations, COIN, Myths About COIN, Counter-Guerrilla Operations, Training Management, and Conclusion. One should keep in mind that the COIN manual had been released two months prior to Hellraiser's talk, and was officially the doctrine of the US Army at the time.

The opening line in the slide on his philosophy is: "We deploy to defeat an armed and aggressive enemy." Regarding the nature of war, he quotes the Bible, and specifically I Samuel 17:48: "As the Philistine moved closer, David ran quickly toward the battle line to meet him. Reaching into his bag and taking out a stone, he slung it and struck the Philistine in the forehead. The stone sank into his forehead, and he fell face down on the ground." Presumably, David symbolizes the US soldier and the Philistine represents the Taliban. In the next slide, he quotes Sergeant Isaac Naylor from a battle in the Indiana Territory in 1811, which was the subject of his book: "The Indians made four or five fierce charges on our lines, yelling and screaming as they advanced, shooting balls and arrows into our ranks. At each charge they were driven off in confusion, carrying their dead and wounded as they retreated." Next, he quotes from a citation regarding the Philippine Insurrection of 1899: "Sergeant Weaver, alone and unaided, charged a body of 15 insurgents, dislodging them, killing 4 and wounding several." Finally, he shows a slide with a quote from Operation Iraqi Freedom in 2003: "Sergeant First Class Oakes dismounted from the vehicle and shot and killed a man 10 meters to his front who was preparing to fire a Rocket Propelled Grenade."

Turning to the section on COIN, Hellraiser begins with basic definitions. He defines insurgency as "an organized movement aimed at the overthrow of a constituted government through the use of subversion and armed conflict." Next, he defines counterinsurgency as "military, paramilitary, political, economic, psychological, and civic actions taken by a government to defeat insurgency." And, he adds: "Counterinsurgents use all instruments of national power to sustain the established or emerging government and reduce the likelihood of another crisis emerging." Of course, these definitions beg the question of what was the "constituted government" in Afghanistan from 2007 to 2010. The media reported that the Karzai government rigged the elections and either tolerated or shared power with the Taliban. It is also curious that counterinsurgency is defined in terms of a government, because the inspiration for COIN, namely, Mao Tse-tung, led an insurgency movement which performed counterinsurgency. Another way of putting this is that COIN movements in China, Vietnam, and other hot spots were population-centric, or vying for winning the hearts and minds of "the people" regardless of who was presumed to constitute the legitimate government. Despite Hellraiser's definitions, many of his subordinate commanders made it clear in the Twitty report that they adopted Mao Tse-tung's vocabulary (without mentioning him) by referring to COIN as a population-centric doctrine.

The key point is that Hellraiser does not define counterinsurgency by quoting from the COIN manual. His definition of counterinsurgency overlaps with his definition of counter-guerrilla doctrine. When he finally quotes from the COIN manual, later in his presentation, it is in the context of attacking the tenets of COIN doctrine as myths.

Hellraiser immediately waters down the problematic definitions of insurgency and COIN by instructing his commanders that the real job of counterinsurgency falls on the shoulders of the Afghan government, not the United States government. A series of slides shows statements such as the following: "Commanders focus on the enemy; select a subordinate to be your expert in other types of engagements."

A slide entitled "And More Popular Mythology" lists three core tenets of orthodox COIN doctrine *as myths*:

> The objective in fighting insurgents isn't to kill every enemy fighter—you simply can't—but to persuade the population to abandon the insurgent's cause.

> The first tenet is that the best weapons don't shoot. Counterinsurgents must excel at finding creative, nonmilitary solutions to military problems.

> Victory is achieved when the people of Afghanistan consent to the legitimacy of their government and stop actively and passively supporting insurgency.

To drive home the point that it is a myth that the United States government must provide food, medical supplies, electricity and other essentials to the local population in Afghanistan, Hellraiser makes an analogy to Ft. Lewis in the United States. A slide reads: "Who really provides services?" He shows that the real provider of electric power to Ft. Lewis is Tacoma Power, *not* the US Department of Energy. He adds that the bill for electric power for Ft. Lewis in the month of July was $698,626.00. His point seems to be that if the US government does not supply free essential services to one of its army bases, Ft. Lewis—why should it be obligated to supply such services to people in Iraq and Afghanistan?

The problem with Hellraiser's analogy is obvious: Ft. Lewis is not under siege by the state of Washington or any other government. By contrast, Iraq and Afghanistan were invaded by the US military. A far more compelling analogy for Hellraiser's slide presentation is the following: Supposed that China had invaded the state of Washington and had laid siege to Ft. Lewis. Would China be obligated to supply essential services to Ft. Lewis?

Another slide reads: "Who really steals services?" It makes the points that in Iraq, "armed groups increasingly control the antiquated switching stations," and "blackouts deeply undermine an Iraqi government whose popular support is already weak." Other points Hellraiser makes are the following:

> Saddam Hussein used energy in a system of punishments and rewards. Energy is a commercial activity—the electricity you want is bought and sold like tea, food, cigarettes or anything else you want. An area has to be safe enough for a business to produce and distribute the electricity. We are

here to find the terrorists and militias who want to prevent production of energy so they can control it like Saddam Hussein did. You must help us find the enemy so people can safely produce energy and sell it to you.

Hellraiser's overall point is that counter-guerrilla operations are the bedrock for COIN operations: "Generally, the purpose of counter guerrilla operations is to provide enough internal security to enable the host country to initiate COIN programs and pursue national objectives." In a direct counter to COIN doctrine, he lectured: "Countering subversion, lawlessness, and insurgency does not equate to merely providing essential services: Don't put the cart before the horse, establish security first." Official COIN doctrine does call for the establishment of security and what are called stability operations, but it calls for a balance of offensive, defensive, and stability efforts. Hellraiser's interpretation was that one could not do COIN without doing counter-guerrilla operations first. One of his slides reads:

> The COIN program is designed to counter the whole insurgency. It does this through alleviating conditions which may cause the insurgency. Counter guerrilla operations are geared towards the active military element of the insurgent movement only. To this end, counter guerrilla operations are viewed as a supporting component of the COIN effort.

Hellraiser's interpretation of the relationship between CG and COIN was undoubtedly convincing to some officers in his brigade. Nevertheless, formal COIN doctrine does *not* state that CG operations are a supporting component of COIN doctrine.

Hellraiser drove his point home (about the primacy of CG operations) in slide after slide in the power point presentation: "First we have to stop the insurgency. Then we can talk about civil services and projects." "Security is the top priority!" "We are going to be victorious." "The enemy is not ten feet tall." "The enemy can and will be beaten." At this point in the presentation, he was far from COIN doctrine, which emphasizes that a population cannot be won by simply killing off the enemy. Hellraiser launched into a full-blown program for CG doctrine: "Strike operations include offensive tactics such as raids, reconnaissance in force, hasty or deliberate attacks, and pursuit and are intended to: Harass guerrilla forces ... destroy the guerrilla force ... [and] demonstrate support for the government."

Hellraiser lectured: "The guerrilla must be understood before he can be defeated." Because "the guerrilla" lacks the personnel and logistics to engage US military forces directly, he will exploit weaknesses "by interdicting supply routes and facilities, forcing desertion because of hardships, and by inflicting combat losses that are hard to replace." Whereas COIN doctrine is often summarized as being "population-centric," the title of one of Hellraiser's slides takes the opposite approach: "The population is important but the enemy is the cog." The following points follow: "Determine who is your enemy; determine where your enemy is located; determine how to gain access to your enemy; attack the enemy; re-assess and refine information; re-attack the enemy."

The title of the next slide reads: "Counter guerrilla operations in the framework of COIN." The information on the slide is conveyed through multiple arrows. Basically, the slide conveys a target with "enemy" as the bulls-eye, with the following topics, in order, as the outlying circles: government; local and national infrastructure; population, culture, religion, history; and geography. In Hellraiser's theory, COIN targets the outer circles of the target, but only CG is aimed directly at the bulls-eye or "enemy." The military is depicted as a broken arrow aimed at the enemy because it "alienates population," causes "war crimes and collateral damage." Supposedly, CG strikes at the enemy without these negative consequences.

The slide entitled "How we fight—vision" has the following bullet points on it: "See first, understand first, act first, engage decisively, re-engage at will." The next slide of the lecture is entitled: "The bottom line for brigades and below." It reads:

> No matter what political atmosphere prevails in the host country, *the Brigade must engage the guerrilla with every asset available.* We must realize that democratic principles may not be immediately applicable. *It is the US Government's responsibility to influence the host government's attitude towards democratic principles.* It is not the responsibility of the Brigade, nor its leaders [emphasis added].

The last slide of the lecture is entitled: "The last word on the military instrument during COIN." It quotes General Ulysses S. Grant: "The art of war is simple enough. Find out where your enemy is. Get at him as soon as you can. Strike him as hard as you can and as often as you can, and keep moving on."

It is clear from the sworn affidavits in the Twitty report that Hellraiser's subordinate commanders understood his intent, even if they did not all agree with him. Hellraiser did not see doing COIN as his job. Doing COIN was the job of everyone else in the US government except his brigade. In his mind, his and his brigade's job in Iraq or Afghanistan was straightforward: "engage the guerrilla with every asset available." Hellraiser's lecture turns COIN on its head. The lecture is sufficiently intellectual to give pause to even the ideal officers who sought to follow the orders of the chain of command. It is not a question of whether or not Hellraiser was right or wrong about COIN doctrine. As of this writing, in the year 2012, the nature of warfare and COIN are still debated—even though the US is fighting a war presumably guided by the principles of

COIN.[11] The more important point is that Hellraiser saw COIN as a fundamentally un-American doctrine, and thereby injected the question of loyalty to America into the COIN debate.

We shall never resolve the mystery of how Hellraiser was allowed to deploy to Afghanistan despite the fact that he openly defied existing COIN doctrine. Let us broaden the social context for this mystery by connecting Hellraiser's aggressive, strike and destroy philosophy to American culture. It is not sufficient to point out that Hellraiser was out of sync with COIN doctrine, because it is possible that COIN doctrine itself is out of sync with American culture (which is something Hellraiser seems to imply). One must search for the ways in which Hellraiser was in sync or in tune with American culture, in order to understand how he succeeded in defying his superiors and confusing his subordinates. The links are easy to find. Variations of strike and destroy philosophy are found throughout American culture. Americans are bombarded with slogans, advertisements, and the rhetoric of declaring war on cancer, terrorism, litter, hate crimes, drugs, poverty, obesity, and just about any problem or issue imaginable. The general rule seems to be: "If there is a social problem, strike and destroy it." This attitude is found in political campaigns, including the presidential campaigns of 2012. The news media routinely uses the rhetoric of war to describe a candidate's "crushing blows" against another candidate, "victories" in primaries, "do or die" primaries, and so on. It is tempting to ignore or dismiss these obvious manifestations of strike and destroy doctrine within American culture. It is wiser to connect these cultural manifestations to Hellraiser's strike and destroy philosophy.

This is because the connections between the aggressive slogans, symbols, and philosophy in American culture as a whole with Hellraiser's opinions help to explain why he was allowed to defy COIN doctrine. COIN doctrine comes across as the philosophy of cooperation, and therefore weakness. Hellraiser also depicts COIN as a foreign import, and this claim resonates with widespread examples of xenophobia and ethnocentrism in the United States during the War on Terror. From burnings of the Koran to protests at the building of mosques to a general suspicion of all Muslims, the multitude of such incidents reflects Hellraiser's military doctrine. The important point is that Hellraiser's views would not have been taken seriously or absorbed had they not resonated with a host of other, similar views in the larger, American culture. Conversely, COIN doctrine could not be taken seriously, absorbed, or assimilated fully because it is at odds with much of American culture. To quote the founding father of American psychology, William James: "True ideas are those that we can assimilate, validate, corroborate, and verify. False ideas are those that we cannot. That is the practical difference it makes to us to have true ideas" (James, 2000, p. 88). In this pragmatic sense, truth did not happen to COIN doctrine.

In a sense, Hellraiser is right in his disturbing assessment of US history: it is largely the history of strike and destroy as a philosophy applied to minorities and "non-believers." Nevertheless, it is a one-sided view, because the opposing COIN-like philosophy of cooperation is also present in American culture. It is found in religion, kindergartens, universities, and other social settings where cooperation is valued more than aggression. However, even in seemingly COIN-like, cooperation-oriented institutions, one will find strike and destroy philosophies. For example, there are university departments where a "publish or perish" mentality dominates, and where professors battle each other as if they were in mortal combat. Following the sociologist Thorstein Veblen (1899), I am not claiming that America or any other culture is either-or barbaric or peaceful. I am proposing that barbaric versus peaceful social currents exist in all cultures, and one current dominates depending upon historical and social circumstances.

CONCLUSIONS

After absorbing the more than 90 pages of documents by the brigade commander that are contained in the report, one is left with the following, somewhat lyrical impression of him: Hellraiser was simultaneously the asocial Lone Wolf and True Believer. He sees himself as the victim, and accepts absolutely no responsibility for the tragedy which engulfed his brigade. He comes across as full of pride, eager to force his thoughts and ideas onto others. But he shows no empathy or caring for his soldiers and officers. Objectively, he was always out of step with his commanders as well as subordinates. He was completely out of touch with the common soldier, and almost literally never saw them—except for his personal bodyguards. In this regard, he was out of step with the army's requirements that leaders must mentor, counsel, and associate with their troops (FM 6-22).

Throughout literature, art, and philosophy, the Lone Wolf, as a social type, is consistently portrayed as dangerous. He is dangerous because he lacks the *loyalty* to others that is the basis for all healthy social life, from families to workplaces and military units. It may seem paradoxical at first blush that the Lone Wolf would also be the True Believer. This is because the True Believer seems to be extremely loyal to an idea or cause. But at bottom, the Lone Wolf and the True Believer are the same, and equally dangerous because of their loyalty to themselves or their dogma is at the expense of the well-being of others.[12] We recognize True Believers in the fundamentalists, crusaders, and dogmatists in social life. Both social types are loyal only to themselves. In sum, Hellraiser created his role as the Lone Wolf by defying, mocking, ignoring, and otherwise severing ties with the official doctrine of the US government, namely, COIN. At the same time, he became the True Believer in counter-guerrilla doctrine, with the consequences that he neglected his prescribed duties as a leader to mentor, circulate with, and be mindful of the welfare of his troops. We have seen that discipline, morale, mentoring, and day-to-day administration (all of which are integral parts of army doctrine) suffered in his brigade.

One must keep in mind that Hellraiser was more than an intellectual—he was the brigade commander. Because he was an intellectual, he was formally asked to review COIN doctrine and comment on it (although he was not asked to contribute to it). Like other intellectuals, he has the right to opine on the alleged flaws of COIN doctrine. But as a brigade commander, he had the formal role obligation to carry out COIN doctrine and the orders of his chain of command. The important caveat is that COIN doctrine might have been so confusing that in his mind, as well as the minds of some of his superiors and subordinates, he could have been perceived as carrying out COIN even though he mocked and criticized it. If his intellectual loyalty to what he perceived to be "the" truth (that his counter-guerrilla doctrine was superior to COIN) clashed with his loyalty to the chain of command, he should have removed himself or been removed from command. This is not an idle observation, given that several of the generals who commanded him expressed regret that they failed to remove him from command. And they expressed their regret in sworn statements! Nevertheless, his superiors failed to remove him from command, despite his insubordination (as a brigade commander) and vehement intellectual criticisms (as an intellectual) of the mission he was given. Why did his superiors fail to remove him from command? Perhaps one of the several, possible, reasons is that they secretly identified with his anti-COIN and pro-CG sentiments. Another possible reason is that they themselves were confused about the meaning of COIN doctrine.

Hellraiser was applying an emotionally-laden vision of warfare from the historical past onto his historical present—a phenomenon I refer to as post-emotional thinking (Mestrovic, 1999). Hellraiser's ethnocentrism, that his way was the traditional and American way of waging war, apparently struck deep chords among many of his subordinates. He wasn't going to take advice from French or other foreign intellectuals, or foreign NATO generals, or anthropologists whose field was established by a European and who oppose ethnocentrism—all of whom urged him to drink tea with the village elders in Afghanistan as a way to build trust and establish cooperation. He claimed that COIN was un-American—the issue was pure and simple for him. The subordinate commanders who opposed him never disagreed with him about these primal sentiments. To the extent that the non-believers opposed Hellraiser, they followed another strong American tradition, to follow the orders of the chain of command, whether they agreed with those orders or not. I cannot repeat too often that none of Hellraiser's commanders claimed that they embraced COIN doctrine fully—only that they were *doing* COIN. And so it came to pass that all of his subordinates were trapped in a moral dilemma concerning the virtue of loyalty from which they could find no exit: Hellraiser defied the chain of command, but he was the most important link in the chain of command for his subordinates. They could not say yes to him without saying no to the rest of the chain of command. And the chain of command above Hellraiser could not say no to him either, because he was one of them. We have seen that many of the officers who defied Hellraiser cited General McChrystal as his counter-weight. Alas, it is a historical fact that President Obama fired General McChrystal, whose task it was to carry out COIN doctrine, because McChrystal mocked COIN doctrine in interviews that were published in a *Rolling Stone* article.[13]

Hellraiser's sworn statement raises numerous questions, which we shall be addressing throughout the remainder of this study: What is COIN doctrine? Was COIN ever fully embraced by the army and the government? And what happened to COIN doctrine between 2007, when it was established, and 2012?

CHAPTER 7. COIN AS A JEKYLL AND HYDE DOCTRINE

General Stanley McChrystal was the ISAF (International Security Assistance Force) Commander in Afghanistan from June 15, 2009 to June 23, 2010, when President Obama fired him. (Because the acronym ISAF is probably meaningless to most readers, it is helpful to explain that McChrystal was basically in charge of all allied troops in Afghanistan.) Hellraiser's brigade deployed to Afghanistan in July, 2009 and returned to the United States in July of 2010. The crimes we are discussing in this book occurred between January and May of 2010 in Afghanistan. In other words, McChrystal was in charge when these crimes occurred. Indeed, President Karzai of Afghanistan summoned General McChrystal to his office after the Maywand District killings had become public, and McChrystal promised justice. As of this writing, General Curtis Scaparrotti is the new ISAF commander in Afghanistan. He relinquished his position as commanding general of I Corps and Ft. Lewis, and assumed his new position as ISAF commander in July of 2011. (Morlock was convicted in March of 2011, and was transferred to the navy brig in July, while the remaining companion case courts-martial would drag on into March of 2012.) Scaparrotti had been Hellraiser's commander. He was also the convening authority for Corporal Morlock's court-martial and the courts-martial for the companion cases under study here. Finally, he ordered General Twitty to investigate the command climate in Hellraiser's brigade. General Twitty—all the while complying with his orders—made a huge detour in studying the reactions to COIN doctrine in that brigade. COIN, McChrystal, Scaparrotti, Twitty, Morlock—these are connections missed by the news media, which we shall explore here.

Let us begin with the account of McChrystal's dispute with President Obama and COIN doctrine found in the aforementioned and infamous *Rolling Stone* article entitled "The Runaway General" by Michael Hastings. Hastings offers a portrait of General McChrystal that is a mirror image of Hellraiser in many regards. For example, Hastings writes:

> Last fall, during the question-and-answer session following a speech he gave in London, McChrystal dismissed the counterterrorism strategy being advocated by Vice President Joe Biden as "shortsighted," saying it would lead to a state of "Chaos-istan." The remarks earned him a smackdown from the president himself, who summoned the general to a terse private meeting aboard Air Force One. The message to McChrystal seemed clear: *Shut the fuck up, and keep a lower profile.*

Apparently, General McChrystal got in trouble with his commander (the president) in much the same way that Hellraiser got in trouble with his commanders: both mocked COIN doctrine publicly at the same time that they were entrusted to carry it out. Hastings continues:

> From the start, McChrystal was determined to place his personal stamp on Afghanistan, to use it as a laboratory for a controversial military strategy known as counterinsurgency. COIN, as the theory is known, is the new gospel of the Pentagon brass, a doctrine that attempts to square the military's preference for high-tech violence with the demands of fighting protracted wars in failed states....In 2006, after Gen. David Petraeus beta-tested the theory during his "surge" in Iraq, it quickly gained a hardcore following of think-tankers, journalists, military officers and civilian officials. Nicknamed "COINdinistas" for their cultish zeal, this influential cadre believed the doctrine would be the perfect solution for Afghanistan. All they needed was a general with enough charisma and political savvy to implement it. As McChrystal leaned on Obama to ramp up the war, he did it with the same fearlessness he used to track down terrorists in Iraq: Figure out how your enemy operates, be faster and more ruthless than everybody else, then take the f___s out. (p. 9)

Could it be true that General McChyrstal used a variant of "strike and destroy" philosophy on the President of the United States in order to get the Commander-in-Chief to commit more troops in the name of COIN? Hastings implies that McChrystal went along with COIN in order to get President Obama to commit 30,000 more troops in Afghanistan. Did General McChrystal embrace COIN doctrine any more or less than his subordinate commanders all the way down the chain of command to Hellraiser and his subordinate commanders? Hastings writes:

> Last fall, with his top general calling for more troops, Obama launched a three-month review to re-evaluate the strategy in Afghanistan. "I found that time painful," McChrystal tells me in one of several lengthy interviews. "I was selling an unsellable position."... "The entire COIN strategy

is a fraud perpetuated on the American people," says Douglas Macgregor, a retired colonel and leading critic of counterinsurgency who attended West Point with McChrystal. "The idea that we are going to spend a trillion dollars to reshape the culture of the Islamic world is utter nonsense." In the end, however, McChrystal got almost exactly what he wanted... Obama announced that he would send an additional 30,000 troops to Afghanistan, almost as many as McChrystal had requested. The president had thrown his weight, however hesitantly, behind the counterinsurgency crowd.

In this account, even the President did not seem to embrace COIN enthusiastically. Hastings quotes soldiers who mocked the acronym, "ISAF as short for 'I suck at Fighting' or 'In Sandals and Flip-Flops'". One of McChrystal's aides referred to one of the president's aides as "a clown." Regarding another aide to the president who supports COIN, Richard Holbrooke, we learn that "The Boss [McChrystal] says he's like a wounded animal." This mockery of the proponents of COIN by McChrystal's staff is not essentially different from similar mockery by Hellraiser and his staff of other COIN supporters. Hastings observes: "Even in his new role as America's leading evangelist for counterinsurgency, McChrystal retains the deep-seated instincts of a terrorist hunter" (p. 11). Similarly, Hellraiser was committed to CG doctrine even though he, too, was supposed to have been an "evangelist" for COIN.

These and other comments quoted by Hastings in this *Rolling Stone* article caused a firestorm in the American news media, and President Obama fired McChrystal. McChrystal's removal from office was portrayed more as the result of his insulting the Commander-in-Chief and his staff than as a dispute over COIN. Hellraiser's similarly insulting comments were not picked up by the media, and while he was almost fired at the NTC exercises, he squeaked through and led an ambivalent deployment of Stryker brigade under the command of an equally (or more) ambivalent commander toward COIN, General McChrystal. The commanders in Hellraiser's brigade who opposed him, and thought they were following McChrystal and the chain-of-command in doing COIN were betrayed. Was anyone in the chain of command sincere in promoting COIN doctrine?[14]

Turning to the COIN Manual

The term, COIN, is used by journalists, politicians, military commanders, and others without a clear sense of what it means. We have seen that Hellraiser's subordinate commanders were genuinely confused about the answer to the questions: *what* is COIN, and *how* should they do COIN? It is instructive to turn to the COIN manual, FM 3-24, in order to grasp the source of confusion.

The COIN manual is a hodge-podge of essays, tables, charts, and appendices authored by military officers as well as scholars. It comes across as one big power point presentation. Indeed, the published power point presentation of COIN doctrine based upon this manual invoked mockery from pundits and journalists. It is incomprehensible.[15] One reads in the manual that "the US military has had to relearn the principles of counterinsurgency (COIN)" and wonders—Why? Why does the US military lack a traditional approach or treatise on COIN? Sentences such as the following help to explain how Hellraiser passed NTC rotation despite his criticisms of COIN: "All full spectrum operations executed overseas—including COIN operations—include offensive, defensive, and stability operations that commanders combine to achieve the desired end state. The exact mix varies depending on the situation and the mission." (p. 1-19). Conceivably, Hellraiser was doing COIN according to this definition, because he was "mixing" it with offensive operations to achieve his goals. One learns that "the conduct of COIN is counterintuitive to the traditional US view of war" (p. 1-26). This is a point that Hellraiser makes repeatedly. If this assertion is true, then why did the government expect COIN to be absorbed by its military commanders?

Chapter 1 also includes an interesting list of maxims to follow, under the heading of "Paradoxes of Counterinsurgency Operations." These maxims are as follows:

- Sometimes, the More You Protect Your Force, the Less Secure You May Be
- Sometimes, the More Force is Used, the Less Effective It Is
- The More Successful the Counterinsurgency Is, the Less Force Can Be Used and the More Risk Must be Accepted
- Sometimes Doing Nothing is the Best Reaction
- Some of the Best Weapons for Counterinsurgents Do Not Shoot
- The Host Nation Doing Something Tolerably is Normally Better than Us Doing It Well
- If a Tactic Works this Week, It Might Not Work Next Week; If It Works in this Province, It Might Not Work in the Next
- Tactical Success Guarantees Nothing
- Many Important Decisions Are Not Made by Generals

These are witty statements, but are not helpful for a commander trying to decide what to do in a specific situation. The statements also contradict each other. If tactical success guarantees nothing, then what is the point of offensive and stability operations? Chapter 3 appears to have been written by a sociologist, or someone with sociological training. This chapter defines the concepts society, social structure, roles, social norms, culture, beliefs, and values. The definitions are correct—from the perspective of a Sociology 101 course—but the author's intent is not in the spirit of sociology. For example, one reads that "commanders can determine whether counterinsurgents can exploit differences in values." (p. 3-7). As a rule, sociologists do not seek to exploit or manipulate the individuals and groups they study. Similarly, the anonymous authors of this chapter assert that "by listening to narratives, counterinsurgents can identify a society's core values" (p. 3-6). Once the values are determined, the COIN strategist will know how to manipulate these values in interrogations. COIN strategists are advised to determine the leadership structures of the village they encounter in order to determine whether they should target the leaders or not. And so on. The sociology in the COIN manual is like the psychology in the manuals on interrogation techniques: military commanders are instructed on how to use the wisdom of the social sciences in order to strike and destroy. This approach is completely at odds with the spirit of the social sciences.

INVOKING SOCIOLOGY

The COIN manual does not resolve the confusion we have documented among commanders about what COIN is and how they should carry it out. The COIN manual is part of a much deeper problem. In theory and in practice, COIN doctrine comes across as a Jekyll and Hyde philosophy from the point of view of the host nation as well as infantry soldiers. What do the Afghan people see in COIN, which is a theory they can comprehend even less than the specialists who devised it and the US commanders who implement it? The Afghans see the Americans having tea with their village elders *and* American soldiers kicking in their doors during night time raids. They see US soldiers offering candy to their children *and* cursing at them. They see projects such as building roads and clinics *and* the aftermath of drone strikes which come in the middle of the night. They are told that the drone strikes kill terrorists, but as the news media reports, they complain that the same strikes kill innocent women and children. In sum, the Afghans see the practical, day-to-day effects of the theory that COIN is a combination of lethal as well as non-lethal operations: they see the composite of a kind, generous American soldier who wants to help them (Dr. Jekyll) who suddenly and without warning turns into the frightening American soldier (Mr. Hyde) who kills them indiscriminately. The practical effects cannot be otherwise, because the theory of COIN has not been disentangled from the traditional US doctrine of "strike and destroy." Instead, COIN has been superimposed upon strike and destroy doctrine.

What the preceding chapters show is that Hellraiser's brigade is only a microcosm of this widespread, societal disjunction. It is true, as one of the generals claimed, that Hellraiser's commanders may be divided into the true believers versus the non-believers. The true believers are believers in traditional, Old School, strike and destroy doctrine. The non believers do not embrace COIN *or* Old School, CG doctrine: they are adherents to *doing* COIN, but COIN doctrine itself is a Frankenstein monster of cooperation and the philosophy of strike and destroy, of lethal and non-lethal doctrines. The internal debate about COIN versus CG doctrine, found in the pages of the Twitty report, is oblivious to how the Afghan people perceived Hellraiser's brigade. It should be obvious from reading the sworn statements that Afghan villagers never knew quite what to expect when the Americans rolled into their villages. Would they encounter Dr. Jekyll or Mr. Hyde on any particular day?

COIN doctrine is built upon a sort of pseudo-sociology, a sociology that itself has been co-opted by a strike and destroy philosophy. Let us set the record straight at this juncture in the discussion about the true nature of sociology as a "doctrine." Sociology was established about a century ago by Emile Durkheim, Max Weber, George Herbert Mead, William James, Georg Simmel, and Karl Marx. Their insights were carried into the twentieth century primarily by Talcott Parsons at Harvard University and Robert Park at the University of Chicago. Obviously, I am not able to review the history of sociology in this limited space. But it is easy enough to summarize sociology with the one word: cooperation. It is not merely the case that sociology is the study of cooperation in its many facets, ranging from the division of labor to all sorts of association. The more important point is that the very idea of "society" *is* cooperation. The interested reader will find this insight in its clearest form in the world's first textbook on sociology, *Introduction to the Science of Sociology* by Robert Park and Everett Burgess, published in 1924. This book is frequently referred to as the "Green Bible," because of its green dust jacket. Indeed, it carries the evangelical connotations of being sociology's sacred text. It is important to note, for the sake of context, that many of the members of the Chicago School of sociology were ministers or the sons of ministers. Mead and Parsons were both the sons of ministers. Durkheim was descended from seven generations of rabbis, and is quoted as saying to his disciples in sociology, "Never forget that I am the son of a rabbi" (in Mestrovic, 1988). The important point is that theology and religion are connected to the birth of sociology.

Durkheim (1912) explicitly argued that real truths (those that are absorbed genuinely) in society are treated as if they were sacred, which is to say, with awe and respect. It should be obvious from the *Rolling Stone* article and the sworn statements in the Twitty report that COIN doctrine is *not* treated with a sense of awe and respect. On the contrary, it is the butt of jokes and the object of bitter mockery. In any case, sociology builds upon the works of the classical theorists I have mentioned above, in addition to the thinker who influenced them—Charles Darwin. Again, there exist important connections among Darwin, sociology, and theology.

The Darwin presented in the Green Bible is not he caricature of Darwin that continues to repel people even today, namely, the Darwin of the "survival of the fittest" philosophy. This phrase—an echo of the strike and destroy philosophy—was not uttered or written by Darwin, but attributed falsely to him. A connection between this false vision of Darwin and the present case is that Sergeant Gibbs saw the Afghans as "savages," and saw himself and other US soldiers as engaged in a struggle for "survival of the fittest." (Numerous soldiers state in their sworn statements that they heard Gibbs express these thoughts.) There is no intent here to place the sin of ethnocentrism (the belief that one's culture is superior to all others) solely on the shoulders of Sergeant Gibbs: a similar ethnocentrism is implied in COIN doctrine, namely, that the US will tame, democratize, and transform the savage host nations. Darwin did not use the phrase, "survival of the fittest." He used the phrase, "struggle for existence," which is ameliorated by "cooperation" and adaptation to a complex, cosmic "interdependence." It was a short step for Durkheim to draw upon Darwin's insights and to conclude, in his classic book, *The Division of Labor in Society* (1893), that the struggle for existence within and among societies is ameliorated by the "cooperation" and the division of labor. Durkheim added that this cooperation or division of labor must be "spontaneous," and he warned against the "forced division of labor"— which is dysfunctional. I ask the unbiased reader: is COIN doctrine, as it has been depicted in theory and practice, a "spontaneous" expression of American and Afghan cultural interdependence, or is it being "forced" upon the Afghan people, not to mention, upon US military commanders?

This concept of "cooperation" in its original, sociological, theological, and Darwinian sense is cosmic in scope. Durkheim regarded it as applying to Nature, societies, and the smallest organisms, down to the cellular level. We have seen in the previous chapter that contemporary society declares a "war on cancer" among its many wars, real and metaphorical, and that cancer is depicted as if it were a terrorist cell. Durkheim's cosmic approach to cooperation would hold the opposite: cancer is more likely a dysfunctional, disorganized, chaotic form of the normal cooperation and division of labor at the cellular level, and instead of declaring war on it, scientists should seek to restore the normal form of cellular and bodily division of labor. Similarly, the strike and destroy doctrine in Afghanistan overlooks the obvious fact that Afghan villagers are in a "struggle for existence" vis-à-vis U.S. soldiers, the Taliban, and other "insurgents." The villagers will "cooperate" with any of these belligerents so long as their long-term survival is ensured. The key concepts of cooperation and the division of labor are applicable to all phenomena, including war.

Indeed, the Green Bible devotes several chapters to war and conflict. Its perspective is that warfare is a form of association and cooperation in its own right. For example, one of sociology's founders, Georg Simmel, writes: "There must be agreement in order to struggle, and the struggle occurs under reciprocal recognition of norms and rules" (Park and Burgess, 1924, p. 588). The authors of the Green Bible extend the idea of "warfare" to include economic competition, political struggles, courtroom trials, and a host of other phenomena in addition to the struggle between armies. They write:

> The result is that war tends to assume the character of litigation, a judicial procedure, in which custom determines the method of procedure, and the issue of the struggle is accepted as a judgment in the case... It was the presence of the public, the ceremonial character of the proceedings, and the conviction that the invisible powers were on the side of truth and justice that gave the trial by ordeal and the trial by battle a significance that neither the duello nor any other form of private vengeance ever had.... An election is a contest in which we count noses when we do not break heads. A trial by jury is a contest in which the parties are represented by champions, as in the judicial duels of an earlier time. (Park and Burgess, 1924, p. 575)

These genuinely sociological insights seem to be as relevant in the current war on terror as they were in 1924. It is still true that world opinion counts heavily in deciding who really "won" this war, and not just militarily. It is still true that all the belligerents, including the Americans, have their ceremonies in preparing for and waging war (recall the symbolism, insignias, mottos, nicknames, scenarios and so on in Stryker brigade). All sides invoke notions of truth and justice based upon various, cultural "sacred" texts and customs—not just memorandums and legal opinions. Ultimately, wars are fought before the "jury of one's peers" that is world opinion. There is "cooperation" and there is a division of labor at every level of discourse, from world opinion down to the circulation of leaders with their troops at the platoon level.

The reason that the Maywand District killings were investigated and went to trial in this larger context is that they violated not only the letter of the law in the Laws of Armed Conflict, but violated customs and perceptions of which side is on the side of truth and justice. Soldiers in Morlock's platoon killed innocent civilians, and such acts are never acceptable to the collective consciousness, even though such act occur in all wars. President Karzai summoned General McChrystal, and both of them promised justice. Morlock's court-martial, like all trials, is itself a microcosm of war: Spinner and LeBlanc were the commanders of their respective teams, and they sparred in and outside of the courtroom. But they also cooperated with each other through disclosures of "discovery" material, reports, and evidence. They did *not* adopt an attitude of strike and destroy toward each other or Morlock. The careful reader will notice the subtle truth woven throughout this story that Captain LeBlanc needed Morlock's "cooperation" (the very word used in the pre-trial agreement) in order to help convict the soldiers in the companion cases. The ultimate winner in any conflict or war—real or metaphorical—is the one who cooperates with his enemy in a profound way, and does not merely annihilate the enemy.

It is obviously beyond the scope of this study to delve any further into the depth and profundity of genuinely sociological insights and their relevance to the present discussion. I have woven these insights into this story. The important point is that the COIN manual is shallow in its misuse of sociological insights, and is fundamentally flawed. The flaw lies in its overall effort to subordinate the cooperative aspects of COIN doctrine to the traditional, strike and destroy doctrine. As we have seen, sociological insights are used in the COIN manual to further the cause of lethal strategies, which is the exact opposite of sociology's perspective that warfare is a form of association. There is no need here to engage in an intellectual argument on this point. The proof is found in the pages of the sworn statements in the Twitty report: officers and soldiers were confused—in a fundamental sort of way—about *how* to *do* COIN in the context of traditional, strike and destroy philosophy. The problem is insoluble: doing COIN in the service of strike and destroy results in the perception of the US military as a Jekyll and Hyde.

In the remainder of this book, I shall refer to the "spirit of COIN" or "COIN-like" ideas and actions to differentiate the noble intent of COIN philosophy from COIN doctrine as it is found in the manual and was carried out in practice. The spirit of COIN is cooperation, and this idea flickers through the pages of the COIN manual like a candle in the wind. But the idea of cooperation, or the spirit of COIN, should be central to winning any war or conflict. This spirit of COIN applies to all forms of association, from the various defense and prosecutorial teams to prisons, platoons, companies, interviews, and other forms of "society." We have seen that General McChrystal, other generals, and Hellraiser failed to implement the spirit of COIN in the process of implementing COIN doctrine and strike and destroy philosophy. In the goal of winning the hearts and minds of the Afghan people, they neglected to win the hearts and minds of their own officers and soldiers. The social dysfunction within Stryker brigade is a microcosm of the larger forms of social dysfunction. The reader of this book at some point in the distant future will perceive this immediately by placing this story in the context of a global recession, seemingly unprecedented mud-slinging in the presidential election of 2012, multiple stories of corruption in the corporate world, and global, political discontent that forms the background for the story at hand.

What Happened to COIN Doctrine?

A future historian will observe that great excitement and collective effervescence surrounded the introduction of COIN doctrine in the year 2007 by General David Petraeus. Petraeus went on to become the director of the CIA in the Obama Administration—and the CIA is hardly known for its COIN-like activities. We have seen the President Obama fired the chief evangelist of COIN doctrine, General McChyrstal in the year 2010. Since 2010, the US has stepped up missions and operations that seem to be in line with strike and destroy philosophy, while references to COIN doctrine have dropped steadily. Examples include the president's plan to bolster drastically the number of special operations forces in Afghanistan in preparation for the eventual withdrawal from that country. Special operations forces are all about strike and destroy, and not about COIN. The most famous strike and destroy mission in this time period was the assassination of Osama bin Laden in Pakistan by Navy Seals on May 2, 2011. The news media reported a dramatic increase in the use of unmanned drones that were carrying out strike and destroy missions throughout Afghanistan between the years 2010 and 2012. The rhetoric of COIN diminished in this time frame. During the same time frame, the visible, documented, actions in line with strike and destroy philosophy increased dramatically. Whatever happened to COIN doctrine?

In this same time frame, the news media reported numerous incidents of desecration and cultural offenses by US forces in Afghanistan. A video of US soldiers urinating on the dead corpses of Taliban fighters made its way around the world on the Internet. There were several instances of Koran book burning, which resulted in riots and deaths in Afghanistan as well as neighboring countries. The latest incident of Koran book burning by American soldiers was reported in the last week of February, 2012.[16] A war crime committed by US soldiers that resulted in the deaths of seventeen Afghans, including women and children, occurred in the wake of the Koran book burnings, and enflamed anti-American passions further in Afghanistan.[17] The public discourse concerning the February incident of Koran book burning (which led to revenge killings against American soldiers) was never connected to COIN doctrine. President Obama apologized for the burning of the Korans by some US soldiers, and the Republican presidential candidates predictably criticized him for apologizing. But the connections between COIN and cultural sensitivity, and problems in implementing COIN and the incidents of book burnings, the urination on corpses, and other similar events—were simply absent from the larger, public discussion.

Consider the news briefing that General Scaparrotti gave to the media at the Pentagon on February 8, 2012.[18] The immediate event preceding this conference was a leaked report by Lieutenant Colonel Dan Davis entitled, "Truth and Lies About Afghanistan."[19] Davis claimed that the US government was lying about alleged progress in Afghanistan, and Scaparrotti predictably dismissed Davis by saying, "it's one person's view of this." The more important point is that no one from the media asked a single question related to COIN doctrine, and Scaparrotti never mentioned COIN doctrine. On the contrary, when asked about his top priority in Afghanistan as commander of ISAF, Scaparrotti answered: "We must relentlessly pursue the enemy and sustain the tactical defeat of the insurgents." Scaparrotti was echoing Hellraiser. There are numerous ironies in Scaparrotti's statement: He was the successor to McChrystal, but did not say that COIN doctrine was his top priority, or that it was a priority at all. Scaparrotti had ordered the 15-6 investigation into Hellraiser's command climate, and learned from it that Hellraiser confused his brigade by pushing relentless pursuit of the enemy at the expense of COIN. Were any lessons learned from the tragedy of Stryker brigade and the subsequent investigations and courts-martial? Here was General Scaparrotti, who was Hellraiser's former commander, echoing Hellraiser! The supreme irony lies in the fact that the army's traditional, strike and destroy philosophy, which preceded COIN doctrine in 2007, emerged again in 2012—it was never truly modified by COIN doctrine.

CONCLUSIONS

It seems to be the case that COIN doctrine was not absorbed by the military or the larger American culture since its birth in the year 2007. Hailed as the only viable way to win the war in Afghanistan, it disappeared from public discourse by the year 2012. Ironically, Hellraiser seems to have been proven right in his searing criticisms of COIN doctrine and refusal to adopt it. The US military began acting out Hellraiser's strike and destroy philosophy in the aftermath of the war crimes under discussion here, not bolstering COIN doctrine. But COIN doctrine is contradictory at its very core, because it allows commanders to mix lethal and non-lethal operations as they see fit. The result is a Jekyll and Hyde doctrine which confuses US officers and troops as well as local Afghans. To be sure, the US government is still *doing* COIN projects (building roads, dams, clinics, and other development projects). However, as the continuous events of desecration, cultural insensitivity, Koran book burnings, and additional war crimes show, the US military never embraced COIN philosophy. Beneath the COIN façade, the goal has always been and continues to be to strike and destroy the enemy. All other considerations, including cultural sensitivity, are subordinate to this overarching philosophy championed by Hellraiser. While these incidents are relatively few, the issue is not one of quantifying incidents that are anti-COIN. The important point is that the incidents listed above carry enormous *symbolic* significance, and are connected to the military's ambiguous, Jekyll and Hyde *philosophy* of war.

I have heard several military prosecutors argue in court that, "This is a war of ideas." They are right, in the broad, sociological sense described earlier. Abu Ghraib, and other sites of torture (including Bagram air force base in Afghanistan and Guantanamo) are more than sites of war crimes. They carry the symbolic significance of failure in the war of ideas, that the United States is morally superior to its enemies. Torture and abuse continued following the Abu Ghraib scandal, and President Obama never kept his campaign promise to shut down Guantanamo. Much like the Abu Ghraib photos symbolized defeat for the United States in Iraq—in the eyes of the global jury of one's peers—the Koran book burnings signaled a similar defeat in Afghanistan. So many years after Abu Ghraib and after the inception of COIN in 2007, the crimes under discussion here, in tandem with the multiple instances of cultural insensitivity, cannot be rationalized away as the actions of a few bad apples or as mistakes. They are the direct result of a strike and destroy philosophy in the American military. It seems that COIN doctrine was merely used as cover for this traditional philosophy, or, at best, COIN doctrine was an interesting experiment. Whatever COIN was or is, it is something other than a sincere policy.

So far in this book, we have examined COIN doctrine in theory and practice. COIN and its antithesis, strike and destroy doctrine, emerged as the central issue in the Twitty report. In the remainder of this book, we shall turn our attention to Corporal Morlock and his fellow soldiers, all the while remaining mindful of connections to the preceding discussion. At this halfway point in the discussion, I remind the reader of my opening lines, and that this is a book about making connections.

CHAPTER 8. MEETING CORPORAL MORLOCK AT THE NAVY BRIG

My research associates (Caldwell and Kerr) and I met Corporal Morlock for the first time on the 25th of September, 2010. It was the weekend prior to his Article 32 hearing (the equivalent of a civilian preliminary hearing). We met him at the brig on a naval base that is approximately an hour and a half's drive from Ft. Lewis. The nearest town to the navy base is Silverdale, Washington. The army sought to keep him segregated from the other accused soldiers, who were confined at Ft. Lewis. Gibbs was segregated from the others by being confined at a civilian, county jail. All members of the so-called kill team were kept in pre-trial confinement. (This is not a hard and fast rule, even in war crime cases involving premeditated murder.) At that particular juncture of this saga, Captain Opachan was Morlock's military attorney, the role he played from start to finish. However, Spinner was not yet on the scene. At the time I met Morlock, Opachan worked with two other civilian attorneys who were representing Morlock until December of 2010. I shall not name these two civilian attorneys. I shall refer to Morlock's initial, lead attorney as the civilian, Attorney X, and he was assisted by civilian Attorney Y. To phrase the matter diplomatically, Morlock's mother was unhappy with Attorney X, and eventually hired Spinner to represent her son.

We have been discussing the lack of communication and resultant confusion within Stryker brigade up to now. Similarly, there was a lack of communication in the initial defense team, and among Morlock, his mother, and Attorney X. Morlock's mother complained that Attorney X never returned her phone calls, so that she had no idea whatsoever of what was in store for her son. Indeed, Attorneys X did not communicate with his defense team either. He met us in the parking lot at the navy brig on that sunny day that we met Morlock—but spent barely two minutes speaking with us. The lack of communication did not change or improve during the subsequent Article 32 hearing, when the two civilian attorneys could have briefed us and Morlock's mother on their strategy and plans for defending Morlock. Attorneys X and Y spent absolutely no time—zero minutes—speaking with my crew or with me about the case even though we were in physical proximity at the time of the pre-trial hearing. I am recording this unpleasant fact for history as well as sociology, because one of the themes in the present study is the spirit of COIN in its broadest sense. The rough equivalent of COIN-directed, "having tea with the village elders" would have been sharing a meal or coffee with the defense team. The spirit of COIN (communication, cooperation) was missing in Morlock's initial defense team as much as it was missing in military missions in Afghanistan. Some attorneys seem to practice law in a "strike and destroy" manner: they are focused solely on the combative aspects of a case, and do not pay attention to the spirit of COIN (negotiating, communicating, cooperating) with the persons with whom they come into contact. I have stated at the outset that Hellraiser is an archetype, a social type—and not only in the military. One can find Hellraisers in other professions as well, including academia (the publish or perish doctrine), the law, medicine, and so on.

Captain Opachan is an exception to these general observations concerning Morlock's initial defense team. He met us in that same parking lot prior to the arrival of Attorneys X and Y. Captain Opachan conversed with my research team and me at length. Some facts concerning Captain Opachan are worth noting, as he would eventually assist Spinner in defending Morlock. Opachan told us that he had been an enlisted soldier, left the army, earned his law degree, and then re-joined the army—this time, as an officer. It was obvious that he understood the army from both points of view, that of the elitist officer as well as the lowly soldier. Opachan was open and transparent about his opinions and feelings. For example, he said, "I like Jeremy Morlock as a person." We had heard rumors that the Twitty report was underway at this time, and Opachan's comment was, "It will be a whitewash." The four of us agreed in that parking lot that we liked Morlock as a person, and that we would have a tough time as a defense team obtaining the Twitty report. He handed us the existing sworn statements from the CID investigation. My crew and I also agreed afterwards that we liked Captain Opachan. But when our conversation came to an end, he visited Morlock with the other two attorneys for about an hour, while my crew and I met with Morlock separately, and for a total of sixteen hours over the course of that weekend.

THE SOCIAL SETTING OF THE NAVY BRIG

It is also important to discuss here, albeit briefly, the general setting, social climate, and ambiance of the navy brig and base versus Ft. Lewis and its detention facility. This is not an idle exercise, dear reader, because the contrast between the two detention facilities is an integral part of the story of the "contagion" that afflicted Ft. Lewis at every level, from Hellraiser's leadership style to the clerks at the visitor's center. Morlock was confined for long periods of time at both the naval brig and the army facility, depending upon various schemes by the government as to whom they wanted to segregate from whom, and when. To get to the point, the contrast between the naval base and Ft. Lewis is as extreme as Dickens's a tale of two cities. For example, my crew and I were always able to get onto the navy base without any problems: we showed our paperwork and identification cards, and we were waived through. At Ft. Lewis, and with the exact same paperwork and identification cards, we always had difficulty getting onto the base. Sometimes the army guards would angrily order us to return to the visitor center, where we were told we would have to obtain oral permission from Captain Opachan in addition to the paperwork. But getting Captain Opachan on the cell phone was sometimes not good enough for the army officials: they required that he call the visitor center from his office phone, and vouch for us. Captain Opachan would have to drop whatever he was doing at Ft. Lewis and run up the stairs to answer his phone in his office, so that my crew and I could get on base. Entering Ft. Lewis was *never* straightforward and was *always* problematic, haphazard, arbitrary, and capricious.

The staff at the navy brig was always courteous, professional, and friendly, even as they followed their protocol. The staff at the army detention center was rarely professional and more often rude and abusive toward me as well as Morlock. I called Morlock on the phone every week for approximately eighteen months, during his entire trial process, at either the navy brig or the army detention facility. The navy staff would consistently connect me with Morlock after asking me to please hold while they went through their protocol of putting him in chains and leg irons so that he would be in compliance with the law to speak with me from a secure phone. While I was waiting on the phone, I could enjoy the music that was played during the hold period: usually it was "golden oldies" music, but it changed to Christmas music during Christmas season. Calling Morlock at the navy brig was more or less like calling him at a hotel (with the exception of the leg irons). On the other hand, the army staff required that Morlock's attorneys and I call for an appointment three days in advance. When I would call at the appointed hour and day, it was hit or miss whether anyone on the other end would pick up the phone.

Sometimes the phone would keep ringing and was never answered on that day. On the days that someone picked up the phone, they would sometime say that Morlock was unavailable, and hang up. There was an incident in which a prison guard refused to let me speak with Morlock because, he said, "You're calling him too much." For a period of time, the staff refused to let me speak with him at all because they said I was not authorized to do so, and Captain Opachan had to go to the facility, in person, to authorize me. Opachan's written authorizations were apparently lost. Similarly, packages that I would send to Morlock at the navy brig, marked as "privileged," would always reach him. On the other hand, similar packages that I would send to Morlock at the army facility would be opened and returned to me, without explanation!

At the army detention facility, Morlock's cell was ransacked, guards would sometimes verbally abuse him, and in general, he felt threatened. Morlock was forced to wear an orange jump suit at the army facility, while he was allowed to wear his army uniform during his entire stay at the navy brig. The army staff referred to him as "Prisoner Morlock." The navy staff referred to him as "Mr. Morlock." The abuse at the army facility was so rampant that I wrote a letter to the base commander, General Scaparrotti, and asked him to intervene. (Of course, I asked Spinner and Opachan for permission to send the letter.) To my great surprise, Scaparrotti called me on my cell phone on the day he received my letter, and promised that he would intervene. The result of Scaparrotti's intervention was that Morlock was mistreated even more after Scaparrotti got involved, than before. In the summer of 2011, the problem was resolved by finally transferring Morlock back to the navy brig. At the court-martial, Captain Opachan brought up the abuse Morlock suffered at the army detention facility. Morlock would often say to me, "The navy brig is like a Hilton hotel compared to the army jail."

It is beyond the scope of this book to venture into a full-fledged study of the navy versus army detention facilities. (This might be an important study for others to pursue.) The more important point is that my experiences with Ft. Lewis were a constant reminder of Hellraiser's aggressive philosophy, while my experiences at the navy base were a constant reminder of the spirit of COIN. Social climates do matter. And social climates percolate through to every tiny detail of social life in a particular location or social institution.

METHODOLOGICAL AND PROFESSIONAL CONSIDERATIONS IN INTERVIEWING CORPORAL MORLOCK

The word "interview" holds widely different meanings in various professions, and is subject to misunderstandings akin to the confusion we have been following concerning the word COIN. My colleagues and I interviewed Morlock in our professional roles as sociologists. Sociologists interview persons under the following guidelines: we attempt "to take the role of the other;" we establish genuine rapport; we withhold judgment; we are always mindful of the social context for what a person says, does, or believes; we listen more than we speak; we try to get a "rich" or "thick" description of events by the interviewee; we do not test hypotheses, but form conclusions based on what emerges out of the situation; and we have no ulterior motives. These are the general guidelines which originate in a body of works that are grouped under the headings "qualitative sociology," "participant-observation," and "symbolic interactionism." Some readers might object to the fact that anyone would show empathy to person who would eventually be convicted of premeditated murder. My professional response is: this is what sociologists are trained to do. This is the tradition established by William James, Charles Horton Cooley, George Herbert Mead, and other sociologists. Pragmatism is an attitude more than cookbook method: one sets conditions for truths to emerge. One does not force, impose, or cajole truths.

In stark contrast to this sociological approach to interviews, CID agents (and criminal investigators in general) use deceit, trickery, and other forms of chicanery to force a person to confess things that the interviewer wants them to admit ahead of time. The criminal investigator is deductive in his approach, while I was inductive. The skeptical reader may do an Internet search for the phrase "Reid Technique" to be convinced of the contrast I am describing. In addition, I became immersed in the issue of how criminal investigators use the Reid and "Reid-like" techniques during the court-martial of Sergeant Michael Leahy in a completely different case. In that case of premeditated murder, Spinner attempted to have the military judge throw out Leahy's videotaped confession, which was obtained by investigators using Reid-like techniques. Spinner argued that these techniques amounted to coercion. The judge ruled otherwise. It is beyond the scope of the present study to delve into this issue, beyond noting it.

In addition, as a sociologist with experience as an expert witness at other war crime trials, I knew that I would ask Morlock about the command and social climate in his platoon, company, battalion, and brigade. A psychologist would not ask such questions, even though a psychologist would be empathetic. To a sociologist, whatever Morlock did, said, and believed was always connected to his social context. In this regard, I am a sociologist like Spinner is a lawyer: we are both simultaneously constrained and enabled by the professional armor we wear.

Another important connection to make is that my sociological (empathetic) approach to interviewing is in line with the spirit of COIN. On the other hand, criminal investigators approach the interview more in line with a "strike and destroy" mentality. There can be no doubt that criminal investigators seek to "nail," target," and "destroy" the accused. These connections, COIN versus CG and the sociological interview versus the CID interrogation, are significant for the present study. They point to the ways in which the doctrines of COIN versus CG resonate with numerous, similar attitudes throughout American culture (although I have by no means exhausted all these connections).

Finally, and from the legal perspective, everything Corporal Morlock told me is privileged information. This means that my account of some of the things he told me has been approved by him and vetted by Spinner. In no way is one able to simply share one's experiences in today's complex world. From the legal perspective, anything Morlock said could, would, and was used against him. From the sociological perspective, I wanted to understand his point of view empathetically. From the criminal investigator's point of view, he was just another target for them, a "mark." For the first defense team, it seems that he was just a client. I leave it up to the reader to imagine what Morlock's narratives—or anybody else's—mean to other professions.

Corporal Morlock's perspective on his videotaped sworn statement

My two colleagues and I took one last look at the outside of the brig, and noticed deer grazing approximately twenty yards from the building which was nestled in a pine forest. "Hey look, it's Bambi," Caldwell joked. It was 8 am on a Saturday morning. The staff inside the building was expecting us and escorted us courteously to Morlock. He was a in holding area with five separate solitary confinement cells, each approximately 10 by 12 feet. I peered inside cell in order to visualize his life in solitary confinement: The door to the cell is made of thick, solid steel, with a narrow slit. The walls inside were painted bleach white. There was one narrow slit on the back wall that served as a window, though it was too high to be able to look through it. There was one vent in the room, directly over the bed. The light was on 24 hours a day, and directly over the prisoner's head. And there was a stainless steel toilet and wash basin. I did not know on that day that this would be Morlock's abode for the next two years. We sat at a table and benches which were made of stainless steel and were bolted to the floor, in the holding area. I introduced myself and my colleagues to Corporal Morlock, and asked him how he would like us to address him. He said, "Call me Jeremy." (For some reason, my brain immediately associated this sentence with "call me Ishmael," the famous line from Melville's *Moby Dick*.) We were all on a first-name basis after that. The first impression he made upon us was, "He's so young!" After we exited the brig, my colleagues and I exclaimed to each other, "He could be one of my students!" Again, this is not an idle observation, given that the persons labeled as war criminals in the current war on terror are predominantly young soldiers in their twenties, which is historically a sharp contrast to the image of old war criminals from the World War II era. Moreover, theories of youth and identity, such as those proposed by Erik Erikson (1963), suggest that these young soldiers simply do not possess the maturity to make consistently wise decisions in their lives in general, much less in a war zone. From start to finish of the interviews, which lasted two days, Jeremy came across as friendly, open, thoughtful, and self-effacing.

Soon after I told him that we would not be tricking or deceiving him, and that contrary to his interrogations with CID agents, we would not be using anything he said against him—he began to talk about his video-taped statement to CID, which took place on May 11, 2010. He said that he was at Kandahar airfield awaiting medical evacuation to the United States. A Navy physician had diagnosed him with "post-concussive syndrome" and recommended further evaluation, as well as entry into the Wounded Warrior Program. Later, I confirmed this in his medical records, and would add that his injuries were diagnosed by subsequent physicians as the more serious TBI or traumatic brain injury. Furthermore, he was also diagnosed with PTSD or Post-traumatic Stress Disorder while he was in Afghanistan. He never made that flight home, because CID agents detained him, and he had been in confinement ever since May 11, 2010 (His court-martial took place in March of 2011). As he spoke, I noticed that his hand was twitching and that he was regularly rubbing his right thigh. When I asked him about his symptoms, he shrugged them off, and said they were nothing.

In general, Jeremy came across as self-effacing, stoical, and someone who consistently minimized his pain, symptoms, and predicament. This is a typical attitude of the American infantry soldier in the current war. They are taught to act tough and "act like a man" regardless of circumstances. I asked him: "Why didn't you invoke your 5th amendment rights with the CID agents?" He said, "I tried. I told them I wanted to speak to a lawyer. They said there were no lawyers at Kandahar." "That's it?" I asked, "You just accepted that explanation?" He said he made a phone call to the JAG office at the US military base at Bagram, Afghanistan, but the person on the other end of the phone said to him, "If you haven't been charged, you've got nothing to worry about." He was not sure if that person was an attorney or a paralegal. It is certain that this person's advice constitutes legal malpractice. Short of a full-scale AR 15-6 investigation, there is no way to ever verify this event. However, I will add that Jeremy's claim that he could not get hold of an attorney is entirely believable to me, based upon my experiences with trying to speak to attorneys on the phone—and I am referring especially to attorneys with whom I have worked as a member of their defense teams! Dear reader, I affirm here for historical record that most of the time when I have called an attorney with whom I work, and left a message on voice mail or with an assistant, the lawyer would take weeks or months to return my call. This is a serious problem with the lack of a COIN-like-spirit in the legal profession, based upon my experience. Jeremy did not have weeks or months to wait for an attorney to step in and protect his Constitutional rights. CID investigators strike while the iron is hot, meaning, while the suspect is fearful, disoriented, and isolated. These strategies are part of the training that CID investigators receive. Investigators strip an accused of his rights within minutes and hours. In this case, Morlock was away from his platoon and isolated on an army base while waiting for his mythical medical evacuation flight—the situation was perfect from the perspective of CID investigators.

I told Jeremy that the last JAG attorney with whom I had worked, Captain James Hill, had a sign framed on his office wall that read: "If someone is reading you your rights, they are not your friend." In response, he looked at me thoughtfully. "So what did CID say to you to get you to waive your rights?" I asked.

"They said that if I signed off on the rights waiver, I'd be on the next flight out for my medical evacuation. They said, 'if you sign off on this form, you'll get to see your unborn daughter.' They said they would protect me from Gibbs. Promises like that."

"And you believed them?"

"Why wouldn't I believe them? They're like me, they're army. They would not lie to me."

Caldwell and I just shook our heads upon hearing this. We had been through the Michael Leahy trial, the army sergeant who also believed in and trusted the army values of honor and telling the truth—he confessed and received a life sentence.

CID interrogators use a soldier's honor as a weapon and turn it on the soldier. They use the establishment of fake rapport as a weapon for obtaining incriminating statements. "Were you sober and drug-free at the time you made the videotaped statement?" I asked. Jeremy was not. He was taking pain-killers, sleeping pills, and prescription muscle relaxants, on top of hashish the night before. In fact, he interrupted his statement by taking one of his prescription medications during the interrogation, in front of the interrogators. This fact is verified in the CID notes that I would read later. Apparently, the CID interrogators did not know or did not care that Jeremy's intoxication on legal and illegal drugs constituted coercion. The end-game is all that matters to the interrogators. Two CID agents are in that videotape, Camero and Wagner. Camero's excitement is evident in his body language, facial expressions, and voice: it is as if Camero had "scored" in the "strike and destroy" mission that was the interrogation. The first few moments of the interrogation are clearly staged:

Camero: Today is 11 May 2010 and the time is 11:21 a.m. Before we begin, I just want to make sure it's clear and understood that you are still under rights advisement; you fully understand all your rights, yes or no?

Morlock: Yes.

Camero: And you currently do not request an attorney?

Morlock: I currently do not request an attorney.

Camero: Outstanding, so if you just want to start off from the beginning—

Wagner: Well, I don't think the consent for the—

Camero: Real quick, I'm sorry, back track; do you consent to a recorded interview of yourself?

Morlock: Yes, yes.

Camero: Ok. So go ahead and just start, you can start from the beginning, as we had spoken before, I'm going to lead you off.

The language in the transcript betrays the lack of affective neutrality that is supposed to characterize the behavior of professionals, including criminal investigators (the video betrays this even more). "Outstanding" is the word Camero uses in response to Jeremy's momentous decision to waive his Constitutional rights. A civil rights attorney might characterize this moment as "Tragic." "Real quick," Camero says, as if such a grave decision should be rushed. "Yes or no," Camero says, as if there is no in-between answer, a "yes and no" (that Jeremy wanted to tell them what happened and wanted to be protected). Note also that in the video, Wagner tries to remind Camero that Jeremy had not signed his rights waiver for the videotaped interrogation.

It should be noted, however, that special agent Wagner would eventually offer to write a letter on behalf of Jeremy's clemency. Approximately two years after the videotaped statement, special agent Wagner concluded that out of all the accused soldiers, Jeremy was the most honest, that he accepted responsibility for what he did, and that he cooperated with the government.

Jeremy's videotaped statement was eventually leaked to the media, and may be found on YouTube. At Jeremy's Article 32 hearing, the IO (Investigative Officer) ruled that it was admissible as evidence, that Jeremy seemed coherent, and that he was not coerced into waiving his rights. Coercion and free will are in the eyes of the beholder. When I later watched that videotaped statement, I did not see a coherent Jeremy Morlock. I saw a young soldier who was leaning against the wall in order to keep himself from collapsing. He was holding his head up with his hand for most of the interview. In the end, the IO's pronouncement created the truth that he was coherent and had waived his rights, and no amount of discussion of this fact can ever undo it.

The background to the statement, as described by Jeremy, is that both he and Winfield were disturbed by the killings which began after Gibbs was assigned to their platoon in December of 2009. Winfield told his father, who reported the first killing to the government and was ignored. Jeremy tried to tell his mother while he was home on leave in March of 2010, but never communicated the full extent of what was happening. Jeremy's mother later confirmed for me that he tried to tell her about "weird things" going on in the platoon, but that she could not believe him. She also blamed herself for the lack of communication. The important point is that there is no hotline and no organized mechanism in the army for a soldier to report war crimes. Jeremy and Winfield felt trapped by Gibbs even though they participated in his scenarios. Like Winfield, Jeremy said that he was afraid that Gibbs would kill him if he ever "ratted" on him.

LEGAL AND ILLEGAL DRUG USE

Because Jeremy had opened the door to the topic of drug use, I asked him to elaborate. He said that "everybody" (except Gibbs) in his platoon smoked hashish. Indeed, fifteen members of his platoon were formally charged with using Hashish, even if this number does not account for the remainder of "everybody." In addition, he described the "cocktails" of drugs that the platoon members would take at the beginning of every day—a mixture of muscle relaxants, anti-depressants, anti-anxiety medications, and pain-killers. The soldiers took the drugs in the morning because their days consisted of two eight-hour missions which involved walking ten to fifteen kilometers per day. Apparently, they were getting themselves ready for the stress, muscle pain, and fear of IEDs that every day brought. They took the pills at the end of the day to "fall asleep." The soldiers were sleep deprived, which is a common pattern among soldiers I have interviewed over the years. I asked him how he and the rest of the platoon obtained these prescription drugs, and he said that the medics and physician assistants handed them out in zip lock bags. We talked at some length how soldiers were never prescribed medications in child-proof safety containers, as they are in civilian America, complete with warning labels not to operate heavy machinery while taking such medications. An army physician later confirmed for me that, indeed, prescriptions are handed out to soldiers in Iraq and Afghanistan in mass, in zip lock bags, and without *bona fide* prescriptions.

How frequently did the soldiers consume these cocktails of legal and illegal drugs? Jeremy wasn't sure, but said it ranged from daily to several times a week. "Didn't that affect your performance?" Here Jeremy reverted to the typical army macho-tough-guy rhetoric that he and all the others could handle it. What was the purpose of the drug use? "It took the edge off," he said. "The edge off what?" I asked. He described the obvious, constant, threat of IEDs and not knowing when they would be blown up or by whom on a mission. Caldwell said to me later, "They were self-medicating."

Jeremy said that no one ever performed the required urinalysis drug testing on them while they were deployed (this would be confirmed later by LT Moye at the Article 32 hearing). Did the officers know about the drug use? "They must have known, but everyone pretended they did not know," Jeremy answered. He also explained how the hashish was readily available from Afghan soldiers as well as civilians and interpreters.

Because drug use in America carries legal stigma, and is a crime, several aspects of Jeremy's description are worth putting into context. First, the drug use was a group phenomenon and was not restricted to a few individual "stoners." Second, the illegal drug use was conjoined to prescription drug use, and the soldiers apparently did not differentiate between the two types of drug use. Finally, several studies suggest that approximately 40% of infantry soldiers in the US Army are taking prescription anti-depressant and anti-anxiety medications while on deployment, and use of illegal drugs is a widespread social problem in the army. In other words, the drug use is not peculiar to Jeremy or his platoon. It is the invisible epidemic in the current war on terror, in which, ironically, the soldiers are terrorized by IEDs.

COIN DOCTRINE (OR ITS ABSENCE) FROM MORLOCK'S POINT OF VIEW

Prior to this interview, I had no idea that COIN doctrine played any role at all in the story of Jeremy Morlock. I stumbled upon it accidentally when I asked him about the Rules of Engagement (ROE) in his platoon and brigade. He answered: "The ROE were different in every AO [area of operations]. There were multiple ROE in place at one time and this confused all of us. The general feeling among everybody was that McChrystal's new COIN rules would get us killed." I asked, "How did the ROE change?" Morlock replied: "Sometimes and in some places it was okay to shoot anybody on a motorcycle, no questions, no EOF, and other times and other places it was not. Sometimes it was ok to shoot vehicles that would not stop at check points, sometimes it was not." I asked him, "What is the difference between ROE and EOF?" He said:

"ROE is the procedure for *why* soldiers engage a target and EOF is the procedure for *how* they engage." The Twitty report displays the "Soldier's Card 5/2 SBCT" which every infantry soldier in Hellraiser's brigade carried with him at all times, and which contains the brigade's ROE. What struck me about the ROE listed on the card is the line, "minimum force includes deadly force." Outside of the military, this sentence makes no sense. Deadly force can never be a part of minimal force, and the use of minimal force was an integral part of McChrystal's new doctrine. "What is COIN?" I asked. "You have to remember I'm about twelve pay grades below the generals, so I couldn't tell you exactly. But it was McChrystal's new way of fighting the war. It was like, 'go have tea with the village elders' instead of the Old School approach. McChrystal's approach put us at risk."

"So what is the Old School approach?" I asked.

"Colonel Tunnell is Old School. His sergeant major is Old School. His sergeant major would try to motivate us by telling us stories like how he killed an Iraqi who was trying to run away from him by bludgeoning him to death with his helmet. Counter-guerrilla is Old School. COIN is McChrystal's new thing, and everybody treated it as a joke. I was in Bravo Company, and our company motto was, 'There is no hunting like the hunting of men.' My platoon motto was 'The Death Dealers.'" I was surprised by the mottos, but soldiers from other units had told me about Old School. Old School is the infantry soldier's phrase for traditional, strike and destroy, army doctrine. Jeremy explained that the enlisted soldiers never had a single lecture or presentation on COIN. In Jeremy's words, "at the time, we didn't know a fucking thing about COIN."

Jeremy went on to explain that COIN put soldiers at risk "because it made everyone timid when making decisions to pull the trigger out for fear of making the wrong decisions, due to the new restraints." Platoon leaders, especially, were always afraid of getting into trouble for ordering their soldiers to engage. He gave the example of the EOF incident with the handicapped Afghanistan man in January 2010. In Jeremy's view, the lieutenant made the right decision to shoot the man because "he went through the entire EOF procedure, from yelling and giving warning shots to finally ordering the platoon to shoot him." But, Jeremy added, the company commander thought that was the wrong decision, and the lieutenant was eventually relieved of his command. Sergeant Gibbs convinced everybody to be ready for such situations by always having drop weapons at hand. In Jeremy's words, "everybody knew about the drop weapons." He emphasized that *the killing scenarios started with the idea of the drop weapons*. Once the soldiers realized that they could make any killing (lawful or not) seem legitimate by planting a drop weapon in "questionable" kills, it was a short step to cross into Gibbs's kill "scenarios" in which killings were deliberately staged to seem legitimate. Again, there was a group dynamic at work here which was conjoined with Gibbs's concept of the "scenario," which in turn emerges out of the "scenarios" Hellraiser used as training aids.

I asked Jeremy to tell me more about the Old School approach. He said that all the brigade infantry soldiers went through "conditioning" for two years prior to deployment. The conditioning involved lectures on not hesitating to shoot and not feeling guilty for killing. "It started at basic training. Within days, sergeants at Ft. Benning would bring out their photographs, which looked just like the ones we were in, and told us their stories." The purpose of the stories was to desensitize the soldiers to killing. He spoke of daily "muscle memory drills" which consisted of pointing loaded as well as unloaded weapons at targets. "Over and over again, we'd hear: Ready, up, aim, pull the trigger, body, body, head. I'll never forget those words: body, body, head. Two to the chest, and one to the head." The purpose of these drills was to condition the brain and the body to kill without thinking or hesitation. As an aside, I should add that I know that ever since the publication of S.L.A. Marshall's World War II study, *Men Against Fire* (1947), the army has been trying relentlessly to turn soldiers into killing machines. Marshall found that in battle, only 20% of a military unit actually open fire, while the remaining 80% freeze. Such a low ratio of soldiers firing their weapons is inefficient by modern standards, so that Jeremy's account seemed to be in line with my reading and research into the army's goal to make as close to 100% of the soldiers open fire as possible.

The de-sensitization of US soldiers to killing and de-humanization of "terrorists" by commanders in lectures was relentless. I mentioned Operation Iron Triangle and Colonel Michael Steele's ROE to kill every military-age Iraqi male on sight. Jeremy said that Colonel Steele gave a motivational speech on killing to Stryker brigade. (This was confirmed in my interview with LTC C.) The title of the speech was "Warrior's Paradise," and after the speech, Colonel Tunnell issued a memorandum to the entire brigade entitled, "Afghanistan: Warrior's Paradise." Jeremy added that Steele handed out "coins" during his visit. He explained that it was an old tradition in the army that soldiers would collect coins from high-ranking officers, and when they went to bars, the soldier with the highest-ranking officer's coin would get his drink free. Further conversation revealed that David Grossman's book, *On Killing*, was used to de-sensitize soldiers to killing in Hellraiser's brigade just like it was used for the same purpose in Steele's brigade.

"Who was not Old School in the brigade?" I asked. He was not sure, because he hardly ever saw his battalion commander. But he was sure that 1-17 had the reputation for being Old School while Jeremy's battalion did not. Jeremy's platoon was most certainly not Old School until Gibbs showed up, and Jeremy described Gibbs as Old School. He described questionable kills by soldiers in 1-17 long before the chaplain would later confirm this fact for me. Jeremy's point was that "everybody" admired and was envious of 1-17 for their reputation of "getting kills." Jeremy also mentioned an incident by the other infantry platoon in A-Troop which shot and killed a 13-year-old boy after an IED went off. Jeremy said that his platoon made the visit to the village in which that killing took place, to pay the father and drop off school supplies. No one investigated the incident. Jeremy also described a mission into Arghandab Valley in which his company was "on loan" to 1-17, and how everyone in his company was thrilled to be doing counter-guerrilla with 1-17, at least temporarily.

Jeremy spoke about "questionable" kills by 1-17. Again, he said that "everybody" heard rumors that 1-17 committed murders, and this was especially true for Bravo Company 1-17, the so-called "murder company." "They were shooting farmers at night," he said. Why? "I don't know. I guess they were told that anyone seen with a shovel after dark was a terrorist." We have seen that the Twitty report makes numerous references to questionable kills by 1-17. And during my examination of the photographs in the Ft. Lewis CID office, I did see numerous photographs of what appeared to be dead Afghan farmers, not terrorists. I also saw members of 1-17 proudly posing with their kills. None of this information about 1-17, which could be pieced together from the Twitty report and the photographs, was ever investigated or charged. But it clearly created an aggressive climate which permeated the ranks of the enlisted men, even if the officers in charge were mostly oblivious to it.

Jeremy described in detail how the word "counter-guerrilla" was stamped on pistols, guidons, memorandums, coins, and other objects. He associated counter-guerrilla with the Old School approach, and did not know how to reconcile it with the references to COIN. We have seen in the Twitty report that commissioned officers were equally if not more confused.

In Jeremy's view, the infantry man's entire existence feels like a never-ending series of tests. The phrases he used to describe these tests were: Are you man enough? Are you tough enough? Can you pull the trigger? Can you kill? Can you survive? He described a daily life of pressure of "having to kill or risk being killed." He added: "It's impossible not to surrender to the insanity of it all."

Getting the Names, Squads, and Units Straight

I asked Jeremy to draw a chart for me that would explain the confusing array of military units in Hellraiser's brigade, and to pinpoint his location and those of his platoon within this large social group. Perhaps this exercise will be helpful to the reader as well. Colonel Tunnell was commander of 5th Brigade, 2nd Infantry Division, abbreviated as 5/2 SBCT or Stryker Brigade Combat Team. This brigade was comprised of 3 infantry battalions and 3 support battalions. The three infantry battalions were 2-1, 4-23, and 1-17. The three support battalions were 8-1, 2-17, and the 402nd Brigade Support Battalion. On paper, Jeremy was in 2-1, formally known as 2nd Battalion, 1st Infantry Regiment. There were four companies within 2-1: A, B, C, and headquarters. On paper, Jeremy was in B Company, which in turn was comprised of four platoons: 1st, 2nd, 3rd, and headquarters. In practice, Jeremy was in Alpha Troop, because of the confusing phenomenon of cross-leveling. Jeremy was in 3rd platoon, which was comprised of four squads: 1st, 2nd, 3rd, and 4th. Jeremy was a team leader in 2nd squad. The four squad leaders in Jeremy's platoon were, respectively, Staff Sergeants Gibbs, Sprague, Bram, and Lee.

The soldiers in 1st squad under the leadership of Sergeant Gibbs were Skinner, Jones, Hefner, Winfield, Ashton Moore, Stoner, and Wagnon. Three members of this squad were involved in some way in the killings under discussion here, namely, Gibbs, Wagnon, and Winfield. Sergeant Sprague was the squad leader of 2nd squad, which consisted of Morlock, Croswell, Perrin, Cicora, Holmes, and Mallet. Morlock and Holmes were the two members from this squad who were involved in the killings. 3rd squad was led by Sergeant Bram, and consisted of Johnston, Quintal, Knapp, Rodriguez, Watkins, and Christy. Bram was charged with some aspects of the killings, but not with murder. Finally, 4th squad was led by Sergeant Lee, and consisted of Corey Moore, Kelly, Willis, Lacroy, Ramer, and Loera. It is important to note that the so-called kill team came from three separate squads in 3rd platoon. It is beyond the scope of this study to review all the charges that were made against other members of this platoon, charges ranging from attempted murder to obstruction of justice, and the various outcomes of those charges. My point is that this story is not about a discrete "kill team" but about an entire platoon that had lost its way.

This neat and tidy description is helpful, but is undermined by the reality of cross-leveling. On paper, Jeremy's company commander was Captain T, but Jeremy was under the command of Captain Q, because his platoon was cross-leveled with Captain Q's Alpha troop. Tactically, Captain Q's troop was under the command of LTC B, but on paper, Captain Q was under the command of COL A and 8-1. In Jeremy's words: "We didn't know which chain of command we were in. We didn't know where our loyalty was." In sworn statements and legal documents, Jeremy is sometimes referred to as being a member of 2-1 and sometimes of

8-1. If this state of affairs seems confusing to the reader, the reason is that it is confusing.

Jeremy explained a profound irony in the consequences of this mind-numbing cross-leveling. It is that Jeremy's former company commander, Captain T, went on to do COIN to such a great extent that he received a letter of commendation from General Petraeus for his COIN work. On the other hand, under the new command of Captain Q, who had worked on Hellraiser's brigade staff, Jeremy's platoon ended up committing war crimes. An additional level of irony is that Captain T invented the company motto, "There is no hunting like the hunting of men"—yet ended up doing COIN with gusto. But Captain Q, whose previous commander was committed to doing COIN, ended up commanding a company that committed war crimes.

OTHER ISSUES

It is impossible to summarize sixteen hours of interviews in this limited space. But it is important to note that Jeremy spoke about other topics that were of intense emotional interest to him: his father, his family, and the coming birth of his daughter (she would be born in December of 2010). Tears came to his eyes as he described wanting to be like his father, who was an army veteran. His father died in a tragic boat accident two years after Jeremy had joined the army. It was clear that his father's death impacted him. It is significant that the cross-leveling and deployment occurred after his father's death such that he was denied guidance from a stable, consistent father-figure in the army at a time when he needed it most. He was lost and forlorn in the army. He spoke affectionately and with excitement about the coming birth of his child. Again, and typically (with regard to convicted soldiers), the mother of their child took legal action to deny him visitation rights and to sever all connections. When Jeremy Morlock's life-story is perceived in a non-legal context, it is the story of a young man from Wasilla, Alaska who was close to his family and idealized his father, thrown into social circumstances which may be described as chaotic, disorganized, and anomic.

CORPORAL MORLOCK'S ARTICLE 32 HEARING

The investigating officer (IO) for the hearing was Colonel Thomas Molloy. The prosecutor was Captain Andre LeBlanc, and he was assisted by two additional prosecutors, Captain Daniel Hill and Captain John D. Riesenberg. (I remembered Riesenberg as the assistant trial counsel in Michael Leahy's court-martial the year before.) The defense counsel were attorneys X and Y, and Captain Opachan. The hearing was called into session at 9:44 a.m. on September 27, 2010. (It was scheduled for 8 am, but delayed because Attorney Y was detained at the visitor's center and had difficulty getting on base.) This was the day following our last interview with Jeremy at the navy brig. The IO "informed the accused that he watched DVD interviews taken by CID and provided to all parties by the government." Then the IO accepted the intention of all the soldiers in Jeremy's platoon to remain silent by invoking their 5th Amendment rights. The first witness was special agent Andy Wagner of the 262nd Military Police Detachment, CID, Kandahar Airfield, Afghanistan. His testimony was that PFC Stoner informed CID that he had been assaulted by his platoon, and referred to the EOF incident in which a handicapped Afghan man was shot to death by the platoon. Wagner continued:

> We had information that an incident about an Escalation of Force incident about an individual that was shot by members of his [Stoner's] platoon.... Stoner wasn't sure, in his mind, if it was a legitimate shoot, but most of our investigation had revealed that proper EOF procedures had been used. He had mentioned that CPL Morlock was involved in some shady circumstances around killing Afghans. That was the extent of the information we had. CPL Morlock was interviewed on the 11th of May. He was here on Kandahar, on his way to Landstuhl to be medically evaluated. We found out he was here on this base, and I was able to coordinate with the unit, track him down and have him brought into the CID office on the 11th of May. I did not initially interact with him, he was advised of his rights by SA Camero, he talked to him one on one for some time, and he told me CPL Morlock had information that he wanted to tell CID but he was afraid for his own safety. He was not revealing any information about any murders... CPL Morlock was afraid of something. When SA Camero and I talked to Morlock, we found that he was afraid of repercussions by Gibbs. He proceeded to tell us of two incidents that he was involved in... After realizing what we were dealing with, and CPL Morlock basically told us he was involved in two murders of local Afghans, we decided the best thing was to record that portion of the interview.... Morlock was very articulate and made eye contact. He was able to recount events that happened several months ago. He was not stumbling; he was not slurring his words. Morlock did not display any symptoms that would have led me to believe that he was under the influence of anything.... CPL Morlock was very cooperative, and the interviews were non confrontational.

During the cross-examination by defense attorney X, special agent Wagner admitted the following: "I was told he [Morlock] suffered concussions from various explosions." Furthermore, Wagner said "I knew this before we interrogated him. I'm sure CID works with numerous people who suffer from brain damage and traumatic brain injury." In addition, Wagner admitted: "I knew that CPL Morlock was taking medication at the time, in the video he said he was on Ibuprofen, flexeril, trazodone, phenergan, a nausea pill, and sleeping aids. I assume it was Ambien.... It might be that special agent Camero took CPL Morlock back to his housing unit to take more pills." Apparently, to the law, none of these admissions meant that Jeremy was coerced into making the videotaped statement. Wagner insisted that "it is not true that he [Morlock] could barely sit up in the chair"—the interested viewer may turn to the video and judge for his or her self. Wagner said, "We don't interview witnesses who are under the influence"—but he did not believe that Jeremy was "under the influence."

Wagner continued: "I wasn't present for the advising of his [Morlock's] rights, and had no indication from SA Camero or CPL Morlock that he requested an attorney." It was Jeremy's word against the CID agents on this point, and apparently, no one bothered to investigate whether Jeremy had in fact made that phone call to Bagram and had requested an attorney. Wagner also admitted: "There is no physical, forensic, or scientific evidence proving that Morlock killed that individual. Morlock's testimony was corroborated by Winfield.... We have only what CPL Morlock told us." It is important to note that to the law, a confession is considered a stronger form of evidence than physical, forensic, or scientific evidence. In fact, none of the subsequent courts-martial of any of the soldiers conclusively proved whose gun, whose bullets, or whose grenades killed whom. And this lack of scientific facts did not matter, and did not prevent convictions. Wagner concluded: "We knew Morlock was on multiple medications and we interrogated him none the less. He looked fine."

Special agent Shannon Richey, of the same CID detachment in Kandahar, testified next. Richey interviewed Jeremy on May 13, 2010 and claimed: "I do not remember having a conversation with Morlock about him incriminating himself or asking for a lawyer. I did not say, 'Don't worry, we're not after you, we're only after Gibbs.' The interview was not recorded." It is convenient that the only portions of Jeremy's several interrogations with CID agents were those in which he incriminated himself, but none of the pre-interview portions were recorded. Jeremy was interrogated on May 11, 13, and 15. He said he called trial defense services at Bagram airfield in Afghanistan immediately following the videotaped statement, but believed that he was not being charged, and therefore waived his rights at the two subsequent interrogations. Soldiers do not understand that when they sign a waiver which states that they are "suspects," they are, in effect, being charged. Again, it was Jeremy's word against the agents on the issue of whether he requested an attorney.

The defense called to the stand an expert witness in toxicology, Dr. David M. Benjamin. Dr. Benjamin's testimony started strong, but fizzled out when he admitted under cross-examination that he had not interviewed Jeremy, had not seen the videotaped statement, and had no way of confirming which drugs (including prescribed medications) Jeremy was taking at what point in time. Dr. Benjamin testified:

> I am a clinical pharmacologist and toxicologist... The defense list of medications provided to me was: ambient, amitriptyline, flexeril, phenergan, Benadryl, trazodone, prazosin, T3 with Codeine, Isometh, Doxycycline, Robaxin, Rizatriptan, Hashish, and Opium... The Hashish in Afghanistan is some of the most potent Hashish ever encountered. It can be 40-50% THC, as opposed to a normal joint being 1.5-3% THC; so it can be up to ten times as concentrated, and can produce psychosis. Many of the medications Morlock was on can cause behavior disorders... These are all psychoactive drugs and can impair an individual's ability to make proper judgment. I recommend to patients who are on these types of medications not to operate machinery... There is no way to link up when Morlock was taking these medications... I do not have a toxicological screen showing what drugs were in his blood at any given time... The accused's statements appeared lucid and coherent to me. There was no indication that any medications impaired his ability during the interviews. I did not review the video made on 11 May, I don't know if it was available to watch.. I did not speak with anyone who saw Morlock during the time of suspected impairments... I have not interviewed Morlock.

My crew and I were baffled as to why we were able to interview Jeremy for sixteen hours while the toxicologist did not interview him at all. We could not understand how the expert could contradict himself by claiming that all those drugs impaired judgment and affected the central nervous system—yet claim that Jeremy appeared coherent even though the toxicologist had not seen the videotaped statement.

Special agent Nicole Fermanis testified that she interviewed Morlock on yet another occasion, on the 15th of May. She said that he did not request a lawyer. Her testimony was brief and did not seem to contribute anything substantial to the testimony. Special agent Israel Camero—who is one of the two special agents interrogating Morlock in the videotape—testified:

> I didn't suspect Morlock of anything when I first brought him in, I just wanted him to corroborate some of the details I got from PFC Stoner. I was interviewing him to see what he knew. I knew there was questionable killing, but there was nothing concrete. I advised him of his rights as soon as I brought him in [and] I advised him for Murder... We discussed his state of mind in the interview and video interview and went over his medications. He told us he was prescribed a wide array of medications. During the interview he told us he was on mild muscle relaxers. He took flexeril while he was at the CID office. If Morlock had asked to speak to an attorney we would have given him an opportunity to do so. I did not say that it would be a waste of time for Morlock to talk to an attorney or call TDS [Trial Defense Services]. Once an individual begins talking and

confessing, they tend to put their head down, open up, start leaning, like they are getting a lot of stress and tension off their chest. I don't think he was having trouble controlling his bodily movements.... We would have stopped the interview if Morlock had asked for an attorney. We made the video recording of Morlock after the paper interview....There was no TDS on Kandahar at the time of the interview, but there is a legal office and there is a TDS in Bagram. If someone asked me if I thought they needed a lawyer, I would tell them that it is their choice and up to them.

If Camero did not see Jeremy as a suspect, then why did he advise him of his rights for the crime of murder? There is no logical answer to this question. The more important point is that Camero's testimony is typical, predictable, legal double-speak used by interrogators to rationalize why they detain persons whom they claim they do not suspect of a crime. I have witnessed similar testimony by special agents over the course of several courts-martial. In my experience, it is also typical for IO's and military judges to accept the statements obtained through trickery and deceit, presumably because the interrogators were following "techniques" which call for trickery and deceit. Why did a major US military base such as Kandahar not have a trial defense office? How could the military assume that having a trial defense office at only one base (Bagram) in all of Afghanistan was sufficient for its thousands of soldiers? How thinly stretched were the military attorneys in Afghanistan? These are some of the sociological issues that emerge out of Camero's testimony. As for the rest of his testimony, it is the same pattern of a law enforcement official's word against the word of the accused. To quote a popular song, "I fought the law, and the law won."

Jeremy's most recent platoon leader (for 3rd platoon, Bravo Company, 2-1) took the stand. LT Stephan Moye testified that he took over the platoon on March 20, 2010 and that he replaced LT Ligsay. Moye's testimony is rich with insights, contradictions, and descriptions. For example, one learns from him that *all* the soldiers are required to take photos of dead bodies with their personal cameras despite the fact that such photography is simultaneously forbidden and required. It is required for the "story board" which LT Moye defined as "a description of the events that take place, it includes date, time, group; where you went, what your mission was; task and purpose and it lays out by time what happens along each step and it has pictures and diagrams." Moye added: "I am aware that General Oder 1 does not allow people to take pictures of bodies on battlefields. We have them [soldiers] use their cameras to take pictures and we use the pictures for their intended purpose then get rid of the pictures once I am done." There is a general pattern here: from Abu Ghraib to all the other war crimes cases on which I have worked, the army requires soldiers to take photos at the same time that it prohibits them from taking photos. Nobody seems to take this contradiction seriously, and it has not been remedied since the war began in Afghanistan. Moreover, the government prosecutes some soldiers for taking the photos, even for the very same photos that are used for the official purpose of "story boards."

As an aside, I will note here that the issue of soldiers routinely taking photographs of bloody, mangled corpses opens many doors other than the one to the legality of taking such photos. Does it not occur to the military that exposure to corpses, in itself, contributes to PTSD? I have observed that in all the cases on which I have worked, soldiers were routinely expected not only to photograph corpses, but to collect decapitated heads and body parts in clean up operations. I will also confess here that when I viewed the photographs of dead bodies in the Maywand District killings case, I felt nauseous, and had to turn away.

Moye also stated that "we did not do any urinalysis tests prior to the allegations being made." Let us take careful note of this contradiction: the army prosecutes illegal drug use as a crime, but failed to perform *any* drug testing at all during the entire deployment in order to prevent this crime! Moye also testified that he never once suspected any of his soldiers as smoking hashish. (My crew and I found this surprising, given that the housing units were all in one area, that soldiers smoked hashish in this area, and that hashish has a distinctive odor.) Moye opened the door to yet another contradiction: "I was attached to a CAV [cavalry] unit, so I had two company commanders." Jeremy was in the same position as LT Moye vis-à-vis cross-leveling. This is what cross-leveling feels like to an individual, as if they had two (or more) commanders and chains of command. But in theory, one is supposed to be responsible to only one commander in one chain of command.

Moye also testified that the incident of May 2nd (which would later be charged as murder) took place in a village in Afghanistan that "wasn't even on the map." He was present for the killing that would later be charged as murder, but did not realize it was murder at the time. Instead, from his point of view, the incident was yet another story board he submitted: "The story board was submitted to higher operations, the document is secret and I cannot keep them. There are digital photos of the deceased on the story board." Let us note that the news media interpreted some of the leaked photos of this incident as proof that soldiers took the photos out of some sadistic motives. In fact, it seems that the photos were a routine part of the story board process. Moye testified: "The story we wanted to provide was that he [the Afghan national] threw a grenade at us.... I did not suspect any US soldiers of wrong doing at the time... I don't see why it wouldn't be believable that he [Afghan national] would come out of the house and throw grenades at soldiers."

The hearing was closed at 5:50 pm on September 27, 2010. A few weeks later, the IO would formally recommend that all the charges against Morlock should be referred to a general court-martial. Because Attorneys X and Y never disclosed their strategy to me at any time, I am not in a position to assess the *meaning* of this hearing from the perspective of what the defense attorneys were trying to achieve.

CONCLUSIONS

From a legal point of view, Morlock's fate was sealed with his video-taped statement. A confession is the highest form of proof known to law, so that all other considerations faded into the background. This includes scientific, factual, or forensic accounts of what truly happened—these issues were never resolved at any of the courts-martial. Had Morlock's defense attorneys gambled on using his drug use and TBI as defenses for the crimes at issue or the coerced videotaped statement, the government would have withdrawn the offer a plea-bargain, and he would have been facing a minimum, mandatory sentence of life imprisonment if convicted. I read in the CID notes (which were a part of discovery) that investigators ordered a full medical examination of Gibbs prior to his interview (he invoked his 5th amendment rights) but deliberately chose not to refer Morlock to a medical doctor prior to his interrogation. In the subsequent plea-bargain, Morlock was forced to sign away as legal defenses a host of factors that are normally considered as mitigating: Traumatic Brain Injury, PTSD, duress, drug use, sleep deprivation and all other defenses except command climate. By the time Spinner got the case, his options for defending Morlock were limited. Spinner did have a strategy, and he shared it with his defense team. We shall see in subsequent chapters how his defense strategy played out in the court room.

Let us set aside the legal social structure and examine the rest of the social structure. Morlock's descriptions of the chaotic, dehumanizing, and disorganized social climate in which he lived and worked is consistent in every way with the sworn statements in the Twitty report. The Twitty report confirms every claim he made, from rampant drug use in his platoon and lack of urinalysis testing to the cross-leveling and failure to mentor and counsel soldiers—among hundreds of other facts. At the time I interviewed him, neither Morlock nor I knew of the contents in the Twitty report.

Chapter 9. The Army's CID Investigation

CID investigators in Afghanistan conducted their inquiries between May and September of 2010. General Scaparrotti instructed General Twitty to begin his AR 15-6 investigation in October of 2010. The CID agents assigned to investigating the Maywand District killings had no access to the vast information on the dysfunctional social climate which we have covered by now. Even if they could have conceived the basic idea that a poisoned command climate plays some role in war crimes, there is no criminological or legal framework in existence for them to express or receive such ideas. The criminal investigator and the law focus solely upon connecting an individual with a crime. In other words, the entire, modern legal edifice is built upon the connection, crime-to-individual, and does not have access to the vocabularies of bad groups, platoons, companies, and brigades. This was not always the case: traditional societies were automatic in connecting criminal responsibility to groups, communities, villages, even nations, when punishing an individual—and entire groups were punished (Fauconnet, 1928). It is beyond the scope of this study to examine the consequences of this chasm between traditional notions of group responsibility and modern notions of solely individual responsibility. Nevertheless, it is important to keep it in mind.

In this chapter, we shall examine some of the raw evidence CID investigators had available to them, in contrast to the polished and prepared testimony they offered at Article 32 hearings. Investigators had enough evidence immediately to notice that at least an entire platoon was involved in the killings to some degree. It was obvious, even to them, that the problem in this case was an entire platoon, and its relationship to the entire brigade. Their typically modernist response was to charge as many separate individuals within the platoon as they could, and to wait and see what charges would "stick" to particular individuals. They selected certain individuals for prosecution while they declined to pursue other individuals who were also connected to the crimes. Sociologists refer to this process as the social construction of reality. Investigators refer to this process as simply following the evidence. In fact, there is nothing obvious about the process of connecting or charging anyone with a crime, even in cases where they seem to be caught "red-handed" or confess.

The CID investigation followed a path of inquiry that is the direct opposite of our line of inquiry in this book: They began with an individual soldier's statement, and did not take into account the social context for the crimes, nor the direct allusions to social climates and command structures in their investigations of individuals. We began this inquiry with the social context, and moved the inquiry down the ladder of social groups to the individual in question. In the case of war crimes, this means starting an investigation with the brigade social climate, and moving down sequentially to the battalion, company, and platoon levels of analysis. Finally, we reach the individual in social context. The consequences of these two opposite ways of approaching and inquiring into crime, as well as assessing responsibility are enormous. The typical, modernist criminal investigator will affix responsibility for war crimes (or any other crimes) onto a particular individual or several distinct individuals. This modern trend basically reduces the idea of responsibility to a vanishing point. In every war crimes case in the current war, low-ranking soldiers have been sent to prison, while the colonels, generals, and other high-ranking officers who created the social climates which precipitated the crimes received written reprimands at worst, or no punishment at all. Beyond noting it, I shall not dwell on this obvious point. This is because it leads into philosophical, theological, sociological and other discussions of the idea of responsibility—and especially the concept of command responsibility. Such discussions are clearly beyond the scope of this study. Instead, I shall review the criminal investigation as it really took place, and point out its inadequacies.

The army first suspected that something was wrong when Private First Class Justin Stoner went to CID on May 9, 2010 to sign a sworn statement that he had been beaten up severely by most of the members of his platoon and some other soldiers as well as non-commissioned officers in B Company, 2-1. Soldiers Morlock, Gibbs, Bram, Quintal, Moore, Jones, and Kelly (among others) were involved in some fashion in the assault on Stoner. Stoner wrote in his sworn statement: "All these individuals then proceeded to beat the hell out of me." They beat him up as a warning and as revenge for "ratting" on them about their habitual drug use. In a second sworn statement, made on May 10, 2010, Stoner told the investigators other things that went beyond the investigation of the use of hashish: that Gibbs showed him severed fingers in order to intimidate him, and that AK-47 magazines and rifles were used to "plant" false evidence on questionable kills. One of the last questions a CID agent asked Stoner was, "Has anyone ever mentioned anything about shooting unarmed locals?" Stoner answered: "PFC Holmes said shit happens but he doesn't go into detail on how it happened, but everything is questionable." One should keep in mind Stoner's exact words: "Everything is questionable."

On the 12th of May, Stoner made another sworn statement, in which he wrote: "The reason that I am worried or felt the need to say something is because *the platoon* has a reputation of going out and finding the right person and finding the means to kill them without reason" (emphasis added). At this early stage in the investigation, Stoner told the investigators that an entire platoon that was out of control, not about particular individuals. The investigators quoted Stoner, but did not absorb the import of what he said to them about the bad platoon. Let us look closely at the CID interview of Stoner concerning the EOF incident (which we have discussed several times):

Q: In January when you were out on mission and the local was shot were all the guys from the inner circle there?

A: Yes, they were not all dismounted but they were all present on the patrol.

Q: Who was in charge of the mission?

A: The LT.

Q: What was the mission?

A: I don't remember what the specifics were.

Q: Was the local national armed?

A: No.

Q: After he was shot, whose idea was it to plant an AK-47 magazine on him?

A: I don't know who specifically it was but the magazine was in 3rd Squad's truck.

Q: Did the incident get reported up the chain of command?

A: I know the commander and 1SG knew about it, but they weren't there with us, they didn't see it....

Q: Can you fully identify the LT that was out in the mission?
A: 1LT Ligsay...

Q: Did he request the AK-47 magazine be planted on the local?

A: No.

Q: Did he go along with planting the magazine?

A: Yes.

Q: Have you been present for any other killings that were staged?

A: No.

Let us review what investigators knew early on: Stoner had already quoted Holmes that *all* the killings seemed equally questionable to the soldiers. They concluded that there was an "inner circle" of soldiers involved in some killings, namely, Gibbs, Morlock, Jones, and Bram. They later added Winfield, Holmes, and Wagnon to the inner circle. But they also knew there were other "circles" of indirect or passive involvement, which included LT L, and that Stevens and Gibbs were both from Hellraiser's security detail. They could have known, had they investigated, that the company commander (CPT Q) was connected to Hellraiser and to COL A. The killing of the handicapped Afghan man was not part of the "inner circle" killings at all, and was not charged as murder, despite the fact that Stoner focused on this incident more than any other. On the one hand, this should have tipped off CID investigators that something was terribly wrong for commanders to "go along" with the planting of false evidence to cover-up a "questionable" kill. On the other hand, investigators do not habitually go after lieutenants and captains or other commanders. Stoner made himself seem irrelevant to the investigators from the moment he told them that he was not present for the "inner circle" killings which were staged. The investigators were at a crossroads: pursue the commanders and the many overlapping "circles" of responsibility, or find someone from the fictitious "inner circle" who was present for the staged killings.

This dilemma was resolved conveniently for CID by the simple fact that Morlock was present at Kandahar Airfield, awaiting a medical evacuation to the United States for his brain injuries due to concussions. On May 13, 2010, Morlock signed another sworn statement in Kandahar. He described the staged "scenarios" which squad leader Gibbs was talking about over the course of several months. One should pay attention to Morlock's exact choice of words: "Initially, Gibbs told *everyone* about this scenario, by pitching it by saying that all these Afghanis were savages, and we had just lost one of our squad leaders because his legs got blown off by an IED" (emphasis added). We shall not analyze the reference to "everyone" in philosophical terms, which is an overly-inclusive term. The more important point is that most of the soldiers interviewed by CID referred to "everyone," by which they clearly meant that more than a handful of "inner circle" soldiers were involved. What should have been clear to CID from the outset was that these crimes were not the result of a handful of individuals acting secretly or alone. This was the false, television model of crime—namely, a crazed individual committing a heinous crime in an idyllic, peaceful setting—that CID was following, in defiance of the facts that were staring them in the face. Layers of circles were involved, from the platoon to company and battalion levels, all of which intersected with other platoons, companies, and battalions, and ultimately connected to Hellraiser's lethal philosophy of strike and destroy. For example, Stoner told the investigators that "Gibbs had pure hatred for all Afghanis and constantly referred to them as savages." Was Gibbs's attitude fundamentally different from Hellraiser's philosophy, which was motivated by revenge against all Afghanis and Iraqis, and viewed all of them as potential insurgents who had to be dealt with lethally?

Morlock told the investigators that Gibbs had carried out similar scenarios in a previous tour in Iraq: "While he was crossing the road as a SAW [squad automatic weapon] gunner, he turned around and sprayed down the vehicle. He told his chain of command that the vehicle never stopped, and that's why he fired on them." It would be important to know how many similar incidents occurred at checkpoints in Iraq and Afghanistan through the entire course of the present wars, with the similar explanation, that the vehicle failed to stop. This data, which is unavailable, would be important in establishing a social context for Gibbs's scenarios. I have come across numerous accounts of such killings from my work in other war crime cases. An investigator asked Morlock: "How many other scenarios did Gibbs discuss with the platoon?" Morlock replied: "They weren't all at one time. He would bring them up as he got props." How did CID manage to fail to notice that Morlock was discussing the involvement of an entire *platoon*, not just a handful of soldiers? And there were many scenarios, not all of which were acted out. An investigator asked: "How many scenarios that Gibbs had created were actually completed?" Morlock answered: "There were the three scenarios that I was aware of and then I had heard of a couple more that Gibbs had tried while I was on leave back to the states."

In a sworn statement dated May 11, 2010, Staff Sergeant Lee reports several incidents in which Sergeant Gibbs shot dogs at random in various Afghan villages. "Everyone" in the platoon knew about the shootings of animals, Lee claimed. On June 1, 2010, Corporal Emmitt Quintal made a sworn statement concerning the several thousand photographs that were taken by platoon members. One line that stands out is the one in which Quintal states that the photographs "were loaded on everyone's computers and hard drives." Again, it would be absurd to enumerate the individuals who comprised the group of "everyone." The important point is that CID had clues from the outset that at least the entire platoon, and possibly other platoons, had the "inside dope" on what was happening, from the shootings to the drug use and photography. Quintal told investigators:

> We went on a couple of serious missions and we all realized how stressful and how mind boggling combat is especially here. After that we went on

a huge, I guess it was, the brigade operation in the Arghandab River Valley. While there we all received small arms contact and witnessed several IED explosions. In that time frame was where the drugs were presented to us and how vulnerable our state was to the stress of being in a combat situation....

Q: OK, and can you tell me the names of the platoon members that were using hashish?

A: Yeah. A lot of people. Myself, Specialist Knapp, Specialist Winfield, Specialist Moore, Specialist Kelly, Sergeant Johnston, Sergeant Watkins, Private Lecroy, Private Willis, Private Rodriguez, Private Stoner, let's see who else, Specialist Pellegrin, Specialist Ciciora, Corporal Morlock.

Knapp committed suicide shortly after returning to Ft. Lewis. Moore and Kelly were sentenced to six months of hard labor. Johnston, Watkins, Rodriguez, Pellegrin, Stoner, and Ciciora were never charged with drug use. Winfield, Lecroy, Willis, and Morlock were charged with drug use. It is also interesting that investigators concluded that Stoner, who reported drug use by other soldiers, also used drugs—but did not charge Stoner. For the sake of context, we shall note that the drug use started after units in the brigade were ordered into the Arghandab River Valley by Hellraiser—in the eyes of some, but not all, subordinate commanders this order violated COIN doctrine. The brigade was supposed to be meeting with villagers and winning their hearts and minds, not chasing invisible or non-existent Taliban in the unpopulated river valley. In a way (but not in any legal or criminal sense), Hellraiser drove this platoon, and other platoons, to illegal drug use. (While 1-17 was the most active battalion in the Arghandab Valley, Morlock's platoon also conducted missions there.) The stress of being exposed to the possibility of death at the hands of an unseen enemy was overwhelming, and the hashish was readily available. The average person can grasp the explanation that the soldiers were self-medicating by using hashish. This social context for the drug use did not make any difference to the CID investigators or the prosecutors. According to the letter of the law, drug use is always equally unlawful, whether it takes place in the comfortable setting of Seattle or the helplessness-inducing context of "Death Valley" in Afghanistan.

"How frequent was the drug use?" Quintal replied: "Bad days, stressful days, days we just needed an escape." The CID agent asked: "How frequent was that?" Quintal answered: "I'd say probably anywhere from three to four—every three to four days."

Turning to the issue of the AK-47 rifles and parts that were always available to be planted on the bodies of Afghans, Quintal said: "I didn't ask questions." The interrogation continued:

Q: Did you tell anybody about the AK-47 and the magazines?

A: I approached my squad leader about it, Staff Sergeant Bram. And he sat me down and he explained to me that it was basically to cover our ass if anything had happened that was an accident so that's pretty much how he explained it to me. I understood and I agreed with that, to *cover the platoon's ass* [emphasis added].

Quintal did not say that the drop-weapons which were used for covering-up questionable kills were kept on behalf of any particular individual or group of individuals. He stated clearly that the drop-weapons existed as cover for the entire platoon. In a real sense, even if not in a strictly legal sense, the entire platoon took part in a *conspiracy* to make any killing seem to fit a legitimate "scenario." Quintal did not participate in any of the killings which were charged as murders. But like all the other platoon members, he did participate—even if indirectly—in covering up all killings. We turn to his explanation of the killing of the handicapped Afghan male which was not charged as murder (the EOF incident), paying particular attention to the subsequent cover-up:

A: We were driving down Highway One and our platoon leader, LT L, at the time seen a guy hunched over kind of on a small hill over watching the highway. He found it to be suspicious. I'm a vehicle commander so I'm stationary in the truck but most of the dismounts in my vehicle, which was third squad, dismounted and I was aware that first squad dismounted as well with the PL. They approached this suspicious individual, they did the proper EOF. I was outside the hatch watching. They did lasers, warning shots, they screamed verbally, they tried everything they could. This man was wearing baggy clothes, he kept approaching the element on the ground. They did a warning shot. They were screaming "Waderega" which is to "stop" in Pashtu. The man wouldn't stop and they engaged this man. An hour or two after the incident I know LT L was pretty stressed out. He was pretty positive that he was going to lose his job at that point. And everybody was getting very stressed out and just tired cause they had us searching and searching trying to find something.

Q; What were they trying to find?

A: Any kind of evidence to prove this man was a bad guy. That we didn't wrongfully kill him. At that point, I don't remember exactly what happened. I was aware of the AK-47 and the magazines in the Stryker and I was either told or Private Stoner was either told to receive a magazine, give it to one of the dismounts and that we did, and that was the last I heard of that. I have seen pictures of a magazine taken in that same time but the weapon was not used, just a magazine.

Q: Was there any kind of information floating around the platoon as to what the magazine was being used for and what the AK-47 was being used for?

A: There really wasn't any information. The magazine we all just figured that it was *for what we planned to use it for, was to cover our ass [emphasis added]*.

The CID agent asked about the arrival of Sergeant Gibbs as a squad leader in December of 2009. Quintal said: "One thing I did notice that before Staff Sergeant Gibbs came into the platoon that there had been no BDA's, no dead guys, nothing of that sort."

Q: What's a BDA?

A: A Battle Damage Assessment. It's when you screw, not screw something up but when anything happens on a combat field you have to go assess the damage of enemy KIA, and anything like that.

Q: Prior to him [Gibbs] arriving to the platoon did you have any KIA's in the platoon?

A: No

Q: Any enemy KIA?

A: No

Q: OK. And since Sergeant Gibbs came onboard, how many have you had in your experience alone?

A: In just my experience I would say three.

Q: And how many with Sergeant Gibbs involved?

A: I believe four or five.

Q: You've been told information that pretty much led you to believe that Sergeant Gibbs was doing immoral things. He was planting evidence at scenes to show that there was a justifiable reason for shooting, things like that. Who told you that information?

A: I had heard it through the grapevine hanging out with my friends, little hints, little rumors, Corporal Morlock, I heard him talking about it and I heard Specialist Winfield talk about it as well.

It seems that the CID agent was constructing the theory that Gibbs was a sort of "contagion" in the platoon: there were absolutely no killings by the platoon prior to his arrival. But was Gibbs the original contagion, or was he merely transmitting the contamination? It was clear that 3rd platoon became lethal after Gibbs's arrival, but the context for the lethal attitude must be explained. It was as if Gibbs acted the role of "typhoid Mary" for Hellraiser's lethal philosophy: Gibbs "contaminated" the platoon with Hellraiser's poisonous doctrine. On the other hand, LT L comes across as hapless, a platoon leader in name only, but in reality, at the mercy of social forces which Gibbs had unleashed. According to Quintal, LT L "strongly believed at the time that we had illegitimately killed a local national and everything was just heated, everybody was stressed and LT L seriously thought that he was going to lose his job over this." In a sense, Gibbs saved the lieutenant's job, at least temporarily, by being prepared with the drop-weapon and magazine.

Quintal could not distinguish the killings that were later charged as murders from the EOF killing. About the first killing that would later be charged as murder, Quintal said: "I heard just guys bragging about it. Private Holmes just saying you know pretty much he was a bad ass for killing a guy for nothing, nothing concrete that 'hey I staged this and got away with murder.' Nothing like that." The investigator said: "OK, back to the highway situation. You said that there was a squad of people that jumped out and they all got on line and they shot and they fired at him?" He was referring to the EOF killing, and Quintal's detailed replies are very important:

A: It wasn't actually on line. It was a wedge formation pushed out. Everybody separated when they got a hunch that it was a suicide bomber.

Q: How many feet away were they? Do you know?

A: Approximately 10 to 15 meters when they engaged the individual.

Q; They fired warning shots?

A: Yes.

Q: How many?

A: Probably 60. A lot of warning shots. About three different occasions they fired warning shots.

Q:And actual shots fired at him with the intent to harm him, how many people do you think fired?

A: I'd say at least eight or nine people engaged the individual.

Q: And how many rounds do you think were fired?

A: Probably about 40. With automatic SAWs, squad automatic weapons, and M4's.

Morlock did not participate in this killing. Let the reader try to visualize the scene: Approximately nine heavily armed soldiers confronted an unarmed, Afghan man who had his hands raised in the air. They were at most 15 meters away from him, fired 60 warning shots, and killed him with 40 rounds using some of the most lethal weapons that exist on this planet. Under these circumstances—which sound more like a scene out of some disturbing war film, such as *Apocalypse Now*—it seems inconceivable that the Afghan could have been perceived as a threat to the soldiers. It is as if some sort of collective madness overcame the platoon. And the entire platoon was involved, directly or indirectly, in this incident. On the other hand, the platoon followed the letter of the law of the EOF rules. The responsibility for the killing was diffused through the entire platoon. Because everybody was responsible, no specific individual was held to be responsible, not even the platoon leader. Despite the legality of the kill under EOF rules, the entire platoon seemed to find it questionable, as evidenced by the fact that they participated in the subsequent cover-up. The CID agent knew all this, and yet, this event would remain forever disconnected from the killings which were later charged as murders. The more important point is this: in the minds of the platoon members, was there really a difference between this killing and the killings that were charged as murders? What was the lesson the platoon learned from this and other killings? The lesson was: all killings must be covered up.

Quintal's description and explanation of the assault by the platoon on Stoner on May 5, 2010 is rich in detail. The striking thing is that most of the entire platoon took part in the assault. The special agent asked Quintal, "Did everybody take part in it?" "Yes," Quintal replied. The term, "everybody," is used frequently in the sworn statements by enlisted soldiers. Quintal added, "I kicked him twice in the calf." Quintal elaborates:

A: After that everybody eased off. I think really quick they realized that they were doing the wrong thing. They stopped and then at that point he was just asked multiple times how he could do that to our platoon [reported the drug use]. Again, Stoner couldn't answer, Specialist Kelly hovered over him, spit in his face and then everybody filed out of the room. After that, I went back to my Stryker. I continued the repairs and parked it. I came back, went in my room for a little while and then I went to Stoner and Knapp's room. I acted like I was talking to Knapp. Realistically, I was checking on Stoner. I felt really bad for what happened and I still do. Talked to Knapp for a little bit and then left the room. An hour or two went by and it was really getting to me so I went in there, Knapp was not present and I sat down and had a talk with Stoner. Basically what was discussed was, I wanted to know why he turned his back on certain individuals specifically, even the platoon. I had never done anything wrong to Stoner and there are several people in the platoon that haven't either. Just explained to him that was happened was fucked up and that everybody was going to recover from it. Little did we know at that point that it would come to this. Me and Stoner came to agreement and I left the room. Went back to my room and hung out and then a few hours went by again, I was outside smoking a cigarette and I seen Gibbs and Morlock on our side. We lived on different sides of the CHU [Container Housing Units] so I automatically knew that something was going on. They filed into Stoner's room and I followed. I felt I needed to be there in case something else was going to happen.

Q: Was anybody else present?

A: Yes. Private Lecroy followed me as well. But, yeah, I went in there to make sure that Stoner wasn't going to get beat again. And just kind of, I guess, mediate. As we went in there, Gibbs sat down casually and told Stoner that if he snitched again he would kill him. And that he has killed people before and he has no problems killing again. At that time, Gibbs had a cloth, he opened it and dropped it and three human body fingers fell on the floor—on the ground. At that point I kind of lost my head and that's really all that I could collect from that incident...We left the room and after that I knew that I wanted nothing to do with any of that. And that was that. The next morning, myself and a whole bunch of other people in the platoon watched Stoner gather all of his belongings and he left. We haven't heard or seen from Stoner since.

In the rest of the interview, CID determined that Quintal's job obligated him to stay in a Stryker most of the time. "So you wouldn't have been present during the shootings or anything else?" "No," Quintal replied. The agent asked him: "Was it pretty much understood throughout the platoon that drop guns were necessary in case mistakes were made?" Quintal answered: "I know a lot of people did know about it." Did Quintal wish to add anything to his statement that was not asked? Quintal said: "I'm scared. I'm scared for my life right now because I was told by multiple people that no matter what happened, not to tell you guys anything." Nevertheless, Quintal waived his rights to an attorney and to invoke the 5th Amendment, and answered questions posed by CID agents. On the one hand, he was following the army values of honor and integrity. On the other, he and others who "ratted" were placing their lives in danger, because it is always perilous to go against one's immediate society, be it a family or a platoon. And his sworn testimony made it very clear that the entire platoon, as well as other platoons, were involved in and knew about the killings, drug use, and drop weapons.

Statement by Specialist Adam Winfield

Winfield also waived all his rights and spoke to CID investigators on May 17, 2010. His story is particularly interesting because he told his parents about the first killing, and his father made several phone calls on or about February 14, 2010 to the Pentagon and to other government offices to report the incidents and to save his son. No one in the government took Winfield's father seriously. A CID agent asked:

Q: Why didn't SSG Gibbs trust you?

A: He thought I was going to tell. Prior to this incident SSG Gibbs fired me from my job as the vehicle commander because I left the hatch open. I was upset about that and called my parents and told them that was not fair because my squad leader murders people and gets away with it. I told them I did not tell anyone about this because I had no one I could trust and talk to, in fear that it would get back to SSG Gibbs.

Q: How did you notify your parents?

A: I called them, emailed them, and through Facebook instant messenger.

Q: Did your parents make any reports pertaining to your conversation about SSG Gibbs murdering people?

A: They said the State Senator's office, Fort Lewis, and CID.

Q: Who knew about the threats on your life?

A: PFC Moore told me that SSG Gibbs was going to kill me if I ratted him out about the murders.

The CID agent had no reaction at all to Winfield's expressed fears. He proceeded to interrogate Winfield about the several killings—some of which were lawful, and some of which were questionable—which involved his platoon as well as other platoons. Regarding one such incident, which occurred in November of 2009, and which involved a platoon other than his own, Winfield said: "There is even a video of a walking patrol taken by a saw gunner and there is a motorcycle and they start shooting the guy at point blank range, and the video is about 30 minutes long." This particular incident was never investigated and did not result in any criminal charges. What is very clear in Winfield's statement is that he saw no real difference among the killings which were charged later as murders and those that were not. Moreover, he made it clear to CID that knowledge of the killings, drug use, and photographs extended well beyond his particular platoon. For example, he stated that Stevens, who was from Hellraiser's security detail, knew about the murders and had photographs. Winfield elaborated on one of the killings in his platoon which was later charged as murder:

> We were on a key leader engagement mission, we pushed into the second town, 1st squad was in front. SSG Gibbs asked me, SGT Jones, and CPL Morlock, if we wanted to get someone, we answered "I don't know." SSG Gibbs walked around and found a guy to kill, he pulled out his grenade, and as he did the rest of the platoon came up so he put it away. We moved forward onto a roof top. Myself and CPL Morlock deemed it clear and started walking out. SSG Gibbs and the rest of the squad showed up at the compound. SSG Gibbs said let's do this guy, this is perfect. SSG Gibbs directed me and CPL Morlock to the guy outside and go behind the berm. We did as SSG Gibbs told us to do. SSG Gibbs set the guy in a ditch on his knees. SSG Gibbs told us he was going to throw the grenade and directed myself and CPL Morlock to shoot at the guy. We did as SSG Gibbs directed. SSG Gibbs told everyone to take cover and get ready to shoot him. SSG Gibbs threw the grenade and a big cloud of dust formed and myself and CPL Morlock fired into the dust where the local national had been kneeling.

> Q: Who is SGT Hefner?

> A: SGT Hefner, B Co, 2-1 IN, 5/2 Striker Brigade, he is a team leader in my squad. He showed up in April 10, and from the beginning he found out about the scenarios and murders, and said he didn't want any part of it.

> Q: Who was the Chaplain you spoke with?

A: Chaplain Burton....

Q: Were Knapp, Ashton, and Moore also on his [Gibbs's] kill team?

A: I wouldn't say directly on his kill team, but he said that he trusted them and they were down to kill. There was an incident in a foot patrol in Zari where Sergeant Gibbs shot at some farmers that had no weapons, said that they had an RPG, and I know that Moore was on the fire team that was doing the shooting of them.

Q: Did Sergeant Gibbs fire at them as well?

A: Yes, Sergeant Gibbs, Sergeant Jones, oh, and there was a medic attached to us on the mission and his name was Sergeant Stevens.

Q: Was the medic involved as well?

A: I know he shot at them.

Q: The medic did?

A: Yes, but he's not in our platoon, he's with A-5-2.

The designation, "A-5-2," which should read more formally as A 5/2, refers to a special company of soldiers who were Hellraiser's bodyguards, or "security detail." Gibbs was a former member of A 5/2. It is clear that the circle of soldiers who knew of or participated in unlawful killings was much larger than the handful of soldiers who were charged—or, more accurately, there were several, distinct circles. Spinner requested the full roster of soldier's names in A 5/2, but the government never released it to the defense team. If Stevens and Gibbs were both from A 5/2 and involved in unlawful shootings, Spinner wondered who else from Hellraiser's security detail might have been involved. One will never know. No one was charged for the probable killings that occurred in the Zari foot patrol incident, and it is not certain that anyone was killed. To his credit, the CID agent probed further:

Q: Can you describe in detail the incident pertaining to the farmers?

A: The commander of A 2-1 said that anyone who you see with a radio is probably a bad guy, and made it seem as if the whole area was full of Taliban.... SSG Gibbs said we were going to shoot at these guys and say they had a radio and an RPG, we are probably going to kill one and say the others got away with the weapons. SSG Gibbs positioned me and SGT Hefner in the rear pulling security because he did not trust us, and he put PFC Moore, SSG Stevens, SGT Jones and SPC Wagnon on the fire line, and everyone present knew that the farmers were not armed and did not have a radio. Everyone on the fire line fired, no one was killed, but after everyone on the fire line moved forward and cleared the field. They found one guy and he didn't have any radios or weapons on him so they cleared him and released him. Later that night there was a second incident in with the farmers... SSG Bram shot his M-4 and CPL Quintal started firing the 240B. At that point A Company told them to cease fire and got mad at SSG Bram because that was A Company's area and they were shooting at random people. No one verified if anyone was killed during that incident.

Perhaps it will be helpful to some readers to explain that the M-4 is the current, lighter version of the M-16 rifle, while the 240B refers to a heavy machine gun. In any case, it is clear that a single "kill team" of permanent soldier-members did *not* exist. Instead, there were soldiers whom Gibbs "trusted" to kill if he called upon them to do so. The membership of the "kill team" in each incident—whether it was charged later as murder or not—varied from incident to incident. The soldiers who were later charged with premeditated murder were Gibbs, Morlock, Holmes, Winfield, and Wagnon (although these charges were later dropped against Wagnon and Winfield). Despite the fact that Winfield named other soldiers and other incidents in addition to the so-called "kill team" incidents, .no one was charged with any crimes with regard to these other incidents.

STATEMENT BY STAFF SERGEANT KRIS SPRAGUE

Sprague was interviewed by CID very late in the investigation, specifically, on November 15, 2010. To remind the reader: Sprague was Morlock's squad leader, and was apparently not aware of the killing scenarios. In his sworn statement, Sprague describes several questionable shooting incidents, in addition to the incidents which resulted in criminal charges. He also notes that "LT L had allowed the soldiers to often shoot local dogs without cause mostly by SSG Gibbs." Sprague tried to stop the shootings of dogs, to no avail. The shooting of dogs did not cease until LT L was replaced in March by LT Moye. (Perhaps it is worth noting that shooting Afghani dogs seems to violate the spirit of COIN doctrine.) Sprague recalls:

> There was an incident where SSG Gibbs had shot a dog for no reason in the village of Biabanak and SFC Ditmer jumped off the truck immediately and made SSG Gibbs stay on the truck during the rest of the mission. After the mission was completed LT Moye and SFC Ditmer had spoken to all the squad leaders and told us that was unacceptable behavior and would no longer be tolerated. LT Moye got more involved with the soldiers and they started feeling like the higher leadership cared about them and their well being... My assessment of SSG Gibbs is that around the soldiers he was charismatic, but he was a loner off mission, back at the FOB. Most of the leadership doors at the CHU's were always unlocked, but SSG Gibbs always had his locked. Only on occasion would he eat a meal with the rest of the squad leaders or other leadership...One incident I remember was

during a period when grooming standards were relaxed by order of the Brigade Commander. SSG Gibbs had a very robust mustache and was told to trim it down. As what I thought was a joke at the time, he combed his hair over in the likeness of Adolf Hitler and shaved his mustache in the likeness of Adolf Hitler. He most of the time referred to Afghan people as "Savages," which I took as a joke as well. SSG Gibbs was responsible for a majority of the dog shootings either directly or through example. In my opinion, SSG Gibbs displayed a Darwinist belief system. SSG Gibbs and I had a couple of debates regarding survival of the fittest and how it applied to the war in Afghanistan and the Afghan people. He made very clear to me that he was not involved in the war to help the Afghan people or protect Americans from terrorism. We were told that SSG Gibbs was moved to us from A-5-2 because there was an incident where he had taken a Gator without permission and drove it around the FOB.

Conclusions

CID investigators did their jobs in accordance with existing protocols and standards in criminology—which may be construed as the application of a sort of "strike and destroy" philosophy toward the accused. They were confronted with numerous stories of questionable killings, attempted killings, and scenarios within and outside the platoon in question. But like lawyers, criminal investigators are tethered by the pragmatic principle that charges must "stick" to the accused. The EOF incident was officially declared lawful, so it would have been difficult for them to charge that incident as murder. Furthermore, and because almost the entire platoon killed that Afghan male in the EOF incident, and killed him with excessive rounds, they could not link a particular soldier to a particular bullet or "cause" of death. Similarly, they could not verify that Afghans were actually killed in the other unlawful shooting incidents. Above all, they eventually learned that almost the entire platoon was involved in various questionable killings, as well as portions of other platoons—but contemporary law has no place for charging entire groups.

Corporal Morlock immediately waived his rights and told the investigators what he did and what others did with regard to three specific incidents of unlawful killing. His videotaped statement counted as the strongest form of evidence known to law—it would "stick." Winfield's confession was more of a problem for the investigators because he told his father about the first killing incident; his father reported the incident to the government; and the government ignored Winfield's father. Because of these mitigating factors—that Winfield wanted out of the killings early on—it would be more difficult to make charges of premeditated murder "stick" to him. In addition, had Winfield's case gone to court-martial, the army would have been embarrassed by the public air-ing of its failure to stop future killings after Winfield's father had tried to alert them on February 14, 2010 as to what was happening. Indeed, after months of legal wrangling, Winfield's attorneys convinced the government to offer him a plea-bargain in which he confessed to involuntary manslaughter, not murder. Gibbs, Holmes, and Wagnon all pleaded not guilty, and invoked the 5th amendment. Eventually, murder charges were dropped against Wagnon. In summary, and in keeping with the teachings of pragmatism, truth happened only partially to the CID's theory of what happened. The "kill team" theory was simultaneously too broad and too narrow. Only three members of this so-called team were eventually convicted of premeditated murder. On the other hand, the theory is too narrow because it ignored the numerous allusions to "everybody" in the platoon as knowing and in that sense, "conspiring" in the charged killings as well as other killings which were never charged.

Lawyers and criminal investigators are limited by the narrow rule of their professions to indict, convict, or defend individuals. But the reader is not constrained by this rule in making sense of this story. It is clear that this is less a story about Corporal Morlock and four other soldiers, and much more a story about a merciless platoon that lived up to its motto, "The Death Dealers." It is also clear that there was a noticeable contagion effect from Hellraiser's security detail, named A 5/2. Gibbs and Stevens were members of that unit, and other soldiers may have been. The bodyguards were the closest to Hellraiser in daily, physical proximity as well as exposure to his strike and destroy doctrine. The incidents of killing dogs and chickens suggest that the spirit of COIN was absent in 3rd platoon regardless of how much or how little COIN they were doing.

Chapter 10. General Twitty's Conclusions and General Scaparrotti's Response

Sociologists routinely make connections between various societies (families, nations, religious groups, social classes, and so on) and various forms of deviance, ranging from murder and suicide to alcoholism and crime. It was precisely this linkage between social function or dysfunction with deviance that established sociology as a science following the publication of sociologist Emile Durkheim's book, *Suicide: A Study in Sociology*, in the year 1897 in France. But this insight has not yet been absorbed by the army or the profession of law or criminal investigators. As I stated from the outset, the contemporary mind-set in criminology and the law is one of "hunting monsters"—and individual monsters at that. The contemporary mind has yet to fathom the phenomena of monstrous brigades, battalions, companies, and platoons. I prefer the words "dysfunctional," "toxic," and "poisoned" to monstrous in describing how entire groups engage in crime. We have seen repeatedly in this study that the crimes in question are connected to various groups (platoons, companies, battalions, the brigade) and group dynamics (cross-leveling, confusion as to which doctrine to follow, lack of group cohesion). The important point is that this seemingly obvious (to sociologists) connection between society and deviance is difficult to grasp for non-sociologists.

Nevertheless, humanity made assessments of criminal responsibility long before Durkheim established sociology in 1897. The army is an ancient social institution, and it is easy to trace its emphasis on group cohesion, loyalty, and leadership to knowledge of how ancient Roman, Greek, and other historical armies functioned (Fauconnet, 1928). All armies focus and focused on "command climates" and "command responsibility." In its own way, the military as a social institution has practiced an implicit sociology before sociology came into existence by its relentless insistence that command climates—good or bad—are connected to victories as well as defeats and deviance by armies. Furthermore, the military insists that leaders are responsible for command climates and therefore, that leaders are ultimately responsible for everything that happens in their units, good or bad. This is an implicit, ancient doctrine of responsibility, and it still operates—albeit, in a latent, hidden form—in the modern US Army.

On February 3, 2011, General Twitty wrote the conclusions to his report. His overall conclusion was: "I found no causal relation between the 5/2 SBCT command climate created and fostered by the 5/2 SBCT commander, COL Harry Tunnell, and the alleged criminal activity, including murder, alleged to have been committed by soldiers from 2-1 Infantry Battalion." Later he added: "I found no evidence that the alleged acts occurred as a result of the overall command climate set by COL Tunnell." For the sake of context, it is important to note that Twitty was responding directly to the commanding general of Ft. Lewis, Lieutenant General Curtis Scaparrotti, who wrote to him in a letter dated October 18, 2010:

> You will investigate issues of command responsibility/accountability and inquire into overall command climate from the brigade level to the platoon level during the unit's deployment....Was any commander or senior leader with the unit—company, battalion, brigade—aware of or should have been aware of the alleged actions of Soldiers in 5/2 who currently are subject to the pending potential courts-martial involving murder, assault, illegal drug use and related charges prior to those alleged offenses becoming known pursuant to the criminal investigation that began in May, 2010? Examine commander/senior leader's responsibility/accountability for the alleged murder, assault, illegal drug use, and related offenses that are currently pending potential courts-martial charges. How frequently did commanders visit and make meaningful contact with the platoon or forward operating base of the Soldiers currently subject to the pending potential courts-martial charges, or otherwise provide command oversight during operations?

The central issue in General Scaparrotti's directions to General Twitty is the doctrine of command responsibility. It is beyond the scope of the present study to delve into the history or legal and military implications of this doctrine, when it has been used and when it has been avoided in the past. For our purposes, it is sufficient to note that the doctrine is real, in a social sense: it exists as a social fact and a tradition, even though it is "just" a social agreement, whose origins date back to the earliest historical accounts of families, towns, and military units. Durkheim's follower, Paul Fauconnet, wrote the best sociological account of the idea of responsibility—ranging from collective to individual—in his book, *La Responsabilite...* (1928), which has not yet been published in English. Let us attempt to avoid getting lost in academic abstractions regarding the idea of responsibility. The important point is this: General Scaparrotti did not invent his instructions to General Twitty privately, but was following an established tradition in the US army. It is routine, traditional, and entirely predictable that the commanding general of Ft. Lewis would order an investigation into the *command responsibility* for the killings under discussion here. The army is still a traditional society in many ways. Traditional societies typically blame a group—ranging from an entire nation or city or family—for the misdeeds of an individual. Group or collective responsibility is the first instinct, the automatic reflex, of society. It is only in latter-day, modern societies that individual responsibility begins to emerge in law and the rest of society.

Let us not get lost in the forest of so-called modernity for the trees of ancient tradition. It is striking that in every single case of war crimes in the US Army, the commanding general is ultimately responsible (in the ancient, not modern, legal sense) and is also the ultimate dispenser of justice. The commanding general orders investigations, recommends courts-martial, holds the power to override some decisions by the military judge, metes out non-judicial punishments such as reprimands, and at the end of the court-martial process, holds the power to commute sentences handed down by military judges or panels. It is beyond the scope of this study to delve into all the ways that the federal court system is superimposed upon or mingled with this ancient system of justice. It is sufficient to note it. In practice, Spinner told me, the chief of military justice—who is basically the highest-ranking military lawyer on base—"whispers into the ear" of the commanding general, advising him what to do or not do. But ultimately, the commanding general dispenses justice as well as mercy, and the courts-martial are just one aspect of that overall justice.

One should note a profound disconnect in this regard. General Scaparrotti ordered an investigation into the command responsibility of various high-ranking officers in Hellraiser's brigade, especially Hellraiser himself. But the information media focused on Morlock and the other individuals in the so-called "kill team." General Twitty's report focused on Hellraiser and the numerous other commanders within the brigade, *not* on Morlock and his comrades. The gulf between General Scaparrotti's focus on command responsibility and the media's focus on a handful of low-ranking individuals is as vast as the gulf between traditional and modern societies. We shall focus on General Scaparrotti's orders and General Twitty's reply, and their mutual focus on Hellraiser and COIN doctrine, precisely because the information media overlooked these connections almost completely.

What sense can we make of General Twitty's reply? On the face of it, it appears that Twitty absolved Hellraiser and the brigade leadership of all command responsibility for the killings under discussion here. Such a conclusion would be premature. On the one hand, one could conclude that the Twitty report is a whitewash, much like Captain Opachan predicted it would be. General Twitty essentially absolved Colonel Tunnel, his superiors, and the US Army of command responsibility for the war crimes in question. One would expect nothing less from a general. On the other hand, and in a very subtle manner, General Twitty injects the ideological battle of COIN versus CG doctrines into his study and his final report. It is remarkable that the army's internal investigation of the war crimes in question is more about COIN doctrine than any other topic or issue. To phrase the matter plainly: General Twitty's report and conclusion are profoundly and implicitly sociological, even though the military court-martial system ended up prosecuting low-ranking soldiers for the crimes in question. General Twitty blames the army and Hellraiser without overtly blaming the army and Hellraiser with regard to the doctrine of command responsibility

I will first give an account of Spinner's concrete, practical, assessment of Twitty's conclusion and how he incorporated it into a defense strategy for Morlock. Spinner made it clear that his first duty as a lawyer is to protect his client and to do nothing to harm him. His attitude, too, is a social fact and stems from a social tradition with regard to the profession of law. Following the account and analysis of how Twitty's conclusions were actually used or not used in Morlock's court-martial, I will move into the more abstract discussion of what his conclusions mean for society and various non-legal professions in assessing responsibility.

SPINNER CONFRONTS THE TWITTY REPORT

It was March of 2010, and Spinner and I were in Opachan's office in the law building at Ft. Lewis. I took the 500+ page long document, which the prosecutor had sent me, out of my briefcase and handed it to Spinner. He took only the 29 pages of Twitty's letter to General Scaparrotti in which he summarized his findings, as well as Scaparrotti's orders. Spinner handed the remaining four hundred some odd pages back to me. "Aren't you going to read the entire report?" I asked. He replied: "You've read the entire report. I just need to read the conclusions."

The next morning, we sat down in Opachan's office to discuss the report and how we would use it in testimony at the court-martial. I said, "Frank, how can General Twitty conclude there is no 'causal relation' between Colonel Tunnell's command climate and the killings when about 500 pages of sworn statements in the report contradict his conclusion?"

Spinner replied: "What General Twitty is saying is that Colonel Tunnell is not criminally liable for the killings."

"Okay," I said, "but the general is not a sociologist, and he's making a false sociological claim that there is no 'causal relation' between the poisoned command climate and the killings. In fact, there is a relation."

"Would sociologists say that the command climate caused the killings?" Spinner asked.

"We avoid the word cause," I said, and immediately a broad grin came over Spinner's face.

"Why is that?" he asked.

"The word 'cause' is like an ocean. It has so many meanings that in the end it has no meaning. Aristotle wrote about apparent causes and final causes. Hume wrote that causes are only appearances and coincidences of events, not necessarily real causes. We sociologists leave the word 'cause' to the philosophers to debate." And I added, "Why are you smiling?"

"I'll tell you in a minute" he said. "So what words do you use?"

"We say that events are correlated or associated with each other. Connected, which is a word you lawyers use. So, for example, studies show that suicide rates suddenly drop when the World Series or the Super Bowl are in progress, and just as suddenly spike after the sporting events end. But we don't say that abstinence from sporting events causes suicide. The ultimate reason for the connections always lies beneath the surface, so in the end, it's isolation and lack of social integration that lead to deviance of all sorts, and we still won't call it a cause. We would say that lack of social integration is correlated with suicide. So in the example of the Super Bowl, it promotes social integration, and is therefore correlated with a drop in suicide rates."

"In the law, the word 'cause' has a very precise meaning," Spinner said. "It means that one is responsible for what happened next"

"So, really, we don't need the word 'cause'?" I asked.

"We don't need the word 'cause,' and it does not matter that General Twitty said that there is no causal relation. You are going to be on the witness stand, not General Twitty, and you have to convince the judge that there is a connection between the bad command climate and what Morlock did."

I have devoted some pages to the one sentence in General Twitty's letter of findings and recommendations which prevented the doctrine of command responsibility from being invoked against Colonel Tunnell or various generals who were his commanders. But the remainder of Twitty's letter is full of damning conclusions against the brigade commander. Twitty also offers keen insights into the mechanisms through which the poisoned command climate in Stryker Brigade set the stage for the killings in terms that fall outside the purview of "the law" and of the military doctrine of command responsibility. For example, General Twitty writes: "Notwithstanding this lack of a causal relation, the overall command climate within 5/2 SBCT was one of frustration with the SBCT commander." Twitty also reports that, against the army's official COIN Manual FM 3-24, "COL Tunnell believed that brigade and below forces should maintain their traditional roles of conducting offensive and defensive operations to degrade leadership, formations, and supply and communication lines of the enemy."

Colonel Tunnell took command of Stryker Brigade on May 4, 2007. However, "the Army published FM 3-24, Counterinsurgency Operations in June 2007, but COL Tunnell was uncomfortable using the manual, as previously discussed." Battalion and company commanders were gradually assigned to Tunnell's newly formed brigade: "As key leaders arrived, he pointedly asked them, 'what is the center of gravity?' and emphasized that it is the enemy, not the population as suggested in FM 3-24." General Twitty tip-toes diplomatically around the impact of Colonel Tunnell's refusal to follow established army doctrine: "Many of COL Tunnell's officers and NCOs were reluctant to challenge his counter-guerrilla philosophy or approach him with issues or concerns." Indeed, General Twitty seems unwilling to challenge the brigade commander's insubordination even in his letter, although he does elaborate:

> Many of his [Colonel Tunnell's] subordinates characterized him as introverted, unapproachable, close-minded, and as a person who thinks that he knows more than most. COL Tunnell had limited social interaction with his officers and NCOs. He rarely counseled or mentored his subordinates, conducted hail and farewells, or participated in team building events. Because of the lack of interaction, many in the command started to perceive COL Tunnell as unapproachable. As a result, confusion and frustration over his counter-guerrilla philosophy starts to surface in the command. Additionally, many who had been exposed to COL Tunnell's philosophy from the beginning were already growing tired of hearing about it, seeing the debate over counter-guerrilla versus counterinsurgency approaches as wasted intellectual energy over what was really just a matter of semantics.

General Twitty displays great tact in his description of the National Training Center rotation in February 2009, which might be undiplomatically labeled as a fiasco. He writes:

> Approximately three weeks prior to the SBCT's deployment to the NTC for their Mission Readiness Exercise (MRE), the unit was notified that it would not be deploying to Iraq, but instead to Afghanistan, causing additional stress, confusion, and frustration. .. Brigadier General Randy Dragon and his cadre felt that 5/2 SBCT's mindset was too aggressive and lethally focused on defeating the enemy instead of adhering to the Army's contemporary population centric doctrine. COL Tunnell disagreed with NTC's observations and this caused heated confrontations between himself and some of his staff members and the NTC cadre... The confrontation got to a point that the NTC Commander, Major General Dana Pittard, requested senior leadership from I Corps to visit the NTC to resolve the dispute as the *unit was on the verge of not being certified to deploy to Afghanistan.* Lieutenant General J.D. Johnson, then Deputy Commanding General of I Corps, traveled to NTC to resolve the dispute and inform COL Tunnell that his approach was too aggressive and that he and his troops must be more balanced (offensive, defensive, and stability operations) during the rotation. ...The rotation resumed after LTG Johnson verbally counseled COL Tunnell and directed him to align with the NTC's training rotation. COL Tunnell *reluctantly agreed* with LTG Johnson and accepted the NTC's approach [emphasis added].

It is a delicate matter for General Twitty to document the fact that his fellow-generals almost gave Colonel Tunnell a failing grade for deploying to Afghanistan, and that they gave him only three weeks to shift his focus from Iraq to Afghanistan. Three weeks! In the rarified air of the stratosphere in which colonels and generals reside, with its traditional gentleman's code, commanders "counsel," but do not order. A high-ranking subordinate such as a colonel "agrees," even if reluctantly, while those in the lower strata simply obey. General Twitty displays remarkable skill in the dexterous exercise of *almost* implying that his fellow generals were responsible for allowing Colonel Tunnell's brigade to deploy when it was out of step with COIN doctrine, and therefore responsible—to some degree—for allowing the toxic command climate to precipitate the tragedy that ensued. Of course, according to the gentleman's code of conduct, General Twitty may not, and does not, make such charges, which would appear clumsy and rude. Colonels and generals are politicians, in addition to their more standard roles as commanders.

General Twitty's delicacy extends to the important fact that Colonel Tunnell decided that "Lieutenant Colonel Demaree's command tour be curtailed" just prior to deployment to NTC. LTC Demaree was the original commander of 2-1, the very battalion to which Corporal Morlock was assigned. Twitty concludes: "I view LTC Demaree's curtailment from command as a separate, unrelated issue having no bearing on this investigation." Note the discretion of using the term, "curtailment from command." In reality, Colonel Tunnell fired LTC Demaree because Demaree disagreed with him openly and vehemently about disobeying COIN doctrine. Twitty did not interview Demaree, even though Demaree's views might have shed important light on the origins of Battalion 2-1's change in command climate after he was relieved of command. Twitty states simply that "LTC Jeffrey French was identified to assume command of 2-1 Infantry Battalion."

Let us be very precise in understanding the context of this transition of command from Demaree and French for the ill-fated 2-1 Infantry Battalion. Tunnell announced Demaree's removal prior to the NTC rotation, but kept Demaree in the humiliating position of going through the NTC rotation as a commander who would not deploy to Afghanistan. General Twitty's tact prevents him from considering the effects of this humiliation on Demaree and on the officers and soldiers in his battalion. But we must consider it. Moreover, the new battalion commander, LTC French, did *not* attend the NTC rotation; was *not* exposed to Tunnell's philosophy prior to deployment; and was firmly under the control of General McChrystal's staff in Afghanistan at the start of his deployment. Twitty lays out the bare essentials of this inauspicious transition:

> Along with LTC French, several other officers and senior NCOs arrived in the SBCT just prior to deployment to Afghanistan. As a result, they did not receive COL Tunnell's ... explanation of his counter-guerrilla philosophy. Many only had brief introductions to COL Tunnell before arriving in Afghanistan. This created further confusion in the SBCT with newly arrived personnel not understanding COL Tunnell's intent. After arriving from their service schools where they had learned the fundamentals of counterinsurgency, FM 3-24, as the Army's current operating doctrine, they found another doctrine in use, but they did not understand why.

What could it mean, in common sense terms, that the 2-1 leaders did not understand Colonel Tunnell's "intent?" It is certain that they grasped his intent ran counter to the chain of command and to COIN. But the soldiers in 2-1 had been exposed to Tunnell's philosophy and witnessed that their commander, Demaree, was removed from command for disagreeing with that philosophy. From the grunt's perspective, Colonel Tunnell's philosophy "won" the day, and LTC French would meet the same fate as Demaree if he bucked Tunnell's philosophy. The seeds of tragedy, not just "confusion," were sown into the origins of 2-1. The grunts were already under the sway of Tunnell's "intent," and the commanders who wished to follow official army doctrine (COIN) were seen by them and by the brigade commander as expendable. 2-1 was dysfunctional and at war with itself from the beginning of its deployment.

DEPLOYMENT IN AFGHANISTAN

General Twitty observes that as soon as Colonel Tunnell and his brigade arrived in Afghanistan, he unleashed 1-17 into an "offensive approach to clear" Arghandab Valley, which "had seen very little combat forces since the war began in 2001." Colonel Tunnell "vehemently disagreed with Major General Carter about the mission." Quickly, "Colonel Tunnell acquired a reputation of not being a team player." Because he could not obey Major General Carter, "the senior US general in RC-South, BG Hodges, took an active role in providing guidance to COL Tunnell." This relationship also deteriorated rapidly:

> Eventually BG Hodges and COL Tunnell's relationship deteriorated because of COL Tunnell's desire *to challenge virtually every order that was issued by the command.* COL Tunnell's refusal or challenge of higher orders impacted his SBCT staff as well. Many of his staff officers and subordinate commanders felt that their commander did not pick his fights appropriately and that he challenged orders too often instead of moving forward and executing them. BG Hodges stated that, 'MG Carter and I had lost confidence in COL Tunnell's ability to command from his failure to follow instructions and intent." (emphasis added)

Why didn't Generals Hodges and Carter act on their loss of confidence in the brigade commander's ability to lead? The tactful General Twitty does not offer any clues. But he does confirm what we have already found, namely, that the officers in closest physical proximity to Colonel Tunnell adopted his counter-COIN and counter-guerrilla philosophy while officers who were more remote from him were caught in the double-bind trap of not being able to obey or disobey him openly:

> At the brigade level, the majority of brigade staff officers understood COL Tunnell's counter-guerrilla philosophy and supported FM 90-8 [which was obsolete] as the appropriate doctrine for 5/2 SBCT while deployed to Afghanistan. The reason for this support by the SBCT staff was that officers close to him had greater access to COL Tunnell. Thus, he was able to explain his philosophy and influence their opinion on counter-guerrilla operations. Even though battalion commanders conducted stability tasks [COIN] at the battalion level, the majority of staff majors and battalion commanders felt hamstrung by having to choose between following the SBCT vision, applying COIN "on the margins" (or without express dialogue with their brigade commander), or openly going against the SBCT CDR's counter-guerrilla approach during the deployment. BG Randy Dragon noticed this same dynamic during the SBCT's NTC rotation. One of the battalion commanders felt that because he openly challenged COL Tunnell's strategy, he was given an average OER [Officer Evaluation Report], effectively ending his career progression.

General Twitty chooses his words carefully to describe the brigade commander's insubordination: "strategy," "philosophy," and "vision." The brigade staff was clearly on the brigade commander's side. The battalion commanders could not say "yes" and could not say "no" openly to any orders that came down from brigade headquarters. Twitty notes that "at the company level ... many of the captains stated that they disagreed with COL Tunnell, but that his philosophy did not impact the way they operated at the company level." Moreover, according to General Twitty, "it should be emphasized, however, that at the platoon level and below, COL Tunnell's counter-guerrilla philosophy had minimal impact on the soldiers." Twitty does not offer any explanation for his crude sociological interpretation: he assumes that lower-ranking officers (captains) and soldiers could not have been influenced by the brigade commander's philosophy. General Twitty makes this conclusion despite observing that:

> In fact, the only reach of COL Tunnell's counter-guerrilla strategy to the Soldier level seemed to come through the identity he attempted to establish for the Brigade as a "counter-guerrilla unit" by creating company guidon streamers that read "counter-guerrilla," commissioning a deployment print by artist James Dietz that included the term "counter-guerrilla," and selling redeployment memorabilia including pistols and Jack Daniels bottles engraved with the term "counter-guerrilla."

It is doubtful that these powerful symbols of the brigade commander's counter-guerrilla "philosophy" were the "only" reach by him into the lives of the grunts. By themselves, the streamers, memorabilia, pistols, and whiskey bottles were more than enough for the low-ranking soldier to grasp what the symbolism meant. Specifically, they surely grasped that the symbolism crystallized the fact that they were a counter-guerrilla brigade. In addition, several officers confirmed for me that it was common practice for command sergeant majors to accompany the commissioned officers to briefings. Obviously, the command sergeant majors were a major conduit for Hellraiser's philosophy to reach the low-ranking soldiers.

General Twitty comes across as a master politician. He absolves Colonel Tunnell of legal and command responsibility for what happened, at the same time that he picks damning quotes from the sworn statements, and interprets those quotes, to suggest that the brigade commander was a failed leader. General Twitty also focuses relentlessly on COIN doctrine, and its opposite, Colonel Tunnell's counter-guerrilla doctrine. General Twitty implies, but never states outright that to be pro-counter-guerrilla was to be counter-COIN, and also to be counter-US-Army. This division and the attendant double-bind strains—that soldiers and officers were damned if they did or did not follow one or the other philosophy—were felt at all levels of the brigade, from the battalions to the companies to the platoons.

General Twitty lists methodically the discipline problems in the brigade during its deployment. For example, "leaders failed to use the urinalysis program while deployed." In plain language, commanders never gave the soldiers the required urinalysis tests for drug use which could have uncovered the widespread use of hashish and other drugs. Furthermore, "commanders generally did not enforce health and welfare inspections." This neglect ranged from not knowing which soldiers sustained brain injuries from IEDs to not inspecting living quarters for contraband (such as drop weapons). Turning to Morlock's company and battalion, General Twitty observes that "3/B/2-1 IN had significantly lower standards and discipline than other units within the SBCT." He elaborates: "In fact, the platoon's standards and discipline were so alarming that one might question how the company and battalion levels of command did not know of many of the incidents that occurred within the platoon." Soldiers negligently discharged grenade launchers; soldiers shot dogs and chickens while on patrols in Afghan villages; "the platoon used excessive force;" soldiers frequently fell asleep without establishing a guard watch; leaders "allowed soldiers to maintain HE grenades, rockets, mortar rounds, clarymores, Det Cord and C4 in their sleeping tents;" "the platoon's privates and specialists routinely called NCO's by first names;" the "platoon was accused of kicking in doors of homes and being disrespectful to the populace by yelling and saying derogatory comments." The general goes on and on, documenting many violations of army discipline standards found in the sworn statements, including this one:

> At least fifteen Soldiers in the platoon allegedly participated in the smoking of hashish, and some of the Soldiers traded prescription drugs amongst each other with the intent of becoming intoxicated. I found no evidence that the platoon, company, and battalion leadership were ever aware of their Soldier's drug use until reported late in the deployment.

The reader should be aware that in the US Army, it is no excuse for a commander at any level to claim that he or she did not know that subordinates were using drugs or committing any other violations. General Scaparrotti's letter to General Twitty ordered him to find leaders who were either aware "or should have been aware" of these and other violations. Similarly, General Twitty seems to express surprise that leaders did not know of the many problems which he lists. At this point, General Twitty's diplomacy has reached its breaking point. It is convenient for leaders to claim that they were not aware of discipline problems, but army doctrine holds that responsibility can never be delegated or shirked. The leaders *should* have known, from the brigade commander on down through the battalion and company and platoon leaders. There can be no doubt that both Generals, Twitty and Scaparrotti, are aware of the meaning of the doctrine of command responsibility.

General Twitty turns to the harrowing cross-leveling that occurred in Morlock's company (specifically, Bravo Company in Battalion 2-1). We have touched on this issue previously, but, it is worth revisiting, and also worth deciphering General Twitty's assessment of its impact.:

> 3/B/2-1 IN's *habitual* company commander and First Sergeant ... operated and resided several miles away on their daily activities. CPT Quiggle had two platoons (3/A/2-1 IN and 3/B/2-1 IN) from two different companies OPCON to A/8-1 CAV SQN during the deployment. Neither of the platoons trained with A/8-1 CAV SQN during home-station training or at the NTC. The Battalion commander was new to the command as well, so he too was unfamiliar with the strengths and weaknesses of the platoon leadership. (emphasis added)

> Note General Twitty's use of the word "habitual" to refer to the original Bravo Company commander, CPT T, versus the new commander, CPT Quiggle, who took charge after the cross-leveling. General Twitty observes that the cross-leveling of units prevented the new company commander (CPT Quiggle) from knowing the strengths and weaknesses of the platoon leaders. He adds that the new battalion commander (LTC French) and the new company commander (CPT Quiggle) had never trained with each other. These are important observations—habits were disrupted by the cross-leveling. However, the general omits the important fact that Captain Quiggle was a former member of Colonel Tunnell's brigade staff, and espoused a pro-counter-guerrilla philosophy, while the battalion commander, LTC French, was in favor of doing COIN. The cross-leveling pitted the two diametrically opposed "philosophies" against each other in the form of the soldiers and officers who were cross-leveled. Moreover, the cross-leveling itself weakened the morale, trust, and camaraderie among the soldiers involved. Samuel Stouffer had established long ago, in his classic work, *The American Soldier* (1949), that soldiers fight for each other and not for abstract philosophies. But they are less likely to fight for each other if they do not know each other habitually and had not trained together, specifically, following cross-leveling. General Twitty does not address these issues pertaining to leadership and group cohesion, even though, presumably, he is aware of them.

General Twitty's conclusions

General Twitty's conclusions, discussion, and recommendations in the final eight pages of his memorandum to General Scaparrotti are ambiguous at best. On the one hand, he reasserts that "the command climate in the SBCT did not impede good order and discipline." On the other, he

adds that "Colonel Tunnell's inattentiveness to administrative matters
... may have helped create an environment in which misconduct could
occur." By administrative matters, he means standard army doctrine regarding communication, circulation, and group cohesion. In a politically
skillful manner, General Twitty blames the brigade commander without
blaming him openly. For example, General Twitty writes:

> I do find that COL Tunnell's ineffective communication with the officers,
> NCOs, and Soldiers significantly impacted the command climate within
> his SBCT. His refusal to adopt the FM3-24 [COIN] contemporary Army
> doctrine created frustration, confusion, and friction at multiple levels in
> his command. His inability to comply and conform to senior leaders' di-
> rectives demonstrates his lack of flexibility, teamwork, and discernment
> required of our senior leaders. COL Tunnell failed to realize the authority
> he has as a senior officer and commander. COL Tunnell's former supervi-
> sors in RC-South, BG Nicholson and BG Hodges, both stated that they
> lacked confidence in his ability to effectively command his brigade. How-
> ever, they did not request relief.

We lack the insider's information as to why General Twitty would
simultaneously absolve and blame Hellraiser and the command climate
he created. The most meaningful conclusions we may draw is that the
Twitty Report is fundamentally ambiguous at the same time that it is a
treasure trove of information. It is a double-edged sword in many regards.
To a sociologist, the ambiguity, ambivalence, and uncertainty in this report, this case, and similar war crimes cases in the long War on Terror
are social facts. This story is characterized by ambiguity at almost every
turn, from ambivalence toward COIN doctrine versus traditional, counter-guerrilla doctrine to ambivalence about responsibility, commanders,
doctrine, and ultimately, the mission in this war.

Moreover, what could it mean for Hellraiser or anyone else "to adopt
the FM 3-24 [COIN] contemporary Army doctrine"—or not adopt it?
We have seen that COIN doctrine itself is ambiguous. By some interpretations of COIN doctrine, Hellraiser was following it (by mixing lethal
and non-lethal strategies as he saw fit). We have seen that General Mc-
Chyrstal was in charge of implementing COIN doctrine, but was fired
over his comments concerning this doctrine.

General Twitty ends with a list of recommended punishments for the
various commanders in the brigade: "I would recommend that COL Tunnell be relieved of his responsibilities as a Brigade commander for the
following reasons." He lists the reasons as follows:

> The loss of confidence by his superiors in his ability to command from
> his failure to follow instructions and intent ... his inability to get along
> with superiors and peers, indicating a lack of maturity needed to com-
> mand at senior levels. His failure to adequately communicate his intent

to his subordinates. The counter-guerrilla strategy he envisioned for his SBCT was the fundamental aspect of his command. He knew that this strategy was going against the mainstream counter-insurgency doctrine that his subordinates had learned in their classrooms and experienced in previous deployments and yet he did not invest the time and attention to ensure that even his key subordinate leaders understood his "outside the box" philosophy ... I do not believe that any adverse administrative action or worse is appropriate. I did not find that any of his actions amounted to misconduct. When people fail in leadership positions in the Army, they are relieved from such duties as a consequence."

The general recommended no action regarding the commander of 2-1, LTC French. Regarding the platoon leader of 3/B/2-1, Twitty writes: "I recommend that LT Ligsay receive a General Officer Memorandum of Reprimand (GOMOR) for dereliction of duty for not enforcing standards within 3/B/2-1 IN that led to a deterioration of standards and discipline in his platoon." Twitty continues: "I further recommend LT Ligsay receive a GOMOR for undisciplined fire control that resulted in an excessive use of force when 6 to 8 soldiers fired, including four 249 SAW gunners, on one unarmed Afghan local." Twitty also recommended GOMOR's for the platoon sergeant and company executive officer in B/2-1. He recommended "a letter of concern" for the company commander and company first sergeant. It is important to note the exact incidents which Twitty found worthy of punishment:

> SFC Bruno, Platoon Sergeant: I recommend that SFC Bruno receive a GOMOR for dereliction of duty for not enforcing standards within 3/B/2-1 that led to a deterioration of standards and discipline in his platoon.

> CPT Mitchell, Troop XO: I recommend that CPT Mitchell receive a GOMOR for dereliction of duty, both in using poor language on the objective at La Muhammad Kalay to communicate what he meant, and for failing to follow up with SSG Sprague and others to review the shooting.

> SSG Sprague: Squad Leader: I recommend considering a GOMOR for SSG Sprague, pending any additional information that may come out of the criminal investigation or courts-martial process.

> CPT Quiggle, Troop Commander: I recommend that CPT Quiggle receive a Letter of Concern for using improper language to articulate his intent when telling LT Ligsay that, "you'd better find something" during the EOF incident on Highway 1. I further recommend that CPT Quiggle receive a Letter of Concern for exercising poor judgment in not living amongst his Soldiers in order to enforce standards and discipline within the troop living area on FOB Ramrod.

> SGM Hagedush, Troop ISG: I recommend that SGM Hagedush receive a Letter of Concern for exercising poor judgment in not living amongst his

Soldiers in order to enforce standards and discipline within the troop living area on FOB Ramrod....

Nothing in my investigation indicated any dereliction by action or omission by any of COL Tunnell's supervisors. Prior to deployment, there was little brought to the attention of I Corps leadership that would indicate command climate or any other issues within the Brigade. At most, he was viewed as not getting along with fellow Brigade commanders and I Corps staff personnel.

GENERAL SCAPARROTTI'S RESPONSE

In response to General Twitty's report, General Scaparrotti issued specific orders in a memorandum dated 8 February 2011. He did not follow all of General Twitty's recommendations, and he made absolutely no mention of the issues of poor command climate or command responsibility. Specifically, General Scaparrotti ordered that Colonel Tunnell "receive a letter of admonition," which would effectively end his chances for further promotion or command. The company executive officer (CPT Mitchell) would receive a GOMOR while the company commander (CPT Quiggle) would receive a "letter of concern." GOMOR's would also be issued to the platoon leader (LT Ligsay) and platoon sergeant (SFC Bruno). Whereas General Twitty recommended no action against the battalion commander (LTC French), General Scaparrotti would issue a "letter of concern" for him and also for the two sergeant majors in the battalion. Regarding the squad leader, Sergeant Sprague, General Scaparrotti ordered further investigations leading to court-martial. (In the end, Sprague was never charged with anything.) Finally, he directed that all commanders and units under his command "are properly equipped and capable of performing periodic inspections, including both urinalysis and health and welfare inspections, especially when deploying."

Let us note that officers were punished with letters of concern, admonition, and reprimand while the lowest-ranking soldiers were court-martialed and sentenced to prison. All of these different reactions constitute some form of punishment. But in the end, it is clear that in the current War on Terror, responsibility for war crimes falls disproportionately on the low-ranking grunt. A letter of admonition will end a career in the army, but the officer in question will keep all of his pay, pension and benefits. Prison time at Ft. Leavenworth is not only one of the most severe forms of imprisonment in the United States: in addition to imprisonment, the soldier in question loses all of his pay, pension, and benefits, not to mention the near impossibility of ever gaining meaningful employment upon release due to the dishonorable discharge. One should note carefully that General Scaparrotti's response is typical of all the other commanding generals in all the war crimes cases in the current war. Historians have documented that in World War II, high-ranking civilian and military leaders were held most accountable for war crimes. Similarly, and based upon my experience as an expert witness at the International Tribunal at the Hague, the outcome in the Maywand District Killings would have been unimaginable at the Hague. International tribunals on war crimes routinely go after high-ranking officials who created the social conditions for war crimes to occur and do not bother with the "small fish" who commit the actual crimes. Decades from now, perhaps some historians will notice the opposite pattern for punishing war crimes committed by US soldiers: high-ranking civilian and military leaders received "slaps on the wrist," while the low-ranking soldiers are sent to prison.

We arrive at this conclusion as a matter of fact, and particularly as a social fact. It is not this or that particular general or colonel who creates this reality. Rather, the high-ranking generals and colonels fall into a social pattern. There has been no exception to this social pattern of judging responsibility for war crimes in the current war. One needs only to reflect on the Abu Ghraib abuse cases, Operation Iron Triangle, and the Baghdad Canal killing: high ranking officers received letters of reprimand or admonition or concern or some other letter as punishment for creating dysfunctional social climates which precipitated war crimes,

Conclusions

There is so much more than meets the eye in General Twitty's conclusions and General Scaparrotti's response. On the surface, it seems that the report, conclusions, and recommendations were a whitewash of command responsibility, so that criminal responsibility fell entirely upon low-ranking soldiers. The army's elite judged that its high-ranking commanders were immune from command responsibility in the legal sense. But a reasonable, objective reader will notice that General Twitty blamed a host of other generals and Hellraiser for creating the dysfunctional command climate which set the stage for the crimes in question, and failed to repair that climate. Both generals, Twitty and Scaparrotti, achieved this double-edged effect through an ingenious strategy of political, gentlemanly tact combined with hard-hitting tactics. Scaparrotti ordered Twitty to obtain sworn statements from everyone who would be questioned, even generals who outranked General Twitty! General Twitty broadened the question of command responsibility into an issue of COIN versus CG strategy. Historically speaking, these moves by Scaparrotti and Twitty are noteworthy achievements. Twitty's study leads to some profound questions, including: What, exactly, was the mission that the chain-of-command was attempting to carry out in Afghanistan? Was it COIN or CG doctrine or some dysfunctional hybrid of the two doctrines? Was COIN some sort of experiment in the army? Is COIN doctrine sufficiently unambiguous to qualify as a doctrine that can be followed? Who was responsible for the resulting confusion as to mission and doctrine? Was the tragedy of Hellraiser's Stryker brigade symptomatic of a wider dysfunction in the army concerning the issue of *how* to *do* COIN in Afghanistan? There are no easy answers to these difficult questions, and these questions emerge from the data we have analyzed.

Chapter 11. The Grunt's Perspectives Found in the Command Climate Surveys

Thus far, we have reviewed the Twitty Report, which gives the reader perspective into the dysfunctional social climate in Hellraiser's brigade from the perspectives of generals, colonels, other high-ranking officers, CID investigators, Hellraiser, and finally—the author of the report, General Twitty. I wanted to balance this important data which comes from the army's elite with the perspectives of the lowest-ranking grunts in the brigade, namely, the infantry soldiers. Perhaps the low-ranking soldiers could not write with erudition on COIN or CG doctrine, but they had beliefs and emotions about their units and the brigade as a whole. I asked Spinner to request the Command Climate Surveys for the entire brigade. Spinner made this request to the prosecutor three months prior to the scheduled court-martial. The prosecutor handed over 3,000 pages of the surveys two days before the court-martial was set to begin. "Sometimes you just have to burn the midnight oil," Spinner said to me, as he handed over the stack of papers. My "crew" (as Spinner called them) and I stayed up most of the first night going over the 3,000 pages of data. We discovered that the data was not complete. The following day, we requested, and received, an additional 4,000 pages of data. We never received all of the data pertaining to all of the command climate surveys from 2007 to 2010. Nevertheless, the data we received opens important doors to the perceptions by low-ranking soldiers of their units and leaders, from platoon level through brigade.

The existence, and importance, of the surveys was known to all concerned ever since General Scaparrotti ordered General Twitty to conduct his investigation. Regarding these surveys, Scaparrotti's exact instructions to Twitty were as follows: "You may also utilize the information gathered in 5-2 SBCT (to include 2-2 SBCT) assessments, to include command climate surveys, and other similar information." The curious reference to 5-2 to include 2-2 stems from the fact that 5/2 Stryker brigade was decommissioned following its deployment and "reflagged" as 2/2 Stryker brigade. We shall not address the issue of what "core" of 5/2 may or may not have remained in this additional example of cross-leveling.[20] For reasons unknown, Twitty did not devote a single word to the surveys in his 500+ page report. We shall not speculate on the reasons why the command climate surveys were omitted, but the defense team was determined not to omit them from testimony.

The army's command climate surveys are given annually to all of its soldiers. They are the rough equivalent of similar surveys of workplace environments given to professors at universities, doctors in hospitals, and other professionals in various social institutions. The army's surveys which we examined asked a wide variety of questions, ranging from perceived sexism and racism to opinions on morale, group cohesion, trust, and army values. Most of the items were in the form of quantifiable multiple-choice answers to specific questions. In addition, there was space provided for the soldiers to express their opinions freely and without restriction.

Overview of the findings

The most striking thing about the surveys given to low-ranking soldiers versus General Twitty's report is the night-versus-day shift in focus. The soldiers complained primarily about low morale, lack of trust, lack of respect, and a hostile work environment. They had next to nothing to say about COIN doctrine, CG doctrine, or any of the military theory issues that consumed the generals, colonels, and other high-ranking commanders. Conversely, in their obsession with COIN doctrine, the high-ranking officers scarcely seem to notice issues pertaining to morale and work environment. As we have seen, Hellraiser's minions believed morale in the brigade was high, when, in fact, it was dismally low. One of several conclusions we may draw is that high-ranking officers and low-ranking soldiers lived and worked in entirely different social worlds, or more formally, "reference groups," in the same brigade. It is the difference between a social climate in the stratosphere of power (the level of the generals and colonels) versus the social climate at the sea level of power (the level of the infantry grunts).

The two key findings of the quantitative analysis of the surveys are as follows: First, ratings pertaining to lack of trust, low morale, lack of respect, poor communication, and poor training remained relatively constant from the year 2008 to the year 2010. This means that the brigade was dysfunctional since its inception, through its deployment, and following the end of its mission in Afghanistan. Second, in data pertaining to the issues named above, Stryker Brigade was worse than the average of all army brigades, and the average of all army brigades was consistently worse than the average of all the other military services. (These comparative averages across the entire US military were conveniently provided in the data analyses provided by the army.) In plain language, Hellraiser's Stryker brigade was among the worst brigades in the US Army in terms of lack of trust, low morale, lack of respect, and the other issues listed above.

ILLUSTRATIONS OF THE OVERALL FINDINGS

An in-depth analysis or complete summary of all the findings in the surveys would require a separate book. Here, I shall merely illustrate the overall findings by quoting the exact language the soldiers used to describe their brigade, battalions, companies, and platoons.

Asked "list three things that most need improvement in this unit," soldiers wrote:

"Nobody gives a shit. Low morale."

"Trust."

"Basic soldier discipline."

"Control over hazing."

"Morale needs improvement."

"Irresponsible commanding officer."

"Non-commissioned officers need to respect peers more."

"Morale."

"New leadership."

"Morale appears low."

"Getting soldiers help for their personal problems."

"Lack of cohesion."

"Treat each other with respect."

"Courtesy."

"The unit is un-organized."

"We need leaders who aren't idiots."

"Quit changing our command so much."

"Command."

"Overall leadership doesn't care."

"Unit cohesion."

"Respect."

"Proper use of sniper teams."

"Caring about soldiers."

"Too many fat people."

"Intimidation people, scary people."

"Property accountability."

"Arms room accountability."

"Communication between higher and lower commands to include soldiers."

"Me not being here."

"Property accountability is a joke."

"Company commander does not listen to criticism."

"We need to work together."

"Bring in a new commander."

"I don't see enough respect."

"I think everyone is frustrated with the leadership."

"Change the damned commanding officer already."

"Lack of leadership."

"Low morale is being pushed down the chain of command to the soldiers."

"The unit needs team cohesion."

"Everything!."

"A lot of non-commissioned officers are leaving and switching to other platoons."

Asked to "list three things that are good or going well in this unit," here is a sample of responses by infantry soldiers:

"I come to work and know that I am not the only one going through this Hell."

"I can't think of anything. I've been in this unit for over three years and I haven't met one person that wanted to stay in it."

"Lunch break is good."

"Certain people are leaving."

"The Battalion commander is leaving."

"I start my week looking forward to the weekend."

In response to the question, "What is the one thing that the leadership can do for you that they currently don't do?" soldiers wrote

"Actually care about what you have to say."

"Time to get things right."

"Care more about soldiers and not themselves."

"Trust each other more."

For the question, "How would you characterize the medical care obtained from on-base providers?" soldiers wrote:

"Not very good. I have seen seven different doctors for my issues."

"Sucks. I never get the same doctor. Medication is the first option."

"Naproxen doesn't fix everything."

"All of them suck."

"Non-existent, the medical care in the US Army is over-worked and over-crowded, it doesn't do anything but drug your Soldiers. It's a joke and a band-aid on an arterial bleed.."

"A pain in the ass just to get an appointment."

"Ridiculous."

"The way medical is run is all messed up."

"They generally rush the patients out with a drink of water and a, 'Here is a pain killer'."

"All they do is give you medicine and you are on your way."

"Get in and out as quickly as possible with as little time taken as possible. I'll do my own surgeries in my own house."

"Lack of care for soldiers."

"The worst care I've ever seen in my entire life. They only care about pushing you through, not your welfare. They give you pills and send you on your way.."

"Civilian doctors actually give a damn about their patients."

In response to the prompt, "Describe how the unit encourages/discourages promotion," soldiers wrote:

"I don't think there is enough mentorship going on."

"If you are buddies with the leadership, you are in. Even if you are a dirt-bag in this company, you will make it to the next rank as long as you're buddies."

"If they like you, i.e., if you haven't pissed off the commanding officer, then you can get promoted, but nobody in my unit wants to get promoted just to turn around and be subjected to the abuse of the next highest rank and nobody wants to stay in the unit."

"It's all political anyway—who cares?"

"F__ this unit's promotion plan."

"No comment."

"Unknown what I need to do."

"It seems that you need to get a DUI [Driving under the influence] to get promoted in this unit. I've seen at least three men get promoted to either E-5 or E-6 who have had DUI's. In my mind, this is not a very good example to set. I have had lower enlisted members ask me why those men were promoted too. So just because no one says anything doesn't mean it goes unnoticed."

"A lot of promos have been based on the long time saying, 'it's not what you know but who you blow.' Heard a lot of the new NCO's say that they wished that they had turned down the promo for this company for the mistreatment they get."

"No one in this company is mentored."

For corroboration, one may turn to the chaplain's observations that the units operated on a "buddy-system" instead of a formal, rational-legal system for promotion. The Twitty report similarly corroborates the views of soldiers that there was no mentorship in the brigade.

Asked, "How satisfied are you with the level of support for you and/or your family that is provided by brigade services?" soldiers wrote:

"I'm not satisfied at all."

"Non-existent, amazed, nothing to add."

In response to the prompt, "How would you rate your level of job satisfaction and why?" soldiers wrote:

"Low, because the chain of command does not give the flow of information nor do they help out with problems of their Soldiers."

"Low. Staffing issues have a handful of people doing a brigade's worth of work."

"The level of my job satisfaction is low due to the lack of respect, envy, and jealousy."

"I would say that I am completely dissatisfied with my job and have extremely low morale and no daily motivation to come to work. "

"Average, job satisfaction starts with the army as a whole, that being said, it's hard to have high satisfaction when the big army constantly has you down."

"I hate it here, too much stress on one or two people while a ton of people are not pulling their weight. Responsibilities are not evenly spread, a lack of command and control makes delegation difficult."

"Low. I cannot state my reasons and details because then this survey will mean that I will no longer remain anonymous."

In response to the question, "What do you know about this unit that leadership does not know but should?" soldiers wrote:

"That they are not helping out their Soldiers when they should try instead of pushing them off, which is causing some Soldiers to not care about their work or have less respect for the higher-ups in the chain of command."

"More often than not my supervisors are aware of issues arising in the unit."

"I believe the company is completely inept at administrative functions."

"The morale is very low."

"Promotion policy is terrible. People that are squared away do not get promoted, but people who cannot pass a physical training test get promoted. People that do the right thing see no reward for it."

"Lack of accountability and lack of flow of information."

"It has people that are shady."

"They need to drug test more."

"Some NCO's abuse their rights to order around Soldiers."

"Haters."

"This unit needs a face lift from the previous command structure and needs to work towards healthy relationships internally and with external organization."

"Stop believing every little thing that the NCO's say. It's pretty bad that they promote Soldiers that clearly are not ready to be leaders. They have serious trust and integrity issues. This coming from someone who is a leader and has been with the unit longer than most of the Soldiers here."

"Many of the Soldiers are hooligans."

In response to the prompt, "What command climate issues does this unit most need to improve?" soldiers wrote:

"Understanding Soldiers"

"How to work as a group."

"Motivation and discipline."

"Unit cohesion, possibly?"

"Low morale."

"Everything about it and care more about the Soldiers and shit."

"Trust from the bottom up."

"It would be great to have less back stabbing."

"The rain in the Pacific Northwest."

"Proper leadership."

"Support disabled Soldiers. If you don't believe the Soldier, go talk to the doctor! MRI's and X-rays don't lie."

In response to the prompt, "Are you proud to be a member of this unit?" soldiers wrote:

"Not really, it's frowned on when you're in the brigade headquarters staff."

"No, there are way too many discrepancies with the leadership."

"I am indifferent to this unit. I have heard a lot of 'Don't judge the Army by this Brigade.' I do not know what that means, but I have not heard many good things about this unit."

"No, we have a very bad reputation."

"No, this is not the type of unit in which I want to be a part of."

"No, I am not a proud member of this unit. I am extremely embarrassed of the way that Soldiers and NCO's conduct themselves on a daily basis. People are backstabbers and liars in this unit and I want nothing to do with that."

"No, just waiting to get out."

"Hell, no! I hate this unit with a passion!"

"No, because of the stigma placed on the Brigade from the Soldiers accused of and going on trial or being investigated for killing civilians."

"No one seems to have any integrity anymore. The leaders only care about themselves and don't care about the Soldiers. Soldiers are lost and don't know anything because leaders don't tell them. You have leaders that are constantly lying to Soldiers about things that they don't even know the answer to."

"Cohesion within the section and unit is rather poor and there is hardly any communication within the leaders, me, and other E-4 and below are running around trying to figure out which way a mission should be accomplished."

"No!!! I hate this place and the people! They are not well organized. They all act like the Army is brand new. They forget everything they knew before we reflagged."

OPEN COMMENTS SECTIONS

A portion of the command climate surveys were left completely open-ended for comments by soldiers. These unprompted responses are very instructive, in that they indicate the topics and issues which soldiers spontaneously regard as the most important to them:

"I think there are a lot of times that NCOs seem to forget the NCO creed about knowing the welfare of the soldier."

"The NCOs need to stop crying and man up."

"People need to quit bitching and just do their damn job already."

"No one wants to be here. The commander is the reason. The morale is very low across the whole unit, especially with the NCOs. I have never been a part of a unit that is totally divided like this one. I wish I would have never come here."

"Overall, the unit needs a lot of work."

"These NCOs should be counseled accordingly and kicked out of the military or out of their leadership positions."

"If I have to fill out another survey, I'll freak."

"The NCO's should never have been taken from platoons and swapped. My platoon seems to have gone downhill since then, lower morale and lower levels of trust among E4 and below. The camaraderie between the E4 and below soldiers is great, we're a family, but we don't really trust our new NCO's like we should."

"Can we all just get along?"

"Too many new leaders that shouldn't have been promoted."

"First Sergeant treats us like children."

"Training has helped minimally."

"Seems like the senior leaders make everything into a crisis."

"This unit has horrific communication."

"I think that the organizational climate in my workplace is very tense and distrusting towards the leadership because of our two main leaders. One doesn't seem to put out the proper information or know what's going on, and the other seems so full of himself, and makes others feel poorly about themselves, that it truly damages morale."

"My NCOs treat us like garbage and have no organization and are hypocritical in everything they do and say."

"Not enough respect."

"Morale of soldiers is incredibly low."

"People don't know where anything is because we switched leadership too quick and it's really hindering the unit. We need stability. I'm sick of shit changing every five minutes."

"Commander needs to come out of his cave and interact with Soldiers."

"The officers are impossible to approach regarding any issue, professional or personal. The commander does not care about the morale of his troops. It's basically, 'The beatings will continue until morale improves.' Senior ranking people play favorites when it comes to anything for the Soldier. Thank God I'm leaving this unit."

THE ARMY'S ANALYSES OF THE COMMAND CLIMATE SURVEYS

Some of the results were analyzed by some—though by no means all—executive officers and first sergeants at company levels. It is instructive to note the conclusions these officers drew from the surveys. One officer writes:

> Much of the data suggests that a focus group needs to be conducted to understand some of the issues: Soldiers have mixed feelings about officers; spread of conflict and stress during combat deployment; uncertainty in the unit that will have a negative impact on command climate; Soldiers not feeling valued by their leadership; Soldiers perceive that leadership does not work well together. The recommendation for focus groups should focus on: communication and information, dissemination, Soldier and unit morale, Soldier perceptions that leadership does not work well together.

Writing with regard to a different company, another officer concluded that the survey results:

> ...point out possible threats or consequences of collected data: reinforcing
> trust in leadership should be a top priority, allowing polarization to oc-
> cur will lead to an unhealthy command climate, higher headquarters must
> show command presence in order to show cohesiveness and capitalize on
> unit cohesiveness and strengthen the command climate

A captain from a different company summarizes the main issues that
emerge from his company's command climate surveys. His summary is
lengthy but worth noting:

> There are mistrust issues. Leadership is constantly being changed out.
> One soldier said his leadership unit was changed out 13 times through his
> time in the company. Some of the soldiers do not like the fact that they are
> referred to as idiots or retards.
>
> Correction of Soldiers: "If they are not an NCO, your comments do not
> matter."
>
> Favoritism: Favoritism is displayed by the First Sergeant, Platoon Ser-
> geant, and Platoon Leader.
>
> Micromanagement: One Soldier says he does not delegate anything be-
> cause he has so many bosses. "I don't need 19 bosses, I just need one."
>
> Approaching leadership: Some have a problem approaching leaders. This
> is mostly due to a lack of trust.
>
> No progression: Many feel like they have gone in a complete circle and are
> back to square one.
>
> Throwing the blame: Soldiers are tired of hearing the NCO's stating, "It's
> the leadership," using this comment to try to save their own hides.
>
> Lack of professionalism: One Soldier gave their NCO constructive criti-
> cism, and the NCO said to him: "Go f__ yourself." This NCO told the Sol-
> dier prior, "Anytime you need to talk one on one, come and get me."
>
> Soldiers are given the comment, "If you don't like something, get the rank
> to fix it."
>
> Hostile work environment: Some feel they are in a hostile work
> environment.
>
> Soldiers want to leave the company due to leadership.

A First Sergeant from an entirely different company offers the following assessment based upon the results of the surveys:

> There are Soldier issues and complaints with the chain of command....
> Witch hunt: there was an apparent for ____, this links back to trust.

Bringing up issues: I used to bring up issues, but now I do not due to reprimand. Another Soldier states that he had been told by LT____ that he will destroy him, that he will make him a private first class. LT____ has sent out an e-mail saying that he will destroy the NCO's. Counseling: Very few have received initial counseling. First names: All of the NCO's do not like the fact being called by their first names. LT____ is very passive aggressive. CPT___ only talks to LT___ and he doesn't interact with Soldiers. There is a major separation with the commander. Soldier. We didn't even know that the commander was on leave. Platoon meetings: Platoon meetings are worthless. Bringing up issues is a joke. When I bring things up they just get rejected. Removal: If I speak up, I will be removed. No guidance: I don't ask for guidance because I don't receive any guidance. Reprimand: We are going to get reprimanded for this survey. Getting out of the military: I have been told, "Oh well, you are getting out of the military." What kind of a comment is that?

Another First Sergeant from another company offers the following summary of his company's survey results:

Company events: There are no company events. There was one football game and one card game. What do we do as a company if we have identified that there is a morale problem? You are just frustrated then want to have a release. Punishment: One of the NCO's spoke up and now she is removed. Mental health issues: So many soldiers had to go to mental health from stress. PTSD comes from the constant mental stress. Derogatory terms: The commander has used the term retarded to describe some of us. For leadership, you have two factors: capability and care. There is also the "us" and "them." Sergeant First Class___ stated you can't trust your soldiers. Open door policy: Open door policy brought nothing but heartache.

CHAPTER 12. THE COURT-MARTIAL, PART I: FINDINGS

On March 23, 2011, shortly after the court-martial convened at 9:34 am, Corporal Morlock pleaded guilty to three charges of premeditated murder, two charges of conspiracy (to commit murder and separately, to assault Stoner), one charge of drug use, and one charge of obstruction of justice. He was not charged with assaulting Stoner. The military judge was Lieutenant Colonel Kwasi Hawks. The three prosecutors at the trial were Captain Andre LeBlanc Captain Dan Mazzone, and Captain Dan Hill. Morlock's defense attorneys in the court room were Mr. Frank Spinner and Captain Mark Opachan. The military officers were required to wear the equivalent of their Sunday best clothes, namely, Class A uniforms. The small, unventilated and aged court room was packed, mostly by over twenty-five members of Morlock's family. The news media was crowded into a separate room, where they watched the trial proceedings via closed circuit television. A court room is arranged as if it were a church, with the judge as the priest on his altar. All the actors behave ceremoniously according to rituals, including those that demarcate sacred words, objects, and spaces from profane ones. This is not surprising, given that the institution of law evolved out of religion. The sacred is that which is treated with awe and respect, while the profane is the ordinary. Court room drama consists of more than legal arguments and evidence—it feels like Church.

The military judge (MJ) rested his head upon his right hand, and looked like Rodin's statue of the thinker, albeit in a black robe. He kept this pensive, thoughtful position through most of the court-martial. The first order of business was for the MJ to determine whether or not Morlock was sincere in his pleas of guilty. The MJ said to him, in solemn words that all judges use in these circumstances:

> Now, a plea of guilty is equivalent to a conviction. *It is the strongest form of proof known to the law.* On your plea alone, without receiving any other evidence, this court can find you guilty of the offense to which you've pled guilty. So, I'm not going to accept your plea unless it's clear that you are admitting every act or omission, and every element of the offenses to which you have pled guilty. And Specialist Morlock, if you do not believe you are guilty, you should not plead guilty for any reason [emphasis added].

We shall set aside explaining the history of or reasons for the traditional belief that a plea of guilty is the "strongest form of proof known to the law." Suffice it to say that the accused's plea of guilty would be transformed by the MJ into a sacred, legal covenant of sorts, and thereby close almost all doors to defenses. The MJ read the list of rights that Morlock would be giving up by pleading guilty: the right against self-incrimination, the right to a trial of the facts by a court-martial, and the right to confront and cross-examine witnesses. Next, the MJ directed, "trial counsel, please place the accused under oath." At this point, the MJ turned to a 10-page document which was the "stipulation of fact" and entered it as Prosecution exhibit 1. The MJ explained: "Basically, Specialist Morlock, a stipulation of fact is an agreement. It's an agreement between you, between your lawyer, and between the trial counsel that the contents are true and if they are entered into evidence they become the uncontradicted facts in this case." The MJ had Morlock read the stipulation of fact and to affirm that he had signed it voluntarily and with the advice of defense counsel.

The MJ then reviewed basic facts about Morlock's stay in the army. Morlock joined the army in June of 2006, did his basic training in Fort Benning, Georgia, and went directly to airborne school. Morlock told me earlier that his father had pinned his "blood-wings" (airborne badge) onto his chest. Following airborne school, he was assigned to 5th Stryker Brigade, did not re-enlist, and was due to be released from the army in November of 2010. (His contract with the army was for four years and 19 weeks.)

The MJ asked: "Specialist Morlock, do you agree that ordinarily you would have ETS-ed, but you are still in the Army as you sit here right now?" "Yes, sir," Morlock replied.

The MJ then listed the charges against Morlock to which he had pled guilty: That he used hashish while deployed in Afghanistan. That he committed premeditated murder against three unnamed males "of apparent Afghan descent" on three separate occasions: the first on or about 1 January 2010 and 31 January 2010, the second on 22 February 2010, and the third on 2 May 2010. That he engaged in conspiracy or "entered into an agreement with members of B Company, 2-1 Infantry Regiment, 5th Stryker Brigade Combat Team, 2d Infantry Division, to commit premeditated murder of Afghan noncombatants." That, as an added element of the charge of conspiracy, Morlock, along with "Staff Sergeant Gibbs, Private First Class Holmes, Specialist Wagnon, Specialist Winfield performed one or more of the overt acts alleged, which are specifically of throwing grenades, and shooting with firearms three males of apparent Afghan descent for the purpose of bringing about the object of the agreement." That Morlock engaged in conspiracy to assault on Private Stoner on 5 May 2010 along with Staff Sergeant Gibbs, Staff Sergeant Bram, Specialist Kelly, Specialist Moore, Sergeant Jones, and Corporal Quintal. Finally, that he did obstruct justice by striking Stoner in order to impede an investigation into hashish use.

One should note that in addition to pleading guilty to offenses with which he had been charged, Morlock was involving a host of his comrades as co-conspirators in murder, assault, and drug use. This overt ritual of admitting his guilt served the covert function of making it easier for the government to prosecute his comrades. Without Morlock's cooperation, the government had a weak case or no case at all against Gibbs and Holmes. Most soldiers had invoked their 5th amendment against self-incrimination, and the government had no forensic or physical evidence of the killings. Furthermore, and despite the focus on Morlock's individual responsibility for what happened, this legal ritual was implicitly attributing collective responsibility onto his platoon and B Company. One should not overlook the obvious fact here that in getting Morlock to admit to his private guilt and his individual responsibility, the government was gaining the upper hand against his comrades.

In response to the MJ's question, Morlock replied that he understood all the charges against him. In keeping with the legal ritual—which is as predictable as any religious rite in any society—the MJ directed Morlock, "tell me in your own words" what happened. The MJ began with the charge of drug use. Morlock said that he began smoking hashish in September of 2009, when he deployed to Afghanistan.

MJ: You said a number of times, if you had to just give me a—kind of your best estimation, how many times between September 09 and May of 2010, 11 May 2010 would you say you've smoked?

Accused: I would say probably at least three or four times a week, sir.

Morlock further explained that the hashish "was rolled up into a tobacco cigarette, mixed in, Sir." He smoked hashish "in different places throughout the FOB, Sir, either in guys' individual living quarters, or in vehicles." By FOB, he was referring to Forward Operating Base Ramrod.

Morlock's explanation of the conspiracy to commit the killings, in his own words, is particularly important. The conspiracy involved Gibbs, Holmes, Wagnon, and Winfield, but not at the same time.

MJ: What was the agreement?

Accused: I don't think any of the guys that I conspired with were all together at one individual point, Sir, but conversations took on separately amongst all of us, I guess. Discussions generally were how previously, I mean, for lack of better term using, "drop weapons," Sir, throughout the battlefield to kind of justify and legitimize killing Afghans, Sir.

MJ: What's a "drop weapon"?

Accused: Drop weapon, Sir, is generally a weapon that's acquired on the battlefield, whether it be an AK-47, or a pistol, whether it be a raid or a cache, and it's a term that I guess gets commonly used around, especially in Iraq or Afghanistan, for situations that I am kind of involved in, Sir.

MJ: And just to be clear about that, it's a weapon that's been captured or found on the battlefield, and you use it to—you drop it on someone that you have engaged to legitimize shooting them to say they had a weapon?

Accused: Yes, Sir.

MJ: And you guys had some discussions that you are going to select targets, use these drop weapons—so, you would select a target, you would kill them, and then you would use the drop weapon to establish later when there was an investigation, "Hey, they had a weapon, and that's why I shot or killed them?"

Accused: Yes, Sir.

MJ: When was the first time you had a discussion with any of those people you discussed about this?

Accused: It would be sometime in November, Sir, of 2009, when Staff Sergeant Gibbs showed up to the platoon.

MJ: When was the first time you are sure in your mind that you had an agreement? In other words, it wasn't just kind of idle talk, you and somebody else had a plan that you are going to use a drop weapon to kill someone who was a noncombatant?

Accused: I'd probably say, you know, within a month or so after Staff Sergeant Gibbs showed up, Sir, so I mean, October to December, I believe, sometime around then, Sir, I guess.

MJ: Did he show up in October?

Accused: He showed up in November, Sir, I believe, mid-November.

MJ: and so maybe a month after that, so maybe late November to December?

Accused: Yes, Sir.

It is important to take careful note of the exact and precise characterization of *how* the killing "agreement" emerged. The media's characterization of a "kill team" as a set of specific individuals who spontaneously decided to murder civilians is misleading. The judge's questions and Morlock's replies point to the following, more accurate, version of what happened: The conspiracy to kill civilians began as part of a larger discussion of using drop weapons. The conspiracy did not begin as an agreement to kill, but as an agreement to use drop weapons, which snowballed into killing civilians. This insight is extremely important. We have seen that this discussion concerning drop weapons consumed the entire platoon: the entire platoon was involved, directly or indirectly (through the use of drop weapons) in the killing of the mentally handicapped Afghan in mid-January, a killing that never resulted in any criminal charges, because a (planted) magazine was found on the body. This means that the drop weapons were already in place, along with a plan to use them with regard to "legitimate" killings, prior to two of the killings which were charged as murder, and concurrently with one of the charged killings. There was a continuum of understanding in the entire platoon, which ranged from "idle talk" to "agreement," concerning the use of drop weapons. There was also a continuum of understanding regarding the "agreement" as to what constitutes a "legitimate" versus "questionable" kill—the presence of a weapon on the body legitimized the killing. Thus, there seems to have been an agreement that the labeling of "legitimate" versus "questionable" killing would be settled by the presence of a weapon on the body. Given this set of social agreements, which were already in place in the entire platoon, Gibbs acted as the catalyst for the final leap into collective madness: to deliberately kill civilians and then plant drop weapons to legitimize the kills. The "kill team" consisted of different soldiers on different occasions because this agreement was widespread in the platoon, and was not limited to a specific set of individuals who acted without the knowledge, tacit or explicit, of their comrades. The MJ continued with his questioning:

MJ: You had mentioned that members of the conspiracy were probably never in one place at one time, you know, having a formal agreement, and in this proceeding you can tell me anything you know even if you didn't see it yourself. In other words, if later reviewing things with your counsel, and other things that you have heard, you know something, it's fine to tell me that, but as far as you know right now, who all was a member of this conspiracy?

Accused: Three general ranks, Sir, I mean, it was almost an entire platoon for the most part, give or take a handful of Soldiers, Sir.

Again, let us be precise in our understanding. According to Morlock, almost the entire platoon was involved in the actual, formal conspiracy to kill unarmed Afghans even though only five of the twenty-five members of the platoon were charged with conspiracy to commit murder.

This suggests complicated group dynamics which the military judge, of course, would not pursue sociologically, because American law only punishes individuals. The MJ continued with his probing questions:

MJ: Let me ask you this, the alleged overt acts are throwing grenades and shooting firearms at three males of apparent Afghan descent. Staff Sergeant Gibbs, PFC Holmes, Specialist Wagnon, and Specialist Winfield all do—and you, all do either shoot or throw a grenade at Afghans?

Accused: Yes, sir.

MJ: Did they do it as—when they did that, was it part of this plan you guys had to use the drop weapons and kill people?

Accused: Yes, Sir. It was all part of prior conversations, Sir.

MJ: I just want to be crystal clear about what the agreement was. Were you going to shoot at people to scare them, and it got out of hand, or was the plan, "We are going kill people, no doubt about it?"

Accused: The plan was to kill people, Sir....

MJ: With regard to the agreement that you and Staff Sergeant Gibbs were in, you said members of your platoon, a lot of members of your platoon, most of them. What's the plan—did everybody know it was unlawful? Was there anybody who thought, "We have some guys who maybe we have been told we're not supposed to shoot them for ROE, but they're really the enemy, too, and we really have a right to engage them," or did everybody know, "We're killing people who are completely innocent and they are not enemies of the United States, we are just killing people?"

Accused: Speaking on behalf of everyone, Sir, I think, you know, some people might have some—their personal opinions about who's innocent in certain villages and what not, Sir, but generally, Sir, yes. Everybody knew what we were doing was unlawful, Sir.

MJ: Was that your opinion?

Accused: Yes, Sir.

Both the question and the reply are important, and complex. Both the judge and the accused are aware that some soldiers, including Morlock, had thoughts along the lines that everyone in the village is the enemy. Yet, the platoon members also knew that killing persons in this manner, whether or not they were the enemy, was unlawful. The news media focused on only one sentence by Morlock in this exchange, specifically, "The plan was to kill people," and used it for that day's headline. The media did not report the context of the exchange between the MJ and Morlock. The MJ continued:

MJ: Did you have an agreement with at least some members of your platoon to again, kill people who you knew were not legitimate enemies of the United States?

Accused: Yes, Sir.

MJ: Tell me why it was, in your view, premeditated?

Accused: We had discussed it prior to putting the action into place, so we knew—we had planned to follow through and commit the things that we did before it actually happened, Sir.

MJ: And have you talked with your lawyers about heat of passion?

Accused: Yes, sir.

MJ: You're on a battlefield, I mean, your unit came under fire from real enemies of the United States.

Accused: Yes, Sir.

MJ: And did your platoon lose anybody?

Accused: No, Sir. We had some fellows lose some limbs, Sir, in my direct platoon, but no lives were lost in my platoon, Sir.

MJ: So, you had some serious casualties?

Accused: Yes, Sir.

MJ: Were any of these discussions or decisions to kill people kind of in the heat of that situation, or were they all things where you were calm, you were cool, you were thinking about it, and you decided, "We're going to kill people who are not our enemies?"

Accused: It might have been used for fuel at that point in time, Sir, it was, you know, maybe exacting some revenge, but at the end of it, Sir, everyone knew that it was just kind of to go out and kill someone, Sir.

MJ: How long—from the time there was an agreement made to the time that there was actually, I think in the stipulation they are called scenarios, how long from that time there was definitely an agreement until the time one of these scenarios went into effect?

Accused: Probably a few weeks, Sir.

MJ: So, no doubt in your mind that during that entire period of weeks, a group of you had an active plan you were going to kill somebody as soon as the situation was right?

Accused: Yes, Sir.

Corporal Morlock explains the January killing

The usual legal defense against the charge of premeditated murder, namely, being under the influence of "heat of passion," does not seem to apply in this case. Morlock added that the desire to exact revenge for the injuries to his comrades played some, but not a major role in the platoon's "agreement" to kill. The MJ then asked Morlock to explain, in his own words, what happened at each of the three killings, starting with the first one, in January of 2010. These passages are important because they offer details that are not found in the CID interrogations and media accounts. Morlock replied:

> Sir, I believe it was January 15th, about, Sir. Our platoon was on an aver-
> age patrol to a village that we made prior trips to. This particular village

had been kind of flagged as pro-Taliban, if you will. We got a lot of ICOM chatter from that town, and some resistance from the locals. It was a typical meet and greet. The lieutenant had to go engage the local elder in the town and ask this questionnaire sheet of, "How's it going in town, what can we help with," and what not. So, that day, while that was taking place with the lieutenant, probably a couple of squad leaders, security was set in kind of the immediate area of the compound they were meeting in. And then myself and PFC Holmes, he was my junior SAW gunner, Sir, on my team, we were just in place pulling up that security, and in the midst of that we were approached by an Afghan male, and then at that time, me and PFC Holmes made an agreement with ourselves to go ahead with one of these scenarios, if you will Sir, that had been previously talked about with Staff Sergeant Gibbs. This involved a fragmentary grenade, Sir, that had been given to me by Staff Sergeant Gibbs in previous weeks, and after me and PFC Holmes went into the agreement of what we were about to do, we were behind a wall, Sir, the Afghani was roughly about 20 meters and to our front, Sir. Holmes was positioned—his weapon was on top of the wall directed towards the Afghani man, and I began to prep the fragmentary grenade, Sir. I asked Holmes if he was ready, I dropped the grenade on the other side of the wall, Holmes let out a burst of his SAW, and then the grenade exploded. I had stood back up to see the Afghani, and fired off a few shots with my weapon, Sir, and made a radio call to my squad leader to give him a situation report on—to what we wanted everyone to believe had happened, Sir. I led to tell him we were approached by an Afghan male, and PFC Holmes had identified the grenade and a threat, and was forced to shoot him, Sir.

The MJ further determined that the village was approximately 20 kilometers from FOB Ramrod, that the platoon arrived in their Stryker vehicles, and that Morlock and Holmes did not perceive the Afghan male to be a threat in any way. Then the MJ asked an intriguing question:

MJ: Any chance that someone else shot these guys? Did you see anybody else, or anybody else ever later say, "Hey, I was firing"?

Accused: Yes, Sir. Not in the direct incident, though, as far as at the time that me and Holmes fired, but after my situation report was called up, Sir, I was reinforced, if you will, Sir, by members of the platoon, and my squad leader. Staff Sergeant Sprague arrived at my location, and I believe he was given an order from the XO who was out with us that day, Captain Mitchell, to—I believe the words were something, to make sure that the individual was dead. And Sergeant Sprague took that as approach the individual and release two shots into the man at pretty close range, Sir.

MJ: Did he shoot him in the head?

Accused: I couldn't tell you exactly, Sir.

MJ: But he fundamentally performed a *coup de grace*—

Accused: Yes, Sir.

MJ: He shot him at close range with the intent of killing him?

Accused: Yes, Sir.

From a legal perspective, none of the facts disclosed in this exchange made any difference regarding the murder charge against Morlock. Sergeant Sprague and Captain Mitchell were not charged with anything in relation to this incident. Let us set aside the legal perspective, and absorb the import of Morlock's testimony, namely, that the entire platoon "reinforced" Morlock's actions, knowingly or unwittingly. The squad leader, Gibbs, knew that the killing was unlawful, so his support was part of the cover-up. One will never be certain what Sprague, Mitchell, or the others knew or did not know about the conspiracy. But the important point is that the entire platoon supported the killing, partly because they are trained to support each other. In other words, it was *not* the case that Holmes and Morlock killed the Afghan, and the rest of the platoon was startled or that it started challenging Holmes and Morlock about the kill. Various shades of tacit and explicit knowledge about the conspiracy to kill, the conspiracy to use drop weapons, and other "agreements" were already in place in the collective consciousness of the platoon. As another soldier, from a completely different incident, time, and place told me, "Sir, every time we go out on a mission, we are all engaged in conspiracy." What he meant was that by the nature of its function, a combat platoon already has in place numerous, pre-existing social "agreements" about how to engage the enemy and support its members. The conspiracy by Holmes, Morlock, and Gibbs in this incident would have had an entirely different quality had they carried it out against a civilian in some peaceful town in the United States, where the residents would have been startled and shocked. Instead, the conspiracy being described here dovetailed into multiple, other "conspiracies" in the platoon, ranging from lawful through questionable to unlawful (such as the agreement to plant drop weapons). The law is unable to take these complex, *social* factors into account. The fact that it was Sprague, not Morlock or Holmes, who killed the Afghan, makes no difference at all legally. The fact that the platoon, and also the company, battalion, and brigade hold some degrees of collective responsibility for what happened, simply has no place in contemporary American law. For example, Sprague's decision to finish off the Afghan man was not his alone, but is a common practice among US Army infantry soldiers, according to what soldiers have told me in interviews. Even the judge immediately recognized the act as a *coup de grace*, which is a French term that is instantly familiar to American soldiers.

Perhaps some other judge would have left unresolved this issue of who actually killed the Afghan man. But this judge pursued it:

MJ: How do you know that you, or PFC Holmes, who is a member of the conspiracy, killed him?

Accused: I can only assume, Sir, that a burst from an automatic weapon, you know, and comparatively close distance to a fragmentary grenade going off, Sir, that would be the end result.

MJ: Defense, what's your position on if the death resulted from the actions of Specialist Morlock or Staff Sergeant Sprague? If the death resulted from Staff Sergeant Sprague's action, was that an intervening cause or was that—at that point does the manner of death become Specialist Morlock's report that this person is a combatant?

Defense counsel: Can I have a moment, Sir?

[The accused conferred with his defense counsel.]

MJ: Trial counsel, while the defense is talking about this, was there any medical evaluation on this 15 January homicide that establishes exactly whose bullets or what his manner of death was?

TC: No, Sir.

MJ: Well, let me ask you this. What is your theory of liability?

TC: That the death resulted from the actions of PFC Holmes and Specialist Morlock, Sir.

MJ: And when you say, "the actions," do you mean the shooting and grenade throwing?

TC: Right, Sir.

MJ: If it turns out that's not true, is there an alternate theory?

TC: Well, yes, Sir.

MJ: Why do you know that's—he doesn't know whether it's his grenade or the bullets that killed him. Let me ask you this, Specialist Morlock, do you believe when the grenade was dropped near you, and the whole point of it was to simulate that this guy was throwing it at you, do you have any reason to think that its concussive blast injured the man?

Accused: I believe it's possible, Sir, but I wouldn't be able to tell you for sure, though, Sir.

MJ: Can you tell me for sure whether your bullets or Holmes' bullets are definitely the reason why this guy is dead?

Accused: No, Sir.

TC: Well, Sir, in either case, the proximate cause of the death is the actions of Specialist Morlock and Private Holmes, in the respect that either their grenade and bullets resulted in his death. I think, Sir, if you inquire into the position of the body, was he moving after that, or anything like that, I think it would become more clear that he didn't appear to be alive at that point, and even if he wasn't, Sir, if Staff Sergeant Sprague's bullet was the *coup de grace*, as you put it, Specialist Morlock's report to his squad leader that he was engaged by a hostile—by hostile force, and that was the cause for that person to shoot at him, he's still provident to the offense, Sir.... Our view of this and our understanding of the law is that under the law principles, just—a man was killed as an object of the conspiracy, and aiding and abetting whether it was his bullet that killed him or not, or whose bullet killed him, he acted in furtherance of the conspiracy to completeness, and so, the death would be flowing from the conspiracy.

MJ: Would you agree that the killing blow must have been landed by a member of the conspiracy?

TC: Well, that's—I don't know that it has to be a bullet from a co-conspirator, as long as the object of the conspiracy is completed....

MJ: Thank you. Specialist Morlock, let me ask you, after throwing of the grenade and the burst by PFC Holmes, could you see the man?

Accused: No, Sir. I was, like I said, Holmes's position with his weapon posted on the wall, Sir, and after I released the grenade, I had taken cover behind the wall, Sir.

MJ: Okay... Prior to you issuing the report, do you—either from what you remember that day, or anything you have learned since then, do you have any reason to think any other shooter who was not part of the conspiracy was shooting at the beginning?

Accused: No, Sir....

MJ: And if you had wanted to, at that point, you could have said to your squad leader, "no, don't shoot," you know, "the XO is wrong, my report is wrong, this guy is not an enemy, do not shoot." You could have done that?

Accused: Yes, Sir...

MJ: And so, do you agree with me that whether your bullets directly killed him or whether the situation you created led to this guy's death, he died as a result of what you and PFC Holmes did?

Accused: Yes, Sir.

The government and the judge had Morlock agree that he killed the Afghan man in terms of legal theory. In fact, no one will ever know who killed the Afghan man or how the man died because the victim's body was never recovered and no forensic tests were ever performed on it. But according to legal theory, Morlock is guilty because he was part of a conspiracy to kill the Afghan man, and the man's death was a result of that conspiracy—even if the man died from Sprague's bullets, and Sprague was not part of that particular conspiracy to kill the man.

However, this legal theory of what occurred opened the door for Holmes's attorneys to challenge an essential assumption in the theory, namely, whether Holmes was in "agreement" (or conspiracy) with Morlock to kill the Afghan man. In two separate pre-trial hearings, Holmes's attorneys argued that Holmes did not know what Morlock intended, and that Holmes fired because he thought that Morlock was in danger from a hostile enemy. Moreover, they argued that there was no evidence that Holmes's bullets ever struck the Afghan man, a factual point which, as we have seen, is of no consequence in assessing Holmes's (or anyone's) legal guilt in a conspiracy. Nevertheless, Holmes eventually signed a pre-trial agreement in which he pleaded to premeditated murder in exchange for a sentence of eight years. The prosecution thought they needed Holmes to bolster Morlock's testimony in the eventual court-martial of Gibbs.

CORPORAL MORLOCK EXPLAINS THE FEBRUARY 22ND SHOOTING

The judge asked Morlock to tell him what happened in the February 22, 2010 shooting. Morlock explained:

> It was a similar situation, Sir. It was just another average patrol. We actually had quite a bit more intelligence on this particular village, Sir. I had made prior trips to this village in the previous weeks and months, a lot of Taliban activity in that region. On that specific day, I believe, our LT's specific task was to go out and we were going to try to categorize village members with other corresponding compounds, so we kind of go to put together a roster of the village. So that day, the LT, I think, met up with one of the village elders in the center of town, and then our platoon began to do a rough 360 of that area so the LT could do his thing. Staff Sergeant Gibbs, being in charge of first squad, and myself in second, there was a point in the security where our lines kind of intersected, Sir. So, at the end of first squad's line is kind of where my security picked up, and that's when myself and Specialist Wagnon were those two security elements in that part of the line. We were pulling security on a pretty wide entrance to one of the compounds. We were approached by Staff Sergeant Gibbs. We ultimately went into the compound and found an Afghani individual and had brought him out and Staff Sergeant Gibbs had—he let us know that he had an AK-47 in his assault pack, that he had acquired through a previous engagement, Sir. A vehicle was blown up, and he happened to get an AK-47 out of the ordeal. He asked me and Specialist Wagnon if we were willing to participate with him staging this AK-47 he planted on this guy. And basically, he was going to say that he was shot at or engaged by the individual, and then the end result would—we would have to eliminate the threat, Sir. So, what ultimately ended up happening, I believe, Sergeant Gibbs had us watch the individual while he removed the AK from his assault pack, and then he had set the individual out a few meters from him, and then myself and Specialist Wagnon went back to our security positions, and there were two shots from the AK-47 that Staff Sergeant Gibbs had had. He had fired into a wall behind his position, and then, I believe from there, he tossed the AK at the individual's feet, and engaged the individual with his M4. From my position, Sir, we were probably about 10 meters away, and I couldn't actually see the individual. He was behind him in a corner of the compound when Gibbs had fired.

After Gibbs had fired, a handful of rounds, myself and Specialist Wagnon moved to his immediate location on the corner of this wall, and then we both—Wagnon was carrying a SAW, so I think he let off a few bursts from his SAW, Sir, and then I fired a few shots with my M4 in the direction of the individual who was at the time laying on the ground, Sir. And then from there, I believe Sergeant Gibbs called up a situation report, and laid it out in the same context, Sir, that he was fired upon from the individual and we used force to engage.

MJ: Whose bullets do you think actually killed that person?

Accused: I would have to say Staff Sergeant Gibbs, Sir, because by the time myself and Wagnon got to his location, the individual was already on the ground, Sir.

MJ: And when he did that—when he was doing the firing that brought the guy to the ground, were you and Specialist Wagnon in a conspiracy with Staff Sergeant Gibbs? Were you still in that agreement you told me about earlier?

Accused: Yes, Sir. We had the conversation prior to prepping the AK, if you will, Sir...

MJ: And again, what exactly—who said what in that conversation?

Accused: I believe we were both approached by Staff Sergeant Gibbs around the same time. We were only with a few meters of each other, Sir, and I can't speak exactly what Gibbs's words were, but somewhere along the lines of he asked us if we were willing to assist and be a part of killing this individual, Sir. And I believe a quote from Wagnon that's been—he said something along the lines that it wasn't his first rodeo, Sir, and I agreed with Staff Sergeant Gibbs that I would participate and support him, I guess....

MJ: Counsel, do we know if this person is dead? Anybody?

TC: Sir, I think further inquiry with Specialist Morlock that he returned to the scene and observed the actual body and possibly took a photograph with it.

MJ: Is that true?

Accused: Yes, Sir...

MJ: And it was clear to you when he was put into the body bag that he was dead?

Accused: Yes, Sir.

CORPORAL MORLOCK DESCRIBES THE MAY 2ND KILLING

MJ: Let's talk about 2 May.

Accused: The 2nd of May, Sir. I had been back in country for roughly about a month, Sir, returned from my R&R, I got back, I believe, April 6th or April 7th. I was immediately approached by Staff Sergeant Gibbs pretty quickly upon my return about some other items he had acquired, Sir, explosives, off the books C-4, if you will, and some RPG rockets, and then it had gone into some conversation about more scenarios that would be possibly put into action later on, Sir. May 2nd came along, I believe it was a local village, this one was no more than a few kilometers outside the FOB, Sir. We would be returning to an individual's compound that had previously been arrested for having an IED found in his house. That occurred while I was gone on leave, so I don't know exactly the end result of that, but apparently, this individual had been released. So, the LT's job that day was to go out and reengage that individual and question him. So, that had happened, the LT found this guy, we set in roughly security, a 360 of that building. In the time that the LT was questioning this individual, Gibbs had grabbed a few of us to sweep some of the surrounding buildings, Sir, from this individual's compound. The result of that was, Gibbs had found an individual in a nearby compound living nearby, and then approached myself and Winfield directly about putting in effect the scenario of a Russian grenade that he had found earlier on. And it would be similar to the first incident in January, Sir, as we were approached by an individual holding a grenade and we were forced to engage him as a threat. So, me and Specialist Winfield were directed by Staff Sergeant Gibbs to take up a prone position about 15 to 20 feet away from this individual. He had placed the individual near his compound, near a wall, Sir, and then Gibbs himself had backed up to a corner on the compound. The plan was he was going to release a grenade in intent that this individual had thrown it at us, and then me and Winfield would be forced to engage him. But, what actually happened, apparently Gibbs thrown a grenade too far, Sir, and he had thrown the grenade and it exploded fairly close to the individual and to myself and Winfield. Winfield was on a SAW, and released a burst or two in the direction of the man, as well as I did at the same time, Sir. I fired a few rounds in that individual's direction. After the grenade explosion, and it was clear that the individual was on the ground, myself and Gibbs moved to his position, and that's when I had laid the Russian grenade near him, and at that point, Staff Sergeant Gibbs took two point-blank shots to the individual's head, and then from there, we went back to our security positions, and then we were approached tactically by the rest of the platoon. The LT had wanted to know what was going on in a situation report, and then it was—Sir, what was played out to—what we wanted it to—the scenario, Sir, basically.

MJ: So while your lieutenant was questioning this other person, this person just presented themselves?

Accused: Yes, Sir.

MJ: And again, any intelligence or other reason to believe this person presented a threat?

Accused: Not directly, Sir, no.

MJ: And you say, "not directly." What, if anything?

Accused: Just the dynamic of the battlefield, Sir. It's a warzone, so anyone perceivably could've been a threat.

The MJ determined with further questioning that this Afghan man had his legs blown off by the grenade so that absent any urgent medical intervention, he had assuredly died.

THE CONSPIRACY AND ASSAULT ON PRIVATE STONER

The MJ asked Morlock to explain the conspiracy to assault Stoner. Morlock replied that he was approached by Sergeants Bram and Gibbs shortly after the May 2nd killing, sometime in early May. They told him that Stoner had told the chain of command that he and others in the platoon were smoking hashish. As they walked to Stoner's room, they joined up with additional soldiers: Kelly, Jones, and Quintal. Morlock said:

> We entered Stoner's room, he was sitting there on his cot, I don't know who engaged in conversation with him first, but he had said what he had said about individuals in the platoon using drugs. So, some short conversation was, you know, taken, and then I believe Stoner told us as a group that he understands why we are there, and to go ahead and take place in his ass beating, if you will, Sir. From there, I don't know who grabbed him first, but it didn't take much after that, and someone had thrown him on the ground and everyone kind of took their shots. It was discussed prior to going into his room that no one would hit him in the face, Sir. So, myself, I gave him a few punches to the chest, and other than probably some yelling and screaming that had been going on, that was about it on my end. I know a couple other guys had kicked him, and I think at the end of it, some individual had spit on PFC Stoner. Then after that, Sir, we had left his room

The MJ inquired into the hair-splitting, legal technicalities of which of the other soldiers also engaged in the conspiracy, and whether it was a conspiracy. Morlock said that he did not know what Kelly, Moore, Jones and Quintal had discussed before going into Stoner's room. The judge asked: "Was your prior agreement one to harm PFC Stoner, or were you just going to talk to him?" Morlock replied: "I don't think, Sir, it was ever directly said that, you know, 'Hey, we're going to go and punch Stoner in the chest,' but I think in less words to none, that there was an understanding that we were going to take care of what we had to take care of, and that entailed beating up Stoner." Morlock's explanation fits the legal definition of conspiracy, which does not require an explicit, overt, or verbal plan to engage in an action. "What were you guys trying to accomplish by going in to see Stoner?" Morlock replied:

I have to speak honestly, Sir, obviously, but part of it would definitely be a dislike for his actions and the dislike for him personally, Sir. He is an individual who did not mesh well with the platoon to begin with, and this was kind of why he was on a FOB detail and didn't go on patrols with us. So, that definitely played a part, Sir, but ultimately it was, you know, to have him keep his mouth shut about anything else he might have known about what was going on in our platoon.

In the rest of his questions on this issue, the MJ seems to miss completely the significance of Morlock's remark that the platoon did not want Stoner to talk about "what was going on in our platoon." What was going on in the platoon entailed more than hashish use, and included agreements about drop weapons, keeping explosives, and killing scenarios. But the MJ concentrated solely on the connection between Stoner and hashish. Later in the inquiry, Morlock told the MJ that he went back to Stoner and threatened him further if he "continued with divulging information about our misconduct."

Quite apart from the legal theory and verbiage, the sequence of events is significant. The last killing occurred on May 2nd, Stoner was beaten up on or about May 5th, and by May 10th CID was inquiring into the killings as well as the hashish usage. Presumably, Gibbs was afraid that Stoner knew about and would divulge information on the scenarios and/or killings—in addition to the hashish use—and by this point was threatening to kill Morlock and Winfield if they talked with CID. To miss this point (that inquiry into hashish use opened doors to other misconduct) is to miss the significance of why Morlock and Winfield told CID about the killing shortly after Stoner was beaten up: The assault was a message to Stoner, but also to everyone else in the platoon, to keep their mouths shut. By the first week of May, everyone in the platoon was scared of Gibbs.

DISAVOWAL OF DEFENSES

The MJ went over each and every legal defense that Morlock abandoned in his stipulation of fact, which he had signed prior to the court-martial. The government insisted that Morlock give up these defenses to explain or mitigate his actions, and I know that he was reluctant to do so. But in the end, Spinner, Opachan and Morlock concluded that he had no choice but to give in to the government. The only major legal defense that he did not give up was that his behavior was connected to a dysfunctional command climate. The MJ had Morlock agree that he gave up the defense that he was obeying orders by Gibbs. Next, Morlock agreed that he was not suffering from any mental disease or defect, so he gave up the defense of mental responsibility. The MJ asked: "With regard to voluntary intoxication, were you actively under the effect of hashish for any of the offenses other than the use of hashish?" In other words, was Morlock "stoned" during any of the killings or conspiracies to which he had pled guilty?

Accused: There might have been overlapped time, Sir. The incidents themselves, no, Sir. I don't think that I ever used hashish on mission or prior to patrols, or anything like that, Sir. The assault on Stoner, possibly, you know, the day before, or the night of, possibly, Sir.

MJ: So it may have been in your system?

Accused: Yes, Sir.

MJ: But do you think it affected your judgment?

Accused: No, Sir.

MJ: And withdrawal from conspiracy—and again, prior to May, was there ever a point where you went to Gibbs or anybody else and said, "That's it, I'm done, I'm never participating in any of these scenarios again?"

Accused: I had my own personal incident, Sir, when I went on R&R. I think I left early in March, and spent the better part of that month home, and then in transit back. It was a really hard decision for me to come back to deployment for the simple fact that I didn't want to engage or be a part in anything else that might have occurred in the last two months.

MJ: Did you communicate those misgivings to any member of the conspiracy?

Accused: No, Sir.

MJ: Did you specifically talk about duress with your counsel?

Accused: Yes, Sir, we covered it.

MJ: Do you understand that duress is not a defense to any homicide offense, but it is a possible defense to the others, particularly with regard to everything that happened with Stoner?

Accused: Yes, sir....

MJ: If I hear you, your fear of Gibbs wasn't really a motivation for you in your actions towards Stoner?

Accused: No, Sir.

Morlock was sufficiently upset with the first two killings that he wanted to go AWOL during his R&R rather than return to his unit and remain under Gibbs's command. He did not talk about this with his comrades, but he did discuss it with his mother and brother, who talked him into going back. (To be fair, he did not tell them why he wanted to go AWOL.) But to the law, this psychic anguish did not qualify as motivation "to withdraw from the conspiracy." Similarly, Morlock and the other soldiers were afraid that Gibbs would kill them, but this fear, or "duress" does not qualify as a defense in homicide cases.

Having given up his defenses, the MJ asked both counsel if he had overlooked anything. The prosecutor chimed in that the MJ needed to consider the effects of the prescription medications that Morlock had been taking.

MJ: Did you have a valid prescription for any prescription medication while you were at—really from September of 09 to May of 2010.

Accused: Not a prescription as you would—you would see as far as stateside, Sir. The prescription would entail a trip to the aid station, the Roll 2, and you know, Flexeril, a muscle relaxer, that was pretty, a pretty common over-the-counter from the physician's assistant (PA) to any Soldier as long as, you know, you made a legitimate claim that you needed them. There were quite a few prescription drugs that I was using throughout the entire deployment that was here.... [also] Flexeril, and the common 800 milligram Ibuprofen, which you know, that gets passed around like candy over there. And then our medic prescribed Amitriptyline, and he was kind of handing that out to Solders that needed it.

MJ: And what does that do?

Accused: Amitriptyline, I believe, it's a mild antidepressant, and it also doubled for sleep, Sir... I had been using a few different sleeping medications, Sir, depending on their availability. Ambien was a major one used, and then Trazodone, I believe, Sir, was the other one. Off the top of my head, Sir, that's all I can really remember.

MJ: Specifically with regard to the Amitriptyline, Ambien, and Trazodone, do you think any of those affected your judgment in a way that might have affected your commission of any of these offenses?

Accused: Not directly, Sir.

Intervening Steps in the Legal Process

Having accepted Morlock's formal disavowal of most defenses, the MJ turned to the prosecutor and asked, "What do you calculate to be the maximum punishment based solely on the accused's plea of guilty?" The prosecutor replied: "To be confined for life without the possibility of parole, to be dishonorably discharged from the United States Army, to be reduced to the lowest enlisted grade, and to forfeit all pay and allowances."

Next, the MJ asked to see the pretrial agreement, and explained that "basically, a pretrial agreement is a contract. You agree to plead guilty, the convening authority takes action in return, ultimately in the form of limiting the maximum sentence that they will approve in this case." The MJ also said that he was legally obligated to go over the pretrial agreement with Morlock at this point in the trial. One part of the agreement stated that Morlock would "waive all waivable motions," which is a phrase that is difficult to comprehend for anyone except lawyers (and Spinner never explained to me what it means). The MJ spent some time on this phrase:

MJ: Government, what does that provision mean to you?

TC: Sir, that meant to us that all motions are waived. However, we have come to an agreement about how to resolve that issue with defense counsel....

MJ: Defense, what motions, if any, were waived as a result of this provision?

Defense: As we discussed this, what we saw was some ambiguity in this provision in terms of there were serious points where we had potential discovery issues, but all of those were resolved, and potential other issues that—for appropriate relief, minor issues, but they have all been resolved. So, it's not as though there is some motion that was sitting out there on the table that because of this provision we took off the table....

MJ: Well, I guess that's what this goes to. What would you have filed if this provision did not exist?

Spinner: The potential is that we would have filed a motion to suppress, but I can only say, "potential" because ... as lawyers, we have an obligation to deter—to watch the confession, to determine whether or not it was involuntary to see—so, we considered the potential of filing any suppression to a motion.

MJ: As I understand you, you didn't, in part, because of [this provision], because you decided it would be better to resolve this case and all of the issues surrounding it, through this pretrial agreement?

Spinner: Right, after we reflected upon the full context of the case, we believe that this was the best way to proceed.

In plain language, the government obtained a concession from Morlock that forbade him from filing any motion for any reason to challenge their handling of the case, including the coerced, videotaped statement. But, if Morlock refused to concede this victory to the government, then the government would withdraw the pretrial agreement or contract which limited his sentence to 24 years. Not surprisingly, Spinner resolved these issues with the government through negotiation, in order to avoid the need to file motions and thereby lose "the deal." Had Spinner challenged the coerced videotaped statement, he would have risked his client facing a life sentence without the possibility of parole. Lawyer-ing truly is a form of combat, but the government has the upper hand.

The MJ listed the forthcoming cases in which Morlock would be obligated to testify against his comrades as part of his pretrial agreement, namely, "in the proceedings of United States v. Gibbs, Winfield, Stevens, Wagnon, Holmes, Kelly, Bram, Ashton, Moore, Jones, Quintal, and Corey Moore." The prosecutor added that in addition to these eleven cases, the agreement obligates Morlock to testify in "any other potential cases that might develop out of this investigation." Basically, the government would get unlimited testimony out of Morlock as part of "the deal." The

MJ also noted that the pretrial agreement included provisions that Morlock would be allowed four out-of-state witnesses and two expert witnesses to testify on his behalf.

A dispute arose as to how long Morlock would be obligated to testify against his comrades and when the terms of the pretrial agreement would end. As written, the pretrial agreement gave the government one full year to complete the eleven other cases. However, the prosecutor asked for the period of time to be extended to three years and to allow for additional cases. The MJ ordered a recess at 12:04 pm in order to discuss these issues with counsel behind closed doors. The court-martial resumed at 1:37 pm. The MJ announced that the two parties had agreed that the pretrial agreement would be valid for three years. In effect, this means that Morlock would be obligated to testify as a government witness against his comrades for a period of three years, and if he failed to comply, the government would withdraw from the contract and he would be sentenced to life imprisonment.

THE GUILTY VERDICT

The MJ announced that Morlock had "knowingly, intelligently, and consciously" waived his rights and "accordingly, your plea of guilty is provident and is accepted." The MJ asked defense counsel whether there had been any "illegal pretrial punishment" in Morlock's case. Captain Opachan stated that the government had agreed that Morlock was entitled to a credit of 60 days, and continued:

> Thank you sir. We believe the circumstances surrounding credit for illegal pretrial punishment relate to a number of circumstances. First, when Specialist Morlock was brought back from Afghanistan and into the regional correctional facility here on-post, he was held in solitary confinement. We believe the conditions of the confinement were more onerous than were required under the circumstances. Specifically, he was held in solitary confinement without any personal contact with anybody for 23 hours a day. He was only allowed out of his cell for one hour for recreation. As he was let out of his cell for recreation, he was required to be outside of his cell in a common area within the confinement facility inside, and was required to be in hand and leg irons at that point in time. Additionally, he was subject to taking showers in a facility there that is subject to a push-button control that allows a burst of water for only 10-second intervals and no temperature control, and at times was subjected to certain circumstances where it was only cold water. Additionally, he was allowed virtually no access to anything else, no reading material and the like for that period of time with the exception of a Bible that was there in his cell. At some point in time, Sir, he was transferred to the Naval brig at Bremerton for his pretrial confinement, and was there from a period of approximate-

ly July until the end of November. He was ultimately brought back onto the regional confinement facility here, and when he came back ... he was placed back out in H block instead of being housed where he originally had been housed in a cell that's typically reserved for inmates who haven't lost privileges.... Additionally, Sir, in addition to the conditions of confinement, he was also subject to essentially three incidents or problems that he had with guards that were there. At one point, one of the guards made a disparaging remark to him, essentially calling him, and I'm reciting for the record, Sir, "a fucking murderer," and telling him that he would see his ass at Fort Leavenworth, which was reported and extensively investigated by officials at the facility there.... His cell was placed in disarray....he was verbally berated by one of the guards there in front of his family members whenever they would see him...There was also a similar situation where his cell was "shook down" for lack of a better term. Those circumstances, Sir, are kind of in a nutshell, the ones that we discussed with the government and have reached our agreement. Thank you, Sir.

The government did not dispute these charges, but blamed the mistreatment on the staff of the regional army prison at Ft. Lewis, which is referred to as the RCF [regional correctional facility]. Legally, Morlock held the status of "innocent until proven guilty" during this period of time at RCF. The mistreatment was not unique to him—I have come across similar, routine, pre-trial mistreatment in other war crimes cases. It is worth repeating that, in contrast to the army, the navy brig staff did not mistreat Morlock in any way. Morlock would be given 60 days credit toward his sentence as redress for this mistreatment. In addition, he would be given something called an "Allen credit of 292 days of pretrial confinement credit." In effect, the MJ ruled, Morlock's sentence would be reduced by 352 days.

Chapter 13. The Court-Martial, Part II: Mitigation Phase

Spinner asked the MJ for permission to have Morlock make a personal statement to the court, which is typically referred to as "the unsworn statement." The record of trial reads: "Specialist Jeremy N. Morlock, the accused, remained at counsel table and made the following unsworn statement":

> I want to begin by apologizing to the families of the victims, to the people of Afghanistan, and to my fellow soldiers in the United States Army for my actions. By unlawfully taking innocent lives and becoming involved with drugs, I violated not only the law and Army core values, I also violated the principles my father tried to instill in me. While there is no way for me to directly express an apology to the people of Afghanistan, I want to publicly take responsibility for the deaths and pain I caused.
>
> I have had a lot of time to reflect on my actions in Afghanistan in an attempt to explain to myself how I could have become so insensitive and how I lost my moral compass. I don't know if I will ever be fully able to answer those questions. It is my hope that by sharing information about my upbringing and my hopes and dreams when I entered the Army, everyone who hears these comments or reads them in the transcript will see that I came from a good home and intended to serve honorably in the Army that my father also loved and served.
>
> I grew up in Wasilla, Alaska. I was born in 1988 and was my mother's second child and my dad's third child. We have a large extended family. I felt like I grew up with a relatively normal childhood. We engaged in a lot of outdoor activities, common for those who live in Alaska. I started playing hockey when I was around five or six years old, which was actually late for some kids. By time I reached my senior year in Houston High, I was

elected captain of the varsity team. We won the AAA state championship three years in a row, including my senior year. I did not excel academically, but I was respectful of my teachers and my coaches. Whether I had a part-time job or was assigned chores around the house, I tried to carry my load.

My Dad and I were very close. I had always looked up to him throughout my youth but even more when he was serving as a Master Sergeant in the Army National Guard. He inspired me to follow his path in the military which included going through Airborne School. He was so proud of me when I graduated to join his ranks as a fellow paratrooper. Little did we know, after he pinned on my wings, that he would die from a boating accident only a few months later. His death left a big hole in my life. I want to believe that nothing changed, but the fact is, I missed him terribly and I missed having him as a source of good advice. If he had been alive when I went to Afghanistan, I know that would have made a difference.

When I joined the Army, I was hoping to follow a family tradition of serving during time of war. I realize now that I wasn't fully prepared for the reality of war as it was being fought in Afghanistan. We lost fellow soldiers to IEDs and lived in fear of being killed by IEDs on a daily basis. This does not excuse my misconduct, however. I just wanted to survive and come home in one piece.

Your Honor, please consider my guilty pleas and acceptance of responsibility and the fact I have cooperated with the government. At this point, I just want to return back to Alaska and try to live a life that honors my father's memory.

At this point, most persons in the courtroom were crying openly, men and women alike. Morlock was visibly shaken, and his voice broke when he was speaking about his father.

Testimony by Morlock's Mother

Morlock's mother, Audrey, was sworn in and took the witness stand. Spinner asked her questions that filled in the human and personal side of a person that shows up in transcripts labeled only as "the accused."

Q: I would like you to just take a few minutes to tell the judge about the home environment that Jeremy grew up in, in just his upbringing in Alaska.

A: We had lived in Wasilla. Jeremy was, I think, three when we moved to Wasilla. We are still in the same house, been there for 20 years. It's a hockey town, so I put my boys in hockey.

Q: Can you tell the judge about his brothers and sisters a little bit?

A: Well, his oldest brother is thirty-one, and then he has another brother that's twenty-five, and then he has five sisters, and he has a twenty-year-old sister, and an eighteen-year-old sister, a sixteen-year-old sister, and a thirteen-year-old, and then he has a four-year-old. So, we have a big family. We are a real close family....We do all holidays, activities, we just spend a lot of time together. His sisters love him to death. They have—you know, they got two other brothers, but they can talk to Jeremy. He's easy to talk to.

Q: Was it a loving home that he was raised in?

A: A very loving home. I was a stay-home mom, so my entire life with him I was home, until the last one went to school.

Q: Can you tell the judge a little bit about his father?

A: Well, he served in the military for 22 years. I was 100 percent behind him. We'd always go watch him jump, you know, their father was a jumper, so we would go watch him jump in the military... Their dad worked on the slope, so it was two weeks on, and two weeks off. So he'd work on the slope, which is the pipeline, and then he would come home for two weeks and he didn't have to work at all besides do his Guard, but he was at home on the two weeks and we'd go camping, and fishing. We have a cabin, and the boys would go hunting with him, but the passion was taking—watching the boys play football and hockey. Their dad just loved coming home and, he never missed a game when he was home.

Q: How close was Jeremy to his dad?

A: Very close, Jeremy was very close to his dad. All of the children, when he came home they loved him, and Jeremy was close, and Jeremy just, you know, I have a photo of him I think when he was four or five putting on his dad's Army clothes and I don't think he ever—I think that was his goal in his life to be an Army man like his dad, and he looked up to his dad.

Q: How about his family? What kind of family support has he had?

A: Awesome family support. Friends, everybody, they haven't had any negative feedback from Wasilla at all. His family just, you know, we believe in Jeremy, and we love Jeremy, and we know he went to war for a reason, and we don't know what happened to him over there, but we love him, and every one of his sisters, his brother, we never questioned him, we just know we love him, and we all want him home.

Q: Is there a place for Jeremy in Wasilla when all of this is over?

A: Lots of places. There are lots of people that would take Jeremy, you know, if you get to read those letters, Jeremy had a lot of love, and Wasilla knew he had a lot of love, and they all believe in Jeremy, and there's like, I couldn't even count the doors that would be open for him, and he has a good heart. He was such a happy, happy kid, just, you know, a smile could just—his smile, I just, I don't know, it seems like girls were just magnetized to his smile. I don't know what it is with him, but they would just look at him and go, "Hey, Jeremy." I mean, I don't know, just, there is a lot of love for him in Wasilla.

Mrs. Morlock cried through most of her testimony, along with many others in the courtroom. The prosecutor and the MJ had no questions for her, and she stepped off the witness stand to return to her seat in the gallery.

THE HOCKEY COACH TESTIFIES

Mr. James Smith, the fitness teacher and hockey coach at Houston High School in Wasilla, Alaska, took the stand. He had coached hockey in Wasilla for 21 years. Spinner asked him,

Q: How big a deal is hockey in your community?

A: Well, it's huge. We have a lot of kids that are involved in our community and Jeremy was one of them...I started with a group of kids. When they were five years old, I was teaching school at Big Lake Elementary, and Jeremy, and I had those kids all the way through high school through their senior year... I took over a high school program that was zero to 22 ... The kids stuck together, it was a family, and winning five state championships, and did very well.

Q: Do you feel that you were in a position to maybe measure the quality and the heart of the kids that played on your teams?

A: Well, I had them throughout the day. I guess in our first meeting that I had with parents I said, "I will have your kids this season, and I will see them more hours than you will for the next seven months," since I teach them in school as well as coach them after school, so I knew them very well.

Q: How well did you know Jeremy?

A: I knew Jeremy very well. We spent a lot of time together. Jeremy had mentioned earlier that he was appointed team captain his senior year, and I was the one to appoint him to that. So, he had the qualities and the characteristics that I felt to lead our team. His teammates loved him. We—you know, we were a family, and, we ended up winning the state championship that year. He was a very liked individual, for sure.

Q: Now, you are aware of the allegations in this case?

A: Absolutely.

Q: How does that impact your assessment of Jeremy based on the person you knew?

A: First of all, I'm not wearing Jeremy's boots in Afghanistan, so I don't know what that situation is like, but what I can tell you is that he stood next to me for 12 years, and played for me. He's a great kid, great kid.

Q: If you had the chance to live next door to him or have him work for you in the future, how would you feel about that?

A: He would live with me; that's how I feel about him.

MORLOCK'S HIGH SCHOOL PRINCIPAL TAKES THE STAND

Mr. Rex Weltz, who was Jeremy's principal at Houston High School in Wasilla, took the stand. He had been an educator for 15 years. Spinner asked him,

Q: So, how well did you know Jeremy compared to other students?

A: I think as I reflect back on the students that I have had in the past 15 years, there are students that come and go, but there are several that stand out. And as an administrator right now, for the last four years, you realize those students that make a difference in your educational community, leadership, respect, who they are and how they treat people. Jeremy was one of those individuals that, in 15 years stood out—if I could put five kids into that group, you know, Jeremy would be one of those. And I've taught in three states, and I could tell you five or six students that stand out as somebody that you would want in your school.

Q: I take it that when these allegations came out, it caught you by surprise?

A: It did.

Q: It's not consistent with the Jeremy that you knew?

A: Absolutely not. It was—actually, I was driving into Seattle, and I heard it on the radio, and I didn't believe it was the same one that I knew.

Q: Were you around when his father passed away?

A: I was. We were still in Alaska. We heard of the accident. Several days had gone by, and I know that Jeremy was going to fly in. I believe that at that time, Jeremy had called his mother to contact me to help set and organize the services at a local business there in town.

Q: How hard did it impact him from your perspective and knowing Jeremy as you did?

A: As a person who had lost my own father, you could see, I could see similar holes, that, you know, the loss that there was a change in Jeremy and his demeanor, from going to that kid you saw that was so excited about making his announcement that he was going into the military, that youthfulness, and that joy to, there's a loss, and, you know, and I think his mother had said he grew up instantly through the nature of the event.

Q: Did you know how close he had been to his father?

A: Absolutely, so, as an administrator, and as a teacher, you end up in a small community, you get to know everyone. It was very easy to see, well, we were at a football game, or a hockey game, or a baseball game, his dad, when he could be there, as we heard he had two weeks on and two weeks off, those weeks that he was home, he never missed an event. And not only that, as a coach for many years, as well, you can see when your student athletes have that look in their eye, they are making sure that their parents are there, and it was obvious that Jeremy was making sure that dad was there to watch.

Q: Is there anything else that you would like to share with the judge about Jeremy?

A: Well, obviously, as a high school administrator, we see kids, we see young adults making bad decisions. However, I think a lot of times, as you do, Your Honor, we weigh in and look at their—how well they will react to adversity. There is no question that Jeremy will react positively to this adversity, and I am not minimizing it by any means, but as far as him getting back into society, and being a productive person, James had said he could move in with him. I feel that same way, but, I have kids. I would—I trust him with not only mine but yours. He's got good values. Before he left, he was an incredible person. I know that he could be that again.

The prosecutor had no questions and did not cross-examine Mr. Weltz. He stepped down and returned to his seat in the gallery. Most of the gallery was still sobbing.

UNCLE BOB

Mr. Robert Juliussen was sworn in, and took the witness stand. He was Jeremy's uncle by marriage, and everyone referred to him as Uncle Bob. Mr. Juliussen looked and behaved every part of what one would expect from an Uncle Bob. He began his testimony with some background: he works as a construction manager for a housing authority in Anchorage, Alaska. Uncle Bob made it clear very quickly that he "filled in" for Jeremy's dad for the two weeks of every month that his dad was absent. In a sense, Uncle Bob was Jeremy's other dad. He was married to Jeremy's mother's twin sister. Spinner began the questioning:

Q: How close have you been to Jeremy since he was born?

A: I've been very close with Jeremy. Again, the big family, we're all there in Anchorage and Wasilla, so we are all in Alaska, and the mothers of—excuse me, my wife and his mom are twins, and that's just is a different dynamic, I think, a lot of times, so you are more involved than normal, and you know, I had the opportunity—waited to have kids for a little while, so I was able to spend like 10 years before I had my own children. So, the two boys were the oldest ones before Jeremy. So, I got a lot of time that was kind of different, almost—one, his dad was gone and two, so there was a lot to fill in, and I was involved with a lot of that stuff, just because it was so much fun, and they were so much fun. And so, that was kind of a neat thing. There were times he, you know, lived with us and my family, and so I spent a lot of time with Jeremy, and the whole family at different times for different reasons, but it was always—we're just definitely very close and they are like my own children.

Q: So obviously you knew his dad?

A: Yeah, his dad and me were good friends. His dad was a super neat guy. He—you know, as you've heard here today, he was a 20-year Army vet. He was a vet, joined the National Guard after that, and was a master sergeant with them, a jumpmaster. But the Army's really what defined Rick Morlock. I mean his—he had a lot of friends, but a good bulk of his friends were Army. The Army was really kind of his life, and he obviously, it was just really—just defined who he was. And I think that was a big inspiration for Jeremy. I mean, he had seen what it was like, the camaraderie, and the friends that his dad had, and the activities that his dad had. He would play on a rugby team with a bunch of these guys, and he was kind of a larger-than-life guy. When you'd see his photos at his service, there was mountain climbing, there was rugby, there was love, there was—he was doing all kinds of things, and it was—just a real positive guy. He definitely had a great relationship with all of his kids individually, and Jeremy—Jeremy, you know, personality-wise, was kind of the closest to his dad, really. A strength about him, his dad was a man-to-man guy, knew who he was, didn't mess around, I mean, he just was. Jeremy [witness started crying] excuse me, so, Jeremy was the same way. I mean, he just has a quiet confidence... There's just a certain confidence now and later manliness that's just natural. So, a lot like his father ... they had a special bond. And so Jeremy had this good example to follow, and so going into the Army—everybody that knew him knew that it was a decision that he was making and wanted to make. We went—the families being as close as we are, we all traveled to his basic training graduation.

Q: Even your wife went?

A: Me and my wife, and children, it was ... he was proud to do what he was doing, and we were proud of him.

Q: How did the news of these events impact you based on what you knew of Jeremy?

A: Well, you know, it was devastating, of course, and shocking—it's difficult I think for all of us to really think about what it is or what happened. I guess to answer your question, and it's just been very difficult. Based on the person I knew, I knew him, he went to boot camp, and then ended up here in Washington and was—I know he wanted to serve in a war, and was ready to go, wanting to go the whole time, and that was a short period... Well, I think Jeremy has the strength that we have seen today to, you know, to take responsibility for this to—I mean, he has so much potential. I mean, you know, that's a difficult one for me to say. I mean, I think he's a warm, beautiful, smart, bright-type of guy, and his potential is, I think, good. He's doing the right thing even now.

Again, the prosecutor declined to cross-examine the uncle. Uncle Bob stepped down and took his seat in the weeping gallery, wiping and trying to contain his own tears.

Morlock's original squad leader takes the stand

Staff Sergeant Jon King was sworn in and took the stand. At the time of the trial, King was stationed at Ft. Sill, Oklahoma, but he had been Morlock's original squad leader in the year 2006. In other words, King would have held the position that Sprague had in Afghanistan, had it not been for the massive, complex, and multiple instances of cross-leveling that occurred since 2006.Captain Opachan asked questions which clarified the artificial history of Stryker brigade, in that it had no real history but was constructed from the start through cross-leveling:

Q: Can you tell the military judge how you knew Specialist Morlock?

A: Specialist Morlock came to [Battalion] 2-1 Infantry at the end of 2006 when I got there. After I initially went to Iraq the second time, I took over as one of the 10 NCO's that were starting a brigade, and Specialist Morlock and the group of the soldiers he came with were soldiers there.

Q: Can you explain to the military judge, what do you mean by, "starting a brigade"?

A: Well, it was a new Stryker brigade, so we were just restarting a new Stryker brigade here at Fort Lewis at the time, 5th Brigade.

Q: Can you tell the military judge how he performed for you when he first got to the unit?

A: Well, when we first got—we got a batch of new soldiers and they were the normal out-of-basic-training soldiers.

Q: When you say that, what do you mean? If you could just give the military judge a sense of what you mean by that?

A: They didn't really know what to expect because they were just coming out of basic training, and so, it was more of—it was a different environment for the soldiers because we were just starting a brigade, and this was the second time that I had restarted with a brigade, and so they quickly realized that for their part they were in competition to become leaders, because we weren't getting any more NCOs in at the time.

Q: How did Specialist Morlock fit in with that group of new soldiers that you got?

A: From my knowledge, they all went to basic training together, they all went to Ranger School, stuff like that. So, when they got to us they came together, so they were a strong group of kids because they all knew each other for a couple of months already as it was, and we just started picking and deciding who were the stronger soldiers out of the group that we had gotten. Specialist Morlock became one of the stronger of the group. So, he ended up being a team leader as a PFC, and a couple of other fellow soldiers with him.

Q: And in the course of—so how much time did you have the opportunity to spend with Specialist Morlock?

A: I got to—when I got to the brigade in December 20th of 2006, I believe Morlock was there before I was until around December of '08. I had Specialist Morlock under me in first platoon, and then he got switched to third platoon as a team leader out of necessity because their platoon was short.

Q: Sergeant King, I would like to talk to you a little bit more about the time that he was with you in the unit. You indicated that he was one of the stronger soldiers that you had had?

A: Yes, Sir.

Q: Did you attempt to mentor him in any way?

A: Yes, Sir, me and the late Sergeant McConnell, he passed away in Afghanistan. He was pretty much Sergeant McConnell's go-to guy for Sergeant McConnell and his team. Because once we got Sergeant McConnell, he was an E5 and Morlock fell under him, and he worked pretty well with Sergeant McConnell. We never had any issues with them....

Q: Were you aware of the issues that he had back home when his father went missing?

A: Yes, Sir. On the day that he found out that his father was missing, he informs me that his sisters were with their father, and they—I believe his dad went to get supplies, or—from what I remember, but he never had come back. We were having an issue of getting him back up to Alaska, and I think through me complaining about it, mostly about getting him there because no one knew what was going on. He finally got there, and as he called me, I could hear his sister—one of his sisters in the background screaming because they had just pulled his dad out of the water, so he had just got there on time.

Q: And you were on the phone with him when that happened?

A: Yes, Sir.

This was the first time that I had heard that Jeremy was present at the very moment that his father's body was being dragged out of an icy Alaskan lake. Jeremy had never shared that poignant detail with me. When Sergeant King disclosed it in court, one could hear a soft, collective gasp in the room, followed by more sobbing. By this point, it was clear to everyone in the court room that Jeremy's father was his first and only hero. Those who take Freud seriously see that this is common: every boy's father is a hero to him. Jeremy wanted to be like his father and to make his father proud of him. It cannot be a coincidence that his hero was replaced by the surrogate father-figure of Hellraiser at about this time in his life. (One imagines, immediately, that given his antipathy toward foreign intellectuals, Hellraiser would no doubt question Freud's credentials on the grounds that Freud was not an American.) Opachan continued his poignant questioning:

Q: In the course of that time after he came back, was the unit doing any kind of train up for deployment?

A: After he came back, we got word that we were supposed to be getting deployed and NTC was coming up in California, and we were just prepping for that. We were doing our normal rotations to Yakima just to get ready for deployment, but we didn't know exactly when we were leaving.

Q: Was he training with you as one of your soldiers in preparation for that deployment?

A: Yes, Sir.

Q: At any point in time, was he—you mentioned that he left his position under you. Why was that that he left you?

A: Well, again, for necessity for third platoon. They were short on team leaders, so he got moved over to third platoon, again reluctantly, because at the time, his issue with his dad was—he was just coming out of the issue with his dad. He just got married, and again, due to reluctance, we were trying to get him out of dealing with his new wife, because that's when he started having issues with her, more so. So, I think his concentration was set on dealing with his wife at the time. Then he ended up moving over to third platoon, and ever since—the day he moved over to third platoon to the time we go to Afghanistan, he tried to get back to first platoon.

Q: When he left to go over to third platoon, was that something you wanted to have happen?

A: No, Sir.

Q: Do you remember how soon before the deployment that he was actually moved over to that new platoon?

A: I believe he was moved around January of '09, right before we headed out to NTC

Q: I have no further questions, thank you.

The prosecution had no questions for Sergeant King. Sergeant King's squad in first platoon remained in Bravo Company 2-1, and had no problems in Afghanistan. It seems reasonable to conclude, given all that we have learned about third platoon, that had Jeremy stayed in Sergeant King's squad and in first platoon—the tragedy we are analyzing here might not have happened. Spinner requested a recess, which the judge granted at 2:42 pm. The court-martial was called to order again at 2:54 pm.

Most studies of crime, including war crimes, focus on various theories, criminal investigations, and legal evidence. They rarely acknowledge the families of the accused. Spinner made sure that the perspectives of Morlock's family, coach, principal, and original squad leader would be inscribed forever in the trial and historical record. I want to add a few observations based upon my interactions with his family and support group. I got to know them considerably well over the course of the Article 32 hearing, the aborted court-martial, and the final court-martial. I also travelled to Wasilla, Alaska in September of 2011 for further interviews and to see his home and high school.

In conversations with Jeremy's family members, I learned that his mother's side of the family is Alaskan Native. Jeremy's maternal grandfather (who is also a military veteran) reminisced how his mother spoke a Native Alaskan language, but he could no longer speak it. I accompanied most of Jeremy's extended family to the Alaska State Fair, and I can attest that they seem to be as close and supportive as the testimony suggests that they are. I also spoke with the coach, Mr. Smith, at great length. Smith was basically a surrogate father to Jeremy and all the members of the championship hockey team that was mentioned in testimony. When Smith retired from his position as coach, the team stopped its winning streak. It was clear to me, from visiting the high school, that Smith was the sole reason for those championships. None of the members of that team got in trouble with the law, in large measure because Smith was watching over them when their parents were not. Smith said to me, "All you'd have to do is drop a puck in the parking lot of a grocery store, and the guys would go at it. They lived and breathed hockey." Smith also said to me: "Jeremy really has only one character flaw. He's too honest. He's honest to a fault, and will tell the truth even when the truth will get him in trouble. He has always been that way." Smith's remarks were made in one of those moments that one can never forget.

How can I summarize the impressions of all those conversations and the visit to Wasilla? First, that had Jeremy stayed in Wasilla under the guidance of Smith and other authority figures, instead of joining the army, he most likely would have been like his best friend Larry. I met Larry and his family in Wasilla. Larry was attending college and working on a fishing boat during the summers. I got the same impression from Larry's father that I obtained from all the others I had met: the group of boys on that hockey team was basically raised by an "extended" family of authority figures in Wasilla, and they protected and guided "their boys." But all these authority figures also said that Jeremy's father was "larger than life." "He climbed Mount McKinley, you know?"—they told me repeatedly. Everyone with whom I spoke expressed great admiration for Rick Morlock, and the inevitability that Jeremy would follow his father's footsteps by joining the army. They also made it clear that had his father not died in the boat accident, Jeremy would never have become involved in the killings under discussion here.

In summary, the possible trajectories of Morlock's life in Wasilla that did not involve the U.S. Army gave no indications of a young man who would be convicted one day of premeditated murder. In line with a host of sociological studies on the importance of peer groups and one's immediate society, it seems that the key variable for explaining Morlock's involvement in these tragic killings is—Stryker Brigade. Lieutenant William Calley's (of the My Lai massacre) mother is quoted as saying, "I gave them [the army] a good boy and they sent me back a murderer."[21] The coach, the principal, Uncle Bob, Sergeant King, and Jeremy's mother never used the same words, but in so many words, expressed the same sentiment. The clear import of their testimony was: We remember Jeremy as a good boy. What happened to him in Stryker Brigade? It would be up to my testimony to explain that connection.

My testimony

I was sworn in, and Spinner began what is known in the field of law as the *voir dire*, or evidence that I was qualified as an expert witness in "sociology and war crimes." He asked me to recite my university degrees, some of my publications, and experience in other war crimes trials.

Q: Can you highlight some of those things in your vita that are relevant to why you are involved in this case today?

A: Sure. Well, I began my career as an expert in the sociology of Emile Durkheim. He's like the George Washington of sociology. He's like our founding father. So, he was the focus of my doctoral dissertation and my early publications. So, I am an expert—prior to getting into war crimes—in just what makes society tick, and what makes society disintegrate, or make it dysfunctional. And I was teaching, until I got a phone call one day from The Hague, and they asked me, because I had published a book on the Balkans, if I would go over there and testify. After that, I was asked to testify at the trials of Lynndie England, Sabrina Harman, and Javal Davis, all pertaining to Abu Ghraib. And I started to apply my theoretical knowledge of what makes a society tick versus dysfunction in this new context that I had never thought about before. So, the answer to your question is, I started as an expert in very orthodox, mainstream sociology, and moved into an interest in research in the area of war crimes....

Q: Have you written about these incidents?

MJ: Counsel, I'm going to interrupt you. It appears you are heading towards a request for recognition for Dr. Mestrovic as an expert. Is that true?

Spinner: That's correct.

MJ: In what areas?

Spinner: Sociology and war crimes.

MJ: Any objections?

TC: No objection, Your Honor.

MJ: Please proceed.

This was the fastest *voir dire* in my history as an expert witness. Given the particular context for this particular case, I should add the following reflections. The gist of Hellraiser's contempt for COIN doctrine is that it was inspired and written by non-Americans. I am a US citizen, but my career was inspired by the French Jew with a German surname, Emile Durkheim, and my first war crimes case involved genocide in Bosnia-Herzegovina. There is an irony here that should not be ignored, namely: the expert witness in sociology and war crimes in this American war crimes case was foreign-born and unavoidably informed by foreign-born social theorists and knowledge about a foreign genocidal war against Bosnian Muslims. I was facing an African-American military judge, and had thought about what his history might have been in attaining this position and the rank of lieutenant colonel in the US Army. None of this mattered in the courtroom only because he was a no-nonsense judge who treated me with respect for my social role just as I treated him respectfully for his social role. But readers of this book in the distant future should note carefully that the larger social context for this moment in the courtroom was one of widespread xenophobia and ethnocentrism in the United States and Europe aimed at all foreigners, immigrants, and especially Muslims.

Spinner asked me to tell the judge what documents I had studied to prepare for my testimony. I answered that I had read all the Article 32 transcripts, sworn statements, General Twitty's report, and the command climate surveys. In addition, I had interviewed Lieutenant Colonel Jeffrey French, the 2-1 Battalion commander; Lieutenant Colonel Richard Demaree, the former 2-1 Battalion commander, Colonel William Clark, the 8-1 Cavalry Battalion commander, and Chaplain Gary Lewis of 1-17. And I added: "I also read the COIN manual, 3-24, which I have here, and Colonel Tunnell's Guerrilla Hunter Killer Operations manual, which I have a copy of here, and then Colonel Tunnell's book, *To Compel With Armed Force*."

Q: Who is Colonel Tunnell?

A: He was the brigade commander.

Q: But you have not actually interviewed Colonel Tunnell?

A: I have not.

Q: Now, let's go back to the 15-6 [Twitty Report]. On top of just the findings and recommendations, what was the data underlying the 15-6 that you had access to?

A: The 15-6 was shocking to me. It's different from the Taguba report in that it had—

Q: And the Taguba report is what?

A: The 15-6 for Abu Ghraib was written by Major General Taguba. What was shocking was the level of chaos and disorganization; the level of mistrust among the lieutenant colonels, the battalion commanders, which was confirmed to me by the ones I spoke with; the level of lack of mentoring; and the lack of "circulation," which is the term that was used.

I anticipated that one of the prosecutors would object very soon into my testimony, because that had been the pattern in all previous courts-martial. Prosecutors seem resolute in keeping the internal reports written by their high-ranking generals out of the trial record. In this trial the task fell to Captain Mazzone, who was the assistant trial counsel [ATC].

ATC: Sir, objection. I thought the question was innocuous enough, but listening to Dr. Mestrovic's answer, it's entirely hearsay. The government objects that it is hearsay, and lack of authentication.

Spinner: We would ask to relax the rule of evidence, Your Honor, for sentencing.

MJ: With regard to the relaxation of the rules of evidence, I mean, it's not documentary evidence. Ordinarily, the rules are relaxed for documentary evidence and affidavits, however—

Spinner: Correct.

MJ: It might be—being given this information to understand the full basis of the doctor's opinion or opinions he's going to render—

Spinner: Yes, Your Honor, as an expert witness.

MJ: I'm not going to consider it for the truth of the matter, but certainly I will consider it as it informs his opinions.

ATC: Yes, Sir.

MJ: Please proceed.

I recognized the familiar lawspeak from previous cases. The outcome was clear: the judge overruled the prosecutor's objection and allowed me to continue speaking. Spinner had predicted that this would happen, because experts are given "leeway" with regard to the legal rule against "hearsay." But the reasoning remains perplexing. How can it be, in the legal profession, that internal army reports (such as the Taguba report and the Twitty report) are not considered "documentary evidence?" How can it be that these investigative reports are consistently dismissed in courtroom as "hearsay?" These reports are chock-full of documents, evidence, and sworn statements. In the past, some judges have sided with the prosecutor and absolutely forbade any mention of the Taguba or other reports. But this judge sided with Spinner—albeit cautiously. To the outsider, the logic of these legal decisions does not appear to be consistent. What could it possibly mean, outside of lawspeak, that the judge would not consider my reading of the Twitty report with regard to "the truth of the matter?" Spinner and I have had many discussions about this issue, but in the end, his explanations never made sense to me. Spinner is the perennial pragmatist: he would get me to be able to speak on the report, and that was all that mattered to him. And because I had faith in his ability to do this, I hardly paid attention to what the judge or lawyers were saying. I knew the prosecutor would object, and I trusted Spinner that the judge would allow me to speak. Spinner continued, almost on cue:

Q: But before you go through the things that you found in the report, I just want to make sure that—because the report's not here and the judge doesn't know what's in the report, there were interviews of the battalion commanders, and—

A: Correct. Sworn statements, yes.

Q: Right. And other senior officers that worked under Colonel Tunnell?

A: Correct.

Q: And so, you read all of their sworn statement that were considered by the investigative officer?

A: Yes, it's about 500 pages, and it includes Colonel Tunnell's supervisors, General Johnson, General Hodges, and General Nicholson. It also includes the battalion commanders, and it also includes several captains, lieutenants, majors, sergeants, so it's a full range—because that was the request given by General Scaparrotti, to go from brigade level and also the brigade commander's superiors, down to the level of the platoon.

Q: And the point of the 15-6 was to get into issue surrounding the command during the time that these offenses occurred?

A: Correct, and also, based on my reading, it seemed like General Scaparrotti was asking questions pertaining to command responsibility. He specifically asked, "Could these leaders have known, should they have known," some of the issues pertaining to the drug use and the murders. It was a very clear and a very pointed question.

Q: Now, you talked about some climate surveys that you had access to. How many pages are we talking about and who provided the information in the climate surveys?

A: The government provided them to me. It's about 3,000 pages, I really couldn't give an exact number, and they were done as a routine part of Army doctrine, although I noted in the 15-6, they were not done according to schedule. And so, in other words, I have—I've seen a lot of them, but I'm not sure about how systemic they were.

MJ: Before you continue, counsel, it appears under the request to relax the rules of evidence that the underlying statements that are the subject of the 15-6 as being described would be admissible. However, based on some prior 802s, and the representations, particularly the government in prior cases, do you want those entered into evidence in this case?

ATC: Your Honor, our position would be no.

What was going on here? First, and based upon Spinner's questions, the judge realized that I would not be summarizing General Twitty's opinion (which would be hearsay) but would be analyzing the underlying documents which informed Twitty's opinion. My opinion would be based upon admissible documents, but would not necessarily reflect General Twitty's opinion. Second, the judge's reference to "prior 802s" is an allusion to private discussions he had with both defense and prosecution counsel. Although the US system of justice is supposed to be open and transparent, in fact, it is not so entirely due to the legality of these secret discussions. "802s" are a historical, cultural relic of the Starchamber system, which was invented by the Puritans in England, and was entirely secret. Third, the judge knew from these secret meetings that the government would object to entering the sworn statements in General Twitty's report into evidence. Spinner knew this as well, and did not want to get embroiled in that fight, which he might have lost on the legal battlefield, because he wanted me to speak about the report whether or not it was admitted into evidence. Let us be as clear as possible on what this means. Not entering General Twitty's report into evidence means, concretely, that his 500-page report would *not* be physically, concretely a part of the attachments which are routinely placed into a defendant's packet of documents, and which follow him or her for the rest of his or her career as a convicted criminal. However, Spinner would make sure that my opinions on this report would be entered into the trial record and in effect would bypass the prosecutor's objections. In layperson's terms, the Twitty report would and would not be entered into evidence simultaneously: concretely, the document would never appear for anyone to ever read or review it pertaining to Morlock; but in a different and also concrete sense, my expert opinion on the Twitty report would be a part of Morlock's trial record. These are the subtleties and strategies that determine victories versus losses, as well as compromise, upon the legal battlefield that is a courtroom trial. I leave it up to the reader to speculate as to why the prosecutor would not allow the sworn statements in Twitty's report into evidence. What did the government not want the public to know? The legal drama continued:

MJ: Then, in that event, any objection to the court's considering the doctor's review of those statements for what they purport given that they are based on otherwise admissible material?

ATC: Sir, I am sorry, I missed it if you posed the question to me.

MJ: Sure. Any objection to me considering what the doctor's review of those otherwise admissible reports are, even though I don't have the reports, because it's my understanding that you all have those reports as well as the defense. So, if he makes a description of one that is incorrect, you certainly can correct the record.

ATC: Absolutely, Sir, but I would still maintain that it's hearsay. And in this case, we're talking about double hearsay.

MJ: Well, I'm going to relax the rules of evidence, so I am going to consider it. Again, if, in an abundance of caution, you want to put hundreds or perhaps even thousands of pages of evidence into the record so that I have, and the record has, a full report, I will certainly entertain that motion from either side. But, at this point, I'm going to consider what the doctor—his review of that evidence that you have access to.

ATC: Roger, Sir.

MJ: Your objection to hearsay is overruled.

I sat on the witness stand with some anticipation as to which way the tide would turn, and felt some relief that the judge was giving Spinner and me the green light to continue discussing the report. I had been in a similar position before, and the tide had gone against the defense. But I also knew, based upon previous experience, that the prosecutor would continue to object along the way. This hunch proved to be correct. Spinner carefully laid out my path through the metaphorical minefield that would follow. I trusted Spinner like a soldier trusts a leader. He would "insulate" me from some possible objections by the prosecution by keeping me on the straight and narrow path of sociology without the slightest deviation into psychology or my interviews with Morlock.

Q: Now, and again, we are going to get into the meat of what you found in a minute. There are still a couple of preliminary things I would like to address. I mean, obviously you described thousands of pages. Have you had the assistance of anyone in going through all of this information?

A: Yes, two of my former graduate students, Dr. Caldwell and Dr. Kerr, who assisted me.

Q: Estimate the number of hours that between you and them have been put in going though all of these documents?

A: I would say at least a total of 200. But I would think more.

Q: So, in terms of formulating the opinions that you are going to express today, do you feel now that you have had adequate time to go through all that information to be able to form the conclusions that you have?

A: I would have preferred more time, but yes, I feel prepared, but I would have liked more time, Your Honor, but I feel prepared.

Q: Before we get to your opinions and the justifications for those opinions, because you have degrees in psychology, you are not here to testify as a psychologist, correct?

A: That's my understanding, correct.

Q: You are not addressing any issues of mental responsibility, right?

A: Correct.

Q: You are applying the principles of sociology, which go to the issue whether or not the brigade was a functional or dysfunctional organization, right?

A: Correct.

Q: And so, you're not, in that sense, relying on anything that Specialist Morlock has said, other than the fact that you have viewed his videotape that he gave to the CID?

A: Correct.

Q: Now, how does sociology help us understand—how could we understand what happened here?

ATC: Sir, the government objects. Based on the proffer that Mr. Spinner just articulated for the court that this entire line of testimony is irrelevant to the sentencing proceedings.

MJ: Any other basis?

ATC: Sir, yes, that is a starting point.

MJ: I'll tell you what I'm going to do. Your initial—I'm going to reserve ruling. I will hear the answer. I'm going to consider your objection as a continuing objection of relevance, and if at any point I believe that I have heard irrelevant testimony, I will note it on the record and disregard it.

ATC: Yes, Sir.

MJ: Please proceed.

Basically, the prosecutor was arguing that sociology is irrelevant to this court-martial. Again, I was relieved that the judge, in layperson's terms, ruled that the prosecutor should keep quiet and that he, the judge, would determine whether my sociological opinions were relevant or not. In effect, the judge would stop further objections by transforming them all into one "continuing objection," which he would consider only after I had had my say. I glanced at the prosecutor's table, and saw a look of helplessness, frustration, and surprise—all mixed into one pained expression—on the prosecutor's face. I glanced at the faces of my "crew," and read their intense expressions as signifying, "Which way will this go?" Spinner seemed calm, as always. I turned to look straight at the judge and answered Spinner's earlier question, in response to the judge's directive to proceed. From this point onward, I would speak directly to the judge, who seemed frozen in his thoughts, like Rodin's "Thinker." I said:

A: Your Honor, what I found striking was that the Twitty report constantly refers to the conflict between COIN versus counter-guerrilla doctrines. Then, when I read the COIN manual, I saw a lot of sociology in this COIN manual. There is an entire chapter on sociology. I recognize it. It's my language. It's exactly what I lecture on all the time. So, the relevance that I see here is that the definitions used by Generals McChrystal and Petraeus, in understanding the United States mission in Afghanistan is commensurate with what I know about sociology in terms of, and these are the exact phrases they and I use, "norms," "values," "sanctions," and "beliefs," and how they hang together to provide good morale and ensure victory for certain goals. I will define these terms if you'd like. "Norms" are social agreements about what is expected. "Beliefs" are social agreements about what is true. "Sanctions" are social agreements about how to enforce them. And "values" are social agreements about what is preferred. It's how these hang together in synchronicity that makes for not just a better unit, a synchronized, integrated unit, but ultimately ensures victory. So, I see a real overlap here between what sociology does, in other words, we explain how societies work, and the COIN document, which in turn, is the object of a lot of focus in the 15-6 report.

Q: In that regard, what conclusions, and we're going to come back to this, but what conclusions have you drawn from your examination of all the materials that you have been provided in this case?

A: My conclusion is that Colonel Tunnell's leadership style contributed to a dysfunctional social climate in the brigade. Which, in turn, created the environment that led to these crimes, and that, in turn, it also led to a certain dysfunction in the values or the way the United States is represented, because the Afghan people are going to respond to these crimes in a way that will promote vengeance against soldiers in the future. So, I am looking at a macro-level analysis, a large-level picture of U.S. versus Afghani society, which in turn, is part of the COIN doctrine, and on a more narrow level, the brigade level, as well as down to the platoon and company level, all the dysfunctions that were caused by his leadership.

Q: In that respect, I would like to ask you to explain the conflict you saw within the brigade in terms of the pro-COIN versus the anti-COIN conflict.

A: Am I allowed here to talk about interviews with the battalion commanders? Because I asked them about these issues.

Q: Yes.

A: Your Honor, I had honest conversations with the battalion commanders. At a certain point, they acknowledged to me that there was tremendous conflict with the brigade commander. I asked them very bluntly, "Which side are you on? Are you on the side of General McChrystal, or are you on the side of Colonel Tunnell?" Every one of the battalion commanders—

Q: Let's be clear now, General McChrystal's side is?

A: COIN.

Q: And Colonel Tunnell's side is?

A: Counter-guerrilla. And these are incompatible according to the Twitty report, and according to the battalion commanders I interviewed.

Q: Explain how they are incompatible?

A: They are incompatible in that, according to the report and these battalion commanders, Colonel Tunnell was only focused on the aggressive offensive aspect, and not on the defensive as well as the strategic, hold, and other governance aspects of COIN. In other words, COIN is an interrelated system which includes some offensive elements, but intends for US soldiers to basically act as ambassadors of the United States, and that was not a concern or a priority for Colonel Tunnell. So, in that sense, it was like Team A versus Team B, "choose your side." You were either on Colonel Tunnell's side, or you were on the side of the chain of command. And that caused confusion down the ranks, down from battalion through the company commanders, to the sergeants. And that impression was confirmed to me by the battalion commanders. I can give you an illustration, if you like.

Q: Yes, please.

A: In the 15-6, it basically said that the units performed COIN not because of—but despite Colonel Tunnell. I asked Lieutenant Colonel Demaree about this, and he said, indeed, at the NTC, that he handed in two separate reports. One was to appease Colonel Tunnell, and the other one was to appease the NTC trainers, and they were totally different.

Q: And to be clear, because you were working very closely with this, the brigade went to NTC just before their deployment?

A: Yes.

Q: So, this was the place where they were supposed to work out any issues or bugs as far as how they were going to operate in Afghanistan?

A: Yes, and be certified to go to Afghanistan. Now, furthermore, the generals in the 15-6 state in their sworn statements that Stryker Brigade almost failed getting certified to be deployed. I personally found that shocking. And they said that they gave him another chance, and then afterwards, General Johnson and General Nicholson wrote in their reports that they regret that they did not remove him from command. And if you look at the conclusion by General Twitty, after he notes this fact, that four generals expressed regret, one of his conclusions is that Colonel Tunnell should be removed from command.

Q: And why did they almost fail NTC?

A: Because he did not want to listen to the advice of these generals who told them he must follow chain of command General McChrystal's directives.

Q: COIN?

A: COIN. Lieutenant General Johnson was sent in because of the dispute, to try to appease the situation, and in his sworn statement, he states that he had an interview with Colonel Tunnell, and he bluntly told him, "You must do what the trainers want of you. You must comply with the chain of command."

Q: So, when the unit arrives to Afghanistan, was there still this con-flict between COIN and non-COIN commanders?

A: Yes. It only got exacerbated. Lieutenant Colonel French told me that when he arrived there, he was initially, for the first two months, not under the direct control of Colonel Tunnell. He was doing COIN without Colonel's Tunnell's knowledge. A number of other statements indicate basically that they were sneaking COIN. I mean, it's just very unusual to think of an Army unit that's being dishonest, that has to feel like they have to hide something from the boss which is in compliance with the larger chain of command. And they said this was very confusing. So, yes, it was exacerbated, it got worse.

Q: What, in practical terms, as the brigade operated, at the times that these offenses occurred, what was Colonel Tunnell pushing in terms of anti-guerrilla activities, or his approach? Or his philosophy, however you want to put it?

A: The words that I saw used were "strike and destroy." Chief War-rant Officer 2 Picinich, his sworn statement states that he was appointed to maintain a body count board. And several others also mentioned the fact that it was a matter—you were good in Colonel Tunnell's eyes if you were aggressive, and if the body count was high.

Q: How did that—now, I mean, that's at Colonel Tunnell's level, okay?

A: Yes.

Q: Specialist Morlock is down at the platoon level. And looking at all of these statements and looking at the 15-6, and all of the information that you have been provided, how did that—did it work its way down to the platoon level?

A: Well, that's what I focused on. And so, I asked Colonel French very bluntly after we had talked a little bit, I said, "look, I saw your statement, you were trying to protect your men, you were looking out for your men," perhaps before I answer your question, just so I have the sequence right, Specialist Morlock was in a cross-leveled company, Captain Quiggle's, that came from Colonel Clark's cavalry unit. So, when Captain Quiggle came in, two platoons were taken out, two new ones were put in, one of those was Specialist Morlock's. Now, in that situation, I asked in that context, because Colonel Clark told me that Captain Quiggle was one of his best commanders. Colonel French told me that Captain Quiggle was one of his best commanders. I asked the obvious question, "He's one of your best commanders, so how did this happen?" And Colonel French basically said there were no problems whatsoever until Sergeant Gibbs was appointed as squad leader. I then asked, what does he know about that appointment, and he said he was left out of the loop, that he didn't think anything of it, but he wasn't told anything about it, but he knows that the problems all started after that. And then I realized, after talking with these colonels, and also what I had read, that Sergeant Gibbs came from Colonel Tunnell's private security detail. And I started to inductively develop a theory, that here you have Colonel Tunnell, who has some very unorthodox views—

Q: Aggressive?

A: Yes, but also unorthodox. May I give you some examples of unorthodox?

Q: Sure.

A: In the 15-6 report, Colonel Tunnell refers to Condoleezza Rice, and to the authors of COIN, as promoting an "imperialist colonialist philosophy." I just find it very odd that a United States Army colonel would refer to his superiors in very derogatory terms.

The assistant prosecutor objected, and said to me, "Your reaction to what you read is not relevant, sir." The judge sustained this objection. But in the book that you are reading, dear reader, I am allowed to repeat that it is very odd for an American colonel to refer to his commanders as espousing an imperialist, colonialist philosophy by promoting COIN. I confess that I was surprised Spinner had gotten this far without a word from the prosecution desk. After all, a protective order had been placed on General Twitty's report, yet there I was, summarizing it in open court. Spinner had succeeded in two of his major objectives: to enter into evidence the fact that the brigade was dysfunctional, and to connect the dysfunction in Morlock's platoon to the dysfunction in the brigade via Gibbs. This seemed to be sufficient victory—but not for Spinner. He wanted the connections between Colonel Tunnell and Morlock to be spelled out in more detail:

Q: You said he [Colonel Tunnell] had unusual views?

A: The words used to describe him by the lieutenant colonels I spoke with and in the documents are, "odd," "asocial," "strange," "does not fit in." Similar kinds of words were used to describe the brigade, that it was like the odd man out that nobody liked. Members of the brigade, the other people in Afghanistan, other units, other officers, mocked the brigade. So, I see a parallel between the adjectives used to describe the brigade commander, and the adjectives used to describe the brigade. So, now backtracking to Sergeant Gibbs, I started to inquire further on what direct links I could make to Colonel Tunnell and this company. Well, it turns out another direct link is Captain Quiggle himself. It turns out, according to the documents, that he had spent a year in brigade headquarters serving directly under Colonel Tunnell, and he helped write the counter-guerrilla manual. Then I found another piece of data in the Article 32s, and that is that Stevens, I forget his rank, I'm sorry, Soldier Stevens was also on Colonel Tunnell's personal bodyguard team. And then I read further that Stevens was involved in two drive-by shootings which were never fully resolved, where he shot out of a truck, and they never went back to see if somebody was hit, and a grenade was thrown out of another truck. So I inductively came to see that there seemed to be connections here with direct proximity to Colonel Tunnell, and the chaos that ensued in this company, in this platoon.

Q: Did you conclude that—first of all, that the brigade was dysfunctional?

A: Yes.

Q: And what does that mean in terms of how they performed their mission in Afghanistan?

A: For a society to be functional, the norms, values, sanctions, and beliefs have to be synchronized with each other.... The dysfunction comes in when you have a brigade commander whose stated goal in his publications and in his statements to his men are at odds with the overall system, and yet, he has the honor and respect due to him as a brigade commander. That's the dysfunction. It's what in sociology we call "a rule that is a lack of rule," because the rule is you honor and respect him because of his status and position, and yet, he's espousing a position that goes contrary to the larger normative structure. In other words, he was out of touch and out of step with the larger chain of command. That's the dysfunction.

Q: How does that translate then back to Sergeant Gibbs coming from his personal security detachment down to the platoon—did you find any evidence that Sergeant Gibbs knew Specialist Morlock before he was assigned in his same unit?

A: I did not, no.

Q: Tying this together, then, this dysfunction that you found, in the fact that Sergeant Gibbs was put down there, what did he take with him?

ATC: Objection, Your Honor. He just indicated that he's speculating as to what his answer is, there's no foundation for it.

MJ: Overruled. Counsel, part of him being an expert witness is that he can now give opinions within his area of expertise. So, while he can't say, "I find this shocking," he can certainly say, "I think that this unit is dysfunctional because of my training and expertise."

ATC: Yes, sir, I agree with that. I believe that his answer is outside what you just described for us. I believe that he is not giving an opinion based on what his expertise is, he's speculating as to what definitively happened within the unit, which is not what he was recognized for today, sir.

MJ: Overruled.

Q: So, what did he [Gibbs] bring with him that is part of that dysfunction?

A: Yes. The report, and the lieutenant colonels told me that there was a lack of mentoring. I can be very specific about this. Colonel Clarke told me that he saw Colonel Tunnell only four times during the entire deployment. However, he was visited weekly by the general staff of General McChrystal. So, I see a real polarity here between the values and orientation of Colonel Clarke, who is 108 kilometers away from Ramrod, and he's closely aligned with the core COIN values. There were no problems with Colonel Clarke's units. On the other hand, Colonel Tunnell's favorite battalion was 1-17. He went there weekly. They were his favorite because they were the most aggressive, and they also took the most casualties. So, wherever Colonel Tunnell had a lot of interaction, there were a lot of problems.... To answer your question, wherever Colonel Tunnell seems to have been a point of contact, through Sergeant Gibbs, or through 1-17, or Captain Quiggle, problems arose, because he seemed to have transmitted his dysfunctional perspective on things as opposed to the COIN doctrine.

Q: Relating this back now to sociology, and having a functional unit and a dysfunctional unit, and the likelihood that you might see war crimes or—is there another term you could use for war crimes in sociological language?

A: War crimes fall under the general category of deviance, which is the breaking of social norms.

Q: In functional units, what do you see relative to dysfunctional units as it relates to deviance as further defined as war crimes?

A: A functional unit is able to self-correct. It will have some deviance, but not much deviance, because it will self-correct. A dysfunctional unit has a problem with the self-correcting mechanism, and once it has deviance, the deviance tends to continue until there is outside intervention. And that's a general pattern not just in theory, but in the cases I have seen. For example, Abu Ghraib did not self-correct until the photos were leaked. The situation in this brigade did not self-correct until Specialist Morlock made the videotape. So, until something drastic happens, a dysfunctional unit cannot self-correct, by definition.

Q: So, in terms of looking at this brigade, are you surprised that these types of crimes were committed?

A: No, they were inevitable.

Q: What do you mean by "inevitable?"

A: We cannot predict who will be the deviant. But we do predict that there will be various forms of deviance in a dysfunctional unit. By "deviance," I mean things ranging from suicide, accidents, murders, all kinds of things a society recognizes as breaking of social norms.

Q: Taking this back now, again, now to Specialist Morlock. How is he—I mean, if you take a soldier from Wasilla High School whose dad was a military vet, who was a hero in his eyes, and then you put him into a dysfunctional unit, which I presume he has no control over, in Afghanistan in a deployed combat environment, what choice does he have to be able to correct those dysfunctions, or how does he—is there anything he could have done to protect himself from this dysfunction?

A: There are several choices that he and other soldiers did not have. They did not choose their brigade commander. They did not choose to be cross-leveled. They did not choose that Gibbs would come in, or that Gibbs had the connections with Colonel Tunnell. They did not choose this ongoing conflict among the commanding generals of Colonel Tunnell and his subordinates. So, he and others in his situation were caught in a situation which they, as individuals, could not change. It's really a leadership issue....

Q: In expressing the opinions that you have expressed, you are not saying that any of this rises to any kind of legal defense for Specialist Morlock? He's still responsible for his—for what he did?

A: I agree with that.

Q: But in terms of extenuation and mitigation, what conclusions would you draw about this broader dysfunction?

A: In sociology, we have a notion of collective responsibility as well as individual responsibility, and they offset each other. I'm not sure how that would fit in with the law, but speaking as a sociologist, it is my opinion that to some extent the responsibility falls on the brigade.

Q: You've prepared an article about lessons learned from Abu Ghraib, and the Baghdad Canal killings. What if you had to write a story about this case, and what lessons have you learned, what would that sound or look like?

A: I think the Army needs to seriously address leadership issues. It's an organization, and what happened here is in some ways an element of workplace dysfunction.

Spinner: No further questions at this time, Your Honor.

Before the prosecutor could cross-examine me, the judge ruled on what he would consider relevant versus irrelevant in my testimony, as he had promised the prosecutor he would. To Spinner's relief, the judge ruled as relevant the sociological explanation that the dysfunctional brigade climate contributed to the crimes—albeit, in legal language.

MJ: Counsel, before you begin your cross-examination, the court is going to disregard as irrelevant the forward-looking prescription of Dr. Mestrovic for the Army. It's not relevant to this proceeding. Likewise, the court is going to disregard under Military Rules of Evidence 403 Dr. Mestrovic's conclusion of the inevitability of deviance in this case which led to the subject's offenses.

ATC: Yes, sir.

Spinner: May I then, Your Honor, with that ruling just obtain some clarification regarding what the doctor meant by "inevitability?"

MJ: Well, let me tell you what I am going to consider. I'm going to consider that dysfunctional norms within the brigade precipitated an environment that deviance, particularly in the form of both the violations of Article 112a, and the violence which occurred in this case were more likely, and there was a greater likelihood they would have been prevented with more active leadership measures. That's what I am going to consider.

Spinner: That's what you are going to consider?

MJ: Correct.

Spinner: That's all I needed to know.

Spinner smiled, because he had clearly won this legal battle with the prosecution. I have no arguments with the judge's decision not to accept my other two points, because his reasoning is based upon the law. However, media accounts later found that Ft. Lewis truly does seem to be a troubled place, judging by reported suicides, murders, undiagnosed PTSD, and finally, the March 2012 war crime committed by yet another soldier from yet another Stryker brigade at Ft. Lewis.[22] This and similar news accounts between the years 2010 and 2012 support my hypothesis that the social dysfunction at Ft. Lewis would "inevitably" cause numerous social problems, and not just the deviance in Morlock's platoon. And I hope that some readers will take seriously my call for the army to rethink its leadership training in order to prevent toxic leaders like Hellraiser from creating other, similar, dysfunctional brigades. Perhaps these assertions are not "relevant" in a courtroom, but they are very relevant in real life.

The cross-examination which followed was the shortest and easiest in my experience. The assistant trial counsel began:

Q: You spoke earlier that, and you can correct me if my terminology is wrong, but in the normal sociological setting, there is going to be some kind of synchronization between norms, values, beliefs, and sanctions, correct?

A: Correct.

Q: And that's what you would call a normal functioning environment, is that correct?

A: Correct.

Q: So, there is a concept that sanctions are a necessary part of society, is that correct?

A: Correct.

Q: And so, you would agree that an individual makes his own decisions, correct?

A: No.

Q: So, there's no concept of free will in a society?

A: I'm a sociologist. We talk about groupthink, group influences on decisions. I'm being honest. I cannot answer in any sense about a person in a vacuum making a decision.

MJ: Counsel, with regard to your question regarding free will, I would note the doctor has a significant background in theology. Do you want him recognized as an expert in theology to fully answer your question?

ATC: No, sir.

MJ: Or do you want to save your arguments for closing argument?

ATC: I'll save my arguments for argument, sir.

MJ: Please.

And it was over for my testimony. Speaking as a professor, I found the prosecutor's question regarding the notion of free will in sociology a fascinating one. It would have made for great classroom discussion. There is no space here to pursue the interesting issues of fate, destiny, and determinism on the one hand, versus choice, free will, and freedom on the other, all in relation to crime.

But what surprised both the prosecutor and me was the judge's invocation of my theological background! The judge was right: theologians debate the idea of free will. Sociologists cannot imagine the idea of choice without a social context. And the legal profession assumes the existence of free will to commit crime without philosophical debate or social context. There was an unmistakable tone of high-brow sarcasm in the way that the judge dismissed the prosecutor's efforts to have me say that Morlock chose to kill out of his own free will. The prosecutor's face and body language indicated that he was stunned by the judge's comment. I was stunned that the prosecutor gave up so easily. In any case, I was excused, and returned to my seat. There were no more witnesses to call.

Closing arguments and sentencing

There was no break in the proceedings after I sat down. Military trials proceed with the unyielding pace of military missions. Spinner asked that several exhibits be admitted into the trial record: 50 letters of support for Morlock, family photos of the Morlock's family, "a certificate for an Army commendation award that was provided to Specialist Morlock," and Morlock's Combat Infantryman Badge. There were no objections.

The judge asked both sides to give their final arguments, starting with the prosecutor. For the novice to military law, the following explanation may be helpful in deciphering what was at stake. Because of mandatory minimum sentencing laws, Morlock would be sentenced to life imprisonment. The judge had no choice in the matter. True, the pre-trial agreement would cut into that sentence. The judge had one and only one *choice* or decision to make, and that was whether Morlock would be eligible for parole or not. Whether his sentence was a life sentence or 24 years (as per the agreement), only the judge could decide on the possibility of parole. Morlock told me later that, at the time, he had no idea that the possibility of parole was at stake during this section of the trial. Captain LeBlanc made the closing argument for the prosecution, and predictably, asked the judge to impose a sentence that included no possibility of parole:

> May it please the court, Your Honor. Your Honor, the government respectfully requests that Specialist Morlock be sentenced to a life term without the possibility of parole, reduced to E1, forfeitures, and a dishonorable discharge. Your Honor, this case is one where parole eligibility should not be given because of the number of victims, and the horrifying nature of the murders in this case. Your Honor, despite what Dr. Mestrovic just testified about, sir, this is not us. We don't do this. This is not how we are trained. This is not the Army. Your Honor, these are the actions of a few extraordinarily misguided young men, including the accused, they were making a choice to engage a noncombatant. The names of the accountable, sir, you will find on Specialist Morlock's charge sheet. Those are the accountable parties. Sir, three Afghan lives have been needlessly lost to the cruel hands of the accused and his co-conspirators. Three Afghans, randomly selected, completely defenseless, all were completely cooperative during their pre-positioning before they were murdered, fired upon with assault rifles, machine guns, and blown up with fragmentary grenades by the accused and his co-conspirators and nobody else. These events all occurred in their home village right where they lived. Your Honor, the accused then attempted, along with his co-conspirators with some initial success, to paint the innocent as the aggressors. Your Honor, the number of victims, a cold, calculated nature of these murders, the false stories they advocated by the platoon members, those are the factors, that's the aggravation for a life sentence without parole.,,, Sir, this case is obviously about the pointless murder of three innocent Afghan civilians. Instead of providing these people with the security they needed, instead of building relationships and trust, instead of doing the job that we would expect of any professional Soldier, the accused and his co-accused chose to commit acts of unspeakable cruelty with cold calculus. Sir, in every court-martial

we are required to display the American flag as it is here today, it's the symbol of our ideals, our honor, our sense of moral virtue. Sir, the fact that the accused and his co-conspirators wore that flag during the commission of their crimes dishonors it, to all of those who wear it proudly, wearing it proudly while making a hard decision to do the right thing, even in difficult circumstances, unlike the accused and his co-conspirators chose to do. ... For these reasons, Your Honor, we respectfully request a sentence, a sanction for the accused which includes reduction to E1, total forfeitures, a life sentence without the possibility of parole, and a dishonorable discharge. Thank you, sir.

Spinner went next. Spinner's main objective as Morlock's lawyer was to convince the judge not to deny his client the possibility of parole:

> Your Honor, this is a difficult case. It's a difficult case in many respects but it's most difficult because I cannot challenge the fact that innocent lives were taken in my client's hands. And so, we recognize that, and I hope that, as I make the statements in the following argument, you do not lose sight of the fact that we acknowledge that up front. If anything, what I do think sets my client apart is that he has come forward, he has confessed to these crimes, he has pled guilty to these crimes, he has taken responsibility for his role in these crimes. What more can you ask of him to do, than to own up to his own misconduct? Now, another difficult part of this case is the fact that you have really very little discretion. The law does not permit you to adjudge a term of years of confinement. As you explained to Specialist Morlock, there is a mandatory minimum of life with the possibility of parole. And so, at one level, it's very difficult to make an argument given that that's the context in which we are now operating. However, having said that, I really do oppose the government's argument that the sentence should include life without the possibility of parole. This is the one area where you have discretion to say with or without the possibility of parole.

Some readers may not be aware that as a result of mandatory minimum sentencing laws passed by the U.S. Congress since the 1980s and national campaigns to "get tough on crime," all federal judges—including this one—have had their hands tied with regard to the profession of judging. This was the second time that I have seen Spinner announce this national trend in open court. Based upon numerous conversations, I have found that most spectators in the gallery do not truly comprehend the import of what Spinner said. The average person expects a judge or a jury to take into account the numerous mitigating factors which Spinner entered into the record and reduce a sentence accordingly. The judge certainly understood: he sat in his chair in his Rodinesque pose and evidenced a slight smirk at his culturally-imposed impotence when Spinner told him that his hands are mostly tied. Let there be no confusion in the mind of the reader: the only power the judge held at this point was whether or not to grant the possibility of parole as part of the plea-bargain agreement. The entire trial came down to this issue of the possibility of parole, because all the facts, the sentence, and the confession had already been agreed upon prior to trial. Spinner continued:

> I want to argue why that argument by the government is not supported by the sentencing evidence in this case. First of all, but for Sergeant Gibbs, joining Specialist Morlock's unit, you have to ask yourself, would Specialist Morlock have engaged in these acts? In part, that's why we put Dr. Mestrovic on the stand, to show that this was a dysfunctional brigade, to show that Specialist Morlock did not get to choose what brigade he was assigned to, he did not get to choose what battalion he was assigned to, he did not get to choose what company he was assigned to, he did not get to choose what platoon he was assigned to. He had no side in this debate of COIN or non-COIN. He had no choice about going to Afghanistan once he joined the Army. He had no choice when Sergeant Gibbs was placed in his proximity, with Sergeant Gibbs as a superior NCO, could have this kind of influence on Specialist Morlock. So, you have to keep in mind the totality of the circumstances that existed here as you determine what is an appropriate punishment and what level of responsibility to assign to Specialist Morlock.
>
> But I think there is even more than that, Your Honor, that you should consider. Because when you get to sentencing, while the government emphasizes the victims, and emphasizes the drug use, in sentencing, it's time to look at the individual to fashion an appropriate sentence based on that individual and his or her potential for rehabilitation. The government totally ignores the life history of Specialist Morlock in that regard when they make the argument for life without the possibility of parole. You've heard from Specialist Morlock's mother. You heard from his uncle. You heard from his teacher. You heard from his coach. Unfortunately, one person you did not hear from was his father. But what you heard in all their testimony is that Specialist Jeremy Morlock has potential to be a productive member of society, to return back to his community and to make a positive contribution, wherever that may be, whether it's in Alaska, or Washington state, or anywhere else. But you also see, although we did not address it more directly, in the pictures that you have there, is that he has a child, a newborn. When you put someone in prison without the possibility of parole, you are taking away the possibility for him to be a father who is involved in his child's life, just as his father was involved in his life. I think, Your Honor, when you marry those two up, when you marry up the fact that Specialist Morlock, who joined the Army with such high hopes and his history as a student, and as a hockey player, and as a son, and as a cousin, and as a nephew, and as a brother, with the fact that he was, in serving his country, sent to serve in a unit that was where discipline had broken down, where leadership failed him, where there was no professional mentoring, I think those factors all mitigate against the maximum punishment that the government has asked for. And so, in

that sense, we believe that even though the offenses are serious, and even though innocent lives have been taken, that there is something redeeming about Specialist Morlock that is worthy of recognition by the sentence you adjudge. And in that sense, we would argue against a life sentence without the possibility of parole, we would argue that forfeitures are not appropriate given that he has a child, and to the extent that he might have any possibility of providing any support that child, we would ask that forfeitures not be adjudged.... Here's the bottom line, Your Honor.... He has strong rehabilitative potential. He is a young man. And so, in crafting a sentence, we would ask that you craft a sentence that gives him hope; a sentence that gives him a future; a sentence that gives him a chance to return to his family where he will receive the love and the support of not only his family, but the community in which he grew up and has lived. Thank you, Your Honor.

The court-martial recessed at 3:57 pm and reconvened at 5:07 pm. Before the judge passed sentence, he turned to Morlock and asked a question.

"Specialist Morlock, a Ms. Pamela Finnesand alleges that she knows that you have a traumatic brain injury as well as other physical issues including post-traumatic stress disorder. My question to you is, have you received a diagnosis of suffering from a traumatic brain injury?"

A: Yes, sir, I believe I have.

MJ: And defense counsel, have you investigated the effect of that, if any?

Spinner: Yes, we have, Your Honor, with our forensic psychologist. We are satisfied that that's not an issue in this case.

MJ: Thank you.

The judge then sentenced Morlock "to be reduced to the grade of Private E1; to forfeit all of your pay and allowances; to be confined for the remainder of your natural life with the possibility of parole; and to be dishonorably discharged from the armed services." As per the ritual of courts-martial, the judge then opened the envelope containing the pretrial agreement, and said:

I have before me Appellate Exhibit III. It says that the convening authority agrees to disapprove any adjudged confinement in excess of 24 years, and to approve any other lawfully adjudged punishment. So, my understanding is that your sentence, as a result of this trial, will be: to be reduced to the grade of Private E1, to forfeit your pay, to be dishonorably discharged, and to be confined for 24 years. And I should note for the record you have 352 days of confinement credit against the approved sentence. So, of that 24 years, take approximately a year off of it.

The court-martial ended at 5:12 pm on the 23rd of March, 2011. The prosecutor generously gave Morlock several hours to say good-bye to his family. That evening, he would not be returned the navy brig where he had spent most of his pre-trial confinement. He would be transferred to the regional detention facility at Ft. Lewis, where he would stay until August of 2011, and then he would be transferred again to the navy brig until March of 2012. For the next year, he would be at the disposal of the government to cooperate and testify against other accused soldiers in his platoon.

Jeremy Morlock with his brother and sisters

Jeremy Morlock with his father

Jeremy Morlock at Airborne School

Jeremy Morlock and his mother at the presentation of the colors at his father's funeral

Jeremy Morlock recently with his 3 month old daughter, Harlow

Chapter 14. The Courts-Martial of the Other Soldiers

There was a long lull in court-martial activity between March and June of 2011. During this time-frame, Morlock was kept in the maximum level of solitary confinement at the Ft. Lewis detention facility or RCF. Despite the fact that, at the court-martial, Captain Opachan had brought up Morlock's mistreatment at the Ft. Lewis jail—the abuse continued. Captain Opachan again protested the abuse, with no apparent success in improving Morlock's situation. Suddenly, and without warning or explanation to anyone, including the defense attorneys, Morlock was moved out of solitary confinement and placed into general population at the Ft. Lewis jail on June 18, 2010.[23] If one were to speculate on the government's motives, a good guess would be that Morlock had become sleep-deprived, depressed, and had problems with his memory as a result of the solitary confinement. He was required to testify at an Article 32 hearing the following week, and perhaps it occurred to the government that he might be able to fulfill his obligations if he were rested, well-fed, and less lonely. But this respite did not last long. He was placed back into solitary confinement at the RCF after the burst of Article 32 hearings had come to an end.

On June 24, 2011, Morlock testified in Sergeant Bram's re-opened Article 32 hearing. He testified that Bram did not participate in the killings under discussion here, even though Bram took part in discussions of the killing scenarios.[24] From the beginning of the investigation, CID investigators and prosecutors had been pressuring Morlock to point the finger at Bram as a member of the "kill team." Morlock maintained the steadfast position that Bram did not participate in the killings. Captain Ligsay, Morlock's former platoon leader, testified against Bram at this hearing.

This was Ligsay's first court appearance in the drawn-out legal process, and took place because the government gave Ligsay immunity from prosecution in exchange for his testimony. Ligsay had also been promoted from lieutenant to captain in the interim—despite the dark stain of having commanded a platoon that was involved in war crimes. Ligsay gave a different spin to the photos of soldiers posing with the bodies of dead Afghans. He said that he posed in such photos out of a sense of pride and accomplishment at having killed the enemy.[25]

On June 28, 2011, Morlock testified in yet another re-opened Article 32. Morlock was on the witness stand for approximately four hours, most of which were spent being cross-examined by Wagnon's defense attorney. Morlock maintained his position that Wagnon did participate in the second killing by shooting into the direction of where Gibbs had killed the Afghan villager. A month following this hearing, the investigative officer (IO) issued the judgment that there was not sufficient evidence to prosecute Wagnon because of the issue of whether Wagnon knew that the killing was staged.[26] Eventually, the murder charges against Wagnon would be dismissed by the new commanding general of Ft. Lewis, MG Lloyd Miles.

During the week of July 4, 2011, Morlock testified in the court-martial of Sergeant Darren Jones. Jones was the first soldier out of the fifteen who were charged in this overall case to plead not guilty, and to elect a court-martial by military panel (jury). The main charges against him were participating in the assault on Stoner, participating in a drive-by shooting of Afghan farmers which apparently did not result in any deaths, and participating in discussions of killing scenarios. He was facing a maximum sentence of 22 years.[27] The military panel found Jones guilty of assault on Stoner, but not guilty of any of the other charges. He was sentenced to seven months in prison, and remarkably, was not discharged from the army.[28]

Specialist Corey Moore pled guilty to kicking a witness and stabbing one of the corpses. He was sentenced to sixty days hard labor and a bad conduct discharge. Specialist Emmitt Quintal was sentenced to ninety days hard labor as part of a plea-bargain, for drug use and assaulting Stoner.

Gibbs had a second Article 32 or pre-trial hearing during the week of July 18th. At this point in time, the "re-opening" of previous Article 32s was becoming a pattern. The various defense teams were attempting to throw out charges while the government was trying to tack on additional charges for the remaining defendants. Along with about twenty other witnesses, Morlock testified against Gibbs on July 21, 2011. The gist of his testimony was that Gibbs had boasted of other, similar killings in Iraq and that the scenarios began with the theme of using drop-weapons to make all questionable kills seem legitimate.[29] Or, to quote Morlock precisely "The idea of drop weapons had always been around. It was a different spin that these weren't drop weapons to cover your ass. These were drop weapons to kill someone."[30] The medic, Stevens, also testified at this re-opened Article 32. Stevens had already been sentenced to seven months confinement for his part in scenario shootings that did not result in any deaths. Stevens generally corroborated Morlock's testimony, with one small variation: According to Stevens, Gibbs suspected the Afghan man of being a Taliban leader, and was sick and tired of capturing and then releasing Taliban insurgents.[31]

On August 5, 2011, Adam Winfield was court-martialed. He had reached a plea-bargain with the prosecution for 7 years for negligent homicide and drug use. He faced a maximum sentence of 17 years. But in his case, the military judge, Colonel David Conn, reduced the agreement considerably and sentenced Winfield to 3 years in prison. [32] (A military judge may not increase the sentence in a pre-trial agreement, but he has the option to reduce it.) The mitigating factors in Winfield's favor were that his father tried to alert the army about Gibbs and the killings, to no avail, and attested to that at his son's court-martial. Note that Winfield was initially charged with premeditated murder and conspiracy, and the case against him seemed open and shut because he had confessed to CID agents on videotape. But, he was court-martialed for negligent homicide, not premeditated murder. What happened?

By the time Winfield's case went to trial, both the commanding general and the Chief of Military Justice at Ft. Lewis were deployed to Afghanistan. A new commanding general and a new chief were appointed at Ft. Lewis prior to Winfield's court-martial. Captain LeBlanc strongly opposed the change in the charges from premeditated murder to negligent homicide for Winfield. However, the prosecutor had no choice in the matter, as this decision was made by the new commanding general.

On August 15, 2011, Morlock was transferred from the Ft. Lewis prison facility to the navy brig near Silverdale, Washington. He was moved suddenly and without any advance notice to the defense team. Morlock was relieved that he was returning to his version of the Hotel Hilton. He was held in solitary confinement at both the RCF at Ft. Lewis and the navy brig, but even the horror of solitary confinement was more humane at the navy brig. At the navy brig, his cell had ventilation, the showers worked properly, and the food was nutritious. (I was present for one of his meals at the navy brig, and can confirm this.) Morlock told me that he was given fresh fruit at the navy brig, and that Wednesday night was steak night. However, at the RCF at Ft. Lewis, his cell had no ventilation at all, the showers did not work properly, and the food consisted of cold rations, "as if we were out in the field," Morlock said.

The court-martial of Sergeant Gibbs began on Halloween, or October 31, 2011. Gibbs refused the plea-bargain of 99 years which the government had offered, and opted for a full trial by military jury, or panel. His defense attorney was Mr. Philip Stackhouse, who entered a plea of not guilty on behalf of his client. Stackhouse's theory was that Gibbs was directly involved in only one of the charged killings (the third one), which was a legitimate combat killing. Allegedly, Gibbs did not know about the other charged killings. The government's theory was that Gibbs was the ringleader and mastermind behind the killings. The strongest part of the government's theory was the claim that the platoon in question had no killings at all until Gibbs arrived. Stackhouse's strongest argument was that the government had no forensic, ballistic, or physical evidence at all against Gibbs—the entire case hinged on the testimony of over twenty soldiers, including Morlock.

The panel consisted of five members: three commissioned and two non-commissioned officers. The president of the panel was a female lieutenant colonel. Morlock was the first to testify against Gibbs, and his testimony lasted for two days—this is unusually lengthy for a court-martial. Stackhouse tried to make the point that the AK-47 rifle which Gibbs planted as a "drop weapon" on the second victim was a fabrication. He brought an AK-47 rifle into the courtroom and demonstrated that it did not fit into a standard army knapsack. The prosecutor countered with a photograph of Gibbs with a knapsack that seemed to hold an AK-47. Morlock countered on the witness stand that there are many varieties of the AK-47 rifle, and while the one in the courtroom did not fit into the knapsack, the one on the battlefield on the day of the killing did fit. It was an OJ Simpson moment in the courtroom: The defense was making the argument that "if the glove don't fit, you must acquit." More than twenty witnesses followed Morlock in testifying against Gibbs as to what they heard and saw with regard to each of the three killings.

On November 10, 2011, the panel returned a guilty verdict on all sixteen counts, including all the murders, but also including conspiracy, assault on Stoner, obstruction of justice, and other charges. An hour after they rendered their verdict, which carries a mandatory minimum sentence of life in prison, they rendered the second part of their sentence: Gibbs would be allowed the possibility of parole. The media reported the verdict, and the story disappeared from the news. In his closing arguments, the prosecutor stressed the point that Gibbs, who referred to Afghans as savages, "was the real savage." In other words, the government had succeeded in keeping out of the trial record the import of General Twitty's report and issues pertaining to the poisoned command climate in Stryker brigade.

Spinner contacted me via e-mail almost immediately after the verdict was rendered. In his role as Morlock's defense attorney, he was heartened by the government's theory as favorable for his client. The prosecutor had made the point for the trial record that no killings occurred until Gibbs arrived in Morlock's platoon, which meant that Morlock was less guilty than Gibbs from the legal point of view. Moreover, Spinner would pursue Special Agent Wagner's offer to write a letter on behalf of Morlock, asking for a further reduction in Morlock's sentence (Wagner was one of the CID interrogators who obtained the videotaped statement from Morlock).

The following day, I spoke with Morlock by telephone. The staff at the navy brig was courteous, as usual, in connecting me with Morlock. Morlock filled in details which never made their way into the information media. He said that he learned of the verdict while sitting in Captain LeBlanc's office, while the remainder of the more than twenty soldiers waited in the hallway. LeBlanc walked in after the verdict was read, hugged his staff, and hugged Morlock. Then a female civilian prosecutor (who had been assigned to the case) walked up to Morlock and said something to the effect of: "Keep your head down when you go to Leavenworth, because there is a real chance you could be killed in there, but if you keep your head down, you should be okay." Morlock told me that he was speechless. Apparently, she was implying that Gibbs might seek revenge at the USDB at Leavenworth against Morlock for his testimony. Meanwhile, an altercation had erupted in the hallway. Apparently, Stevens was on the verge of assaulting Stoner. The irony of the situation is that Stevens had already served seven months imprisonment. Captain Mazzone returned to whisk Morlock out of the building, into a waiting van, and back to the navy brig. "You're not safe here," Mazzone said to Morlock.

I asked Morlock: "What triggered the brawl?" He replied: "Stoner got excited when the verdict was announced and said something like, 'Convicted on all sixteen counts, yes!'" "Did any of the soldiers come to Stoner's defense?" I asked. "You don't get it," Morlock said, and continued: "Stoner is seen as a snitch, and everyone in the platoon hates him." He went on to elaborate that while waiting to testify, Sergeants Bram, Jones, and Gibbs sat together and maintained their leadership roles among the soldiers in the hallway. Bram was scheduled to be court-martialed approximately a week later, on November 16, 2011. On purely pragmatic grounds, Bram should have been distancing himself from Gibbs instead of maintaining a warm relationship with him. Moreover, the government had initially offered Bram 120 days for assaulting Stoner as a plea-bargain—but Bram's defense team did not act on the offer for over a year. That deal fell through, and the government offered 7 months as a plea-bargain, but again, his defense team did not react to the offer until the day before his scheduled court-martial. By that point, it was too late. The new commanding general rejected the plea-bargain, and Bram was forced to go to trial. The government tacked on eight additional charges against Bram. Stevens, too, had been offered a deal for 120 days—and took it. At his court-martial, Bram was found guilty of assault, solicitation to commit premeditated murder, aggravated assault on Afghan civilians, failing to report crimes, planting evidence, and discussing killing scenarios. He was sentenced to five years in prison.

Then there was the curious case of Wagnon, who was scheduled to be court-martialed in January of 2012 for one of the killings. Wagnon showed up repeatedly in the hallway and the prosecutor's office, requesting to testify on behalf of Gibbs. It was strange that Wagnon kept insisting to testify even after his attorney, Mr. Colby Vokey, had invoked Wagnon's 5th Amendment right against self-incrimination and forbade Wagnon to testify. All this begs the question, "Did Gibbs really have that much charisma, and was part of the platoon still that loyal to him?"

Spinner concluded that Morlock's life was, indeed, in danger. Spinner did not have an immediate solution to this problem. I proposed asking Captain LeBlanc to send Morlock to a naval correctional facility of any sort instead of Ft. Leavenworth. Spinner replied that this was impossible, because the USDB at Ft. Leavenworth is the only long-term correctional facility for all the military branches in the United States. Nevertheless, Spinner would request that Morlock be sent to some prison facility other than Ft. Leavenworth.

Conclusions

Justice is not confined to the outcome of a formal court process. All social groups have their informal forms of justice, including 3rd platoon. These informal forms of "justice" are more often referred to as vendettas. The vendetta in the hallway is not an isolated incident. We have seen that the themes of death threats and assault on the "snitches" have followed this narrative from the start, even though they remained in the background of society's more dominant and formal narrative of justice. And I have seen a similar theme in all the other war crimes cases which I have studied directly. In the Abu Ghraib case, Joseph Darby was the whistleblower, who had to be put into a witness protection program because of all the death threats made against him. In the Baghdad Canal Killings, Sergeant Cunningham was the government's star witness against the three top sergeants who were convicted of murdering Iraqi prisoners (John Hatley, Michael Leahy, and Joseph Mayo). Cunningham was the object of numerous death threats by his platoon. I recall vividly the scene of him sitting alone in a witness room while other soldiers—again, standing in a hallway—made menacing gestures and comments against him. Similarly, in the Operation Iron Triangle case, the government's star witness, Specialist Justin Graber, was the platoon's scapegoat and the object of death threats.

If one examines the vicissitudes of Morlock's imprisonment during the long time period in which he was confined waiting for his final disposition, one confronts a similar pattern. His situation varied in accordance with his relationship to whatever group morality he was confronting at the time. Thus, the staff of the army RCF at Ft. Lewis treated him viciously while the staff at the naval brig treated him correctly, and without a trace of vendetta. This difference can be explained by the fact that the army staff identified with Ft. Lewis, and saw him and the other convicted soldiers as bringing dishonor to their base and overall "collective consciousness." The predictable result was—revenge. On the other hand, the staff at the naval brig perceived and treated him as a stranger, and therefore as more of a guest at their facility, regardless of the crimes for which he was convicted. It is worth repeating that he was allowed to wear an army uniform within the naval facility—in their eyes, he was still an army soldier.

Another interesting group dynamic involved Morlock's relationship to the entire staff of the several prosecutors, and in particular to Captain LeBlanc, who was the chief prosecutor, and more importantly, Morlock's prosecutor. LeBlanc's behavior toward Morlock changed from vengeful to almost "friendly" between March and November of 2011. LeBlanc transferred Morlock from the army correctional facility to the naval brig, and when Morlock was at LeBlanc's office preparing for the courts-martial of other soldiers, he gave him chewing tobacco, shared his ice tea with him, and in general, treated him more kindly as time passed. Some of this behavior could be dismissed as utilitarian and tactical on the part of LeBlanc. But part of the transformation is undoubtedly the result of the hundreds of hours LeBlanc and Morlock spent together preparing for his testimony in the various trials, and sharing in each other's triumphs and defeats at the other trials. Harking back to our earlier discussions of a COIN-like spirit, Morlock and LeBlanc signed a formal agreement to *cooperate* with each other. Through frequent, face-to-face interaction, Morlock gradually became a part of the "prosecutor's team," and came to be treated as such, in opposition to the antagonistic attitudes the prosecutor exhibited toward him while he was a member of the "defense team." It is foolish to regard justice as some dogmatic, absolute phenomenon. Like all other social phenomena, justice comes in many varieties, and is always part of the social context of different groups.

Chapter 15. Conclusions and Recommendations

There is so much more to this story than initially meets the eye. "Questionable kills" were committed by soldiers in Stryker brigade during its deployment in Afghanistan. Winfield's father reported some of these questionable kills to the government, in line with the rule on the Soldier's Card: "All personnel must report any suspected violations of the Law of War committed by any US, friendly or enemy force. Notify your chain of command." But the chain of command ignored Winfield's father. CID first learned of the questionable kills from Morlock while they were investigating the assault on Stoner. Some of the questionable kills were later charged as murders—but no one will ever know the full inventory of questionable kills in Stryker brigade.

General Scaparrotti ordered General Twitty to conduct a formal inquiry into the command climate, and he also served as the convening authority for the courts-martial of five soldiers. General Twitty's investigation was necessarily sociological, because it examined command climate, while the criminal investigations focused upon individuals. The AR 15-6 investigation, conducted by General Twitty, opened up entirely new dimensions to the story: in examining the command climate. Twitty opened the doors for officers and soldiers in the brigade to make sworn statements which were about their brigade commander, COIN doctrine, counter-guerrilla doctrine, and their own confusion as to what they were doing in Afghanistan. On the other hand, the criminal investigators focused exclusively on five soldiers they labeled as the "inner circle," which was renamed "the kill team" by the media. What was considered fringe to the story of these war crimes in the Twitty report became central to the investigators, and vice versa. In other words, the Twitty report pays hardly any attention at all to the five soldiers who were charged for war crimes—they became the fringe element to the story—and is overwhelmingly about COIN versus CG doctrines, Hellraiser, and the command climate. On the other hand, the criminal investigators ignored completely the command climate, COIN and CG doctrines, and even the fact that an entire platoon was involved. They focused exclusively on five soldiers.

Within each of these two grand narratives, there lies yet another center-fringe dichotomy. The Twitty report focuses upon 2-1, because that is the battalion to which the five soldiers were assigned. By the time Twitty began his investigation in November of 2010, he inherited the sworn statements which CID investigators had obtained in the Spring of 2010. Therefore, the Twitty report treats as a fringe element the story of the murderous battalion, 1-17, and especially Bravo company, which emerges from the sworn statements. From the sworn statements contained within the Twitty report, it seems that 1-17 committed many more "questionable" kills than 2-1. But the questionable kills in 1-17 were never investigated, and from the legal point of view, they remain invisible. 1-17 adopted Hellraiser's philosophy, while 2-1 was more COIN oriented. I leave it up to the reader to perform the following thought experiment: suppose that the AR 15-6 investigation had preceded the CID investigation. How would this story have come out differently?

In the narrative created by the criminal investigators, the many attempted scenarios, attempted murders, and questionable kills within Bravo Company, 2-1—especially the EOF incident—become the fringe element, while the three killings described by Morlock in his videotaped statement became central. One could easily argue the opposite: that the killings described by Morlock were a fringe to the story of multiple attempted killings since Gibbs arrived in 2-1.

There are numerous, other fringe-center dichotomies in the entire story. For example, it seems to be the case that officers and soldiers in Stryker brigade were hopelessly confused as to whether their mission was COIN or CG—or weird hybrids of the two doctrines—even though COIN was the official policy of the US Army at the time of their deployment. COIN doctrine itself is defined as a mixture of lethal and non-lethal philosophies as well actions, and the proportion of these ingredients is left up to the brigade commander. In addition, there is the dichotomy between attitude and behavior—in other words, between embracing COIN and doing COIN. Thus, some officers (the true believers) concluded that Hellraiser was doing COIN in his own way, even though he did not believe in it. Other officers (the non-believers) saw him as defying General McChrystal's orders and doing CG, regardless of what he believed about COIN. But General McChrystal, the evangelist of COIN doctrine, was fired by President Obama, for mocking this doctrine and the president's office as well as staff. The distinction between *doing* COIN versus *believing* in COIN haunts this story. Other officers believed that he did not truly believe in CG, even though he ordered that the words "counter-guerrilla" be emblazed on guidons, pistols, cups, stream-ers, and other physical objects—that it was *just a nom de guerre* intended to boost morale.

But I do not intend to end this study in this seemingly postmodern manner: that there were numerous competing narratives and that one could argue that they were all simulacra. In the end, certain truths crys-tallized. Taking up the language with which I began this study, one could say that truth did not happen to some ideas, and truth did happen to other ideas. Let us take up each of these categories in turn.

THE IDEAS TO WHICH TRUTH DID NOT HAPPEN

Truth did not happen to the prosecution's idea that there was a group of five soldiers, the "inner circle," who committed premeditated murder. Charges against Wagnon were dropped completely. Charges against Winfield were reduced drastically to involuntary manslaughter. Holmes and Morlock were convicted based upon pre-trial agreements, so that the prosecution actually proved premeditated murder in open court only in the case of Gibbs, who opted for a full court-martial by military panel.

Truth did not happen to COIN doctrine, in Hellraiser's brigade or in general. It is true that many officers and soldiers were doing COIN, and it is true that COIN doctrine was and remains the official policy of the U.S. Army. But the truth which emerges out of the Twitty report is that officers and soldiers in Hellraiser's brigade were confused as to what they were really doing. Many officers reported that they were "sneaking" COIN behind Hellraiser's back, or in other ways doing COIN despite Hellraiser—it should be obvious that sneaking a doctrine that is sup-posedly normative does not qualify as the acceptance or absorption of a doctrine. It is not enough for COIN or any other doctrine to be stated in a manual, consumed in power-point presentations or to otherwise exist solely as an abstraction. For an idea to "exist" in a common sense way, it must correspond with numerous other ideas and must be absorbed and assimilated. In real life, in the everyday world of interaction and face-to-face contact, COIN doctrine emerged as a Jekyll and Hyde monstrosity. The Afghans as well as US soldiers literally did not know what would happen before, during, or following a meeting to have tea with the village elders. Would an IED go off and kill or wound US soldiers? Would sol-diers threaten and verbally abuse Afghan children, or throw them candy? The Americans wondered, "Is the entire village behind the insurgents who are trying to kill us with IEDs?" The Afghans wondered, "Should we throw our loyalty behind the Americans or the Taliban?"

We have seen that McChrystal's firing does not speak well for the absorption of COIN doctrine in the stratosphere of American power. COIN is the butt of jokes or outright derision in the media and political cartoons. The new ISAF commander, General Scaparrotti, did not even mention COIN when asked about his priorities in Afghanistan. The failure of COIN doctrine in Hellraiser's brigade is mirrored in the overall failure of COIN doctrine in US policy.

THE IDEAS TO WHICH TRUTH DID HAPPEN

Spinner won the battle to enshrine testimony in Morlock's Record of Trial (ROT) that Hellraiser's dysfunctional command climate precipitated the killings. The MJ is on record as accepting the relevance of this testimony. With this testimony, truth also happened to the sociological perspective, that crime in general and war crimes in particular, even though they are committed by individuals, are connected to social climate. Taken in context, it is a small victory, even if it is a real one. The trial process is a metaphorical war, and the prosecutor did his best to prevent Spinner from opening this door. Nevertheless, Spinner opened it—and I walked through the door he opened. However, sociology, as a discipline, is scarcely absorbed by and seems disconnected to what passes for common sense. Realistically, one cannot expect any worthwhile consequences from Spinner's victory in the near future. The "common sense" view that heinous crimes are committed by monstrous individuals still rules in the law and in criminology.

Truth happened to Hellraiser's counter-guerrilla doctrine. Ironically, Hellraiser was proven right by the course of history following his deployment in Afghanistan. His central argument is that counter-guerrilla is the traditional doctrine of the US Army and that COIN was a mythology that could not work. The United States has increased drone strikes in Afghanistan dramatically over the past two years. The exit strategy for leaving Afghanistan rests primarily on a large increase of special operations forces, who are basically trained in "strike and destroy" tactics. The war in Libya was purely of the "strike and destroy" variety. As of this writing, the media is saturated with calls by Senators and Congressmen to commit pre-emptive strikes against Iran. COIN has practically disappeared from political and military discourse.

Finally, truth happened to Hellraiser's CG idea within his own brigade. The "strike and destroy" idea, coupled with the "counter-guerrilla" idea, connected with numerous other ideas within the brigade, and eventually became true. Numerous soldiers *did* strike and destroy Afghans, and many of these kills are described as "questionable." This seems to be especially true for 1-17, the battalion with which Hellraiser was obsessed. The many violent nicknames, mottos, slogans, and symbols in the brigade were bound to emerge as war crimes, and they did. How can one expect young soldiers to absorb mottos such as "Shoot them in the face" and "Death dealers"—among other similar ideas—and not act on them eventually?

The facts in this story show that this was not a simple case of cause and effect. A multitude of factors convinced soldiers and officers that the opposing idea, COIN, was bankrupt. For example, we have seen that soldiers worried that COIN and its new rules of engagement and EOF procedures would get them killed. They worked for sergeants who voiced the opinion that "COIN is crap." They were surrounded by streamers with the word "counter-guerrilla," but not a single officer or soldier mentions streamers with the words, "COIN doctrine"—presumably because there were none. There were no mottos or slogans to "have tea with the village elders"—this phrase was the object of mockery. Soldiers received extensive lethal training, but nobody mentioned any seminars, workshops, or presentations on COIN for the low-ranking soldiers. The presentations which the officers attended basically mocked COIN and glorified CG doctrine. The intervening variable between counter-guerrilla doctrine and the resulting war crimes was the dysfunctional, toxic, social climate that resulted from confusion as to what was the real mission, dismal morale, lack of mentoring, cross-leveling and other factors that have been discussed. I hold to my professional judgment that the war crimes in Stryker brigade—the ones that went to court-martial as well as the "questionable" kills—were inevitable.

On September 19, 2010, Major General John D. Johnson ordered LTC Carl R. Jacquet to conduct an AR 15-6 investigation into the issue of how and why Winfield's father's reports of the killings in Afghanistan were ignored. MG Johnson ordered LTC Jacquet to answer the question: "What is Installation Operations Center (IOC) procedure for handling reports of war crimes or other similar serious misconduct?" Jacquet's finding in the report was that there was no procedure in place, and he documents "the historic lack of attention to detail and complacency" at the Ft. Lewis operations center. Criteria existed at the center for taking phone calls regarding suicides, accidents, and a host of mishaps, and then reporting them up the chain of command. These criteria were depicted on "flip files." But flip files for war crimes "did not exist in February 2010." There was simply no way for the army to *receive* or recognize the truth of war crimes at the time Winfield's father reported them. Yes, the army requires that "suspected violations of the Law of War" be reported to the chain of command, but it had no mechanism for carrying out this rule. And this is true not only for the chain of command which led to Ft. Lewis, but other chains of command as well. LTC Jacquet's AR 15-6 report documents that Winfield's father left messages with the Army Inspector General office, Senator Bill Nelson's office (of Florida), and the CID office at Ft. Lewis—he could only get voice mail, and no one ever called him back.

RECOMMENDATIONS

While I doubt any of them will be taken seriously, I offer some insights gleamed from this study. Sociology has yet to be absorbed in contemporary culture like the disciplines of law, medicine, or the military. Still, perhaps someday in the distant future, some scholar or student at a war college will consider these thoughts and avert the sort of tragedy that has been the subject of this book.

The army should consider reversing the current trend of treating cross-leveling as routine. Cross-leveling destroys group cohesion, and group cohesion is one of the core principles of army doctrine. The concept of group cohesion corresponds to the sociological concept of "social integration." Thousands of studies show that the more socially integrated a group is, the lower its rates of deviance of all sorts will be (suicide, psychosomatic illness, stress, crime, etc.). Soldiers are not machines or chess pieces or other lifeless assets. They are embodied individuals who are sustained by the cohesiveness of the groups to which they belong. No doubt, there will be instances in which cross-leveling will be appropriate, but these should be rare instances. We have seen throughout this study that the army creates hybrid, synthetic units as if out of thin air, with no regard for the loyalties, bonds of trust, friendships, and mentoring relationships established in groups. Such a destructive process should not be routine.

Closely related, the army should put much more emphasis upon its existing requirements that officers circulate, live with, eat with, and in general, that they associate with each other. Interestingly, Durkheim uses exactly the same word, "circulation," to assess the general health and social integration of a group. The higher the circulation, the stronger the social integration will be. This also means that the army needs to emphasize and demand of its officers that they counsel, mentor, and monitor each other and their soldiers.

COIN doctrine needs to be rewritten, from scratch, and it should be constructed upon a genuinely sociological basis. In its current form, it is simply untenable because it mingles lethal with non-lethal philosophies, and leaves the dosage of these philosophies entirely up to commanders. The result, as we have seen, is a Jekyll and Hyde doctrine that does more harm than good: it confuses US soldiers every bit as much as it confuses "locals." By genuine sociology, I am referring to the sociologists I have already discussed, who stress the deep and profound aspects of the ideas, "cooperation" and "division of labor."

In addition, COIN doctrine must be rid of its ethnocentrism. Ethnocentrism is the belief that one's culture is superior to other cultures, and ethnocentrism is something like a mortal sin in anthropology and sociology. Current COIN doctrine definitely assumes that American culture is superior to the culture it confronts in war, and such an attitude can never achieve the desired goals of COIN, namely, to win people's hearts and minds. The opposite of ethnocentrism is cultural relativism, or the belief that all cultures are functional in their own ways; that all religions are true in their own ways because of the social functions they fulfill in giving people a sense of meaning and belonging; and that in general, the goal is for different cultures to enter into a division of labor and cooperate with each other, not that one subjugates the other. And the army must address the issue which emerges from Hellraiser's ethnocentric reaction to COIN as un-American because it relies upon foreign authors, ideas, and theories. How many other officers in the army share Hellraiser's ethnocentrism? How can COIN doctrine be written and presented so that it can be assimilated by American officers?

In general, the army must confront the issue of ethnocentrism head-on. If American brigade commanders balk at working with foreign, NATO commanders; if foreign military theorists are dismissed simply because of their national origin; and if sociology, anthropology, and the other social sciences are not respected because of their national origins—then the tragedy of Hellraiser's brigade will be repeated many times over. War against a foreign enemy is a fundamentally cultural and sociological issue. And modernity requires a cosmopolitan, sophisticated division of labor or spirit of cooperation across numerous dimensions.

The army should consider establishing a hotline or other mechanism for reporting questionable kills and actions. The hotline phone number should not go through any chain of command, but be centralized for the entire army. This hotline should not go to voice mail, but be staffed by humans 24 hours a day. And this staff should have "flip files" for receiving reports of "questionable kills" or other "questionable" acts, not war crimes. War crimes or violations of the Laws of War come at the end of long and protracted investigative and judicial processes, but do not come pre-labeled as war crimes. We have seen that Winfield's father could not get anyone in the government to take him seriously when he reported what his son told him about the killings. At the present time, the only route for soldiers to report war crimes is to go through their chain of command. This is an obviously dysfunctional mechanism when one's superiors in the chain of command are the ones committing or covering up or refusing to investigate questionable kills. Hotlines exist for reporting hate crimes, bullying, and other sorts of social evils. There needs to be a similar mechanism for reporting questionable kills and actions. Otherwise, soldiers are left trapped in dysfunctional and murderous groups.

Symbols matter greatly as a form of communication, and the army does not seem to notice the disconnect between its widespread use of violent, aggressive symbolism and its purported missions to win hearts and minds. If a mission is going to be one of cooperation and having tea with the village elders, the symbols displayed by that unit should be appropriate to the mission.

Finally, the military's theorists of war may wish to consider the tragic story which has just been told as a kind of morality play. Hellraiser's counter-guerrilla doctrine mirrors the archetypical narrative that is *Moby Dick*. Hellraiser and Ahab are social types, representing dogmatism, fundamentalism, and the true believers. The great white whale seems to correspond to terror, as in "the war on terror." The lesson seems to be that one cannot defeat terror, because terror is an idea. Terrorism and terrorists have existed since the dawn of history and cannot be defeated by striking and destroying them. This is an insight that flickers throughout the COIN manual, but it is overwhelmed quickly by recourse to traditional warfare doctrines—meaning some variation of strike and destroy philosophy.

Lethal and non-lethal strategies in making war should be kept distinct. Each has a role to play in the division of labor that is combat. Hellraiser should not have been certified to deploy and sent out to do COIN in Afghanistan, when several of his subordinate commanders were willing to do COIN despite his insubordinate views. Colonel A or LTC B or LTC C, who were the Starbucks in this story, should have led the brigade. If one extrapolates the lesson to be learned in this story to other Hellraisers and other Starbucks in the US military, it is clear: Make officers who fit the Starbuck archetype the commanders for doing COIN.

The reader need only do the thought experiment of how the story in *Moby Dick* would have ended differently had Starbuck been in command instead of Ahab—it would not have ended as a tragedy. The same is true for the story of Hellraiser and his brigade.

APPEALING TO WHAT IS THE BEST AND NOBLEST IN AMERICAN CULTURE

The recommendations listed above address only the most pressing and immediate problems which have emerged from this study, namely, the fundamental confusion as to what constitutes COIN doctrine, the overuse of cross-leveling, and the lack of a viable mechanism for whistleblowing when it comes to reporting wrongdoing in warfare. But no amount of power point slides, refinement of abstract definitions, or other re-conceptualization can fix the problematic issues we have uncovered. What is needed is a fundamental re-examination of traditions, values, and "the big picture" of America's place in current history. This is because COIN and CG doctrines both appeal to the worst parts of human nature and recall the ugliest periods of US history, namely, slavery, the cruelties of how war was waged during the Civil War, and the extermination of Native Americans. New policies, doctrines, and procedures for waging war as well as peace are needed that will appeal to the best in people and what is noblest in American history.

We have seen that in the abstract, CG doctrine pertains only to military tactics aimed at crushing an insurgency. Hellraiser has performed a great service in fleshing out the abstraction of "insurgency" by pointing out that insurgents and insurgencies include embodied individuals and groups ranging historically from Native Americans and US Confederate soldiers to the present-day Taliban. In the abstract, COIN doctrine does not supersede CG doctrine, but absorbs it. As defined in FM 3-24, COIN is supposed to combine lethal as well as non-lethal operations, and purportedly combines offensive, defensive, and stability philosophies.

There is no need here to remind the reader here of the desperate measures to which officers in Stryker brigade resorted in order to reconcile these contradictions. They came up with weird hybrids of COIN and CG doctrines and tactics that did not, and could not, resolve the illogical inconsistency of trying to win hearts and minds while engaging in strike and destroy missions. We have analyzed the agony of individuals in Stryker brigade trying to carry out its impossible missions because we have been blessed with hard-to-get data, especially the Twitty report. It is reasonable to assume that all COIN missions in Iraq and Afghanistan are beset by the same problem. One has only to turn to the episode of President Obama firing General McChrystal, and the ongoing debates about COIN doctrine within the military establishment, to conclude that something is desperately wrong with implementing COIN doctrine in its present form.

The abstract problem of building COIN upon the base of CG is insoluble. One cannot get the most from the least, a moral doctrine from aggressive policy, goodwill from a strike and destroy approach. One cannot get light from darkness. Since the dawn of history, all men and women, and societies have been moved to respect by the virtues of generosity, kindness, reconciliation, and other qualities related to the general, sociological theme of "cooperation." On the other hand, all societies are moved to fear and loathing by the negative "virtues" that Hellraiser describes in great detail as part of a strike and destroy policy. The reader should not suspect me of preaching in these concluding remarks. Sociology and theology are close cousins, and religion is the oldest social institution. According to Durkheim (1912), all other social institutions evolved from religion. Throughout history, all societies have divided social phenomena into the sacred versus the profane. Sacred ideas, policies, actions, and phenomena are those that evoke feelings of awe and respect. The profane is the catch-all category for things, ideas, and phenomena that do not inspire awe and respect.

I will not presume to lay out in any detail how military theorists and officers might develop new war-making doctrines and philosophies that appeal to the best in human nature. Such an undertaking is obviously outside my area of expertise. But I will offer a few generalizations based upon sociological insights. Both CG and COIN doctrines have to fall in line with the broad outlines of humanity's respect for civilians and innocents in warfare. A CG doctrine that evolved out of the army's history of exterminating Native Americans is simply and profoundly out of sync with contemporary sentiments. Few Americans today can look back upon that brutal period of history with admiration or high regard.

Even if we accept that warfare cannot be eliminated and is sometimes necessary, CG doctrines can be written and applied so as to be much more mindful of civilian casualties, and much less likely to result in "questionable" kills, than presently seems to be the case. More than a hundred years after the extermination of Native Americans, one looks back with shame. A hundred years into the future, what will people think of the war doctrines in the current war on terror? In sum, warfare is not immune from the general, cultural law that people respect what is noble, what is sacred, in the manner with which warriors engage the enemy and how they treat non-combatants. This is the reason why humanity repeatedly erects rules of war such as the Geneva Conventions and other Laws of Armed Conflict. But it is not enough for such rules and laws to exist as abstractions. The spirit of these laws must inform all policies in war (including ROE), and CG is decidedly out of sync with this benign spirit.

Similarly, COIN cannot work so long as it incorporates CG doctrine and philosophy. The mingling of these two opposing points of view is something like trying to equate the sacred with the profane. All cultures in all periods of history keep the sacred far removed from the profane through taboos, prohibitions, and rites. The sacred elevates us above the humdrum of daily existence and evokes what is best in human nature. The reader need only imagine the concrete experience for both the Afghans and the American soldiers when they met to have tea (COIN), with multiple Stryker vehicles parked in the village bearing "Strike and Destroy" (CG) streamers. One can scarcely convey the depth of the irony in this typical scene. It almost tragic-comic to imagine a commander saying, "You there, the death-dealers, we need you to guard the village while we have our tea with the village elders. And you there, the shoot-them-in-the-face guys, back them up."

Again, the exact mechanism for putting a genuine COIN policy into action is beyond my area of expertise. Nevertheless, I find Hellraiser's idea of a special battalion for doing COIN a good start. Perhaps its motto and its streamers should be variations of the phrase, "We care." But it is not enough to have special COIN battalions as one more line on a power point slide. We are back to the seemingly insoluble problem that Hellraiser's special battalion was still part of a brigade whose motto was "Strike and Destroy." The other combat battalions that did COIN despite Hellraiser were still doing CG while doing COIN. In sum, COIN doctrine must be completely severed from any and all traces of CG doctrine, in theory as well as practice.

It would be a mistake to reduce the narrative of this book or the task at hand to the narrow issue of re-writing COIN. I have treated COIN and CG doctrines as a vehicle for a much broader discussion of society and social issues. For example, the military theorists who are engaged in this discussion from the narrow, academic perspective of implementing ideas inspired by Mao Tse-Tung, Galula, and other theorists who disturbed Hellraiser because they were foreign overlook completely the Marshall Plan and other ways that America became friends with its enemies following World War II, namely, Germany and Japan. That historical instance of reconciliation and cooperation is not referred to as COIN, but why is not used as an inspiration for COIN? Despite the current efforts to tear down and deconstruct almost everything that is inspirational about American history, it is a fact that there was a time when immigrants did look to America as a refuge from oppression. It is a fact that the post-World War II generation was called "The Greatest Generation." As an important aside, the current doctrine of "deconstruction," which has infected all of academia, holds that all truths must be deconstructed and that one is not permitted to reconstruct truths. This is nothing less than a "Strike and Destroy" doctrine toward truth in universities that prevents anyone from looking up to, admiring, or respecting any truth. My point is that there are plenty of spaces in US history that illustrate what is best about the American people and culture, if only one will be open to them.

Conversely, CG is more than a military doctrine. It resonates with numerous and broad elements in American culture that are not worthy of respect, and that do not elevate us above ourselves. Any consumer of the news knows that the metaphor of "declaring war" on just about everything has become ubiquitous in the present era. It is no exaggeration that in the information media, various factions of Americans have declared war on: women, Christmas, obesity, chocolate milk, potatoes, corporations, the working class, Republicans, Democrats, welfare recipients, abortion, drugs, war, terror, Iran, poverty, guns, and a host of other phenomena. I invite the skeptical reader to Google the phrase, "war on." Postmodernism has declared war on truth. Science has been reduced to proving that hypotheses are false, and not searching for truths. While it is true that these metaphorical wars do not involve military equipment, it is also true that they involve metaphorical military tactics, ranging from baited ambushes and misinformation to "striking and destroying" the presumed enemy. Like real wars, these metaphorical wars do not serve the interests of cooperation and humanity in the long run. As in real wars, there is "collateral damage," and there are "questionable kills." There are metaphorical "war crimes" committed in these culture wars against the weak and vulnerable members of society.

The real world of dust, sweat, and hardship cannot be reduced to an abstract presentation of any sort. This is why I quoted the exact words and phrases used by real, flesh-and-blood officers and soldiers throughout this book—to give the reader concrete examples of what CG and COIN meant to persons engaged in these abstractions. This is why I hold General Twitty's research study in high regard, despite the fact that it was a whitewash of command responsibility: he gave us priceless data on what CG and COIN means to real people. To illustrate the fact that CG doctrine cannot inspire and cannot move people to respect it, one needs only to hark back to how officers and soldiers defined CG, regardless of how it is defined in manuals and slides. They said that CG meant to them: "Let's kill those *@!s," "lethal operations," "enemy-focused," "kill the enemy," "attack," "kill bad guys," "hunt down the insurgents," "search and destroy," "engage and destroy," "hunt down the insurgents," "winning hearts and minds was crap," "[we] began to see every person as an enemy," and "lethal success," among other phrases that evoke fear and loathing but fail to move the human heart in the direction of high esteem.

Conversely, officers and soldiers said that COIN meant to them: "population-focused," "dignity," "respect," "working with the populace," "create a secure environment for the local populace," "to protect the population," "develop ties with the local population" "focus on the population as the center of gravity," "partnering," and "caring." The words dignity and respect were perceived as goals, and these goals are themselves dignified and worthy of respect. LT J describes his COIN-oriented commander, LTC B, as "caring" for the Afghan people. It is ironic that the word "caring" is nowhere to be found in the COIN manual.

In this book, I have expanded the genuine kernel of COIN doctrine that moves people to feel respect—a spirit of generosity and cooperation—to include the treatment of American soldiers, prisoners, and suspects, not just "local nationals." I remind the reader that in focusing exclusively upon CG, Hellraiser failed to do COIN (in this expanded sense) toward his own men. The most extreme example was that some soldiers were forced to drink their own urine during a mission because water and supplies ceased to be regarded as important issues. Numerous soldiers and officers complained about lack of respect for soldiers, poor morale, lack of attentiveness to medical issues such as PTSD and TBI, and other issues up to and including failure to circulate, eat, and sleep with soldiers. The staff at the army detention facility at Ft. Lewis abused Morlock, which can be rephrased as follows: they failed to treat him with the dignity and respect that all prisoners in the US are supposed to be afforded according to social norms, regardless of their crimes. The CID investigators simply did not care about the existing norms that require the suspect to be completely sober and informed of his Constitutional rights. None of these examples will evoke feelings of esteem or admiration in the average reader. Solitary confinement is used routinely in US civilian and military prisons as punishment, despite thousands of studies which demonstrate that it destroys the prisoner's mind. Sociability is the most basic human instinct, and deprivation of social association is the cruelest form of punishment. One should regard solitary confinement as a form of "Strike and Destroy" doctrine applied to prisoners.

On the other hand, the staff at the navy brig treated Morlock and other prisoners with consideration that does evoke respect. Morlock could hardly believe that the navy brig staff offered him a choice of kiwi or other fruits with dinner, whereas the army prison offered no fresh fruit. He told me that on Easter Sunday, the navy staff served him boiled eggs that were dyed with holiday colors. I recall one of the staff at the navy brig saying to me, with some pride, that they try to treat all prisoners with dignity and respect, and he added, "Wednesday night is steak night." Morlock confirmed that this was true. I dwell on these small but concrete examples of kindness because they resonate with thousands of similar acts by soldiers who handed out candy to Afghan children, medics who saved Afghan lives, and scores of others who exhibited the "spirit of COIN" in small but cumulative acts of thoughtfulness and humanity, regardless of how COIN is defined in manuals. Such acts of kindness apparently do not count for promotion or in evaluation reports—but perhaps they should.

The agonizing dysfunction of Stryker brigade mirrors the cultural wars, divisiveness, and war-like mentality in American culture as I write this book. Grasping the problem in this wider social context, and making connections between civilian society and Stryker brigade, would be healthy steps toward healing. But the current state of social anomie cannot be healed without genuine, noble leadership and collective soul-searching, in the military as well as American society as a whole. Future leaders will need to appeal to what is highest and best in human nature and society, and cease using war metaphors to solve social problems. Peace is always preferable to war, real or metaphorical.

Acknowledgements

I am grateful to Lieutenant General Curtis M. Scaparrotti for appointing me as an expert witness in this case. I appreciate the cooperation of Captain Andre LeBlanc and the prosecutorial team at the Ft. Lewis JAG office in providing me with authenticated and unclassified documents pertaining to this and the companion cases. Frank Spinner and Captain Mark Opachan guided me through the legal terminology in making sense of this case. I am grateful to the soldiers and officers—most of whom will remain anonymous—for sharing with me their versions of what happened during the tragic deployment of Stryker brigade in Afghanistan. I would also like to thank the following persons for discussions pertaining to this book: Adam Ashton, Hal Bernton, Ryan Ashley Caldwell, Colonel Edward P. Horvath, Keith Kerr, Ronald Lorenzo, John McDermott, Luke Mogelson, and Rachel Romero. Although he did not attend Morlock's court-martial, Lorenzo deserves special mention and gratitude for the extensive, background research he conducted on various issues pertaining to this case. Jeremy Morlock's extended family was extremely helpful and hospitable in sharing information about Morlock's childhood as well as life in Wasilla, Alaska. The extremely professional and courteous staff at the Navy brig in Silverdale, Washington deserves special mention, because without their cooperation, I could not have communicated as freely as I did with Jeremy Morlock while he was confined there. I am also grateful to my outgoing and incoming department heads, Mark Fossett and Jane Sell, for supporting the research that went into this book, and to Texas A&M University for granting me sabbatical leave to write it. Finally, I would like to acknowledge the editorial help of Jeremy Morlock in proofreading the drafts of the manuscript that went into this book, and for ensuring the accuracy of ranks, acronyms, and military nomenclature. I am solely responsible for any inadvertent errors others may find in this book.

Bibliography

Ashton, Adam (2010) "Army looks at officers who oversaw group of al-leged war criminals," *The News Tribune* November 23

_____ (2011a) "Army review of Stryker deployment stays under wraps," *The News Tribune* March 7

_____ (2011b) "5ᵗʰ Brigade dysfunctional, report says," *The News Tribune* April 10

_____ (2011c) "A commander out of step," *The News Tribune* October 16

Bernton, Hal (2010) "Frustration, pride in a year of danger," *Seattle Times*, August 21.

_____ (2011) "Army report criticizes leaders in brigade involved in alleged war crimes," *Seattle Times* April 4.

Boal, Mark (2011) "The kill team," *Rolling Stone*, March 27

Durkheim, Emile ([1893] 1997) *The Division of Labor in Society*. New York: Free Press.

_____ ([1897] 1951) *Suicide: A Study in Sociology*. New York: Free Press.

_____ ([1912] 1995) *The Elementary Forms of the Religious Life*. New York: Free Press.

Erikson, Erik (1963) *Childhood and Society*. New York: Bantam.

Fauconnet, Paul ([1928] 1978) *Responsibility: A Study in Sociology*. Unpub-lished translation by William Jeffrey, Jr. Cincinnati, OH: University of Cincinnati College of Law.

Golding, William. (1959) *Lord of the Flies*. New York: Perigee Books.

Grossman, Dave (1996) *On Killing: The Psychological Cost of Learning to Kill in War and Society.* New York: Back Bay.

Heller, Joseph. (1955) *Catch-22.* New York: Simon & Schuster.

Jaffe, Greg and Cloud, David (2010) *The Fourth Star: Four Generals and the Epic Struggle for the Future of the United States Army.* New York: Three Rivers.

James, William (2000) *Pragmatism and Other Writings.* New York: Penguin.

Marshall, Samuel L. A. ([1947] 2000) *Men Against Fire: The Problem of Battle Command.* Norman, OK: University of Oklahoma Press

McKanna, Clare (2009) *Court-Martial of Apache Kid: Renegade of Renegades.* Lubbock, TX: Texas Tech University Press.

Melville, Herman ([1851] 1981) *Moby Dick, or The Whale.* New York: Penguin

Mestrovic, Stjepan (1988) *Emile Durkheim and the Reformation of Sociology.* Totowa, NJ: Rowman & Littlefield

____(1997) *Postemotional Society.* London: Routledge.

____ (2007) *The Trials of Abu Ghraib.* Boulder, CO: Paradigm.

____ (2008) *Rules of Engagement? A Social Anatomy of an American War Crime—Operation Iron Triangle, Iraq.* New York: Algora.

____ (2009) *The Good Soldier on Trial: A Sociological Study of Misconduct by the U.S. Military Pertaining to Operation Iron Triangle, Iraq.* New York: Algora

____ (2010) Sociology 657 Cultural Studies—War Crimes. Retrieved March 21, 2012 (http://itunes.apple.com/us/itunes-u/soci-657-cultural-studies/id394384077)

Mestrovic, Stjepan and Caldwell, Ryan (2010) "The war on terrorism in the early 21st century: applying lessons from sociological classics and sites of abuse," in *Handbook of War and Society*, edited by Morton Ender and Steve Carlton-Ford, pp. 88-99. London: Routledge.

Mestrovic, Stjepan and Romero, Rachel (2012) "Poisoned social climate, collective responsibility, and the abuse at Abu Ghraib—Or, the establishment of 'rule that is lack of rule,'" *International Journal of Law and Psychiatry* 35:62-69

Mogelson, Luke (2011) "A beast in the heart of every fighting man." *The New York Times Magazine* April 27

Naylor, Sean D. (2009) "Stryker soldiers say commanders failed them." *Army Times* December 21

Park, Robert E. and Ernest W. Burgess (1924) *Introduction to the Science of Sociology.* Chicago: University of Chicago Press

Parsons, Talcott ([1937] 1968) *The Structure of Social Action.* New York: Free Press.

Ressler, Robert and Schachtman, Thomas (1993) *Whoever Fights Monsters.* New York: St. Martin's.

Royce, Josiah (2010) *The Philosophy of Loyalty.* New York: Nabu Press.

Stouffer, Samuel (1949) *The American Soldier Vol. 1-3.* Princeton: Princeton University Press.

Tan, Michelle (2011) "Report blames lapses on Stryker commander: 532-page report finds colonel ignored doctrine, proper procedure in leading undisciplined BCT." *Army Times* November 27.

Tunnell, Harry D. (2000) *To Compel With Armed Force: A Staff Ride Handbook for the Battle of Tippecanoe.* Ft. Leavenworth, KS: Combat Studies Institute.

_____ (2009) *Guerrilla Hunter Killer Operations Field Manual.* Retrieved March 21, 2012 (http://www.scribd.com/doc/30267328/ghk-fm-v7)

Twitty, Stephen M. (2011) *AR 15-6 Investigation on 5/2 Stryker Brigade Combat Team*

Vaknin, Samuel (2007) *Malignant Self-Love: Narcissism Revisited.* Prague: Narcissus Publications.

Veblen, Thorstein ([1899] 1967) *The Theory of the Leisure Class.* New York: Penguin.

Endnotes

1 http://www.armytimes.com/news/2011/11/army-report-blames-lapses-on-stryker-commander-112711w/

2 See, for example, Ashton (2010, 2011a, 2011b, 2011c) and Bernton (2011) among others. `

3 McKanna (2009) offers one of the best historical accounts of the US court martial system.

4 An interesting anecdote in this regard is the following: Corporal Morlock told me that while he was at the hospital at Ft. Lewis during his pre-trial confinement, he was visited by LTG J's command sergeant major, CSM G. CSM G shook Morlock's hand and seeing Morlock in restraints said, "I didn't realize you were here, Morlock." CSM G turned to Morlock's guards and said, "Does he have to be in those restraints? He's a war hero." This is an unverified anecdote that is not part of the sworn statements. Nevertheless, I include it here for the historical record.

5 http://news.antiwar.com/2010/10/07/eights-months-in-a-full-blown-insurgency-in-marjah/

6 http://www.armytimes.com/news/2009/12/army_afghanistan_mixed_signals_122109w/

7 It may be helpful to note that the chaplain is probably referring to 1-17's mascot, which is a buffalo. All battalions have their own unique symbols and mascots.

8 http://www.csmonitor.com/USA/Military/2012/0328/Afghan-shooting-spree-What-did-Sgt.-Robert-Bales-s-commander-know

9 http://smallwarsjournal.com/blog/2010/11/interview-with-dr-john-nagl/

10 http://www.airpower.maxwell.af.mil/airchronicles/apj/apj07/win07/crane.html

11 See http://warbyanothermeans.cas.sc.edu/hrmcmaster.html; http://public-intelligence.net/ufouo-isaf-cjiatf-shafafiyat-afghan-corruption-information-paper/;

http://www.ndu.edu/press/deconstruction-3-24.html; http://www.ndu.edu/press/constructing-3-24.html

12 For a fuller discussion, see the discussion of loyalty by philosopher Josiah Royce (2010).

13 http://www.rollingstone.com/politics/news/the-runaway-general-20100622

14 http://truth-out.org/index.php?option=com_k2&view=item&id=3588:how-mcchrystal-and-petraeus-built-an-indiscriminate-killing-machine

15 http://msnbcmedia.msn.com/i/MSNBC/Components/Photo/2009/December/091202/091203-engel-big-9a.jpg

16 http://www.huffingtonpost.com/tom-engelhardt/koran-burning_b_1306423.html?ref=world

17 http://news.yahoo.com/us-soldier-kills-16-afghans-deepening-crisis-164242200.html

18 http://www.defense.gov/Transcripts/Transcript.aspx?TranscriptID=4973

19 http://www.armedforcesjournal.com/2012/02/8904030

20 http://www.military.com/news/article/army-news/52-stryker-brigade-re-flagged-as-22.html

21 http://www.nytimes.com/2009/08/28/opinion/28fri3.html

22 http://news.yahoo.com/afghan-killings-troubled-history-american-161221151—abc-news.html

23 http://seattletimes.nwsource.com/html/localnews/2015370754_morlock20m.html

24 http://blog.thenewstribune.com/military/2011/06/22/morlock-distances-sergeant-from-afghan-murder/

25 http://blog.thenewstribune.com/military/2011/06/23/stryker-officer-posed-with-corpse-to-show-battlefield-success/

26 http://blog.thenewstribune.com/military/2011/07/27/for-the-second-time-investigator-finds-scant-evidence-in-kill-team-case-against-wagnon/

27 http://www.thenewstribune.com/2011/07/08/1737214/sergeants-kill-team-case-is-first.html

28 http://www.thenewstribune.com/2011/07/09/1738452/1st-kill-team-verdict-mixed.html

29 http://www.armytimes.com/news/2011/07/ap-hearing-repoens-for-lewis-private-in-afghan-deaths-072111/

30 http://www.thenewstribune.com/2011/07/22/v-lite/1754417_killer-turned-army-witness-alleged.html

31 http://www.sacbee.com/2011/07/22/3787878/stryker-soldier-bragged-about.html

32 http://seattletimes.nwsource.com/html/localnews/2015830986_winfield06m.html

INDEX